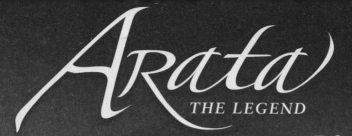

Arata: The Legend

Characters

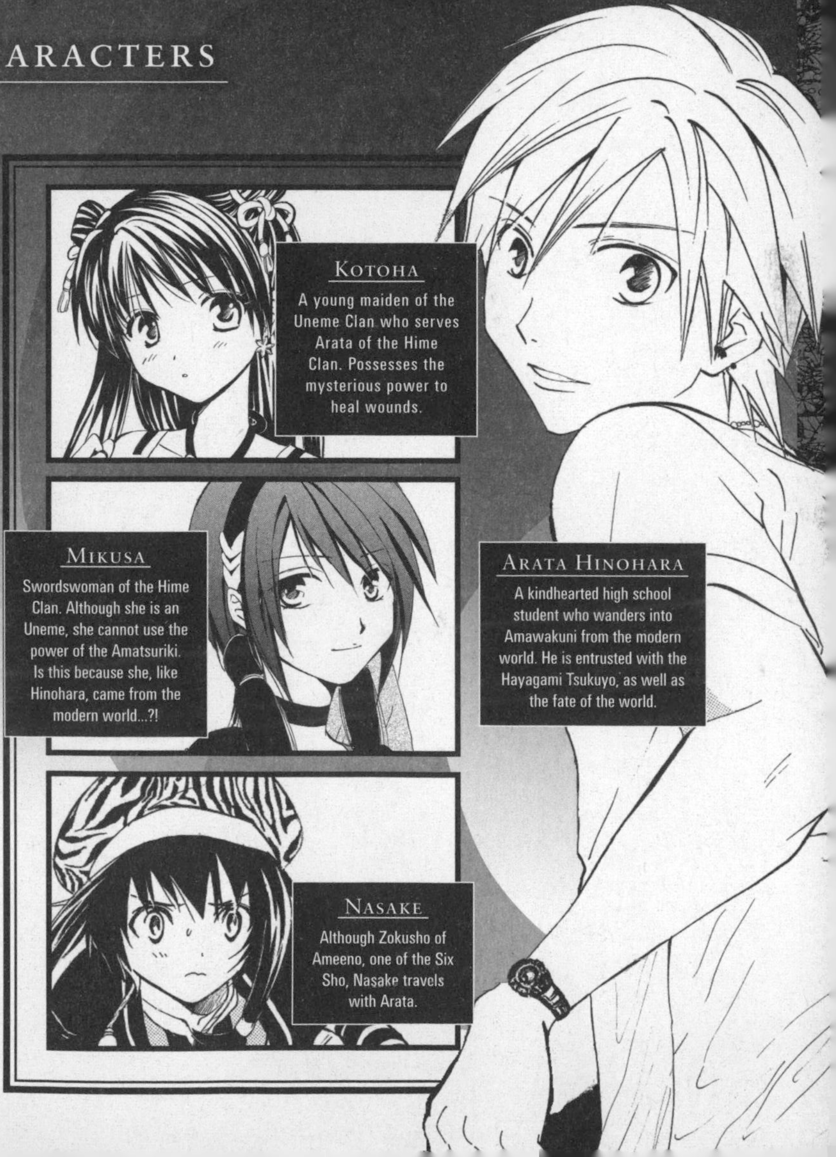

Kotoha
A young maiden of the Uneme Clan who serves Arata of the Hime Clan. Possesses the mysterious power to heal wounds.

Mikusa
Swordswoman of the Hime Clan. Although she is an Uneme, she cannot use the power of the Amatsuriki. Is this because she, like Hinohara, came from the modern world...?!

Arata Hinohara
A kindhearted high school student who wanders into Amawakuni from the modern world. He is entrusted with the Hayagami Tsukuyo, as well as the fate of the world.

Nasake
Although Zokusho of Ameeno, one of the Six Sho, Nasake travels with Arata.

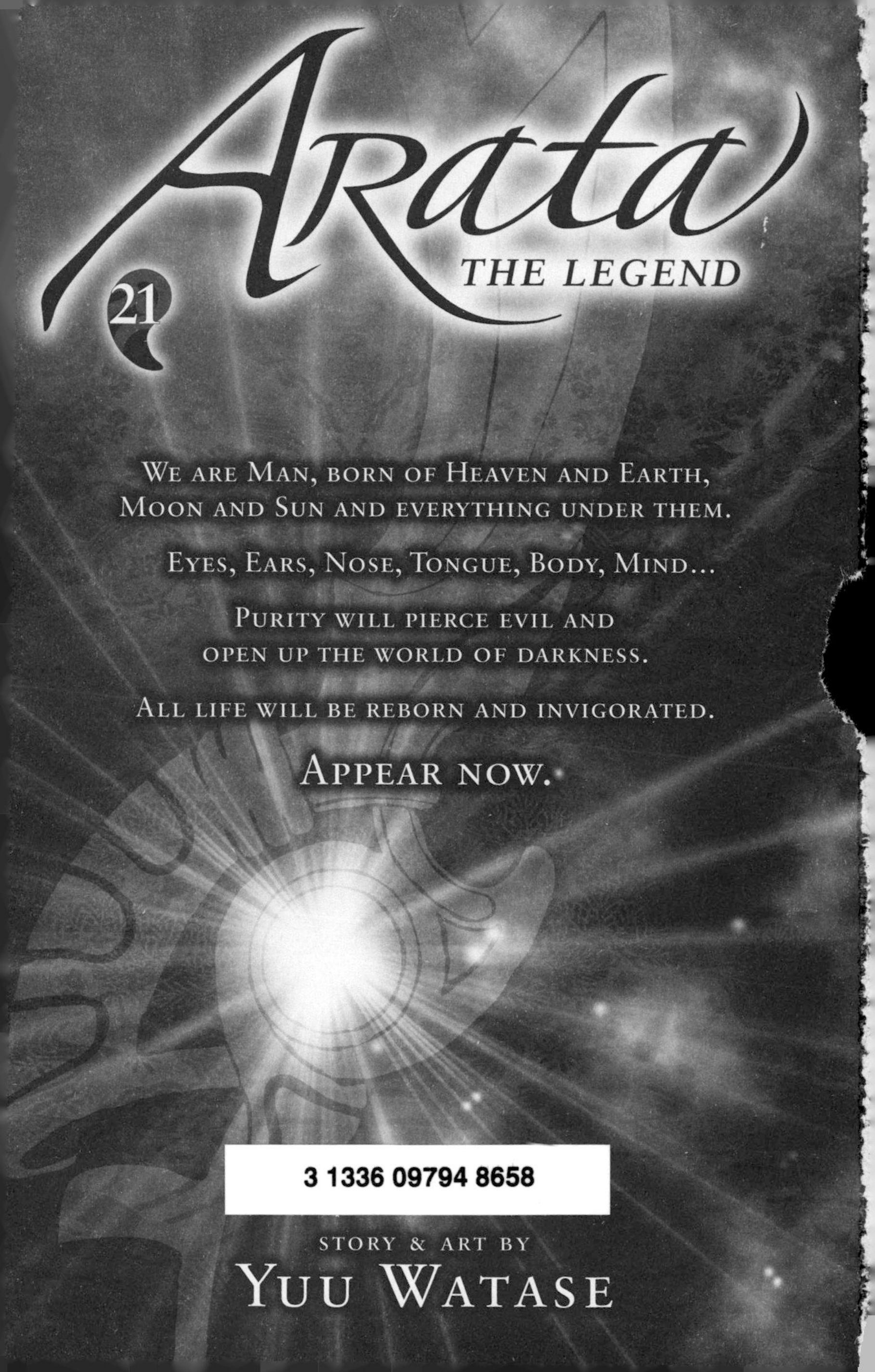
Arata
THE LEGEND
21
We are Man, born of Heaven and Earth,
Moon and Sun and everything under them.
Eyes, Ears, Nose, Tongue, Body, Mind...
Purity will pierce evil and
open up the world of darkness.
All life will be reborn and invigorated.
Appear now.
STORY & ART BY
YUU WATASE

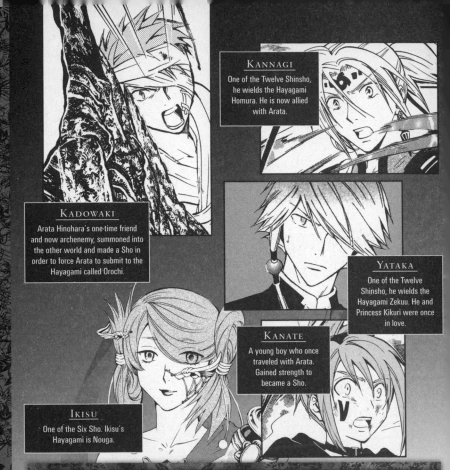

KANNAGI

One of the Twelve Shinsho, he wields the Hayagami Homura. He is now allied with Arata.

KADOWAKI

Arata Hinohara's one-time friend and now archenemy, summoned into the other world and made a Sho in order to force Arata to submit to the Hayagami called Orochi.

YATAKA

One of the Twelve Shinsho, he wields the Hayagami Zekuu. He and Princess Kikuri were once in love.

KANATE

A young boy who once traveled with Arata. Gained strength to became a Sho.

IKISU

One of the Six Sho. Ikisu's Hayagami is Nouga.

THE STORY THUS FAR

Arata Hinohara, finding himself in Amawakuni, a land in another dimension, is chosen as the successor to the legendary Hayagami Tsukuyo. In order to stop the fighting that ensued after Princess Kikuri's collapse, he continues his journey to make all the Sho submit and unify the Hayagami.

Nasake, the Zokusho of Ameeno, one of the Six Sho, appears before Arata and wishes to submit. Accepting Nasake's offer to guide them to Ameeno's domain, Arata and company board a ship. But the ship is wrecked on the shore of an uninhabited island ruled by Ikisu, another of the Six Sho.

Ikisu, meanwhile, has been pursuing Arata. Appearing suddenly on Kadowaki's airship, Ikisu uses his scent Kamui to bewitch Kanate and snatch him away.

21
Arata
THE LEGEND

CONTENTS

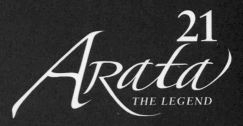

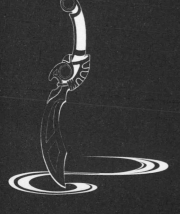

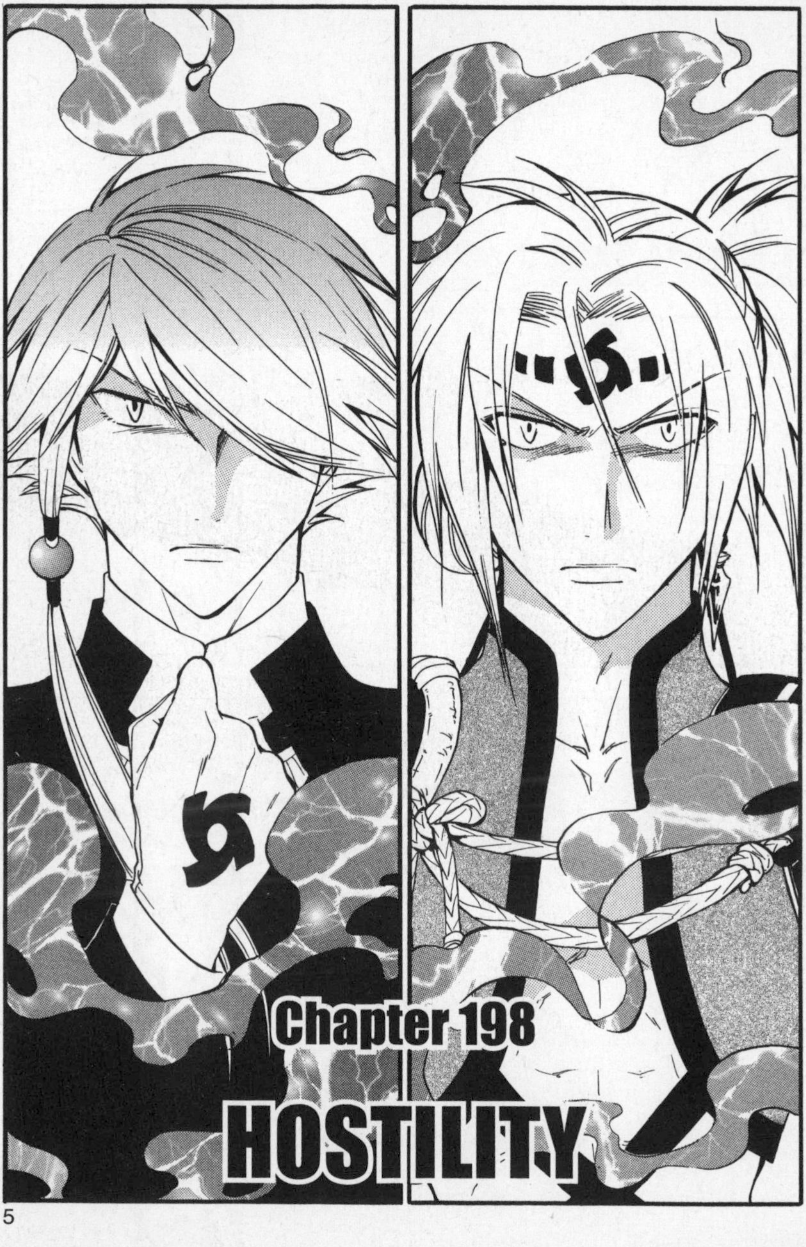
Chapter 198
HOSTILITY

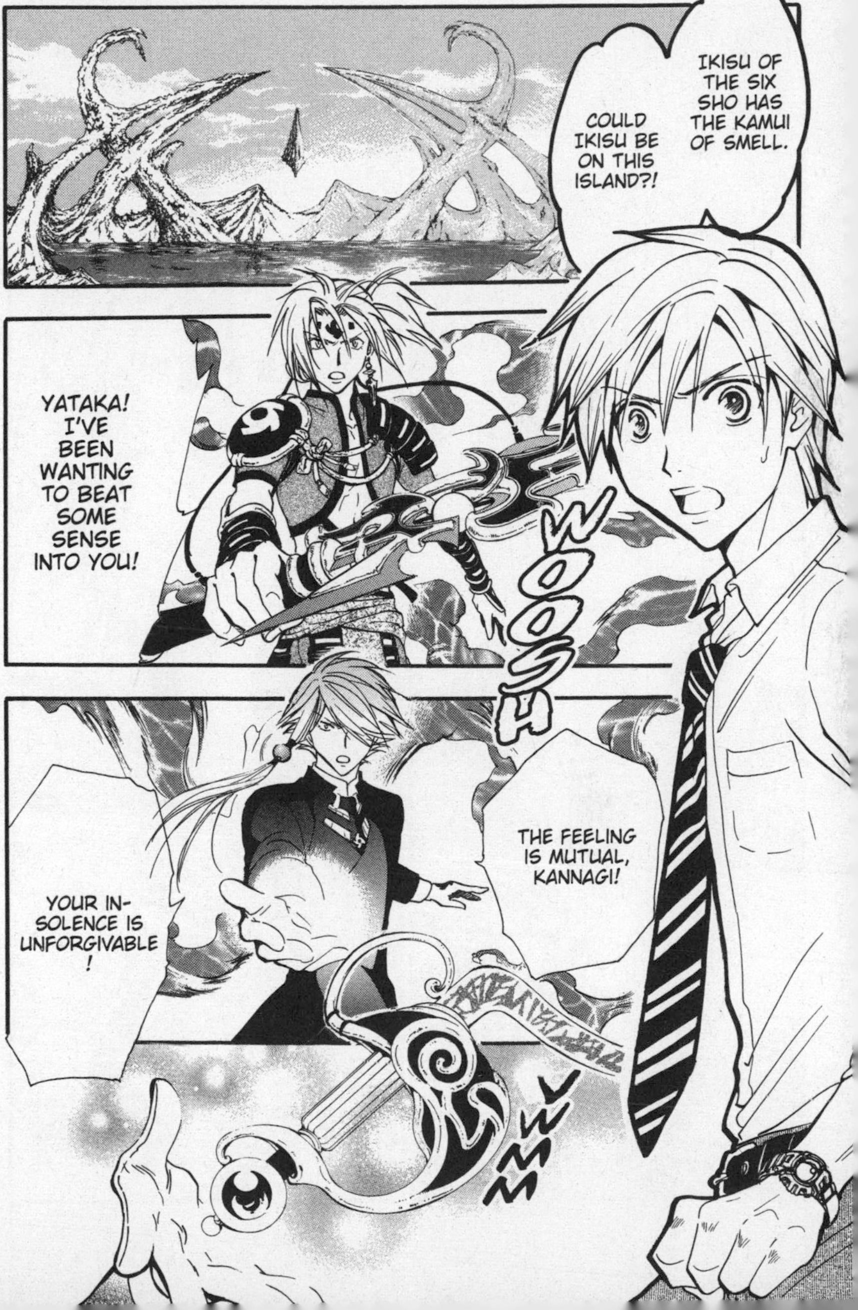
IKISU OF THE SIX SHO HAS THE KAMUI OF SMELL.
COULD IKISU BE ON THIS ISLAND?!
WOOSH
YATAKA! I'VE BEEN WANTING TO BEAT SOME SENSE INTO YOU!
THE FEELING IS MUTUAL, KANNAGI!
YOUR IN-SOLENCE IS UNFORGIVABLE!
VWMM

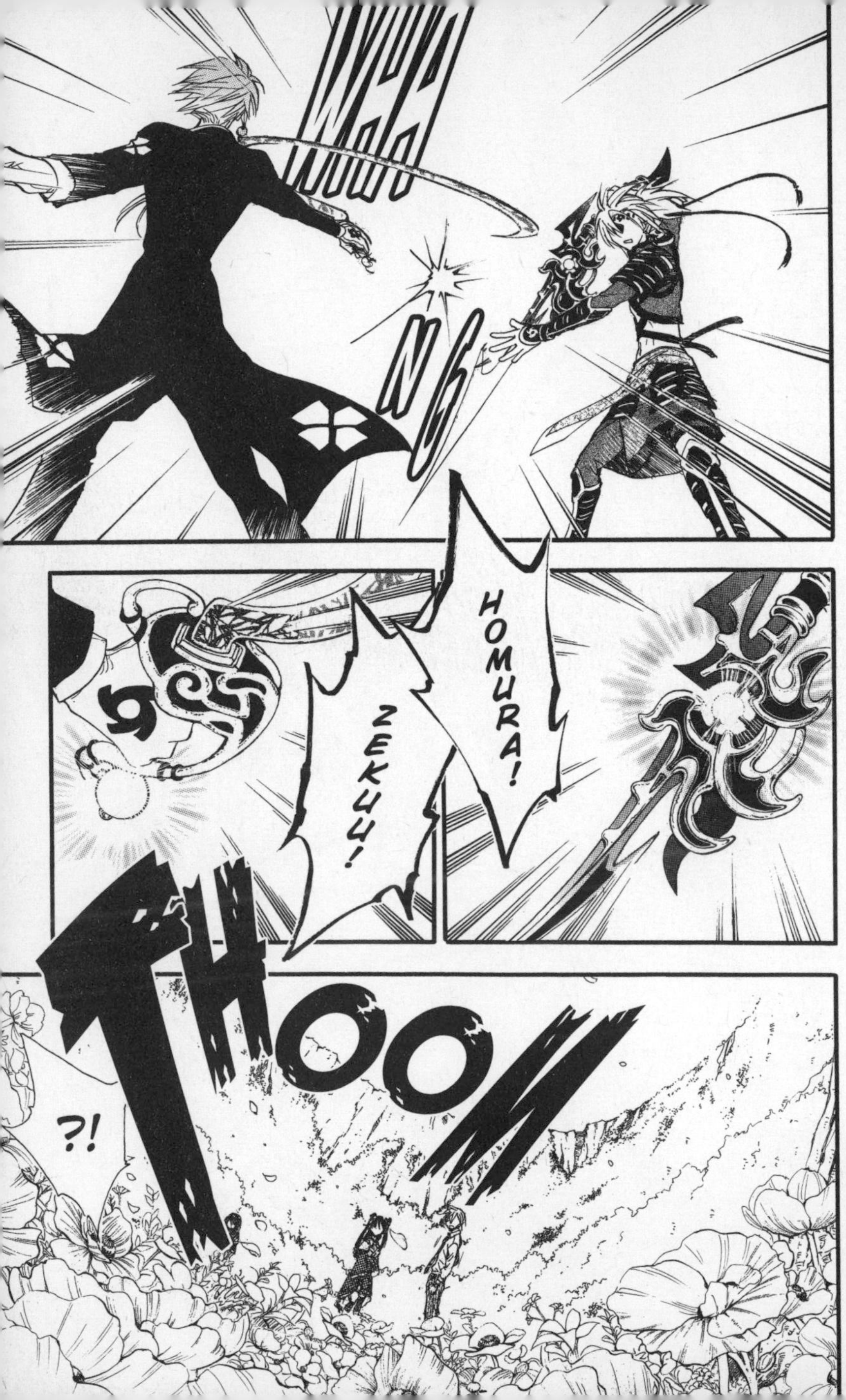
HOMURA!
ZEKUU!
THOOM
?!

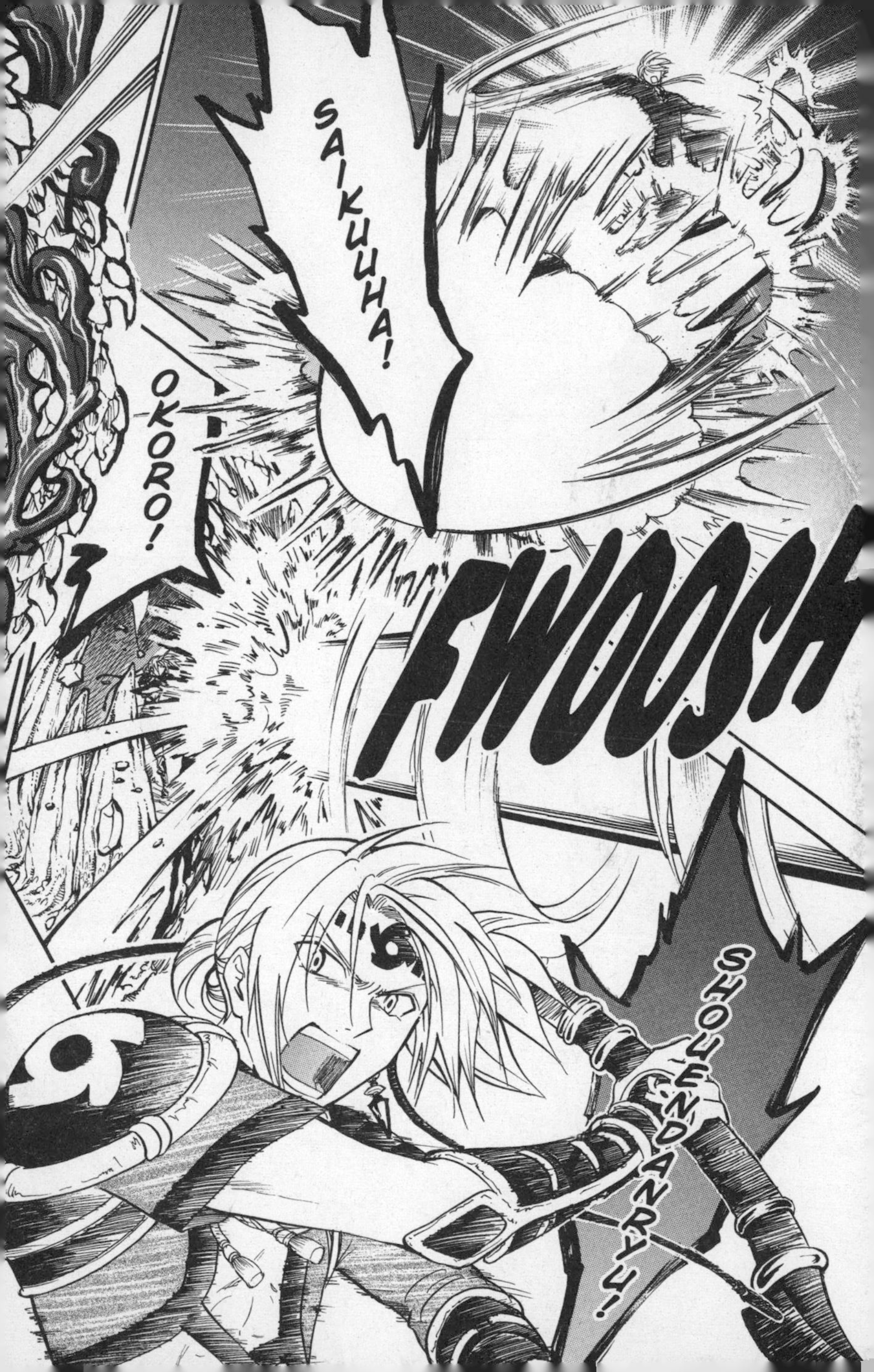
SAIKUUHA!
OKORO!
FWOOSH
SHOUENDANRYU!

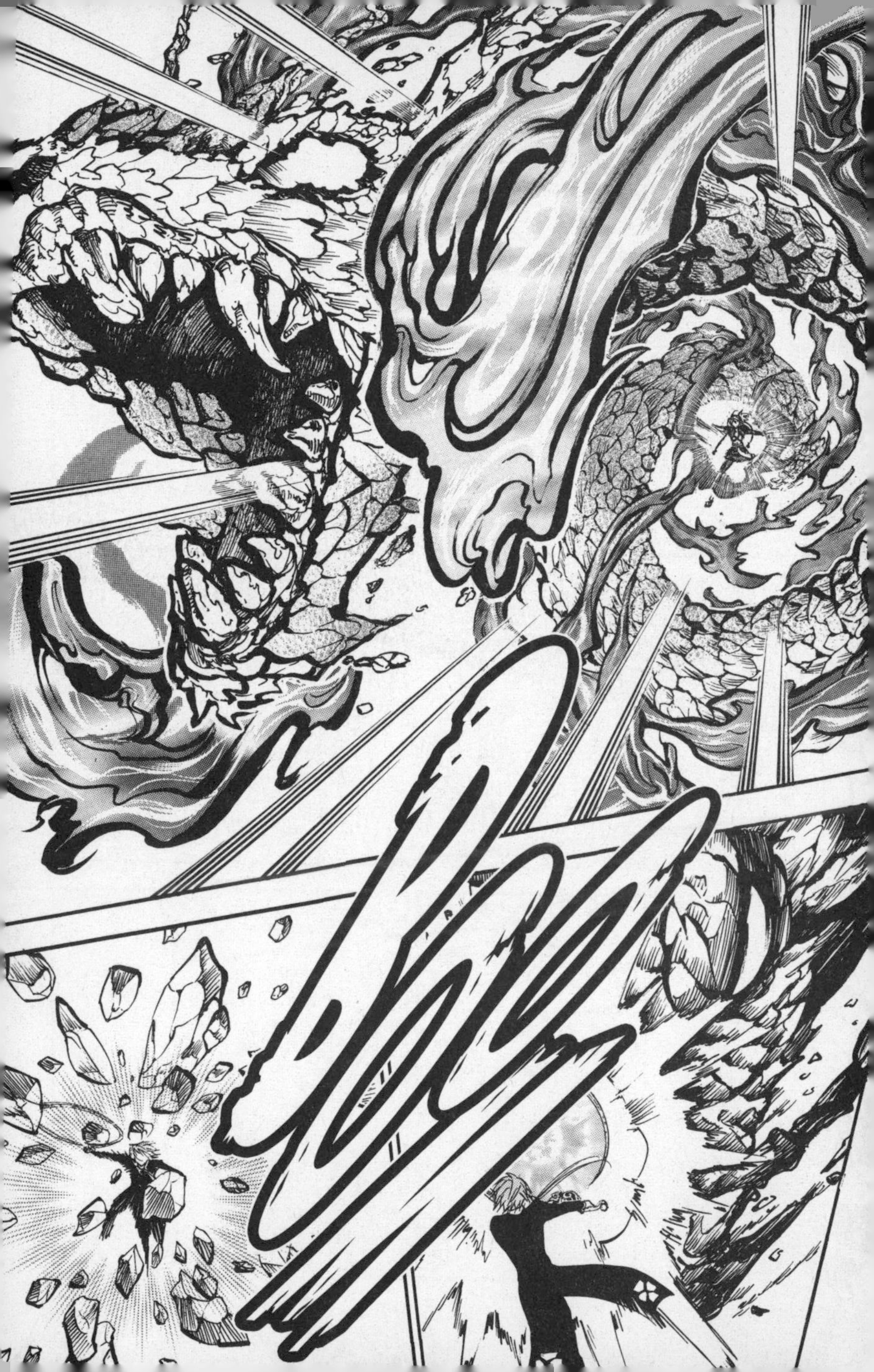

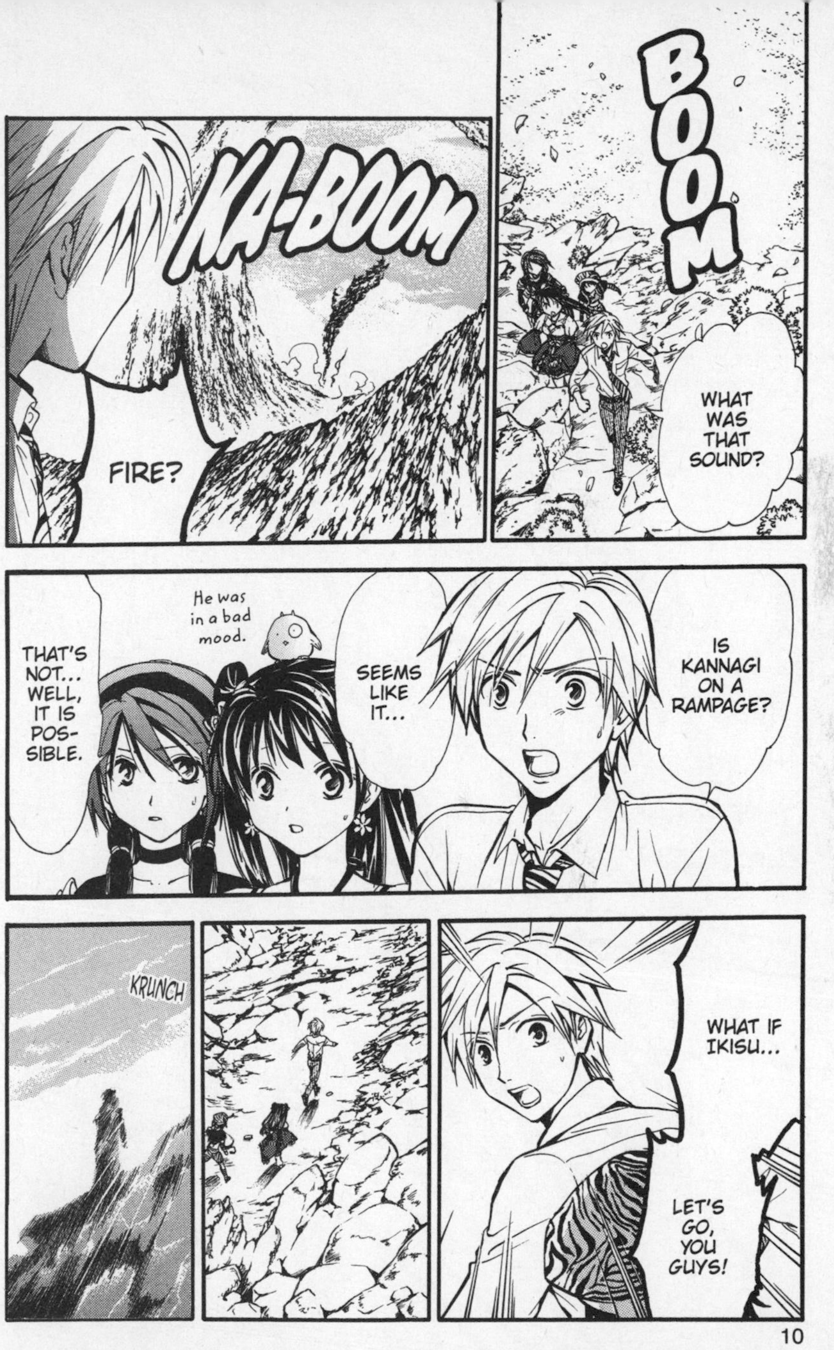
BOOM
WHAT WAS THAT SOUND?
KA-BOOM
FIRE?
IS KANNAGI ON A RAMPAGE?
SEEMS LIKE IT...
He was in a bad mood.
THAT'S NOT... WELL, IT IS POSSIBLE.
WHAT IF IKISU...
LET'S GO, YOU GUYS!
KRUNCH

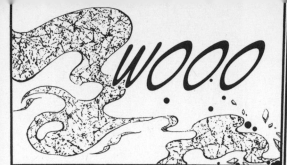

WOOO

SHEEN

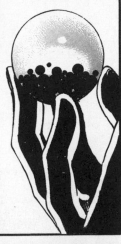

KOTOHA!

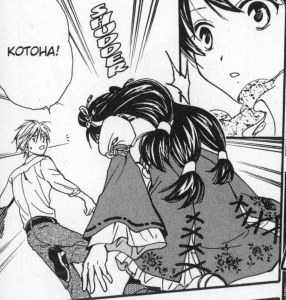

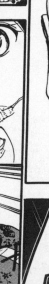

P

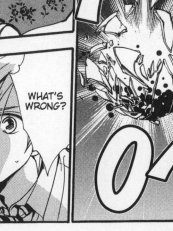

OP

...

WHAT'S
WRONG?

11

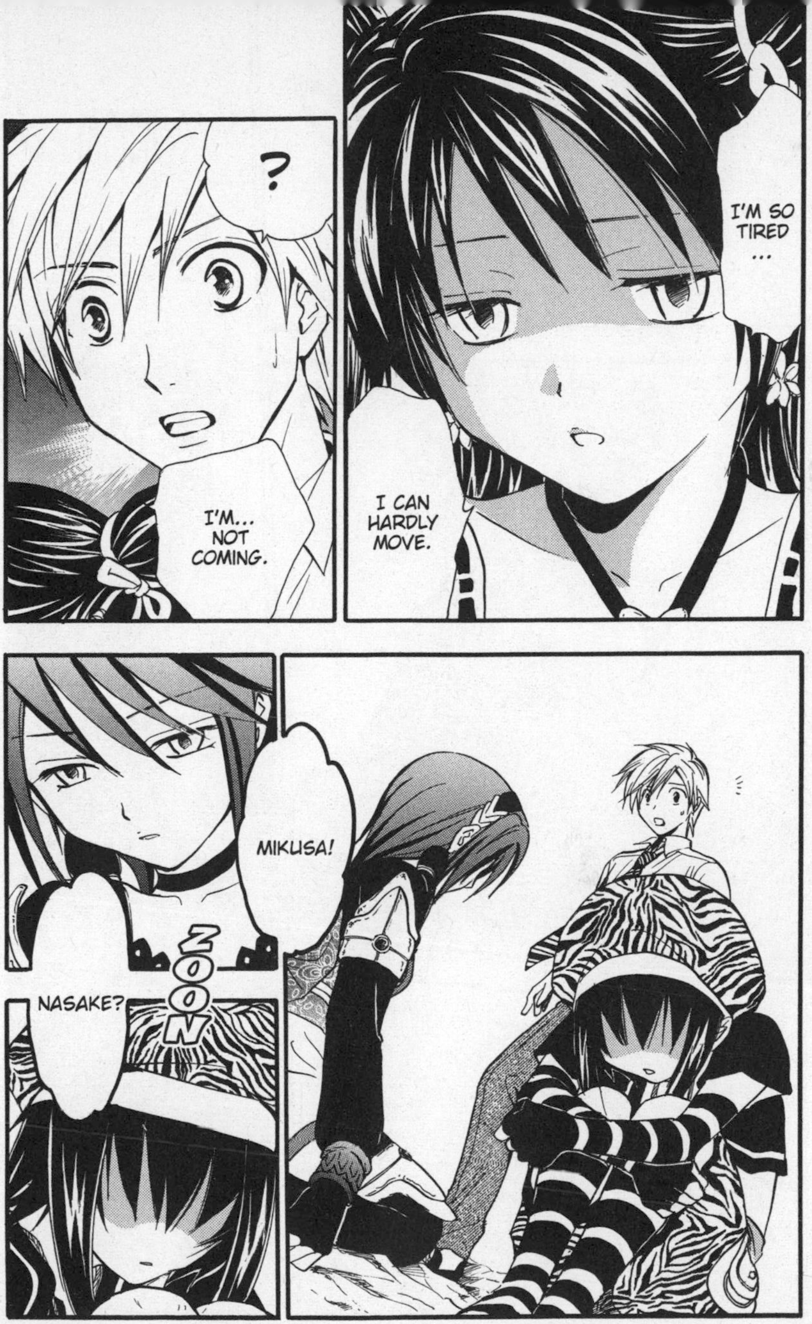
I'M SO TIRED ...
I CAN HARDLY MOVE.
?
I'M... NOT COMING.
MIKUSA!
ZOOON
NASAKE?

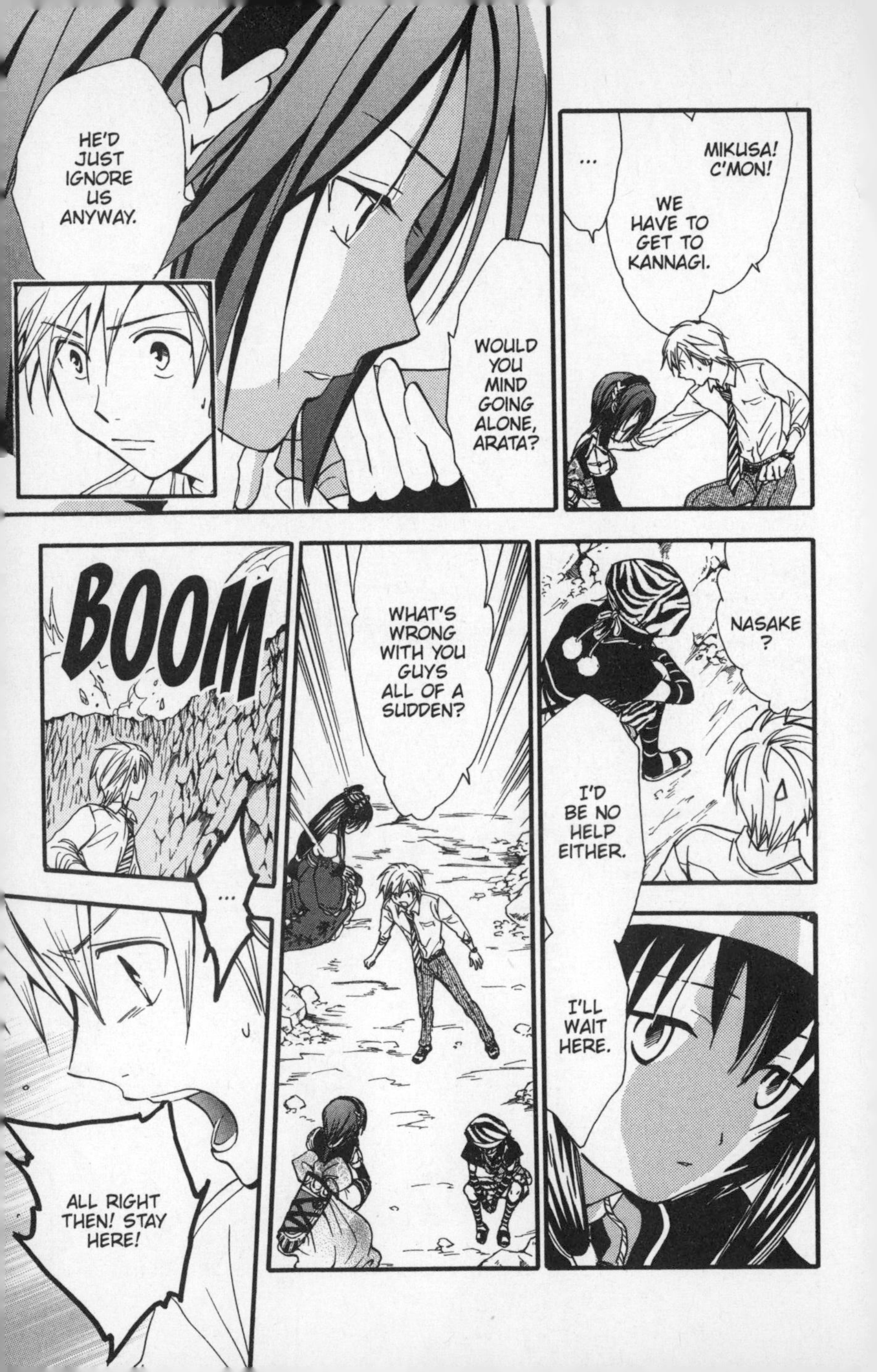
MIKUSA! C'MON!
WE HAVE TO GET TO KANNAGI.
...
WOULD YOU MIND GOING ALONE, ARATA?
HE'D JUST IGNORE US ANYWAY.
NASAKE?
I'D BE NO HELP EITHER.
I'LL WAIT HERE.
WHAT'S WRONG WITH YOU GUYS ALL OF A SUDDEN?
BOOM
...
ALL RIGHT THEN! STAY HERE!

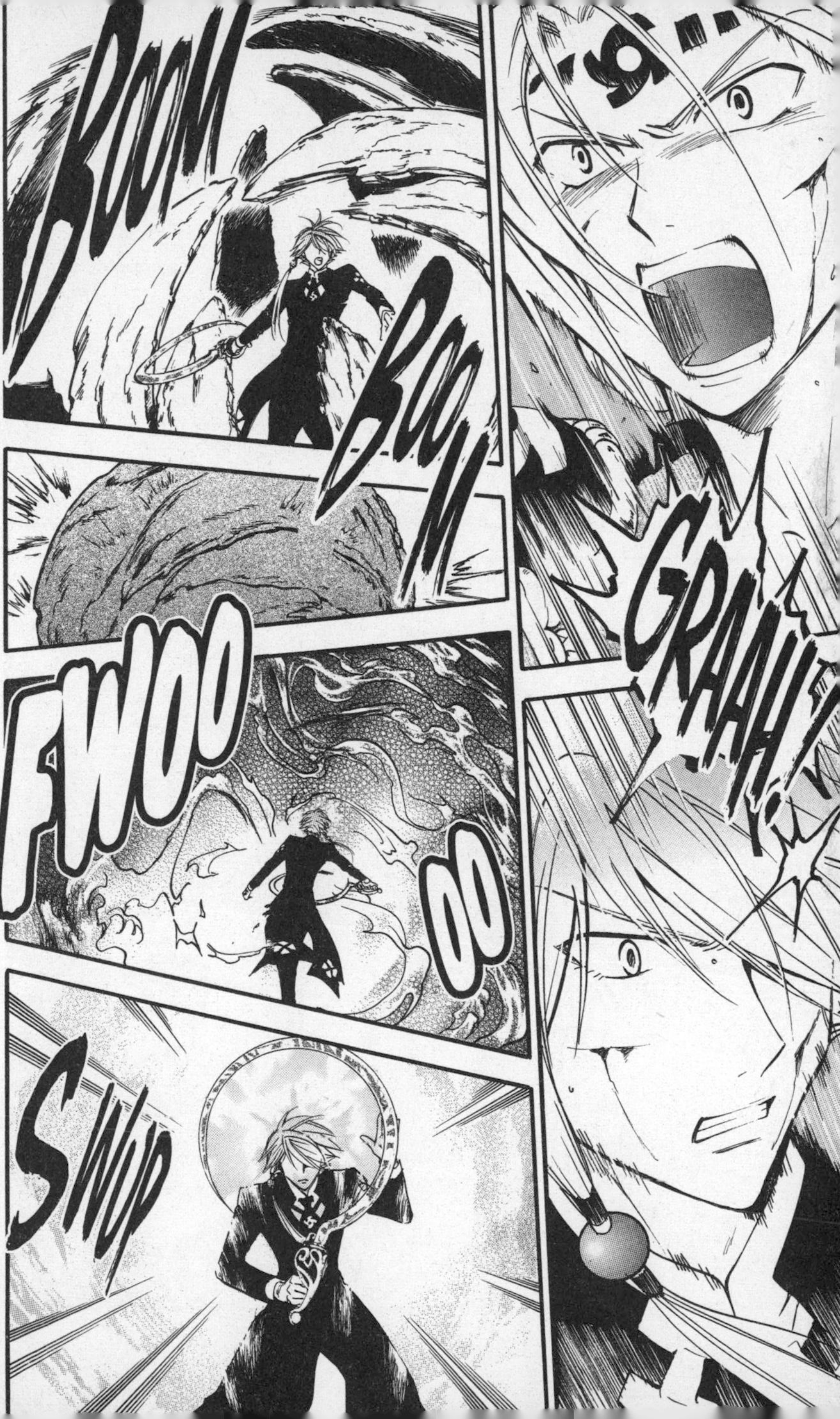
GRAAH!!
BOOM
BOOM
FWOOOO
SWIP

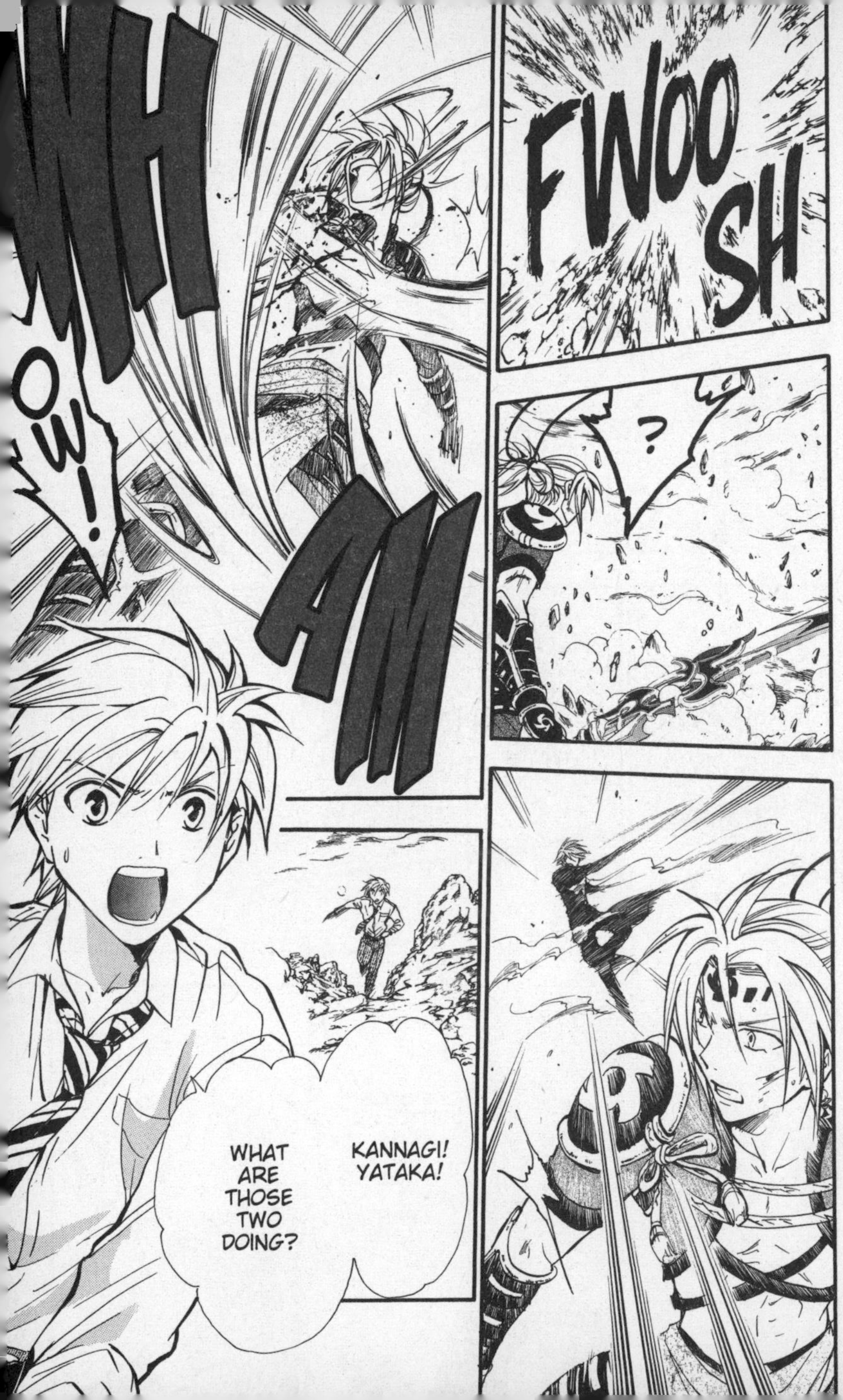
FWOOSH
?
WHAM
OW!
..
KANNAGI! YATAKA!
WHAT ARE THOSE TWO DOING?

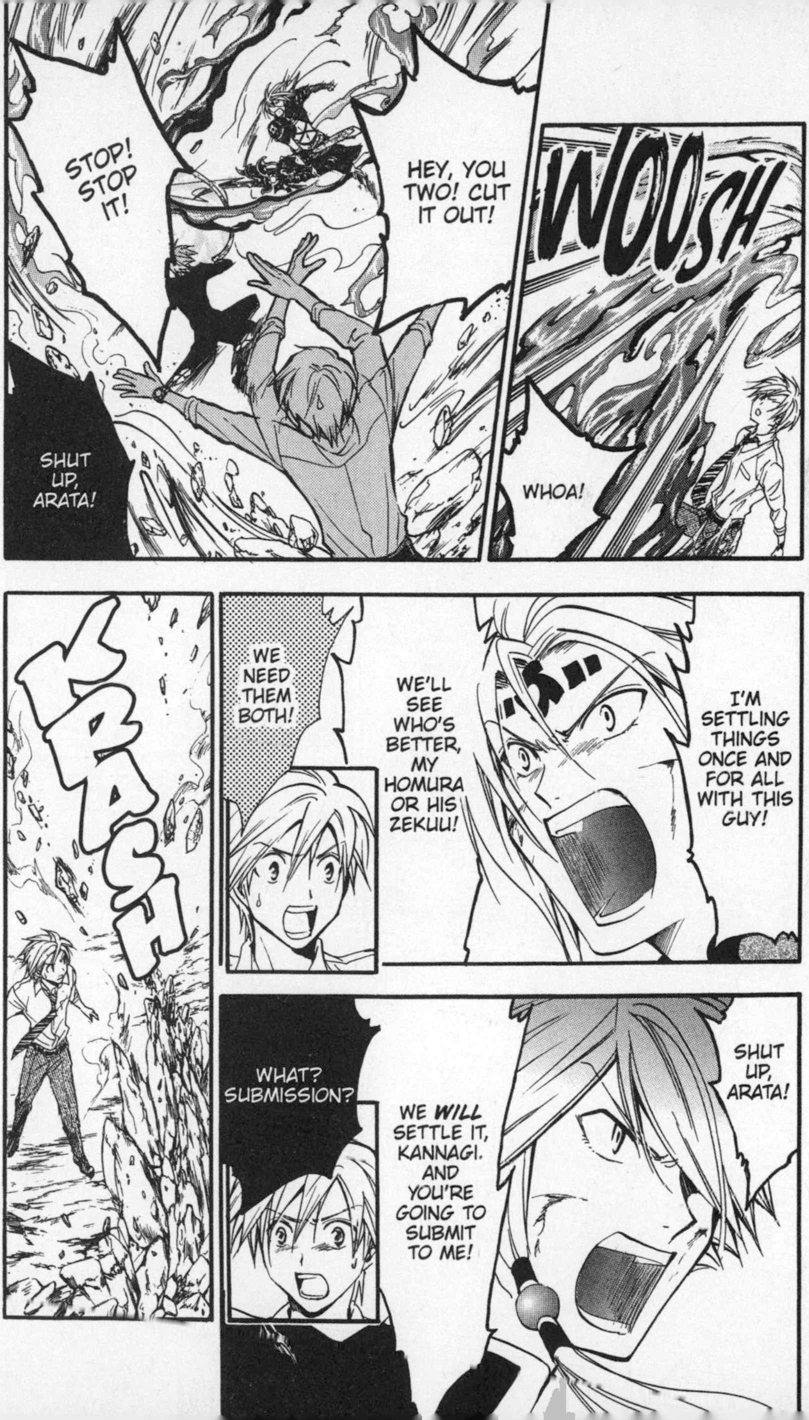
WOOSH
WHOA!
HEY, YOU TWO! CUT IT OUT!
STOP! STOP IT!
SHUT UP, ARATA!
I'M SETTLING THINGS ONCE AND FOR ALL WITH THIS GUY!
WE'LL SEE WHO'S BETTER, MY HOMURA OR HIS ZEKUU!
WE NEED THEM BOTH!
SHUT UP, ARATA!
WE *WILL* SETTLE IT, KANNAGI. AND YOU'RE GOING TO SUBMIT TO ME!
WHAT? SUBMISSION?
KRASH

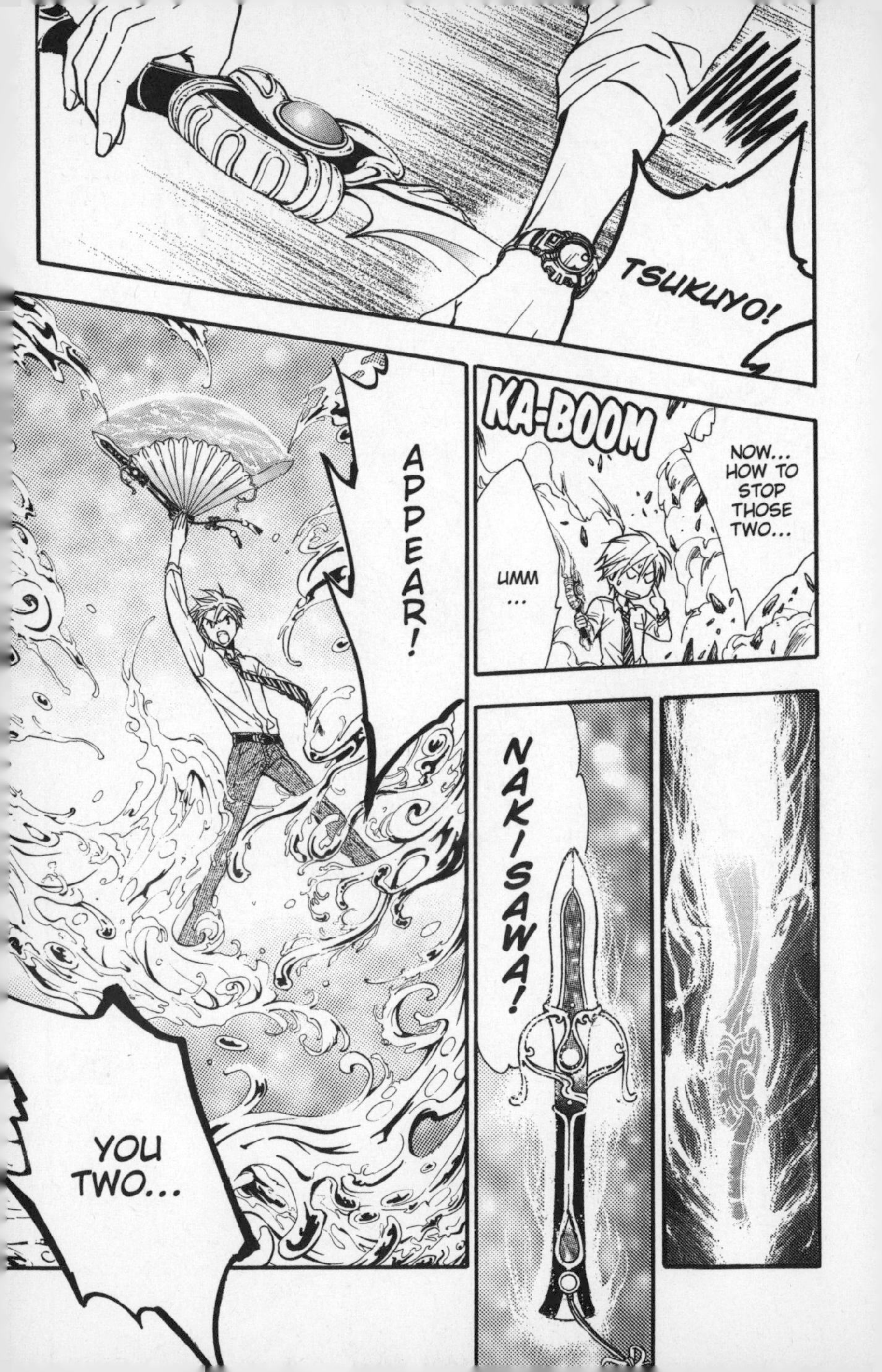
TSUKUYO!
KA-BOOM
NOW... HOW TO STOP THOSE TWO...
UMM ...
NAKISAWA!
APPEAR!
YOU TWO...

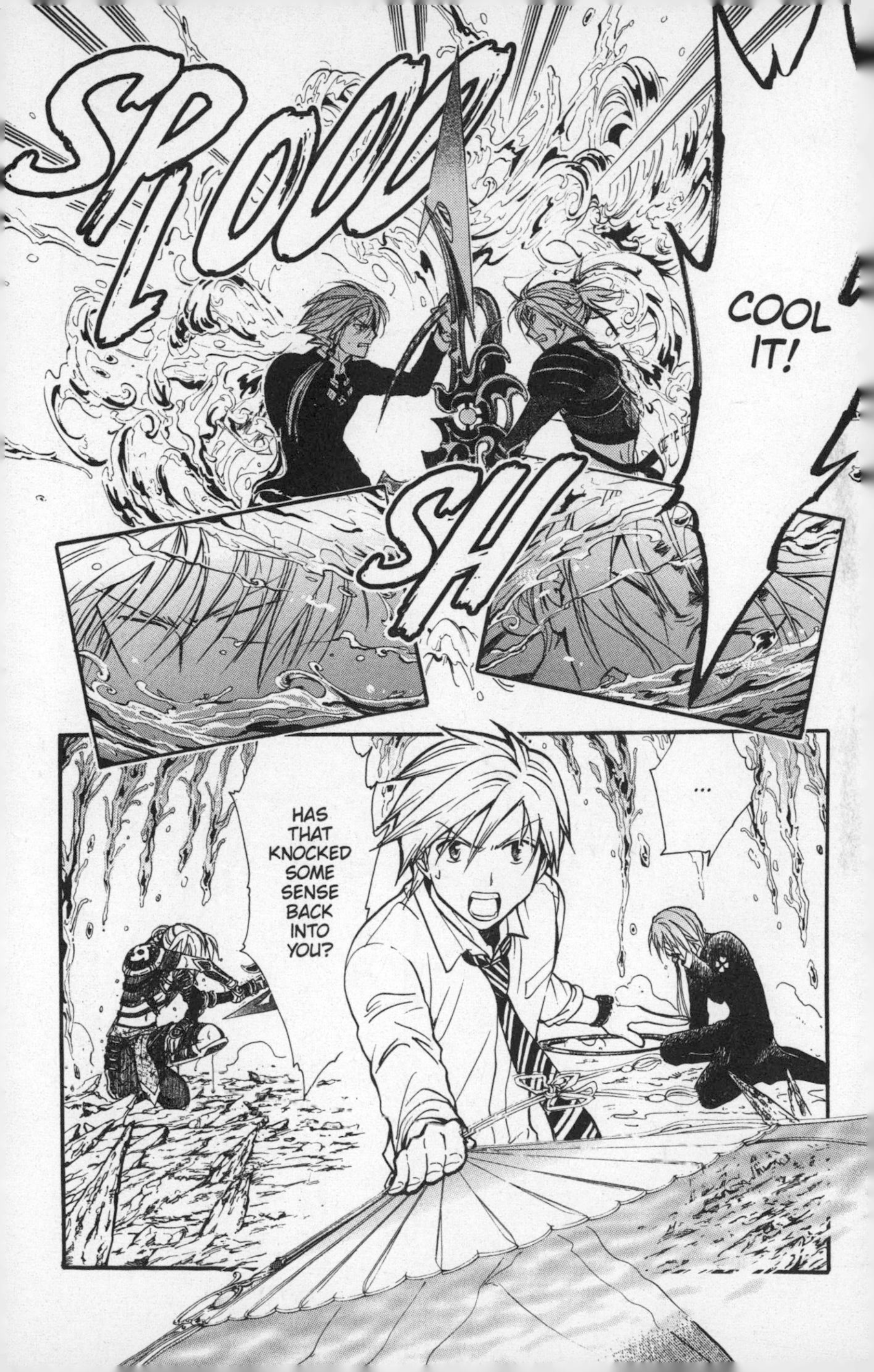
SPOOSH
COOL IT!
...
HAS THAT KNOCKED SOME SENSE BACK INTO YOU?

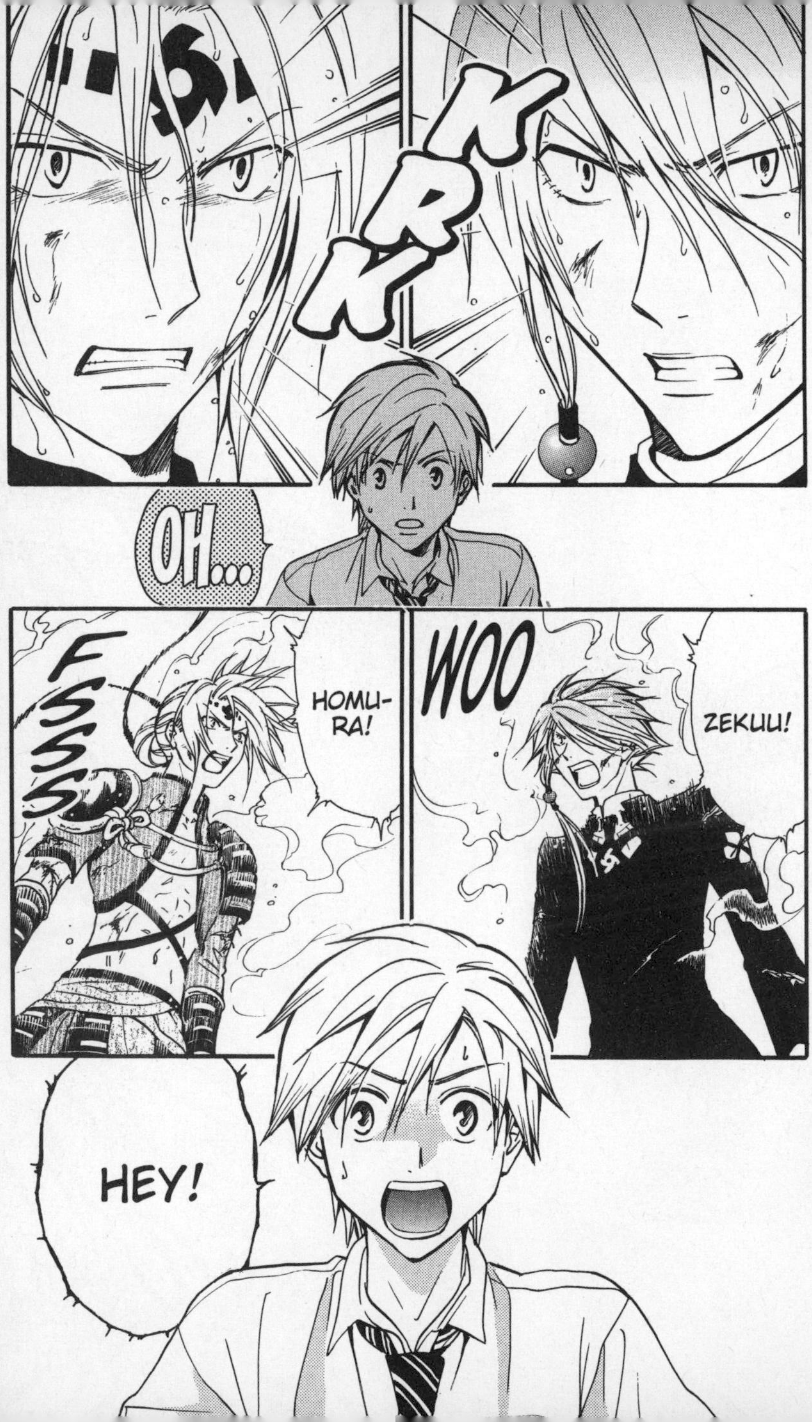
KRK
OH...
WOO
ZEKUU!
FSSSS
HOMU-
RA!
HEY!

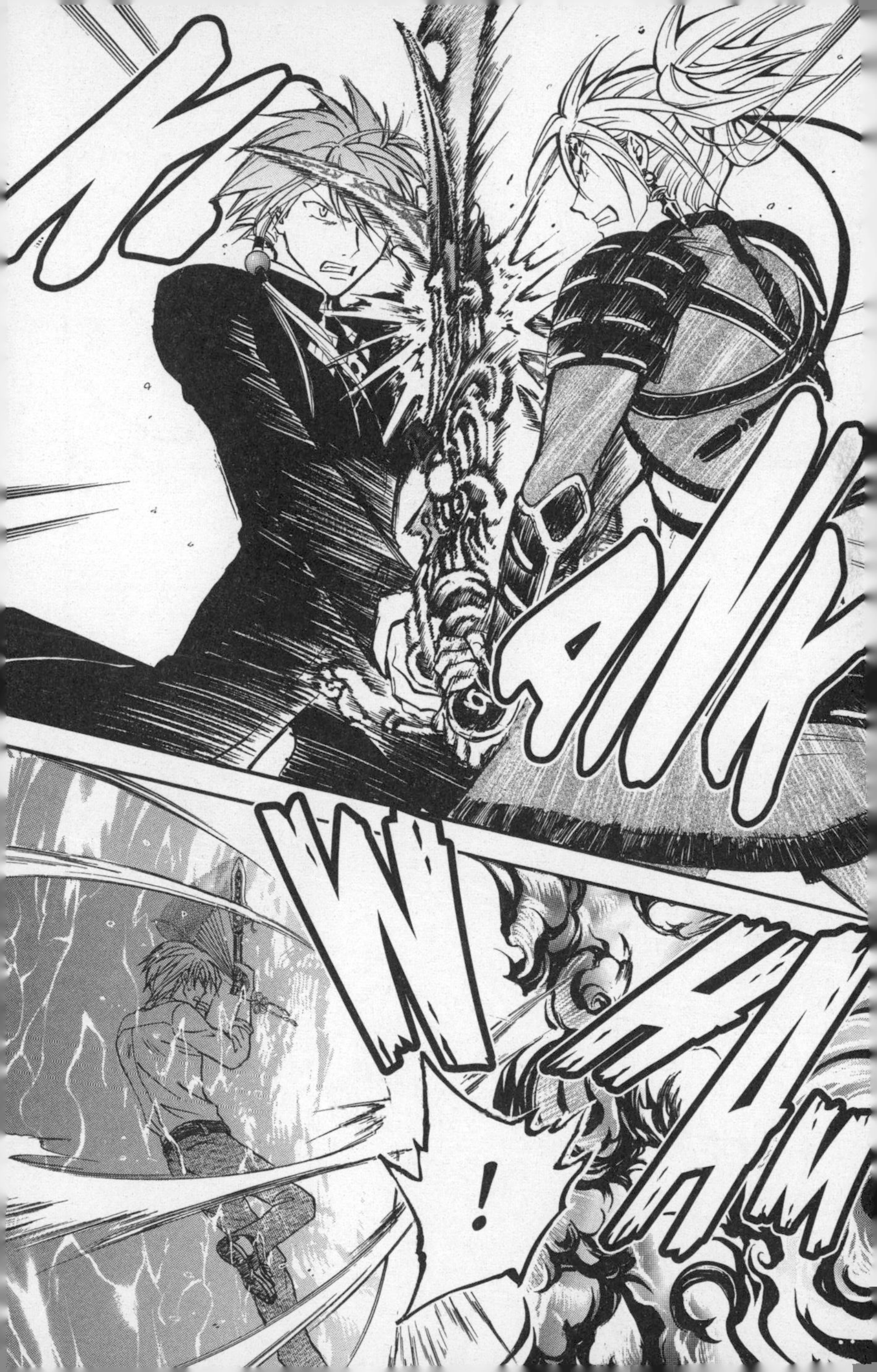
!

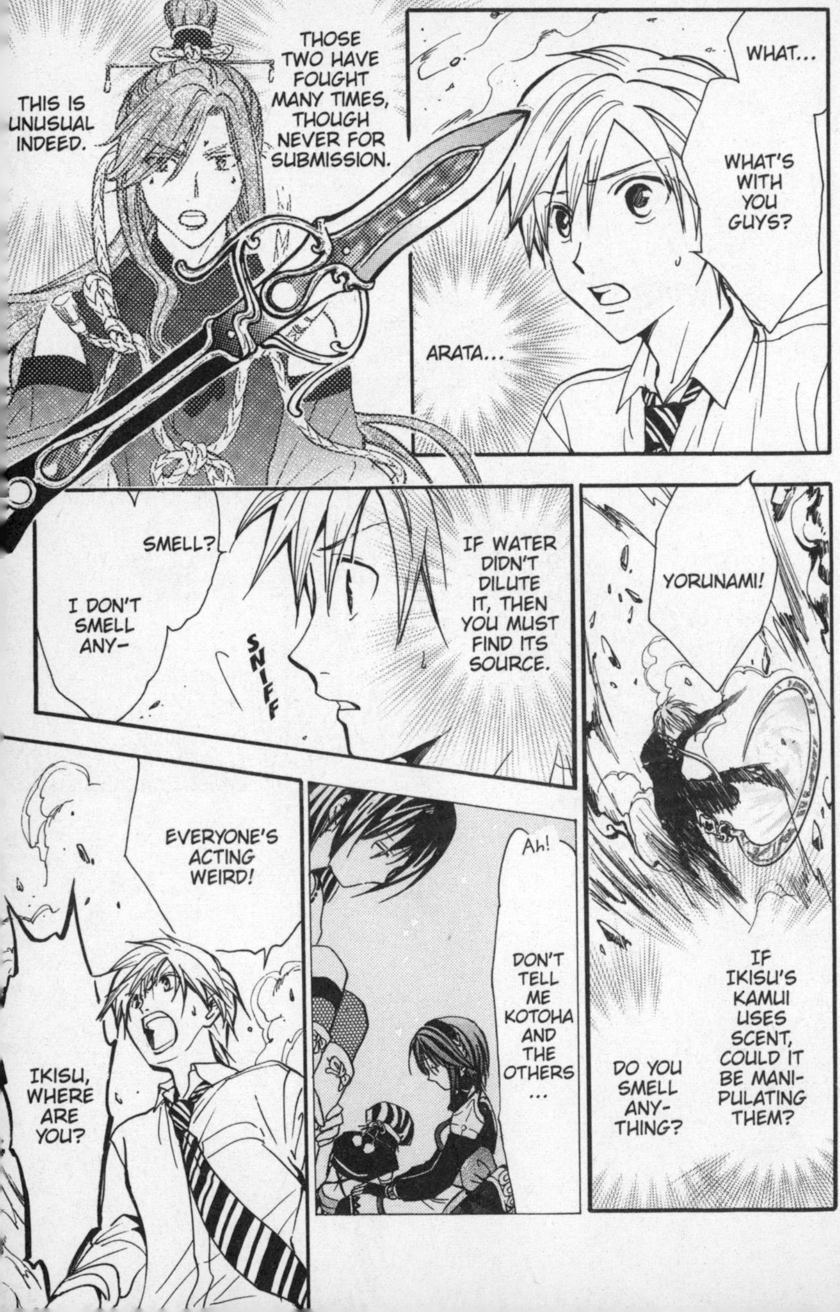
WHAT...
WHAT'S WITH YOU GUYS?
ARATA...
THOSE TWO HAVE FOUGHT MANY TIMES, THOUGH NEVER FOR SUBMISSION.
THIS IS UNUSUAL INDEED.
YORUNAMI!
IF IKISU'S KAMUI USES SCENT, COULD IT BE MANI-PULATING THEM?
DO YOU SMELL ANY-THING?
IF WATER DIDN'T DILUTE IT, THEN YOU MUST FIND ITS SOURCE.
SNIFF
SMELL?
I DON'T SMELL ANY-
Ah!
DON'T TELL ME KOTOHA AND THE OTHERS ...
EVERYONE'S ACTING WEIRD!
IKISU, WHERE ARE YOU?

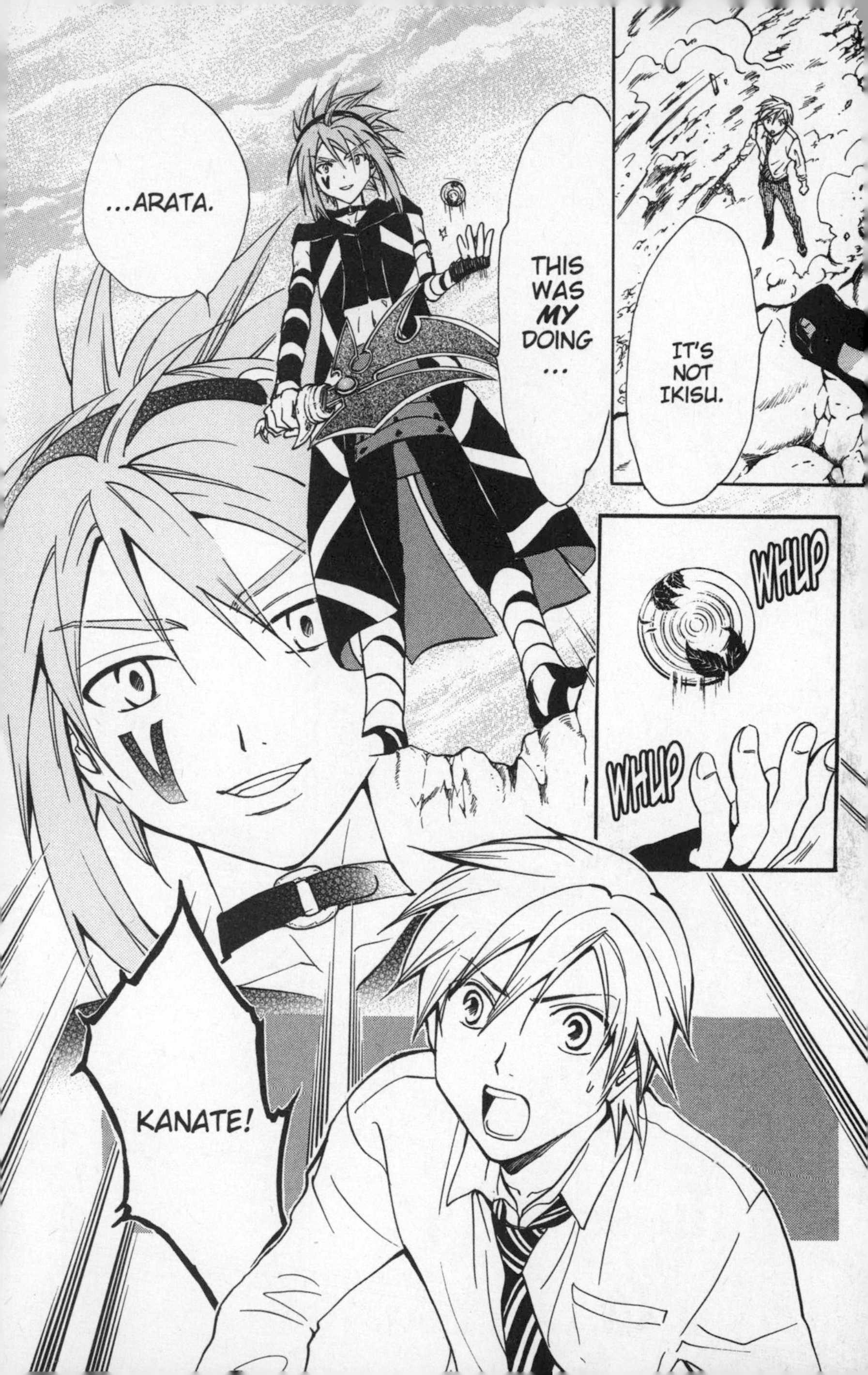
IT'S NOT IKISU.
WHLUP
WHLUP
THIS WAS MY DOING ...
...ARATA.
KANATE!

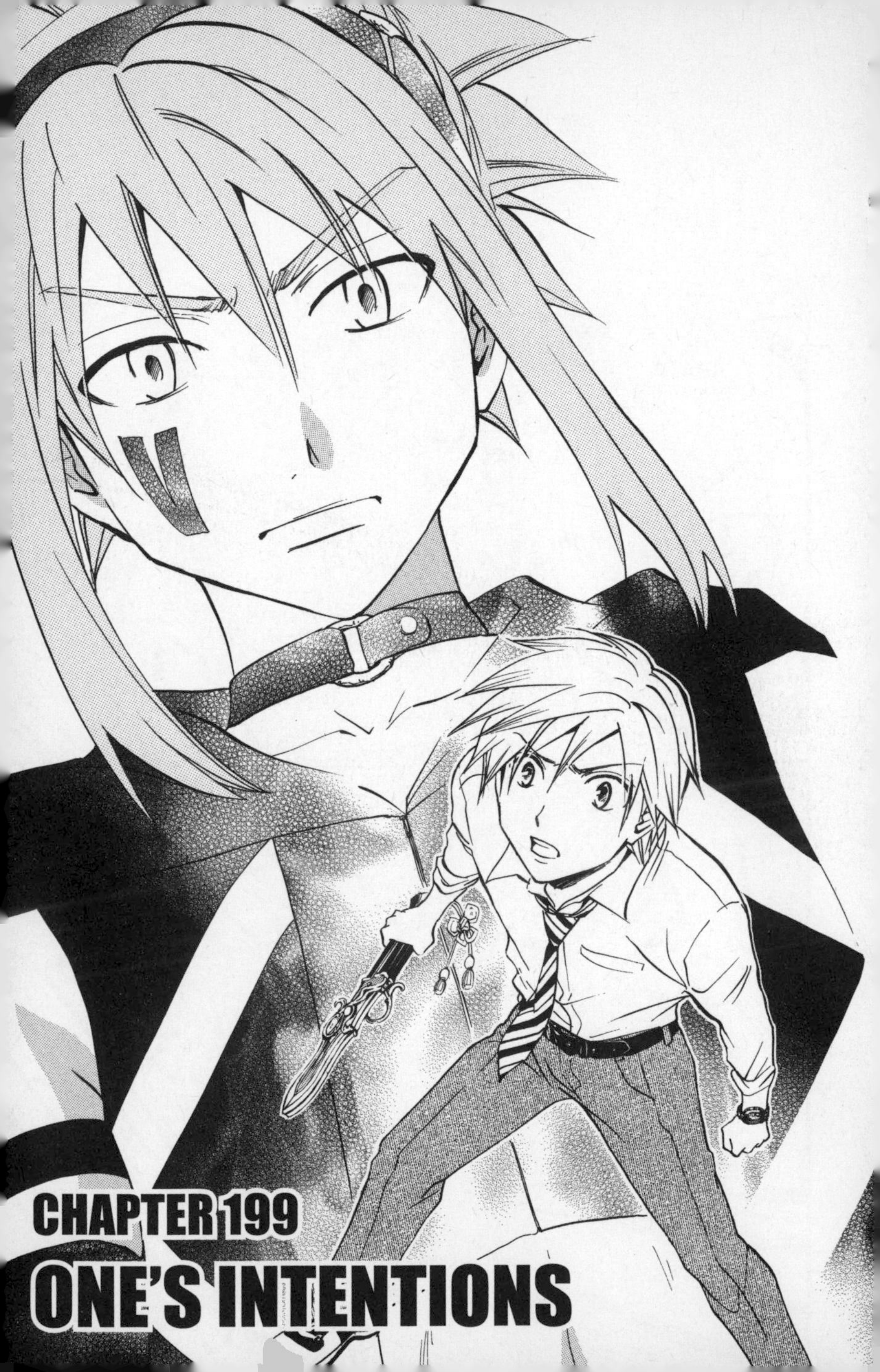
CHAPTER 199
ONE'S INTENTIONS

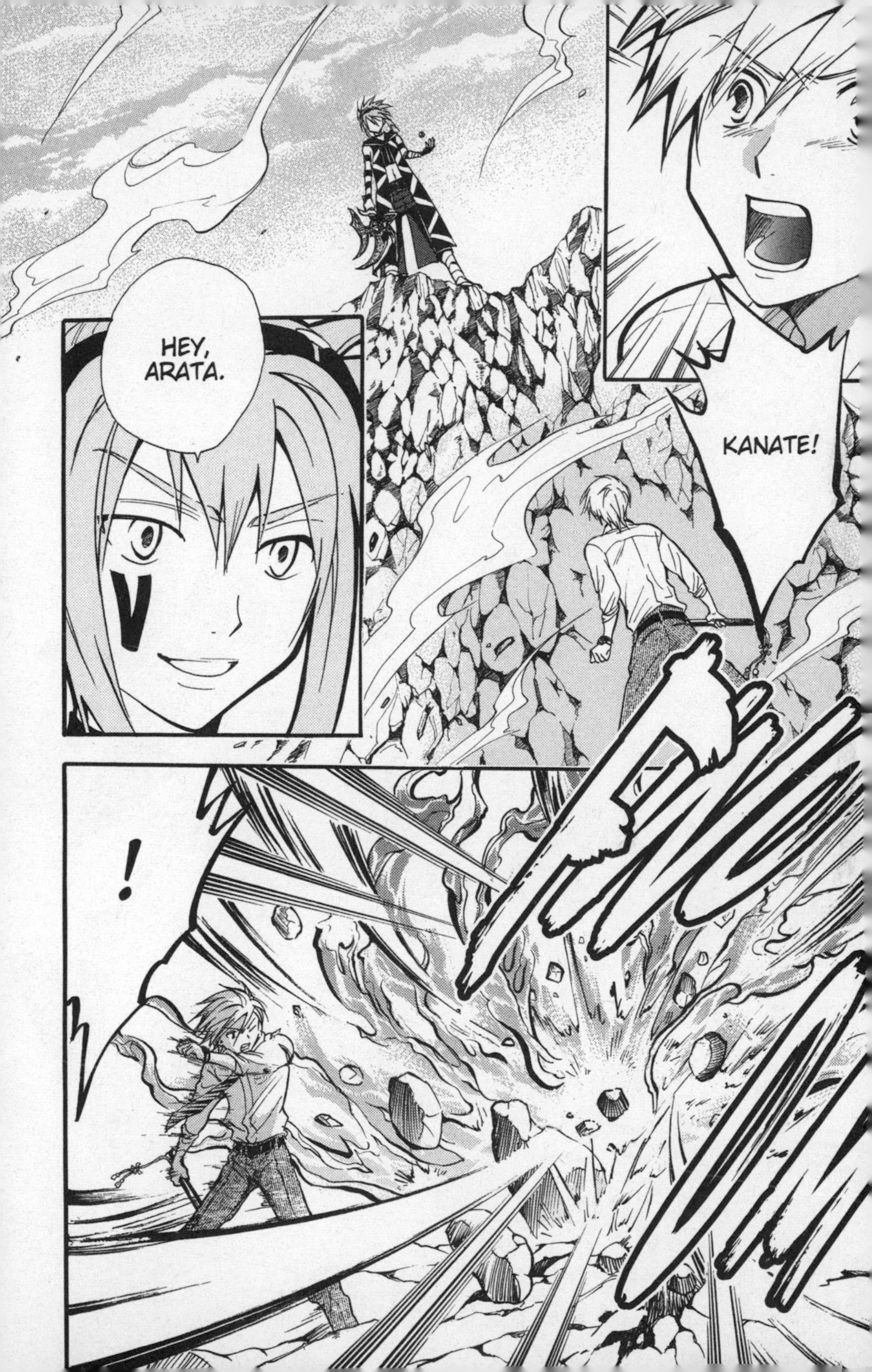
KANATE!
HEY, ARATA.
!

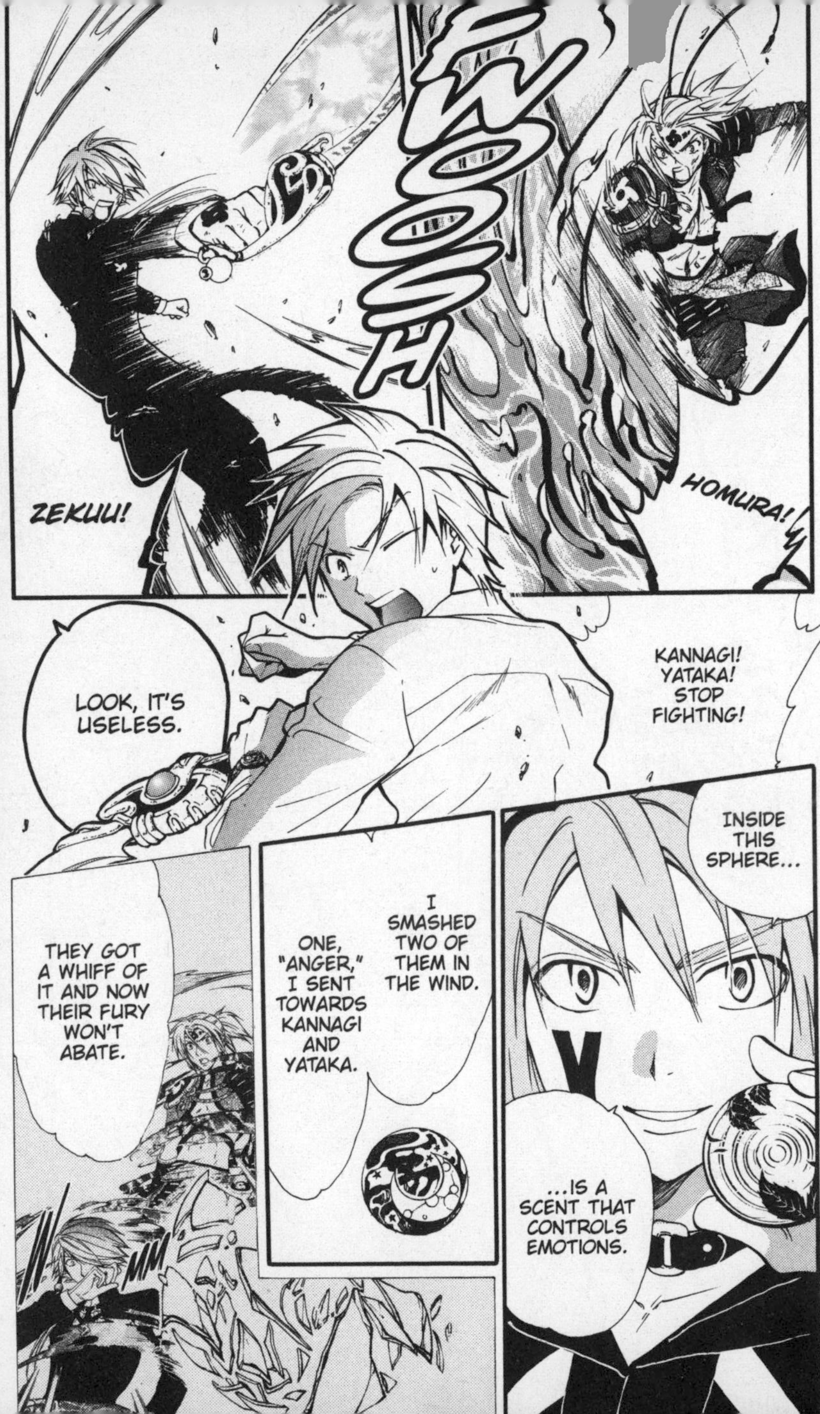
HOMURA!
FWOOSH
ZEKUU!
KANNAGI! YATAKA! STOP FIGHTING!
LOOK, IT'S USELESS.
INSIDE THIS SPHERE...
...IS A SCENT THAT CONTROLS EMOTIONS.
I SMASHED TWO OF THEM IN THE WIND.
ONE, "ANGER," I SENT TOWARDS KANNAGI AND YATAKA.
THEY GOT A WHIFF OF IT AND NOW THEIR FURY WON'T ABATE.
NMM

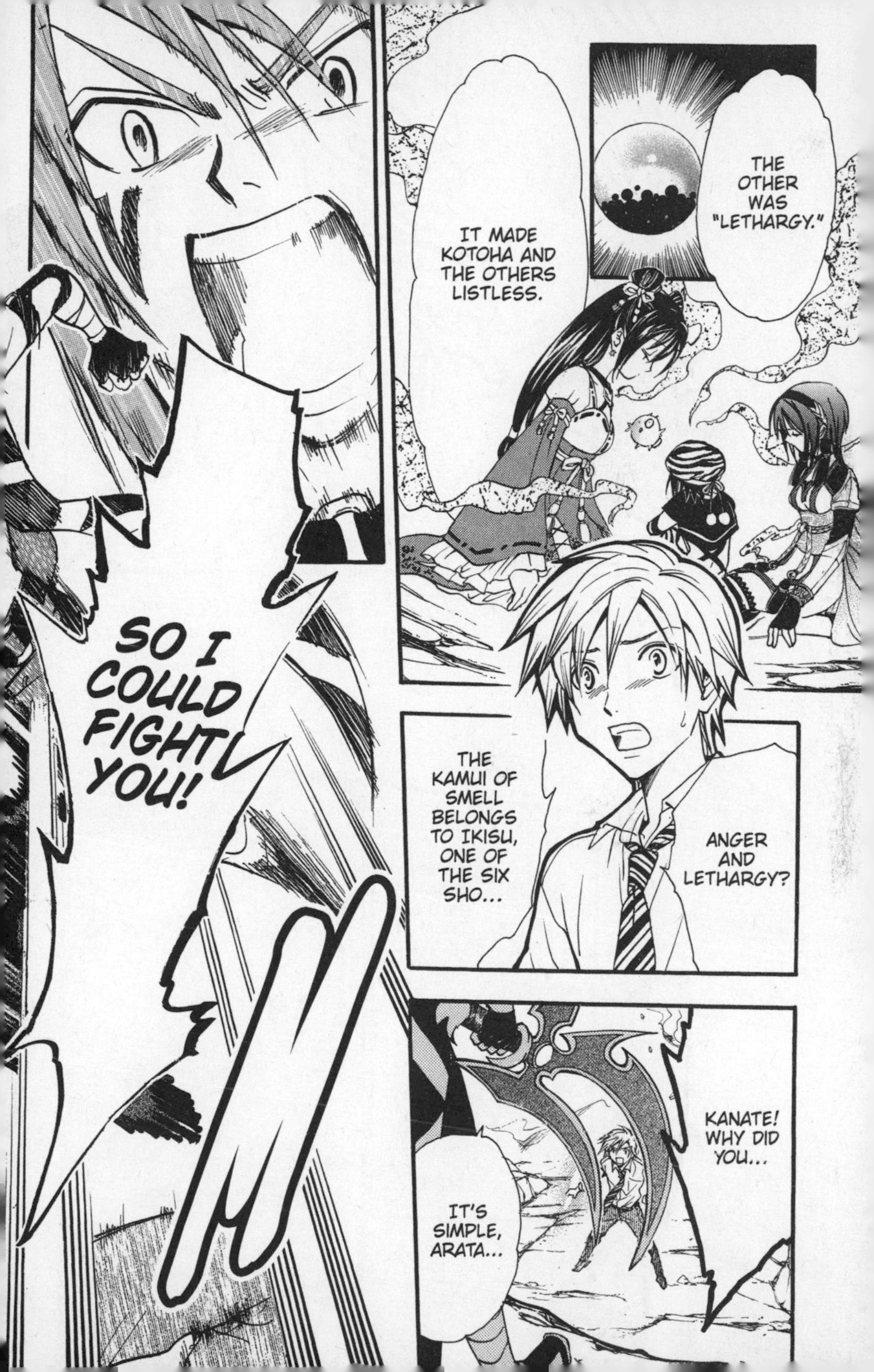
THE OTHER WAS "LETHARGY."
IT MADE KOTOHA AND THE OTHERS LISTLESS.
ANGER AND LETHARGY?
THE KAMUI OF SMELL BELONGS TO IKISU, ONE OF THE SIX SHO...
KANATE! WHY DID YOU...
IT'S SIMPLE, ARATA...
SO I COULD FIGHT YOU!

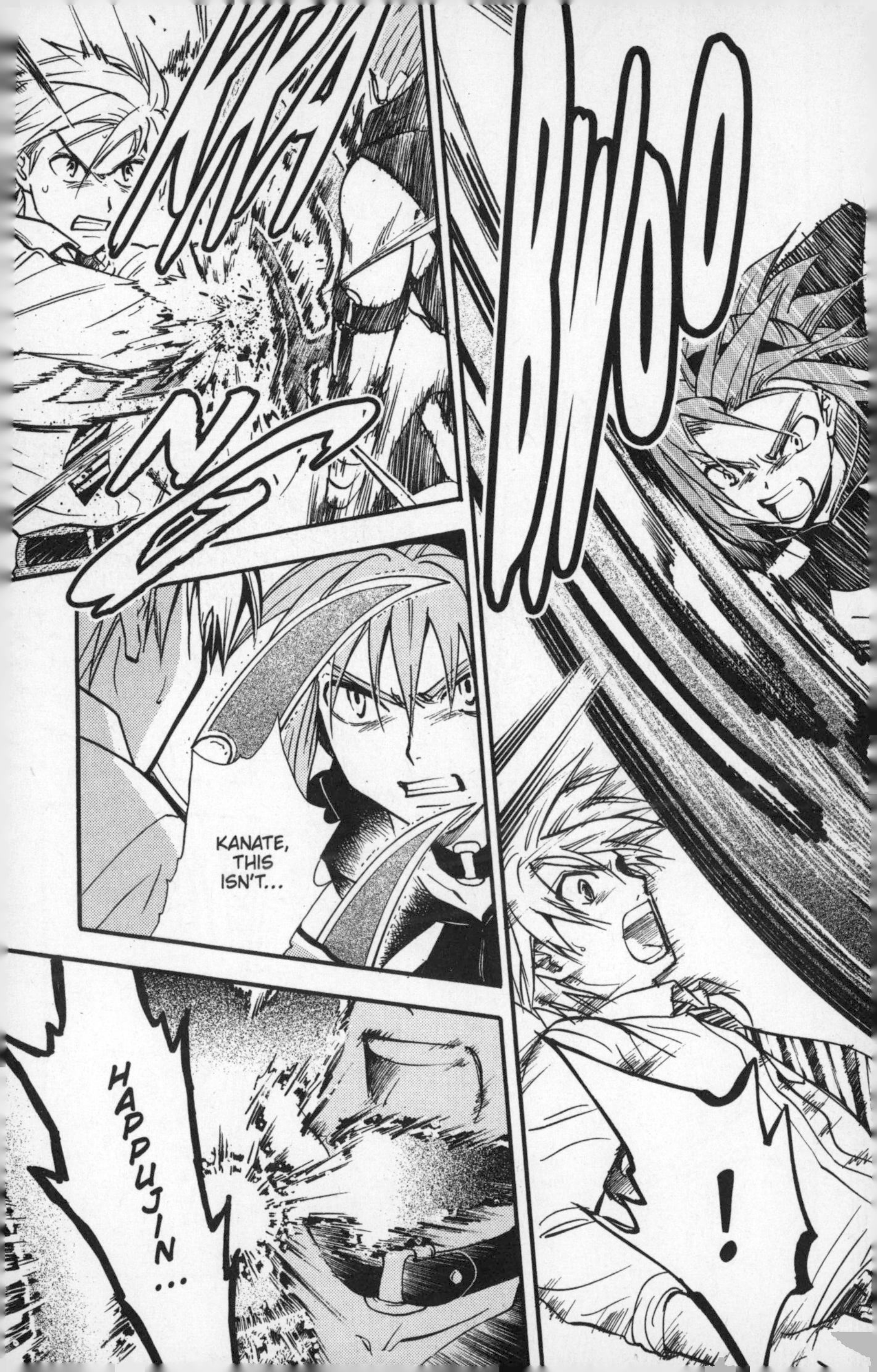
!
KANATE, THIS ISN'T...
HAPPUJIN...

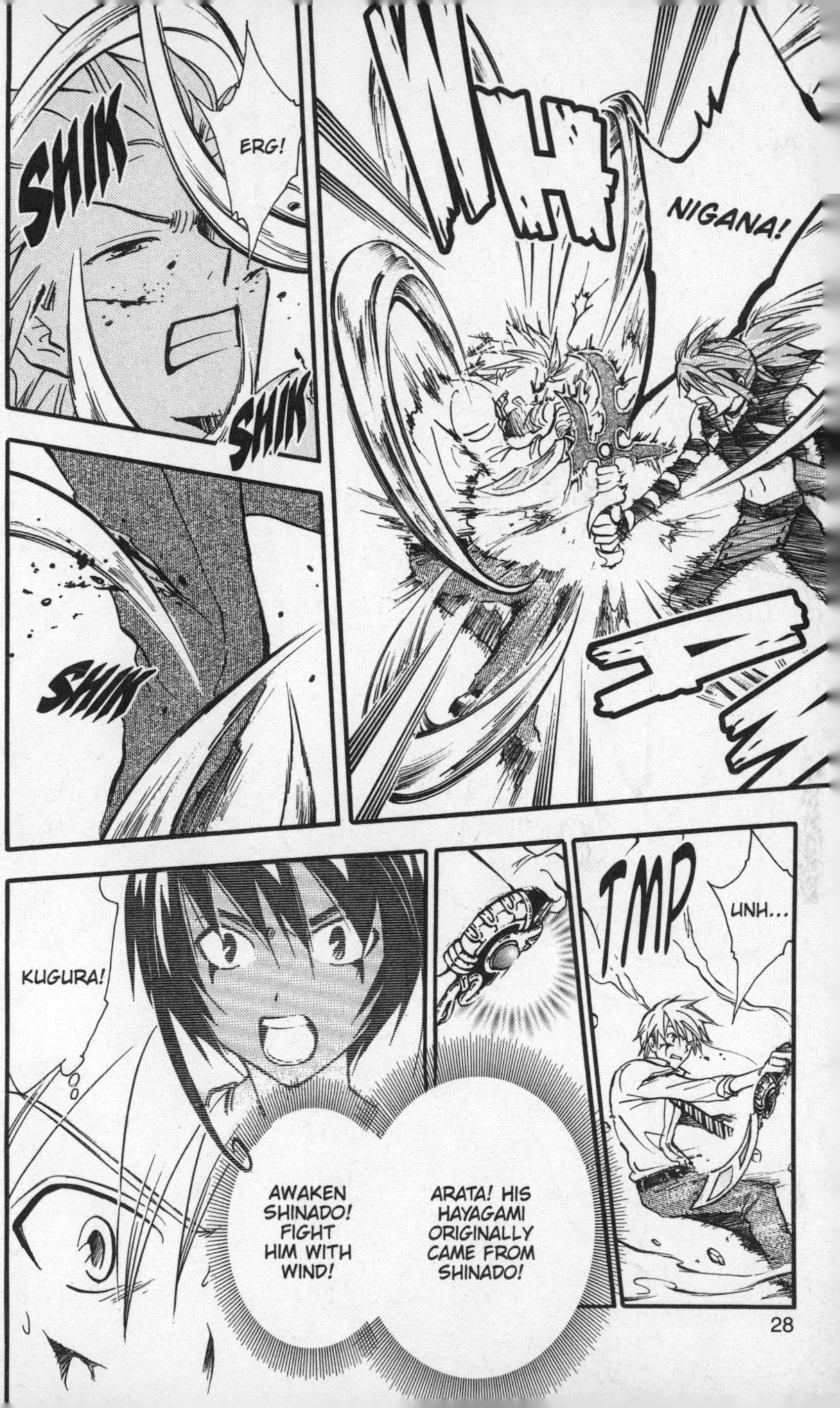
NIGANA!
SHIK
ERG!
SHIK
SHIK
TMP
UNH...
KUGURA!
ARATA! HIS HAYAGAMI ORIGINALLY CAME FROM SHINADO!
AWAKEN SHINADO! FIGHT HIM WITH WIND!

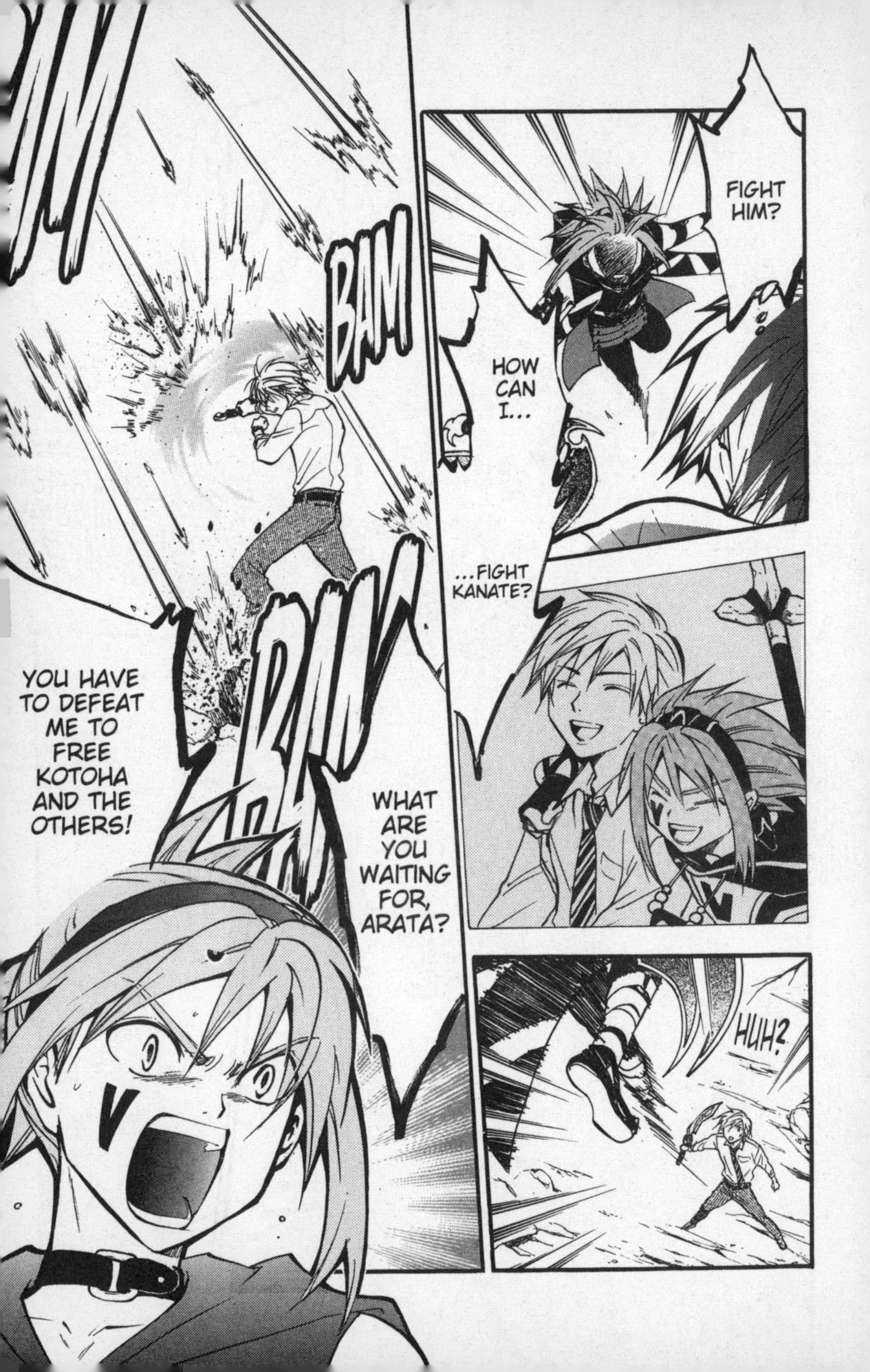
FIGHT HIM?
HOW CAN I...
...FIGHT KANATE?
HUH?
BAM
WHAT ARE YOU WAITING FOR, ARATA?
YOU HAVE TO DEFEAT ME TO FREE KOTOHA AND THE OTHERS!

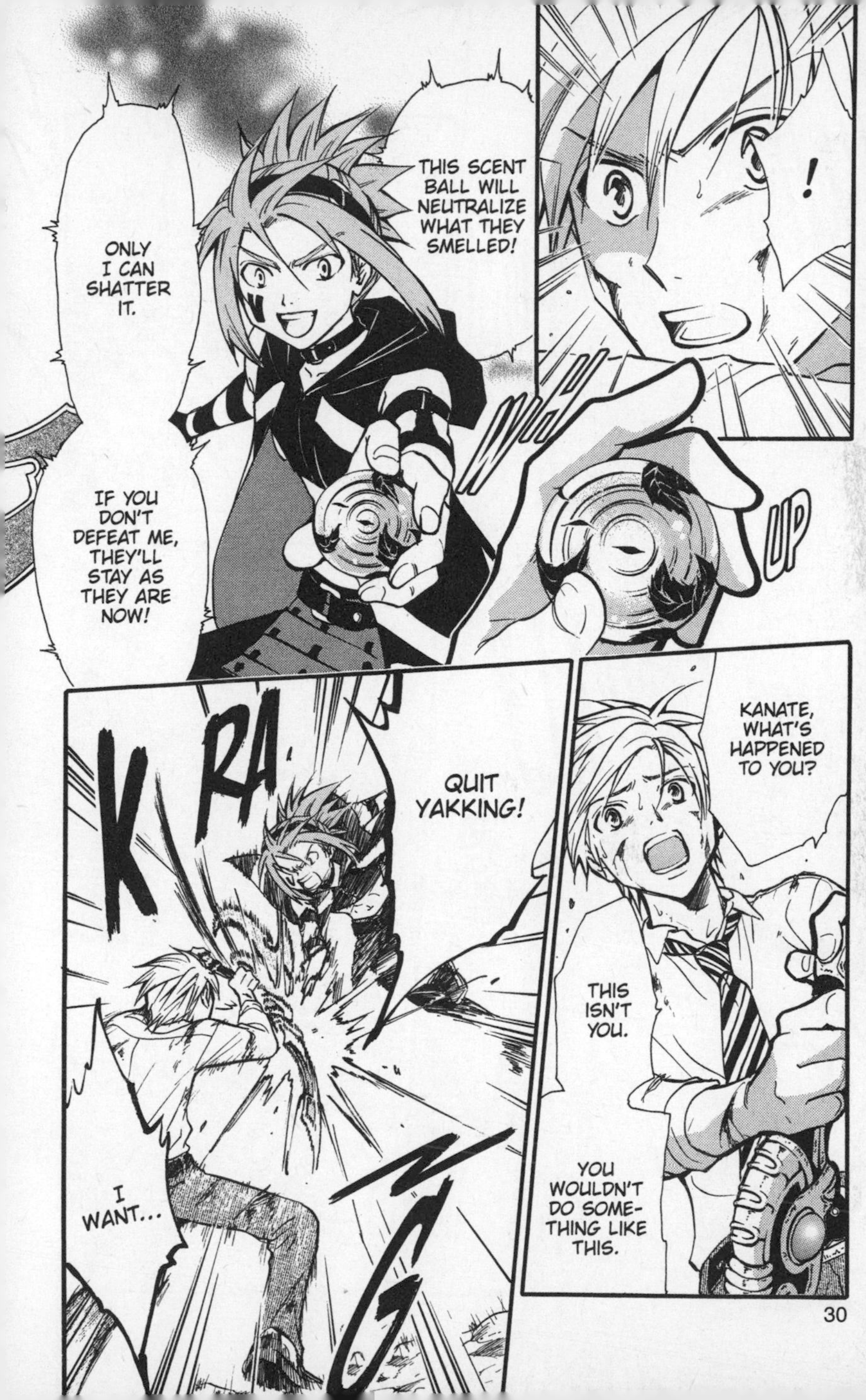
!
THIS SCENT BALL WILL NEUTRALIZE WHAT THEY SMELLED!
ONLY I CAN SHATTER IT.
UP
IF YOU DON'T DEFEAT ME, THEY'LL STAY AS THEY ARE NOW!
KANATE, WHAT'S HAPPENED TO YOU?
THIS ISN'T YOU.
YOU WOULDN'T DO SOME-THING LIKE THIS.
QUIT YAKKING!
KRANG
I WANT...

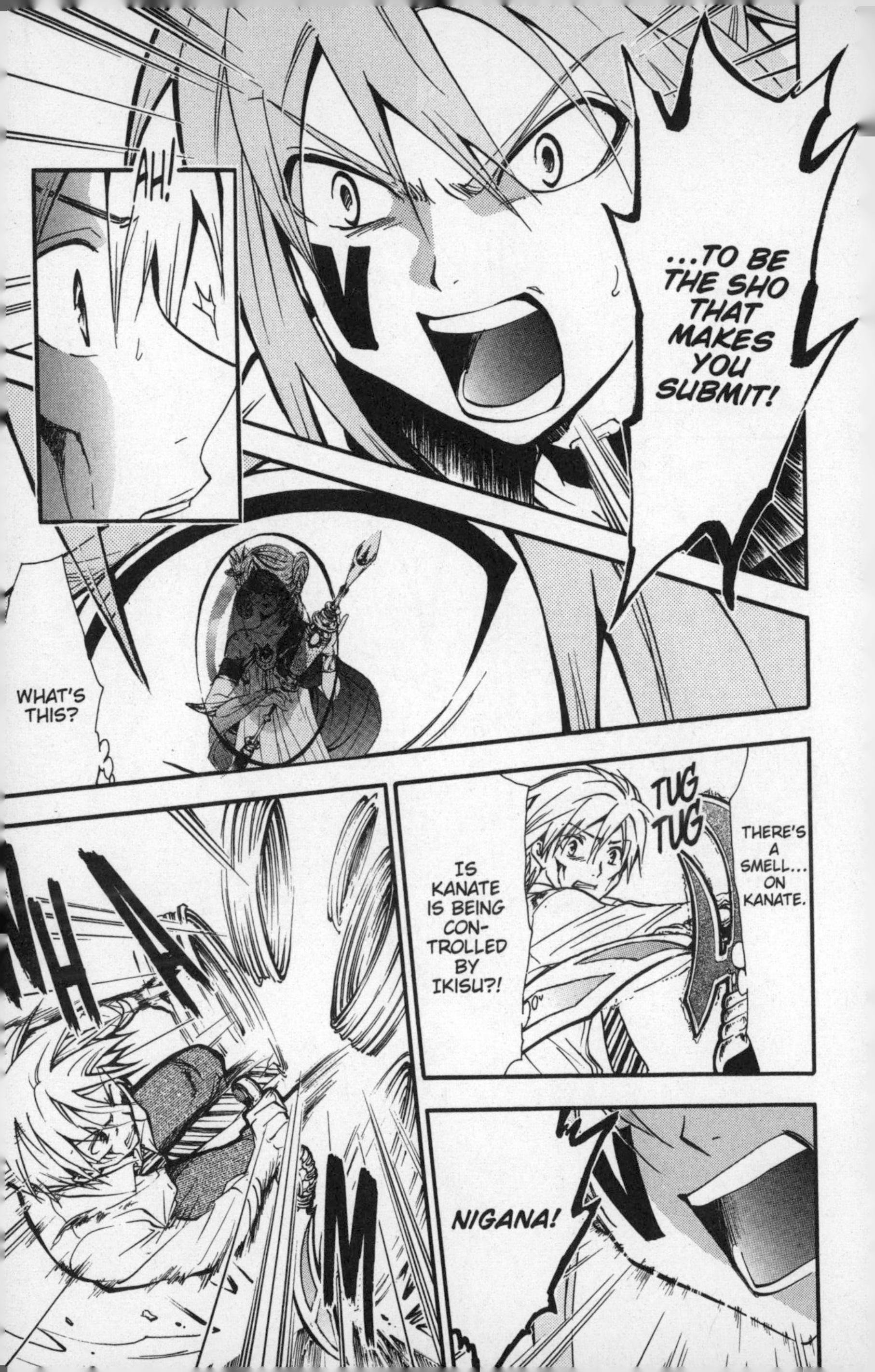
...TO BE THE SHO THAT MAKES YOU SUBMIT!
AH!
WHAT'S THIS?
TUG TUG
THERE'S A SMELL... ON KANATE.
IS KANATE IS BEING CON-TROLLED BY IKISU?!
NIGANA!

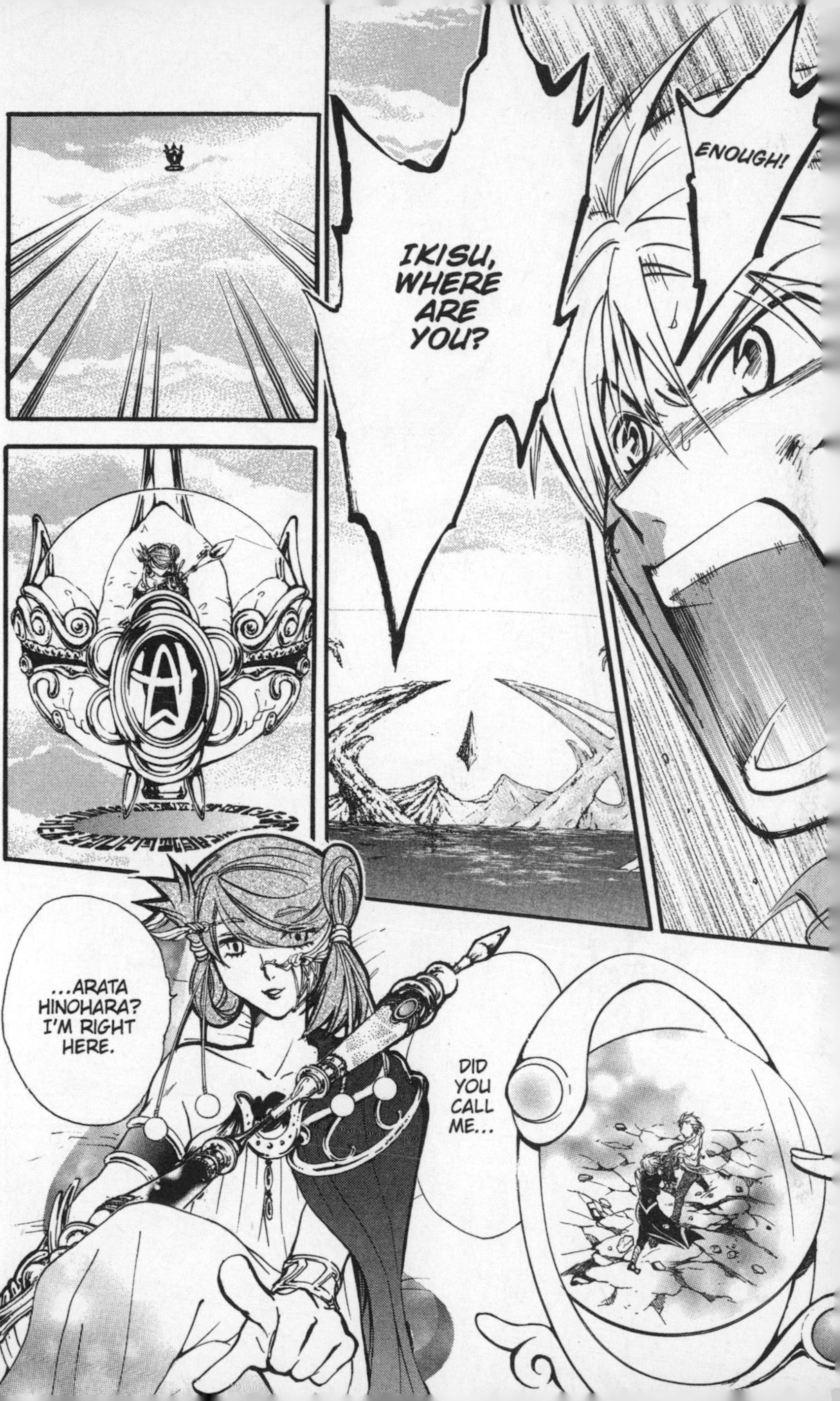
ENOUGH!
IKISU, WHERE ARE YOU?
DID YOU CALL ME...
...ARATA HINOHARA? I'M RIGHT HERE.

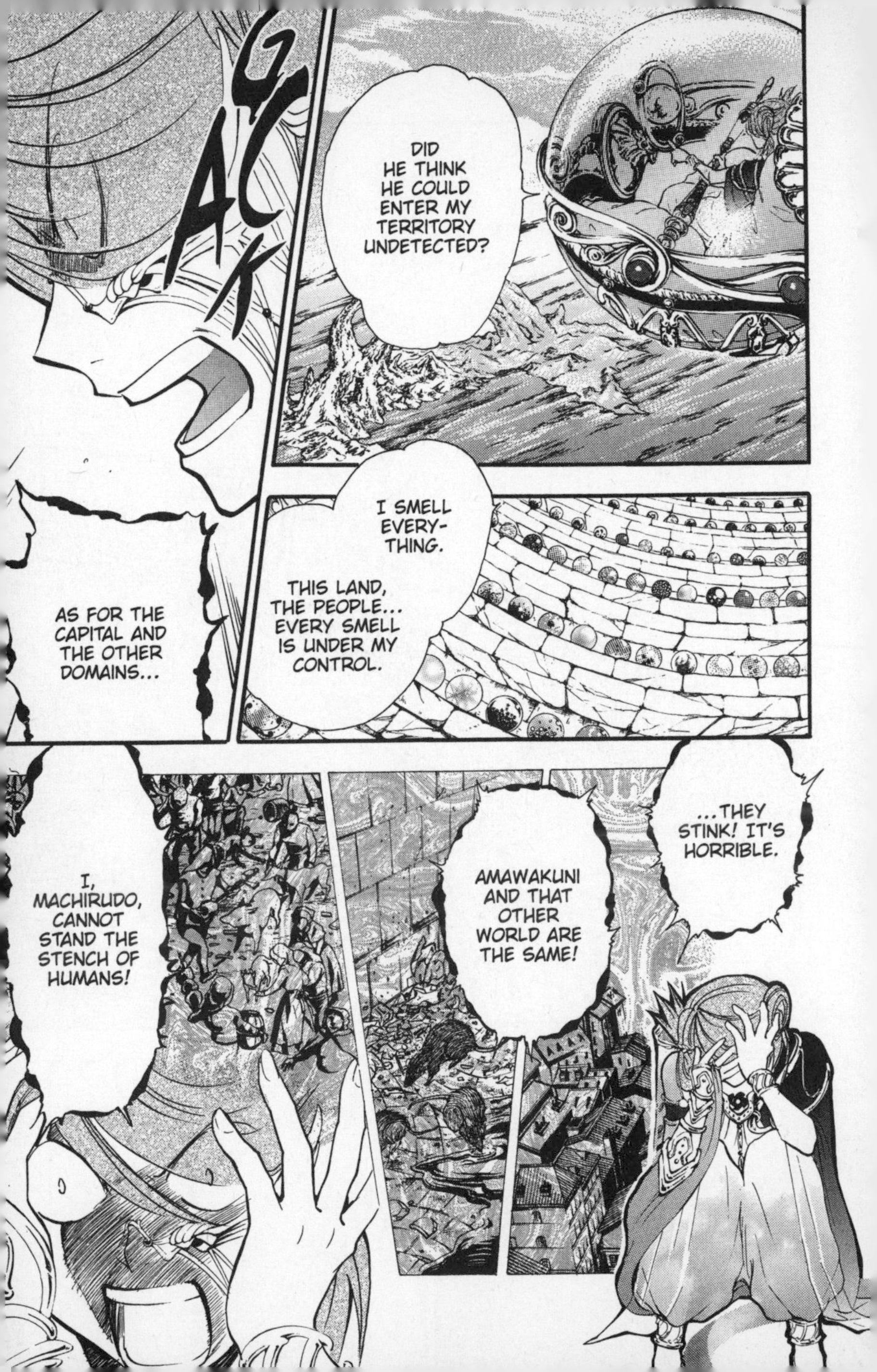
DID HE THINK HE COULD ENTER MY TERRITORY UNDETECTED?
GACK
I SMELL EVERY-THING.
THIS LAND, THE PEOPLE... EVERY SMELL IS UNDER MY CONTROL.
AS FOR THE CAPITAL AND THE OTHER DOMAINS...
...THEY STINK! IT'S HORRIBLE.
AMAWAKUNI AND THAT OTHER WORLD ARE THE SAME!
I, MACHIRUDO, CANNOT STAND THE STENCH OF HUMANS!

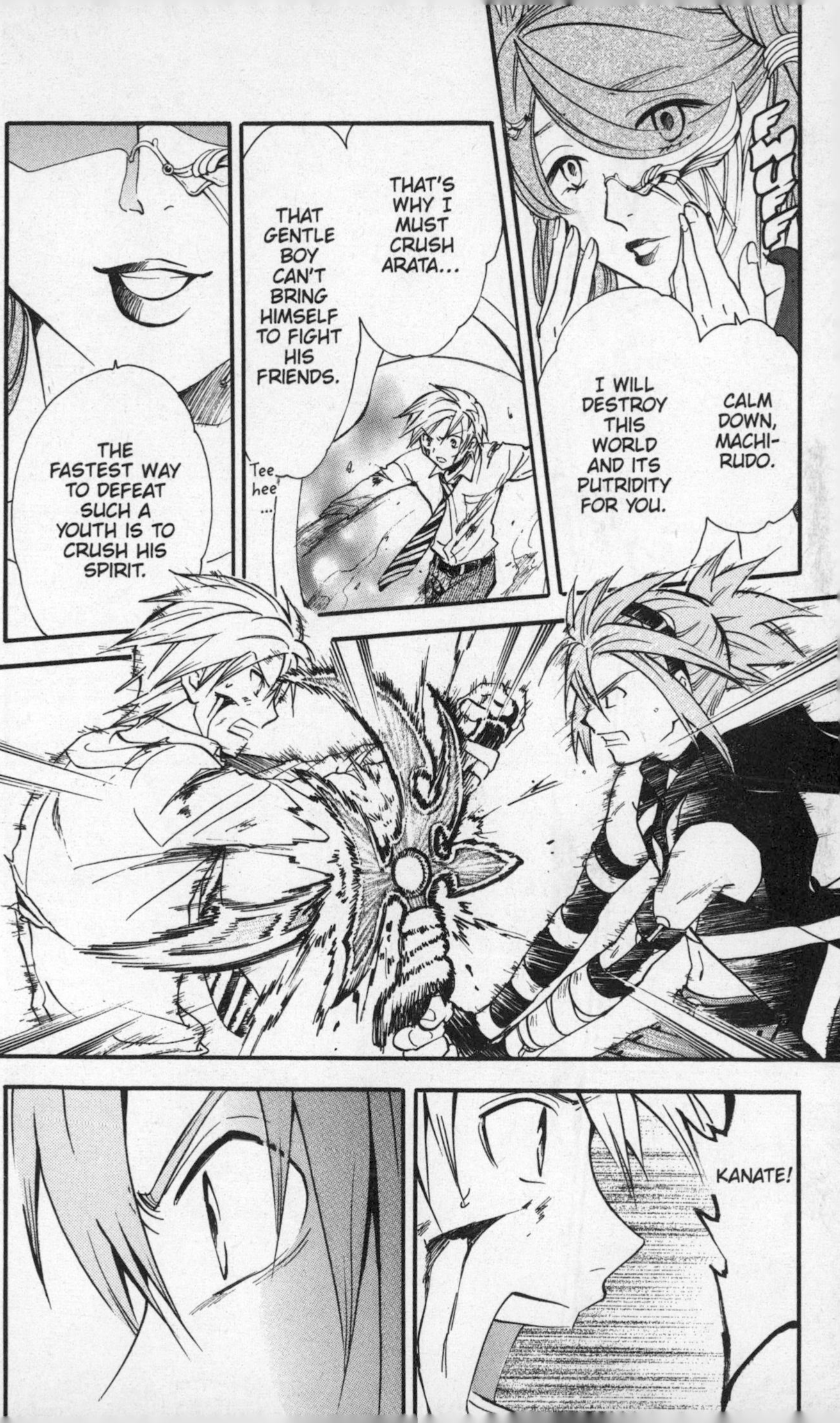
CALM DOWN, MACHI-RUDO.
I WILL DESTROY THIS WORLD AND ITS PUTRIDITY FOR YOU.
THAT'S WHY I MUST CRUSH ARATA...
THAT GENTLE BOY CAN'T BRING HIMSELF TO FIGHT HIS FRIENDS.
Tee hee...
THE FASTEST WAY TO DEFEAT SUCH A YOUTH IS TO CRUSH HIS SPIRIT.
KANATE!

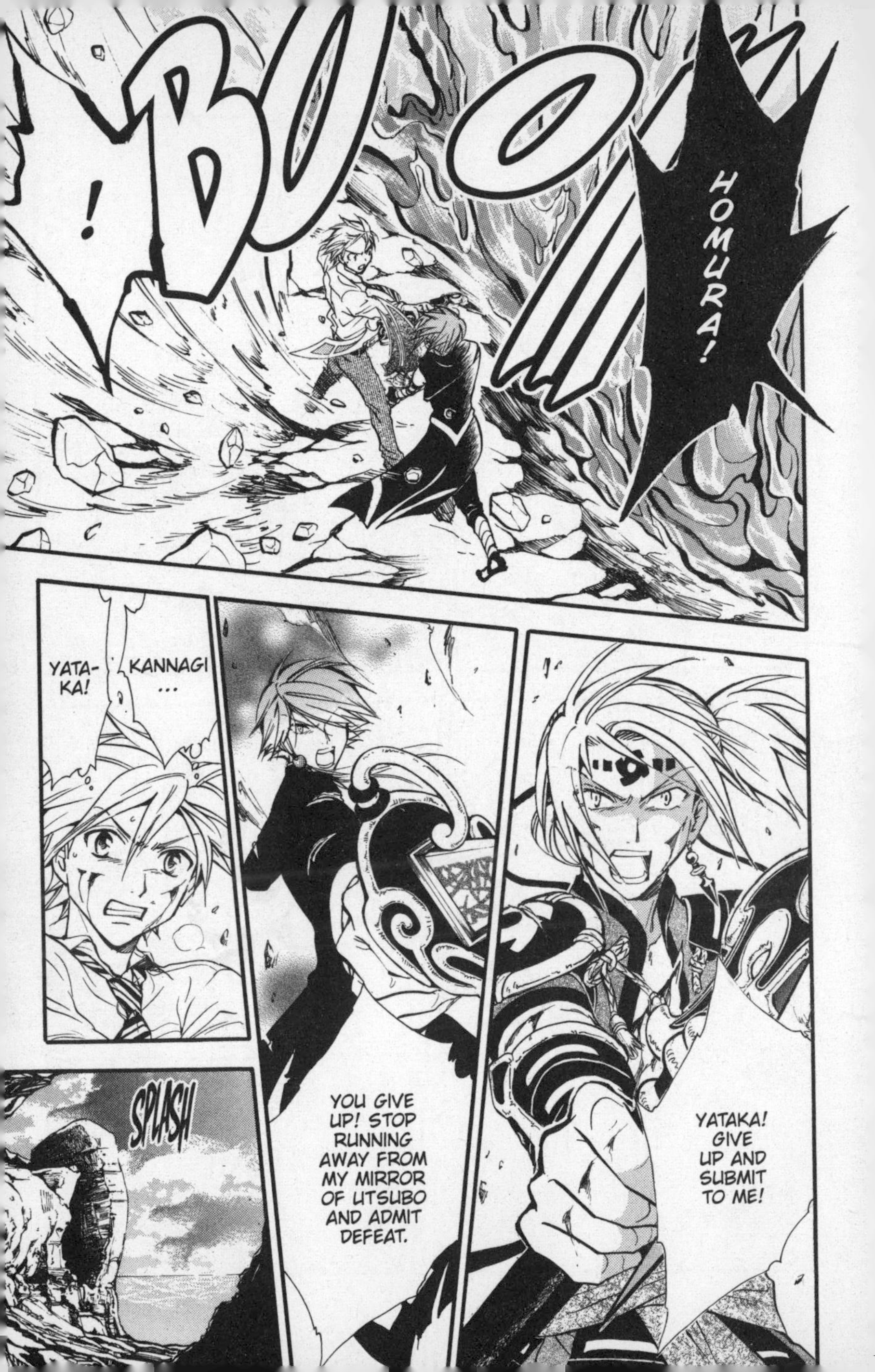
HOMURA!
YATAKA! GIVE UP AND SUBMIT TO ME!
YOU GIVE UP! STOP RUNNING AWAY FROM MY MIRROR OF UTSUBO AND ADMIT DEFEAT.
KANNAGI...
YATA-KA!
SPLASH

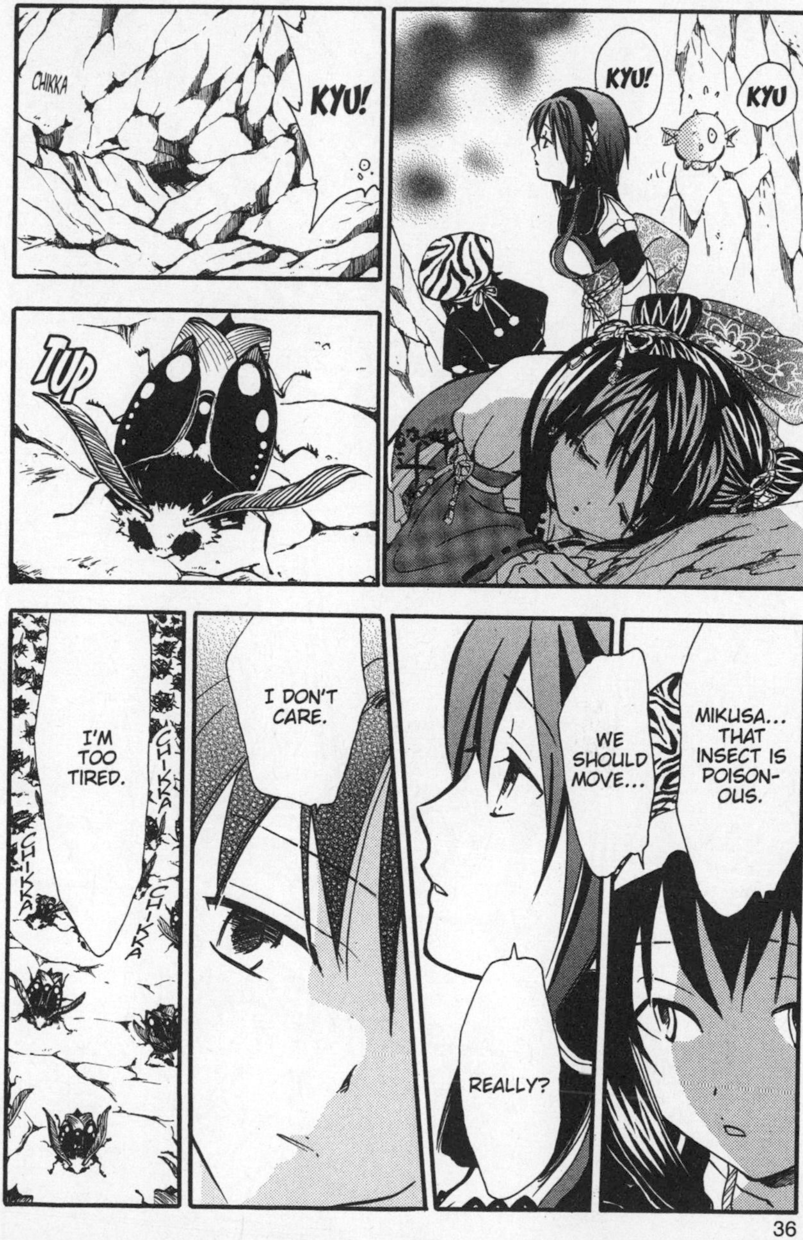
KYU!
KYU
CHIKKA
KYU!
TUP
MIKUSA... THAT INSECT IS POISON-OUS.
WE SHOULD MOVE...
REALLY?
I DON'T CARE.
I'M TOO TIRED.
CHIKKA CHIKKA CHIKKA CHIKKA

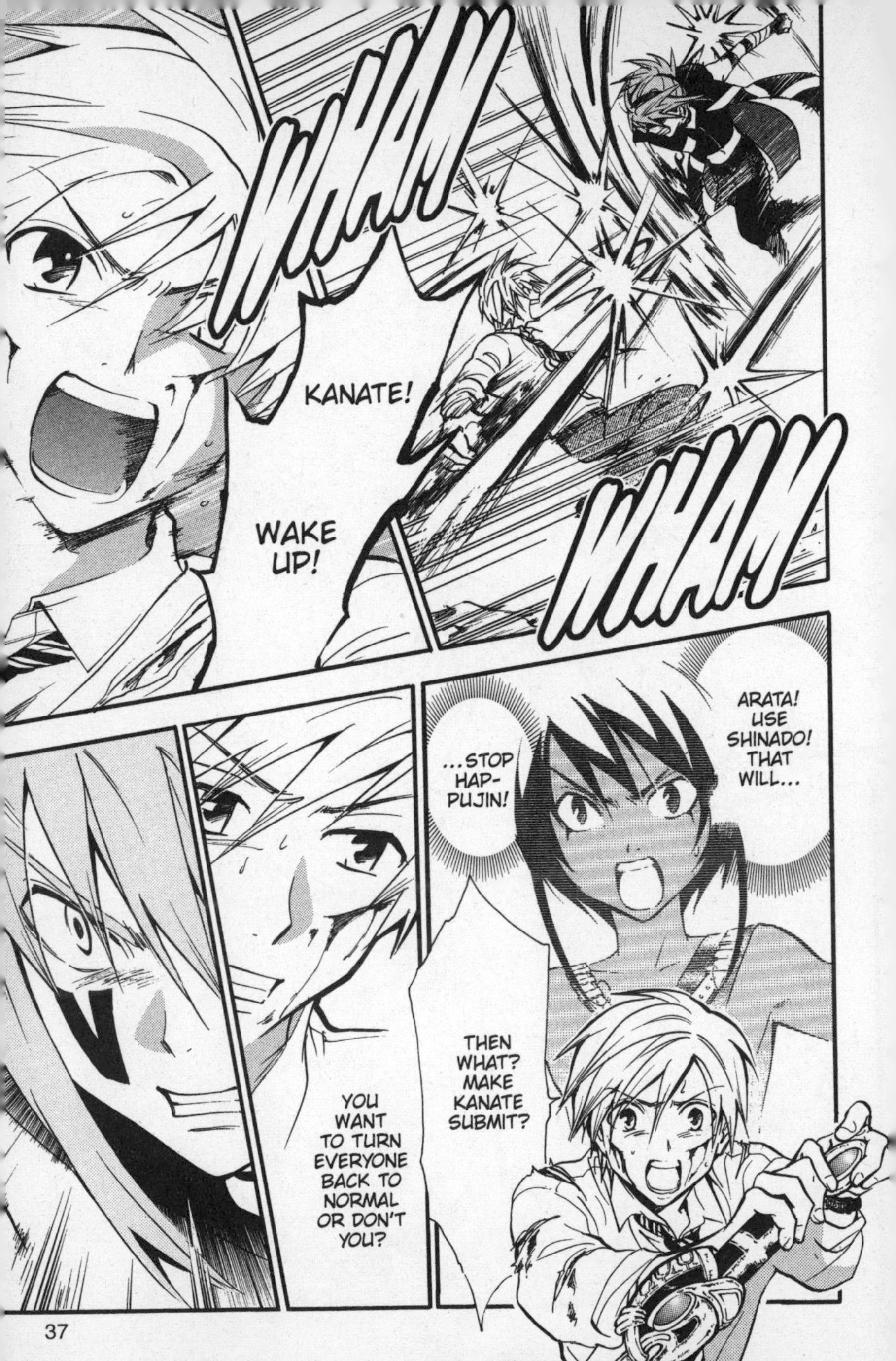
WHAM
WHAM
KANATE!
WAKE UP!
ARATA! USE SHINADO! THAT WILL...
...STOP HAP-PUJIN!
THEN WHAT? MAKE KANATE SUBMIT?
YOU WANT TO TURN EVERYONE BACK TO NORMAL OR DON'T YOU?

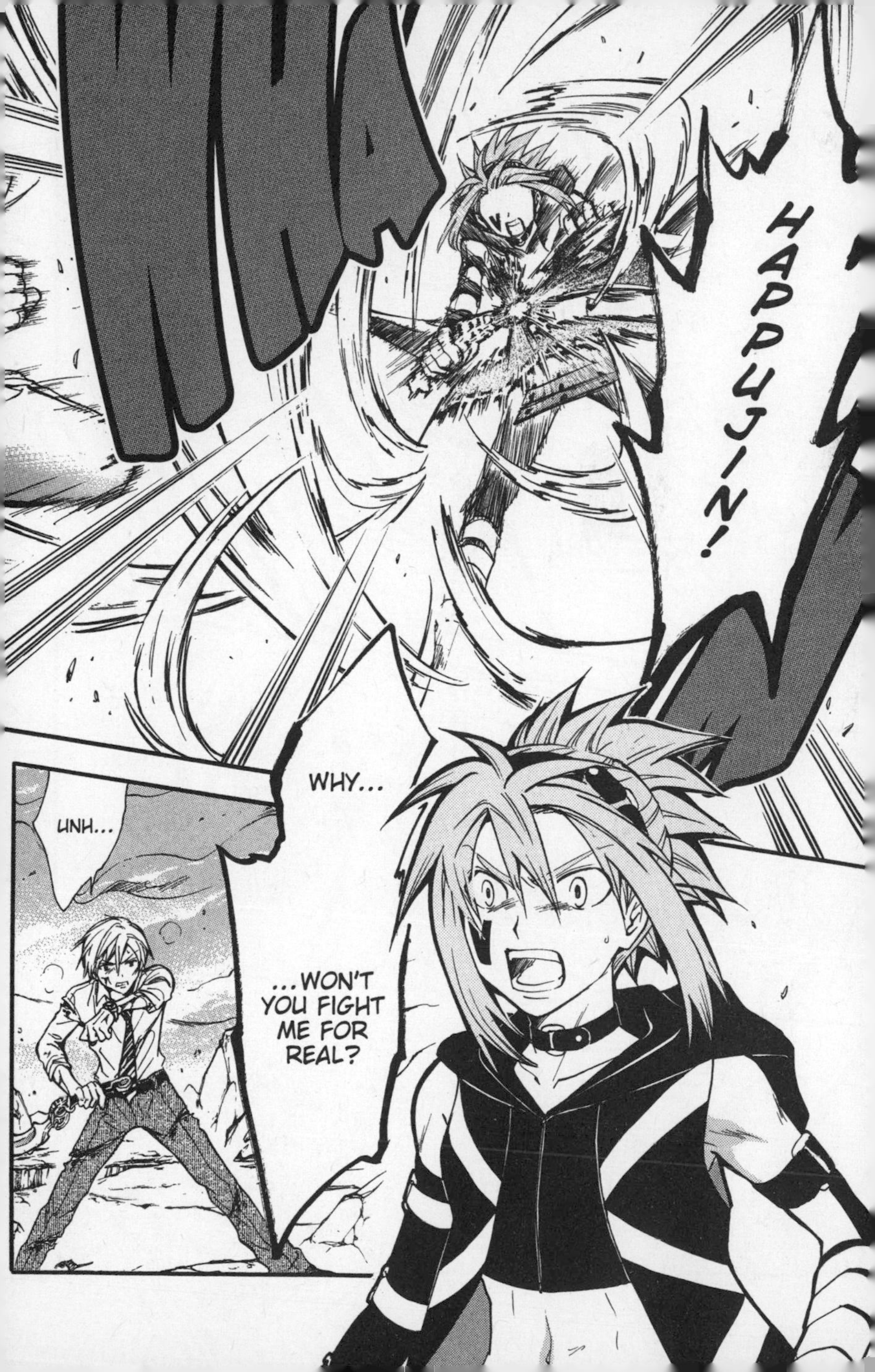
HAPPUJIN!
WHA
WHY...
...WON'T YOU FIGHT ME FOR REAL?
UNH...

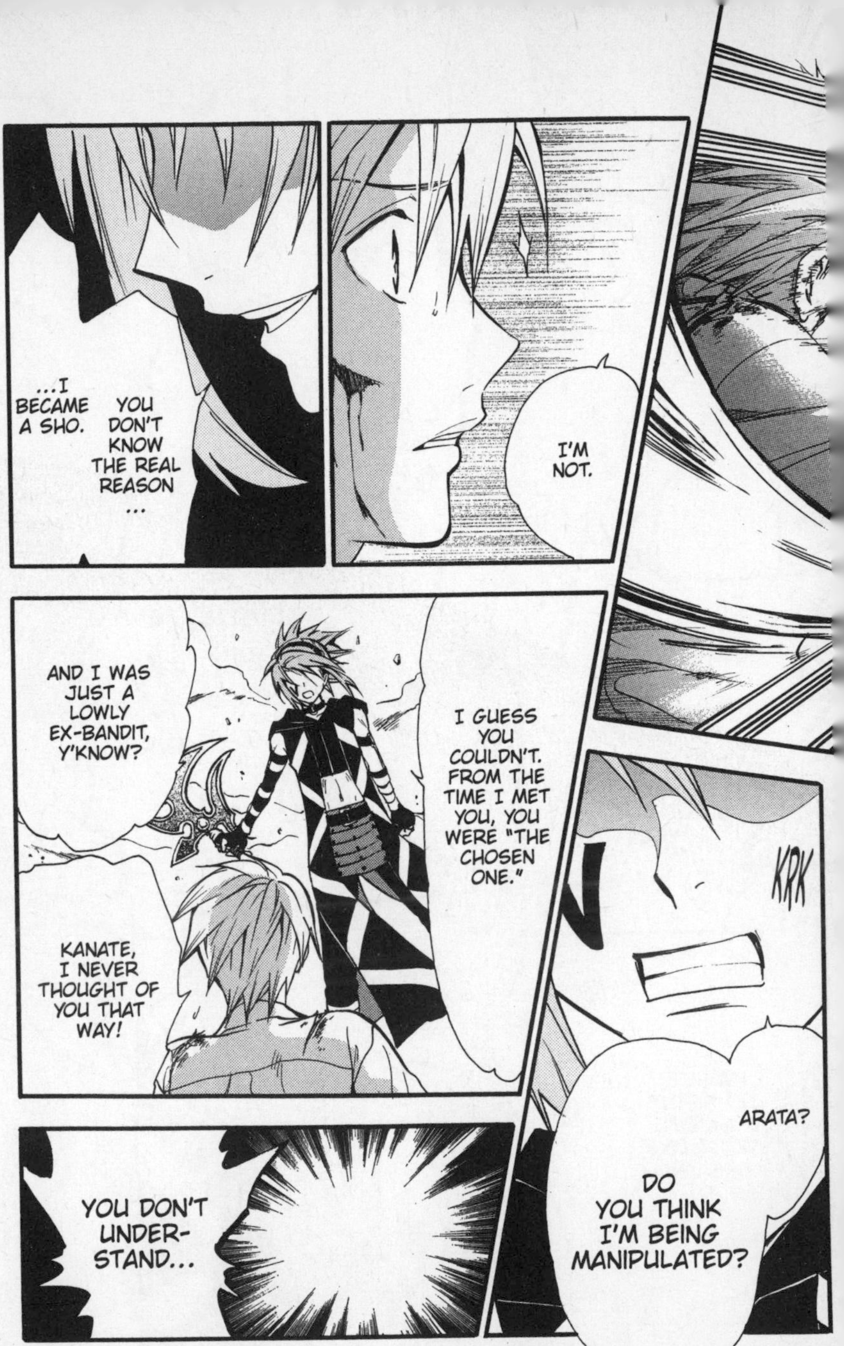
I'M NOT.
YOU DON'T KNOW THE REAL REASON ...
...I BECAME A SHO.
I GUESS YOU COULDN'T. FROM THE TIME I MET YOU, YOU WERE "THE CHOSEN ONE."
AND I WAS JUST A LOWLY EX-BANDIT, Y'KNOW?
KANATE, I NEVER THOUGHT OF YOU THAT WAY!
KRK
ARATA?
DO YOU THINK I'M BEING MANIPULATED?
YOU DON'T UNDER-STAND...

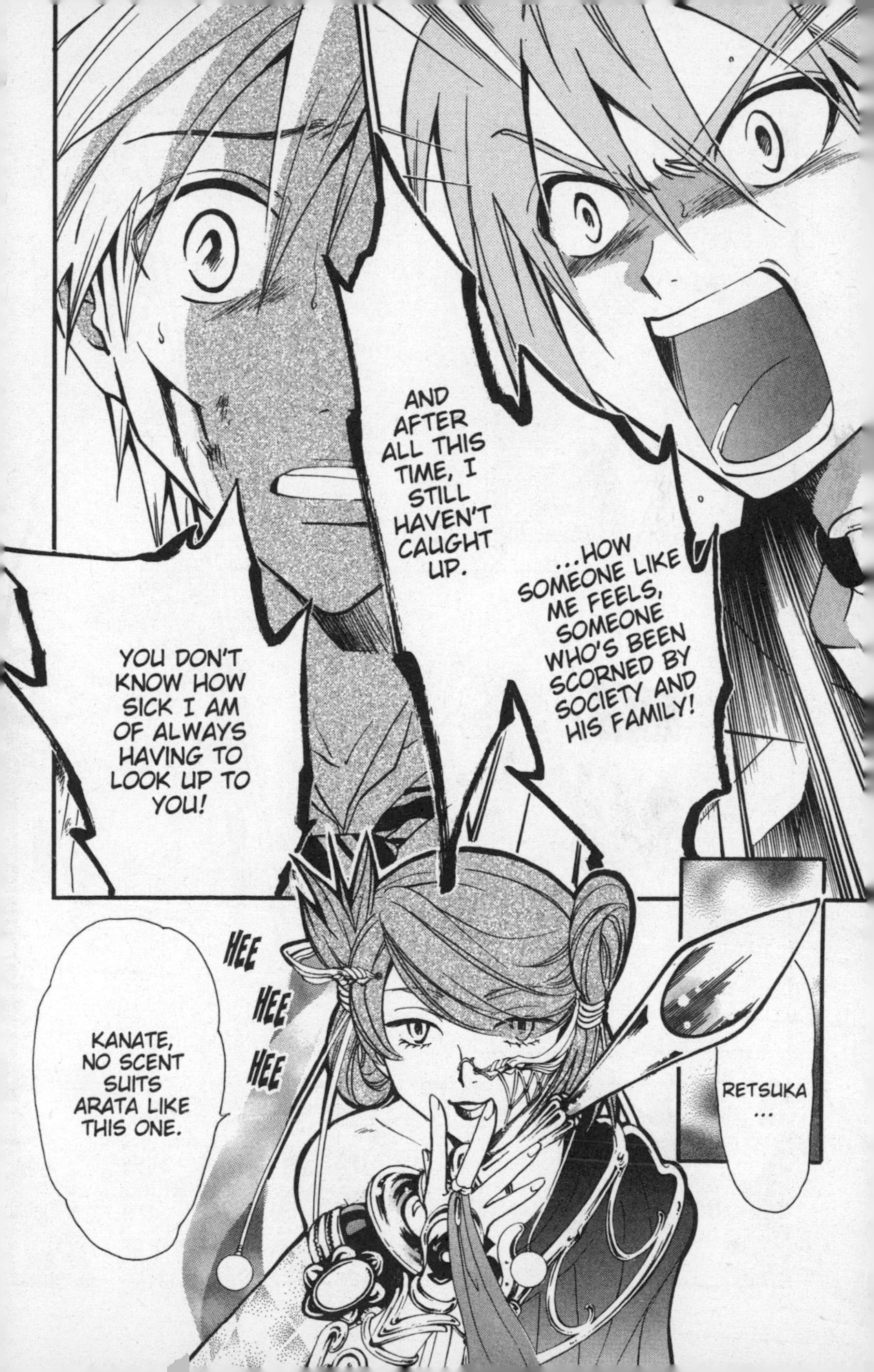
...HOW SOMEONE LIKE ME FEELS, SOMEONE WHO'S BEEN SCORNED BY SOCIETY AND HIS FAMILY!
AND AFTER ALL THIS TIME, I STILL HAVEN'T CAUGHT UP.
YOU DON'T KNOW HOW SICK I AM OF ALWAYS HAVING TO LOOK UP TO YOU!
RETSUKA...
HEE HEE HEE
KANATE, NO SCENT SUITS ARATA LIKE THIS ONE.

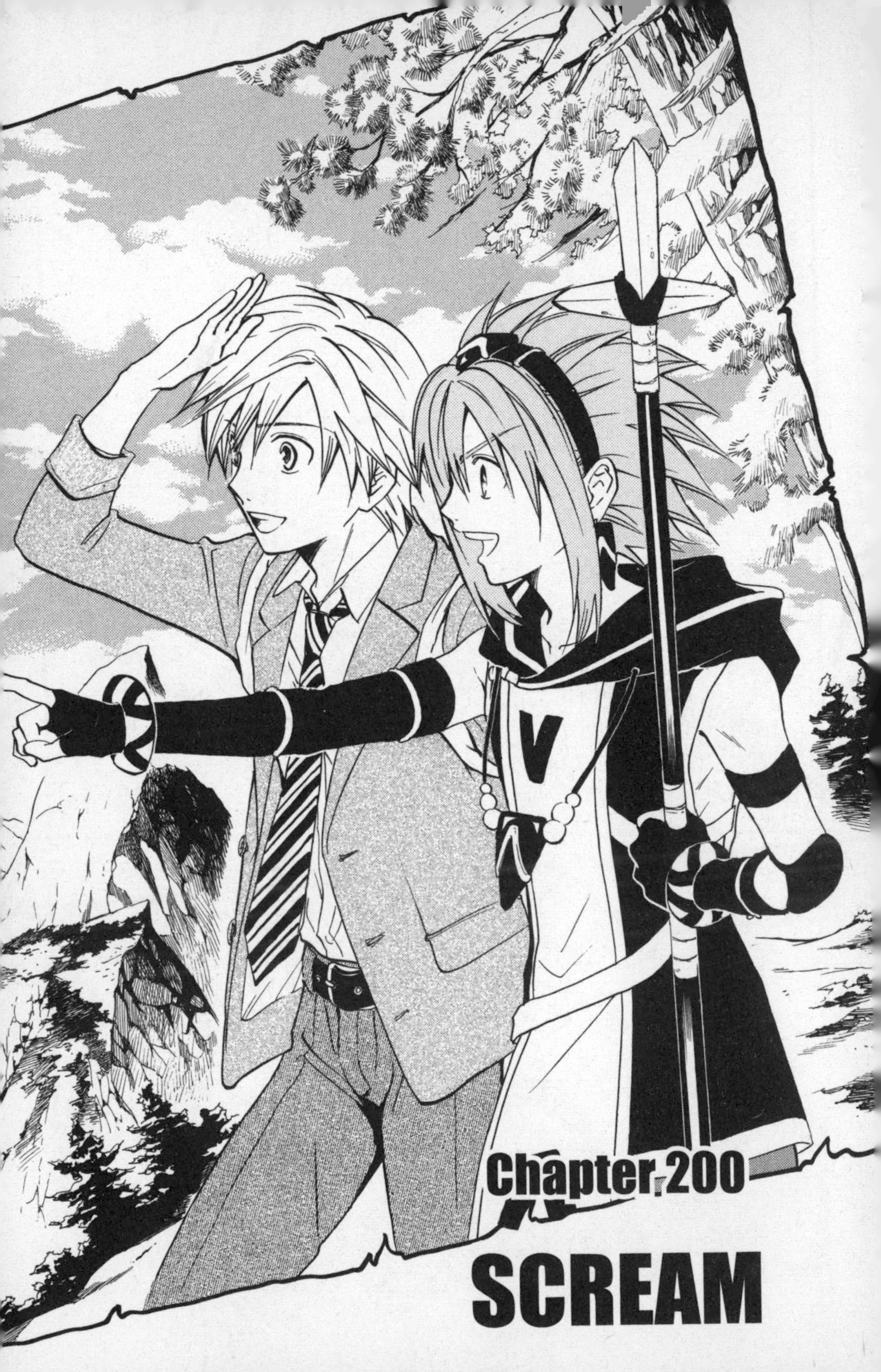
Chapter.200
SCREAM

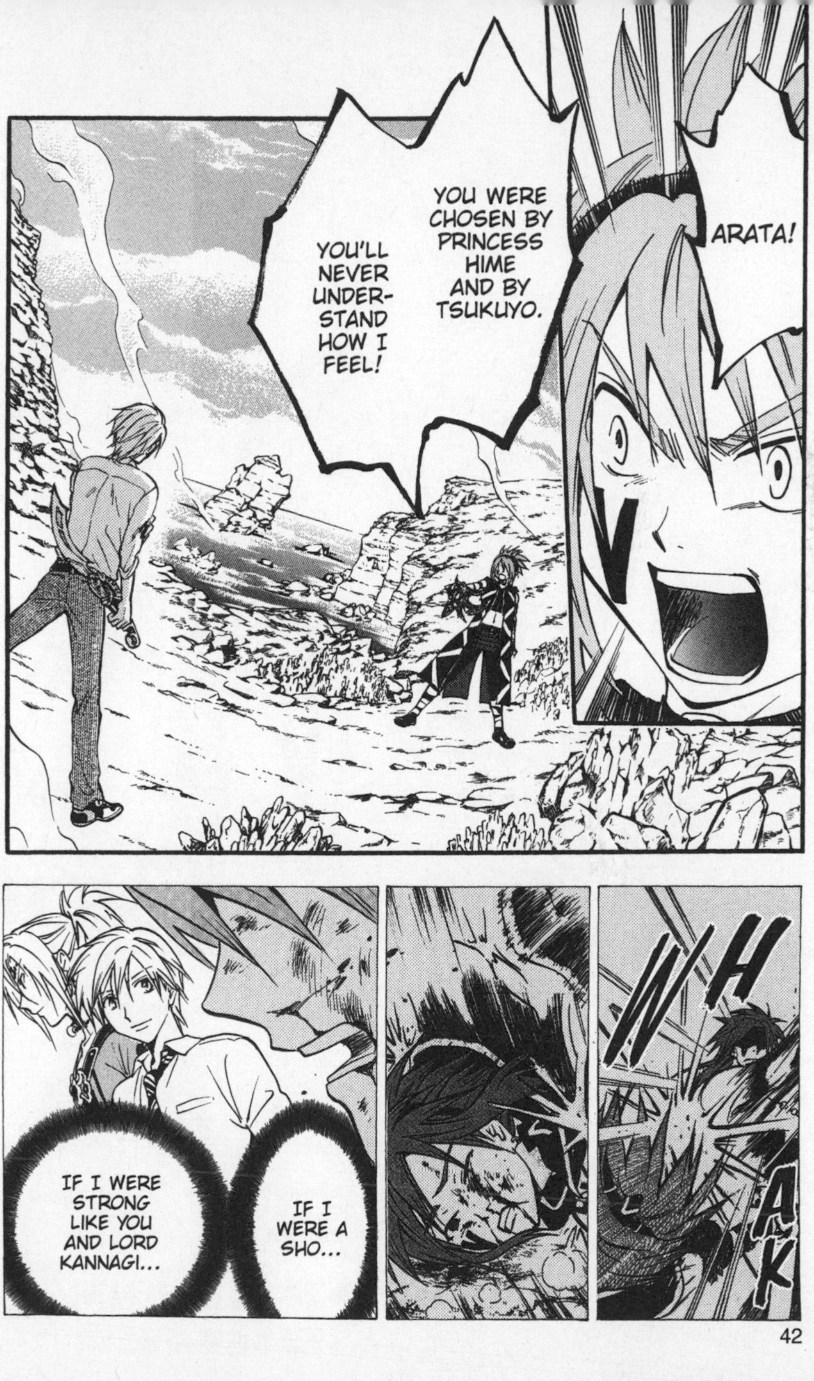
ARATA!
YOU WERE CHOSEN BY PRINCESS HIME AND BY TSUKUYO.
YOU'LL NEVER UNDER-STAND HOW I FEEL!
WHAK
IF I WERE A SHO...
IF I WERE STRONG LIKE YOU AND LORD KANNAGI...

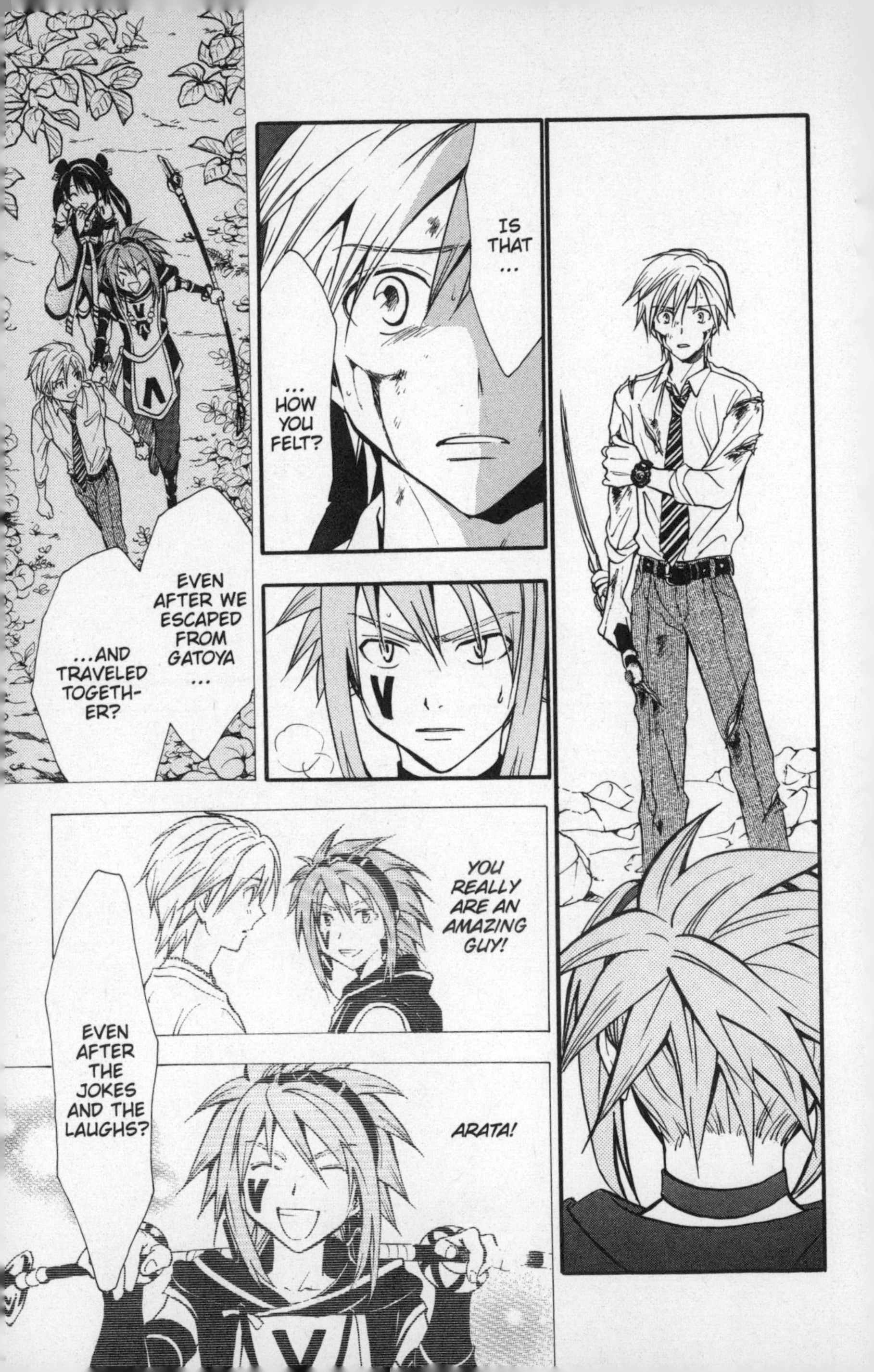
IS THAT ...
... HOW YOU FELT?
EVEN AFTER WE ESCAPED FROM GATOYA ...
...AND TRAVELED TOGETHER?
YOU REALLY ARE AN AMAZING GUY!
EVEN AFTER THE JOKES AND THE LAUGHS?
ARATA!

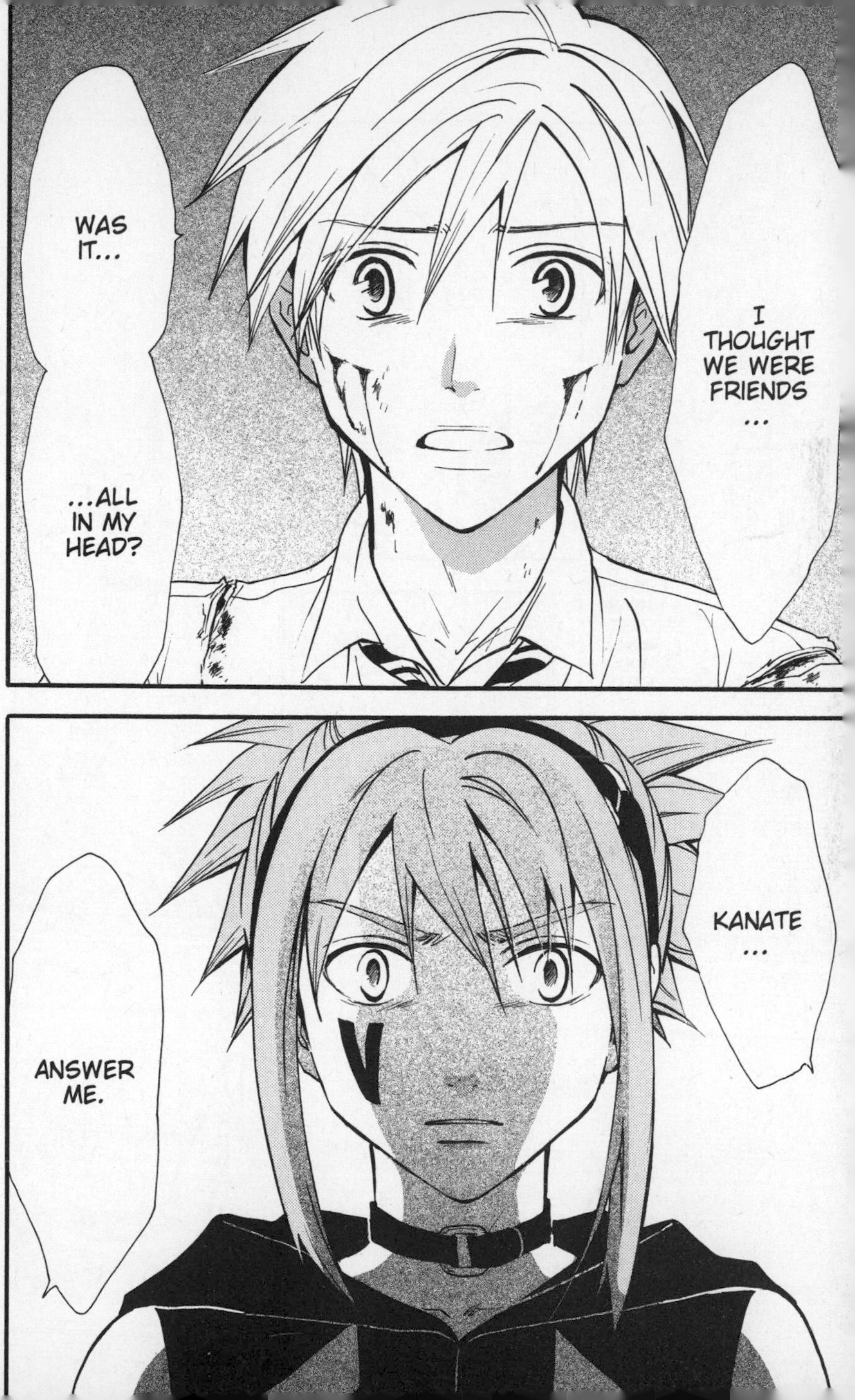
I THOUGHT WE WERE FRIENDS...
WAS IT...
...ALL IN MY HEAD?
KANATE...
ANSWER ME.

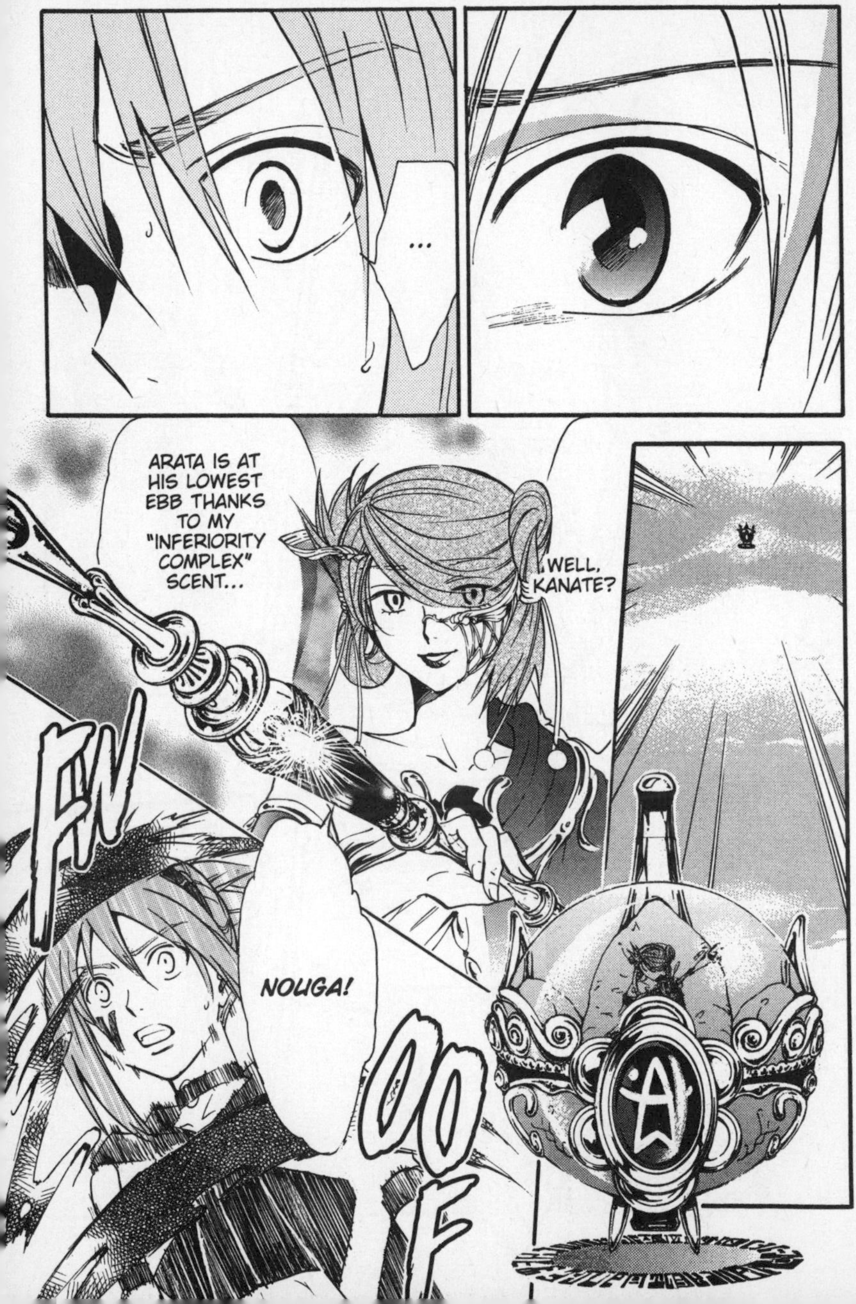
...
WELL, KANATE?
ARATA IS AT HIS LOWEST EBB THANKS TO MY "INFERIORITY COMPLEX" SCENT...
FN
NOUGA!
OOF

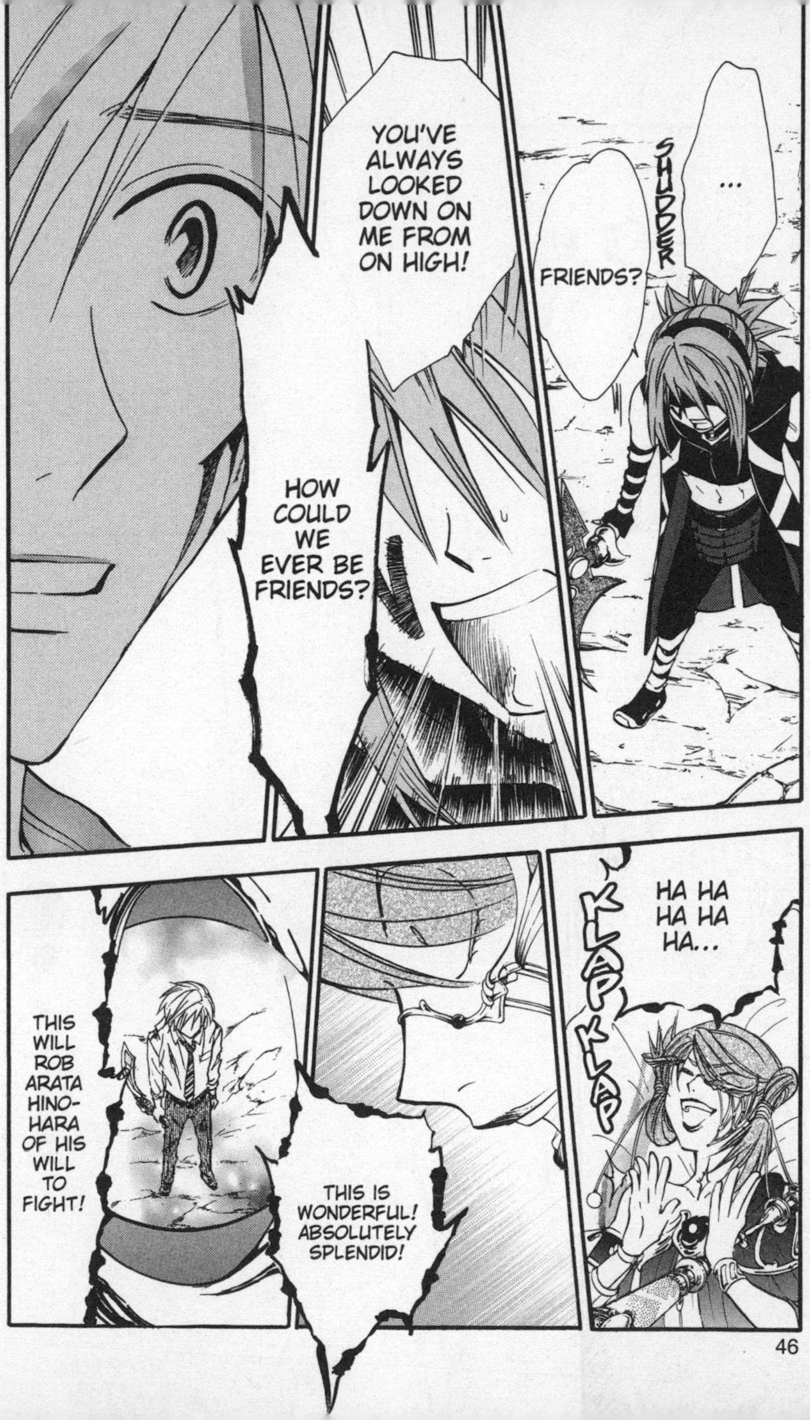
...
SHUDDER
FRIENDS?
YOU'VE ALWAYS LOOKED DOWN ON ME FROM ON HIGH!
HOW COULD WE EVER BE FRIENDS?
KLAP KLAP
HA HA HA HA HA...
THIS IS WONDERFUL! ABSOLUTELY SPLENDID!
THIS WILL ROB ARATA HINO-HARA OF HIS WILL TO FIGHT!

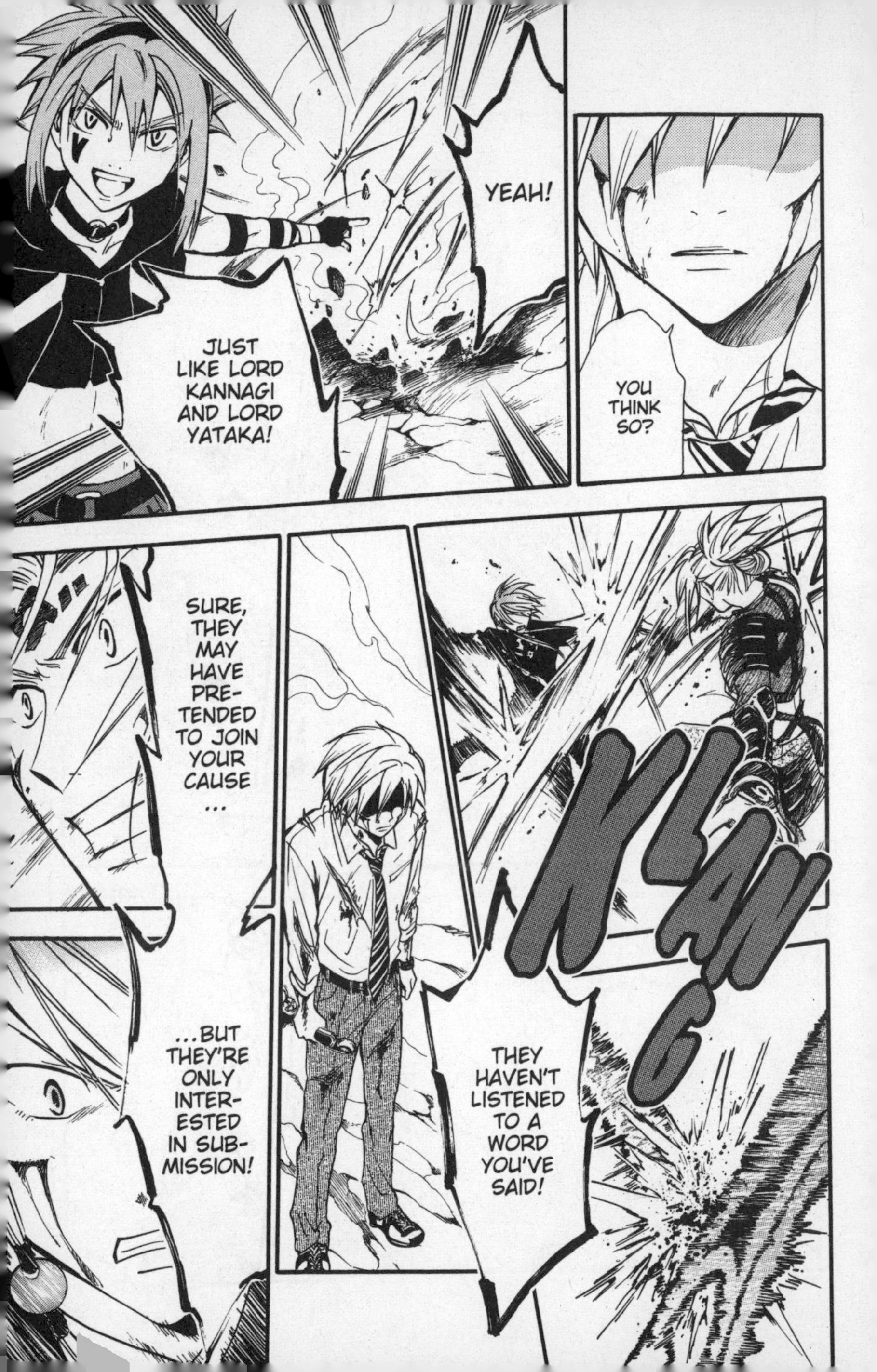
YEAH!
JUST LIKE LORD KANNAGI AND LORD YATAKA!
YOU THINK SO?
KLANG
THEY HAVEN'T LISTENED TO A WORD YOU'VE SAID!
SURE, THEY MAY HAVE PRE-TENDED TO JOIN YOUR CAUSE...
...BUT THEY'RE ONLY INTER-ESTED IN SUB-MISSION!

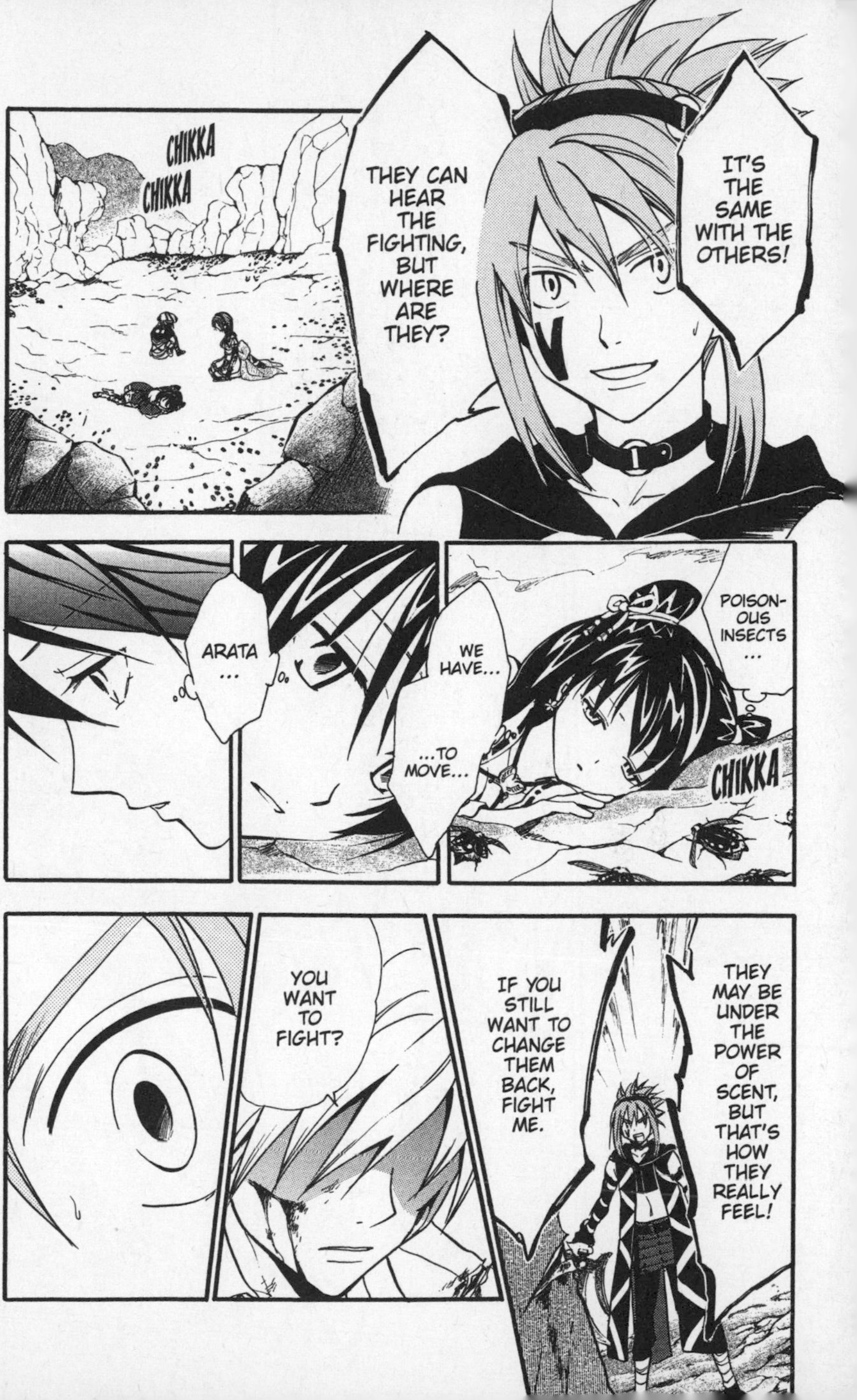
IT'S THE SAME WITH THE OTHERS!
THEY CAN HEAR THE FIGHTING, BUT WHERE ARE THEY?
CHIKKA
CHIKKA
POISON-OUS INSECTS ...
CHIKKA
WE HAVE...
...TO MOVE...
ARATA ...
THEY MAY BE UNDER THE POWER OF SCENT, BUT THAT'S HOW THEY REALLY FEEL!
IF YOU STILL WANT TO CHANGE THEM BACK, FIGHT ME.
YOU WANT TO FIGHT?

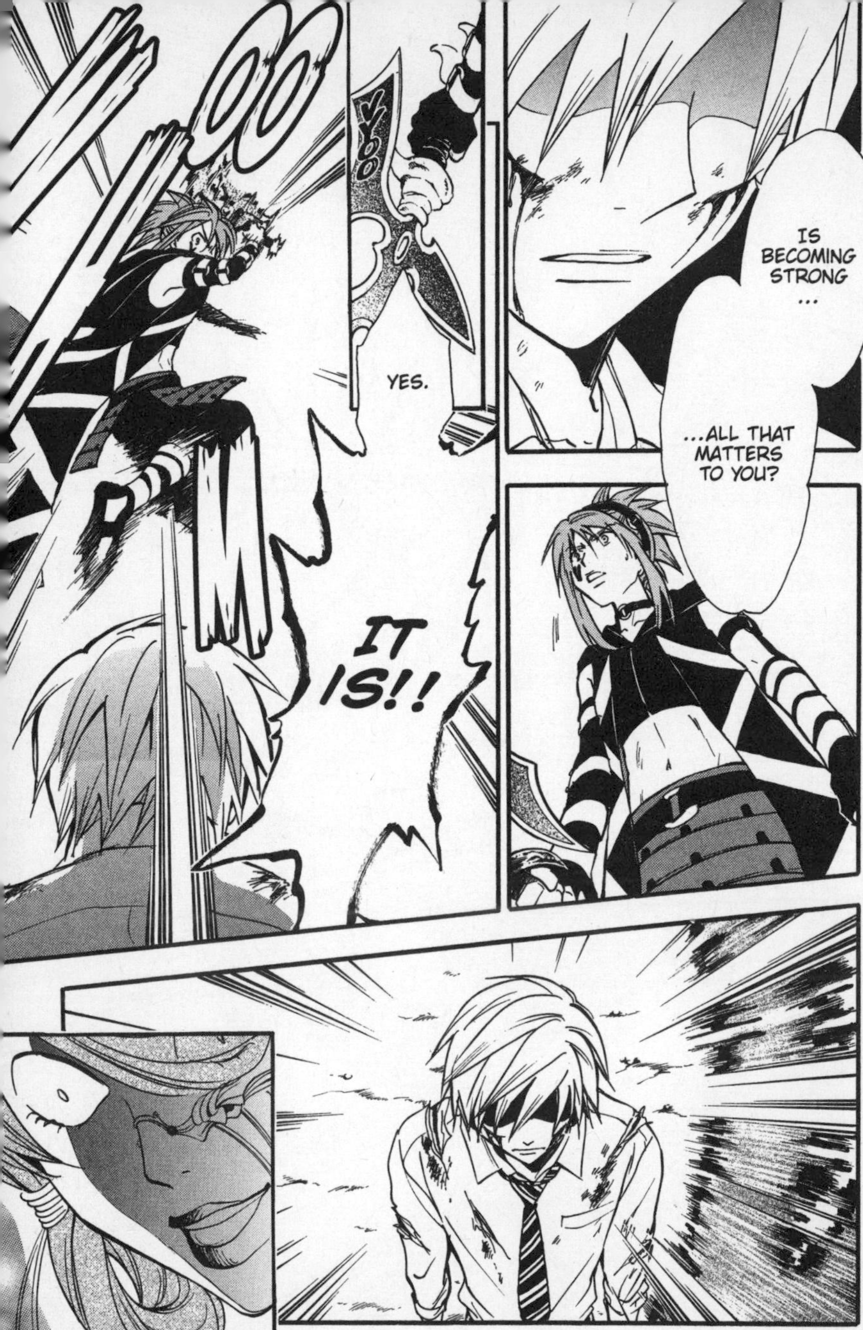
IS BECOMING STRONG ...
...ALL THAT MATTERS TO YOU?
VYOO
YES.
IT IS!!

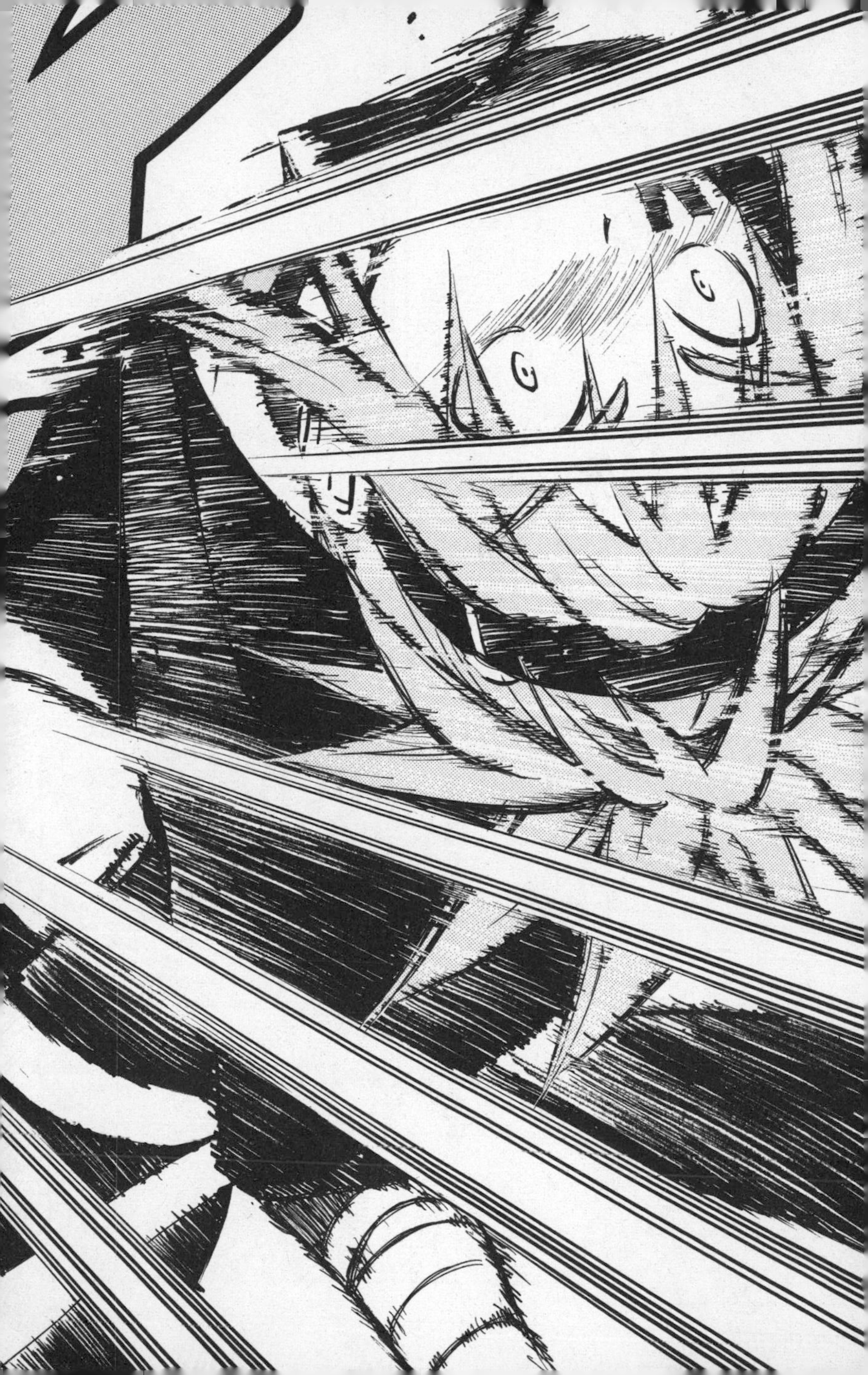

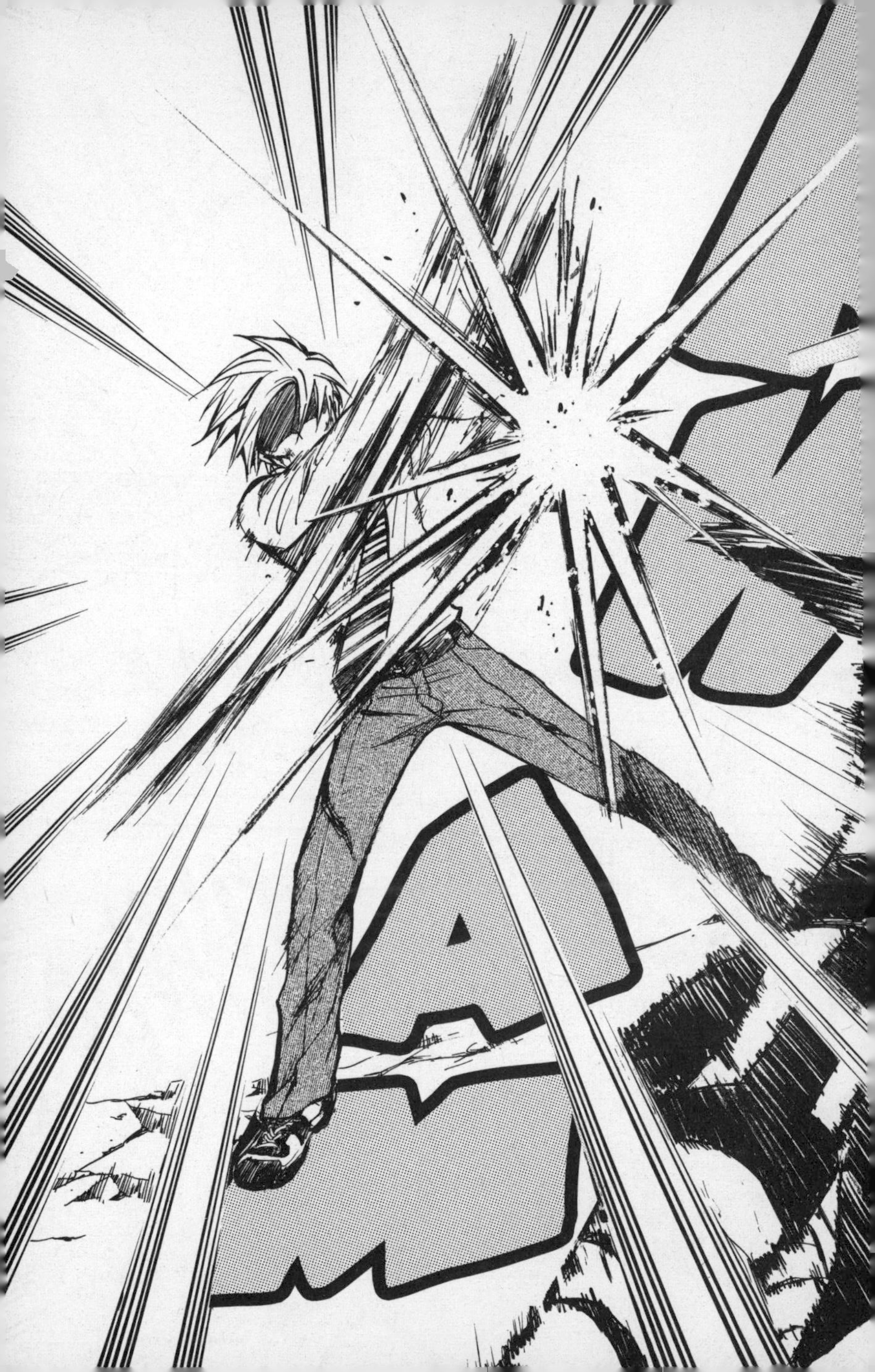

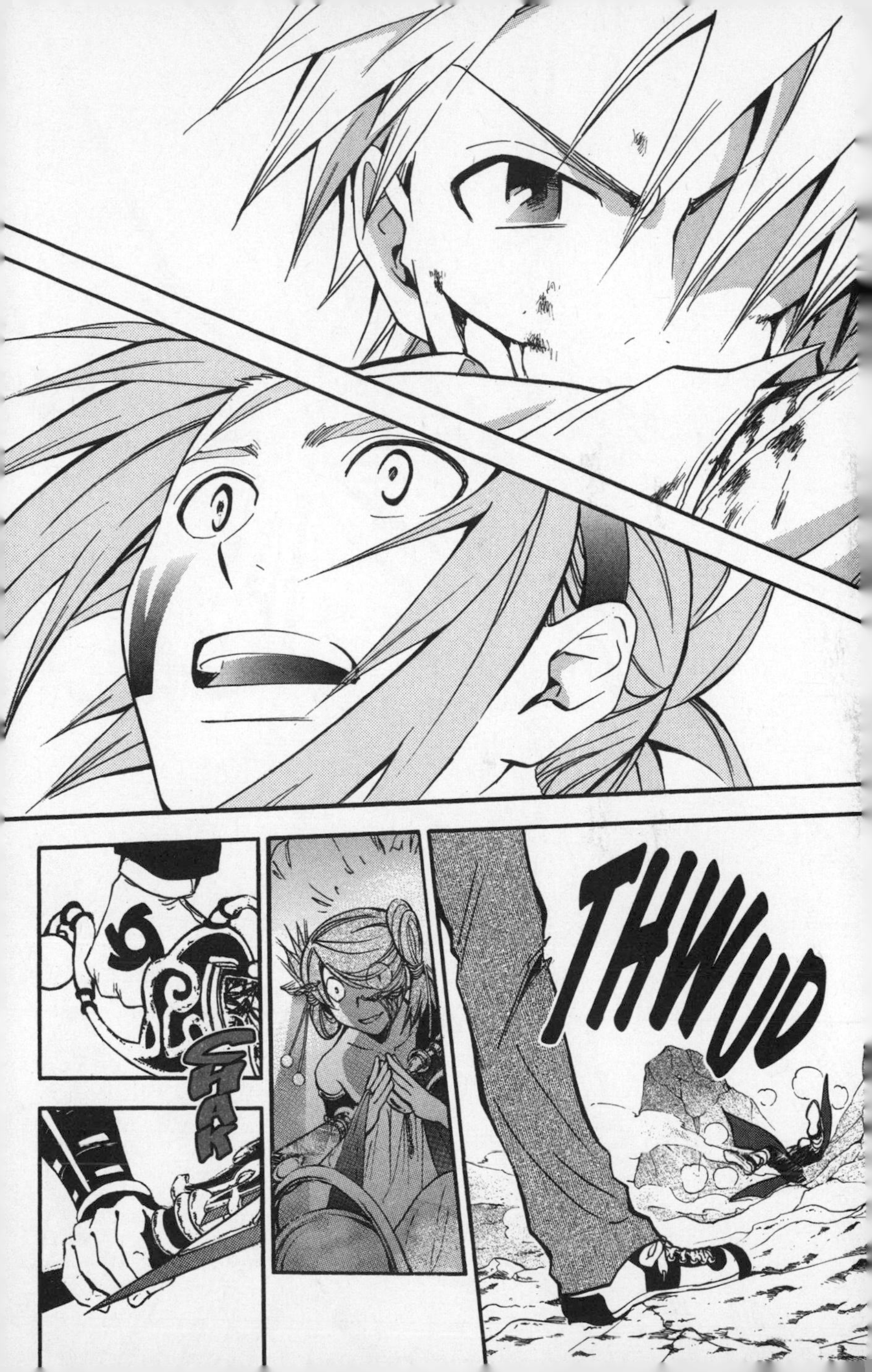
THWUD
CHAK

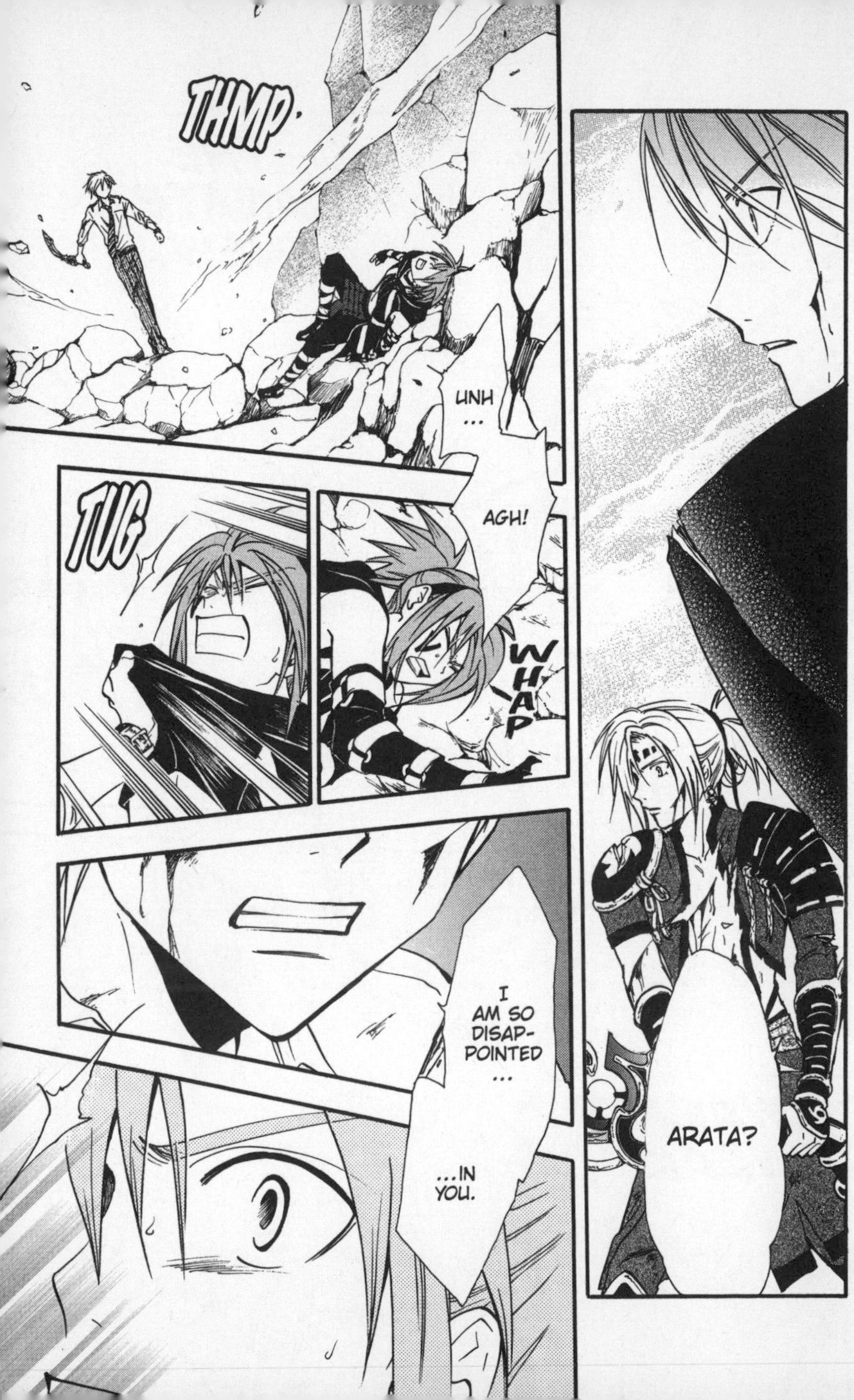
ARATA?
THMP
UNH ...
TUG
AGH!
WHAP
I AM SO DISAP-POINTED ...
...IN YOU.

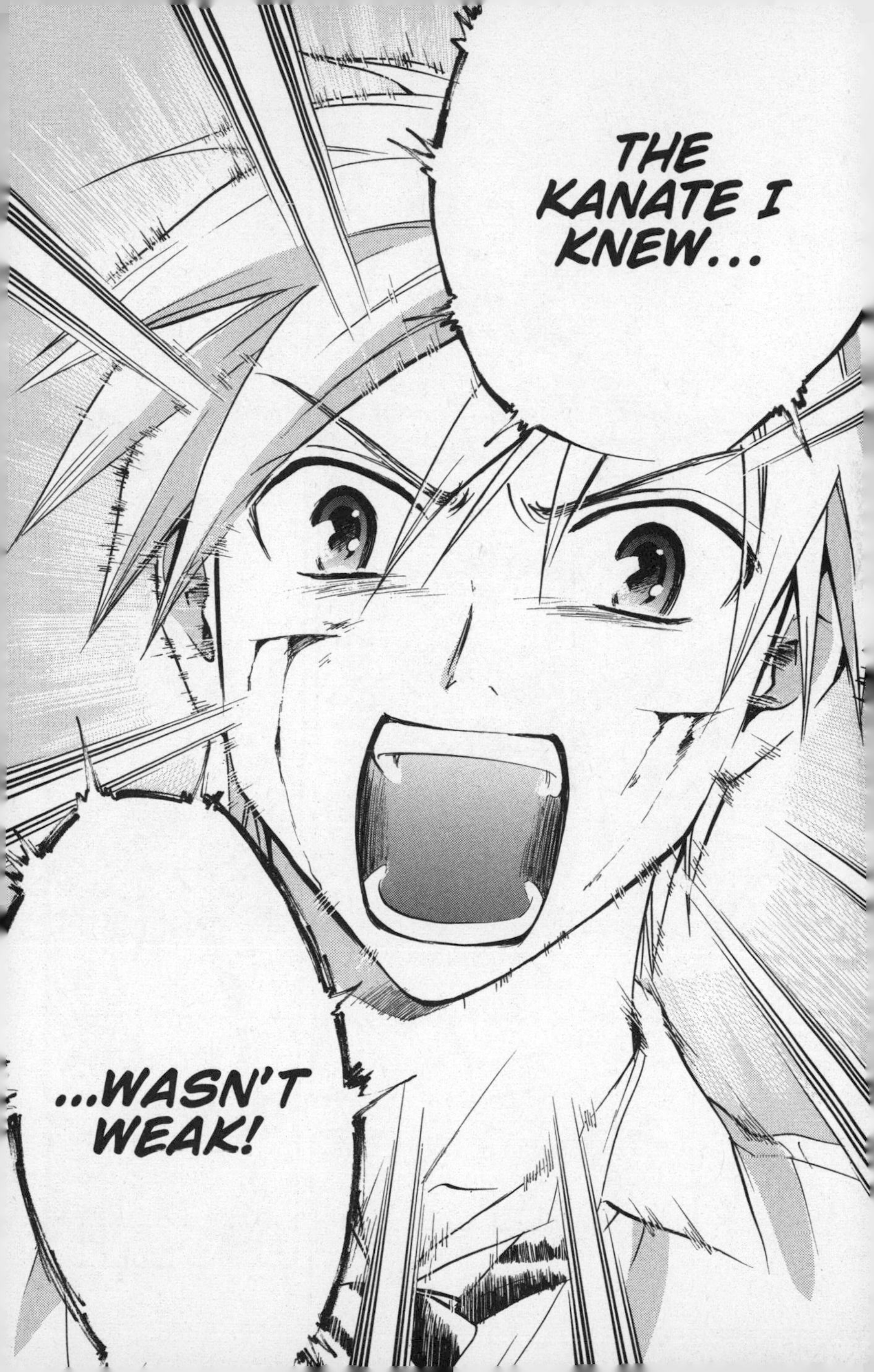
THE KANATE I KNEW...
...WASN'T WEAK!

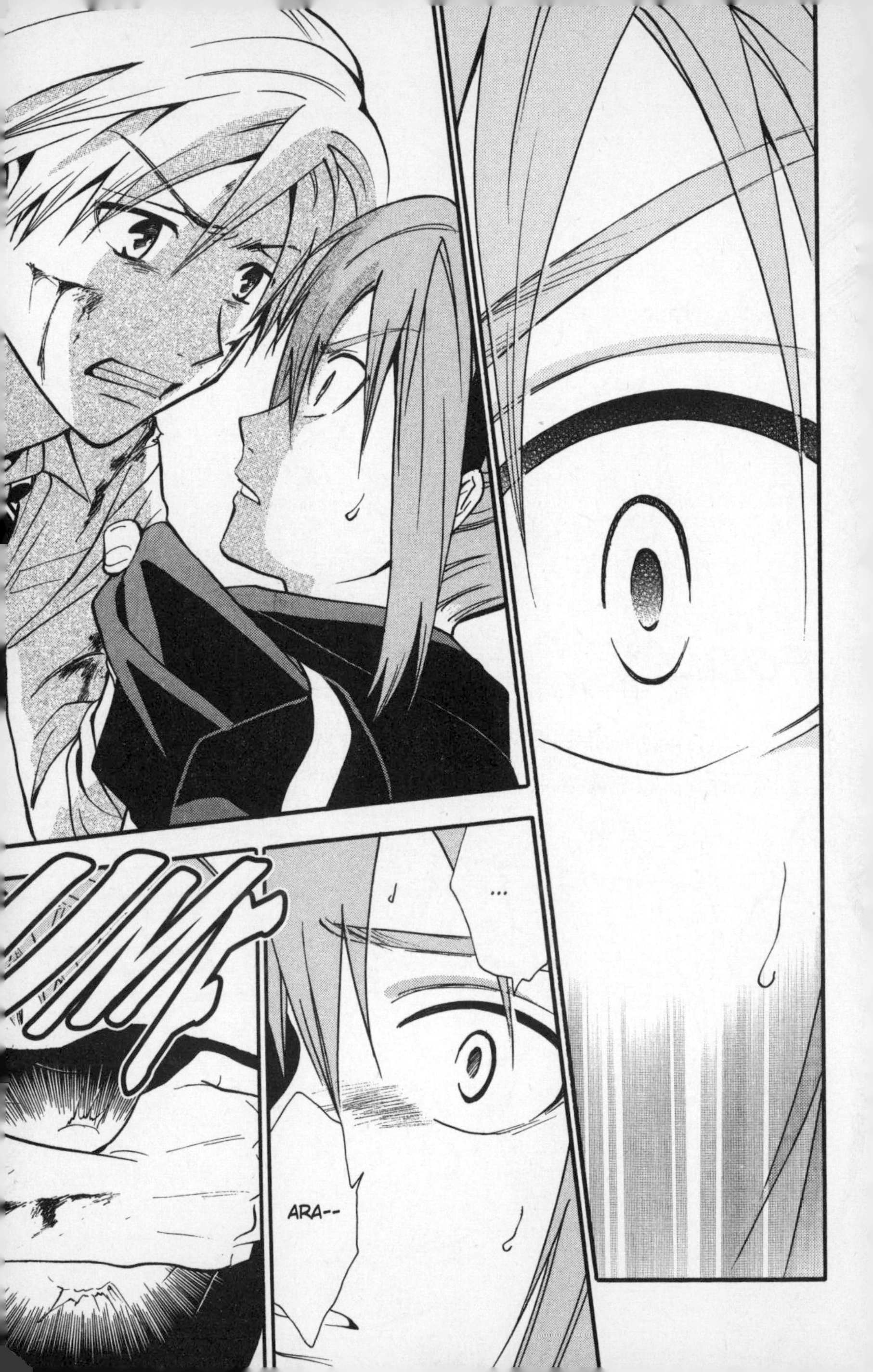
...
ARA--

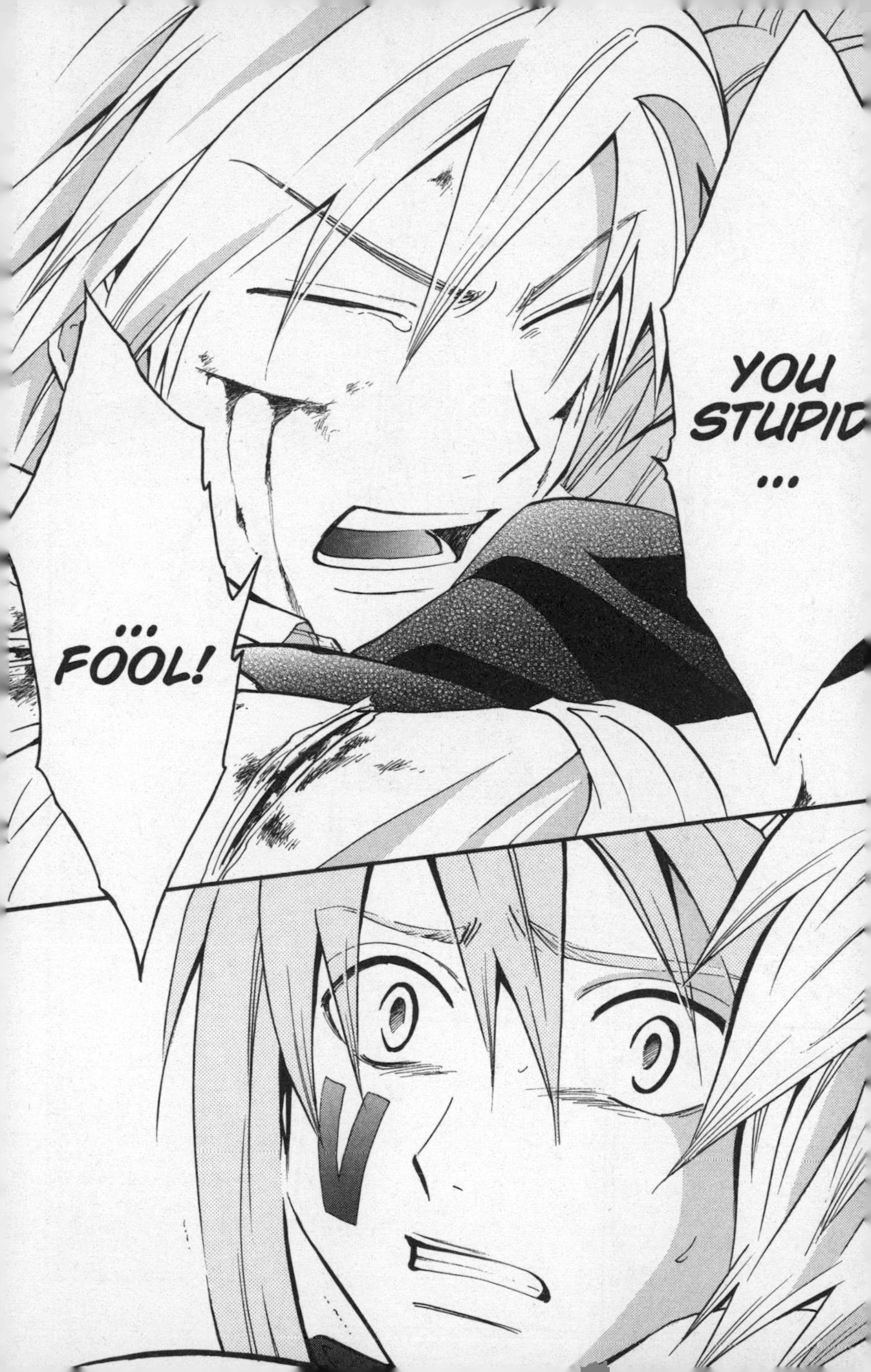
YOU STUPID ...
... FOOL!

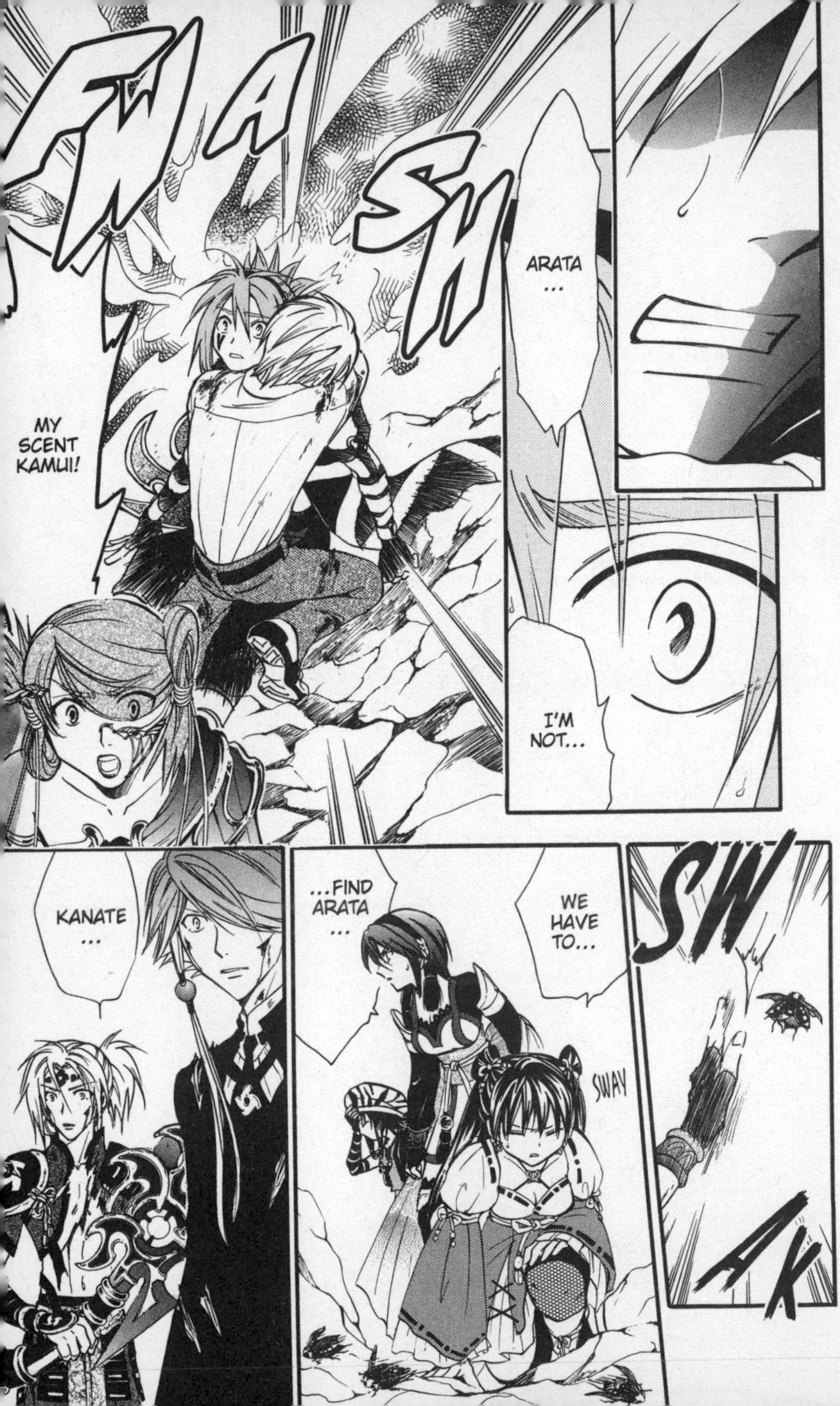
ARATA
...
I'M NOT...
FLASH
MY SCENT KAMUI!
SW
AK
WE HAVE TO...
...FIND ARATA
...
SWAY
KANATE
...

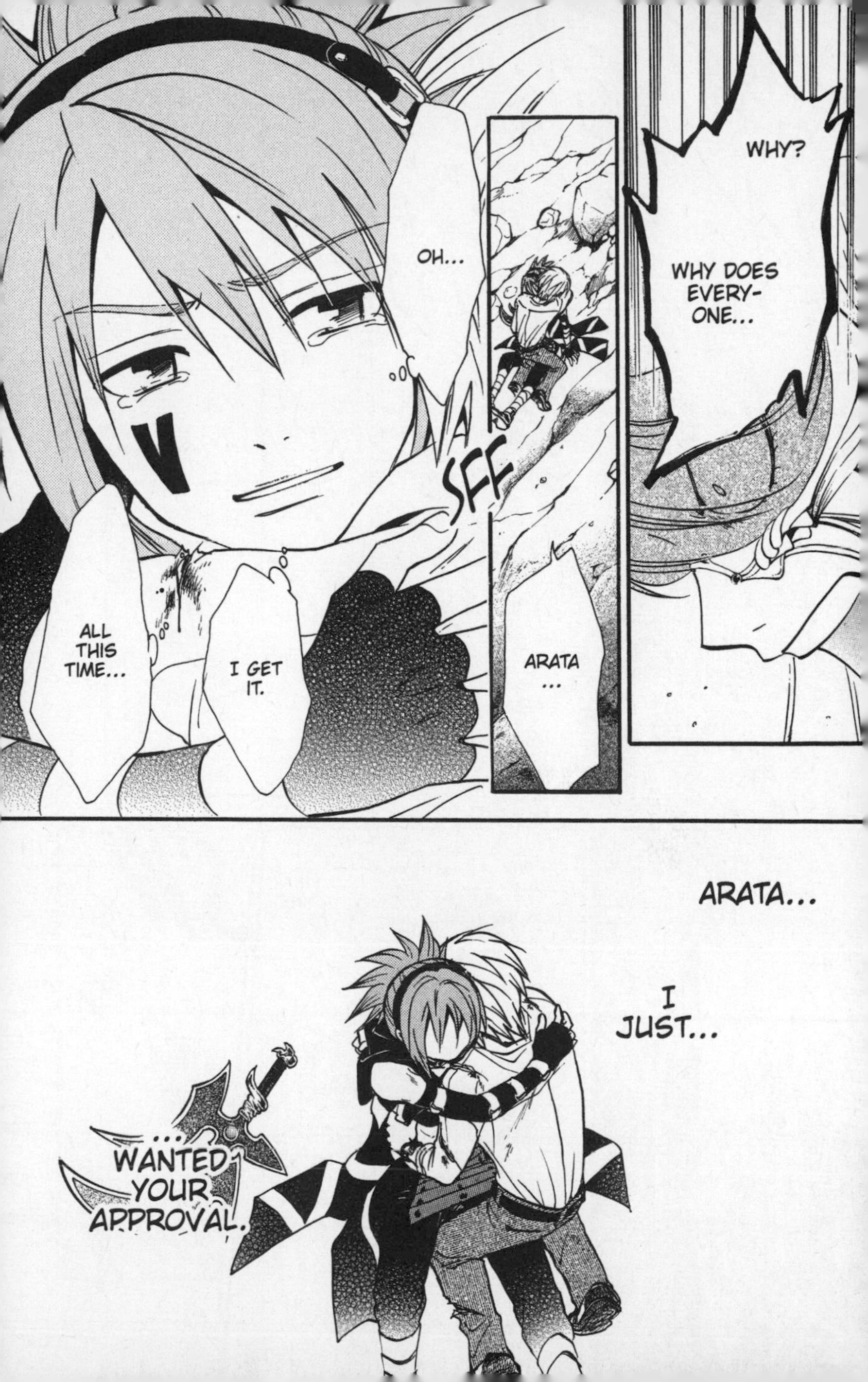
WHY?
WHY DOES EVERY-ONE...
ARATA...
OH...
SFF
I GET IT.
ALL THIS TIME...
ARATA...
I JUST...
...WANTED YOUR APPROVAL.

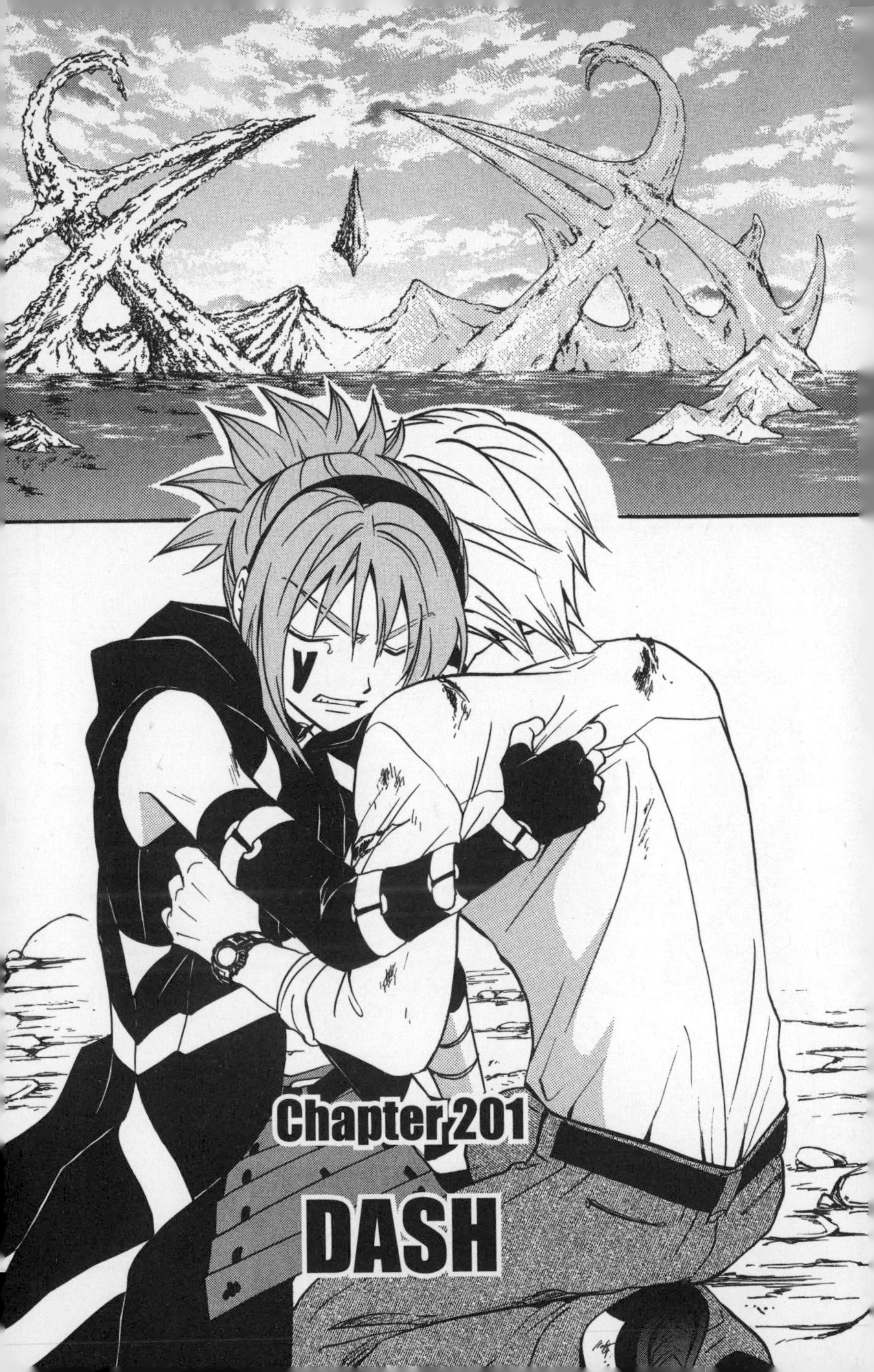
Chapter 201
DASH

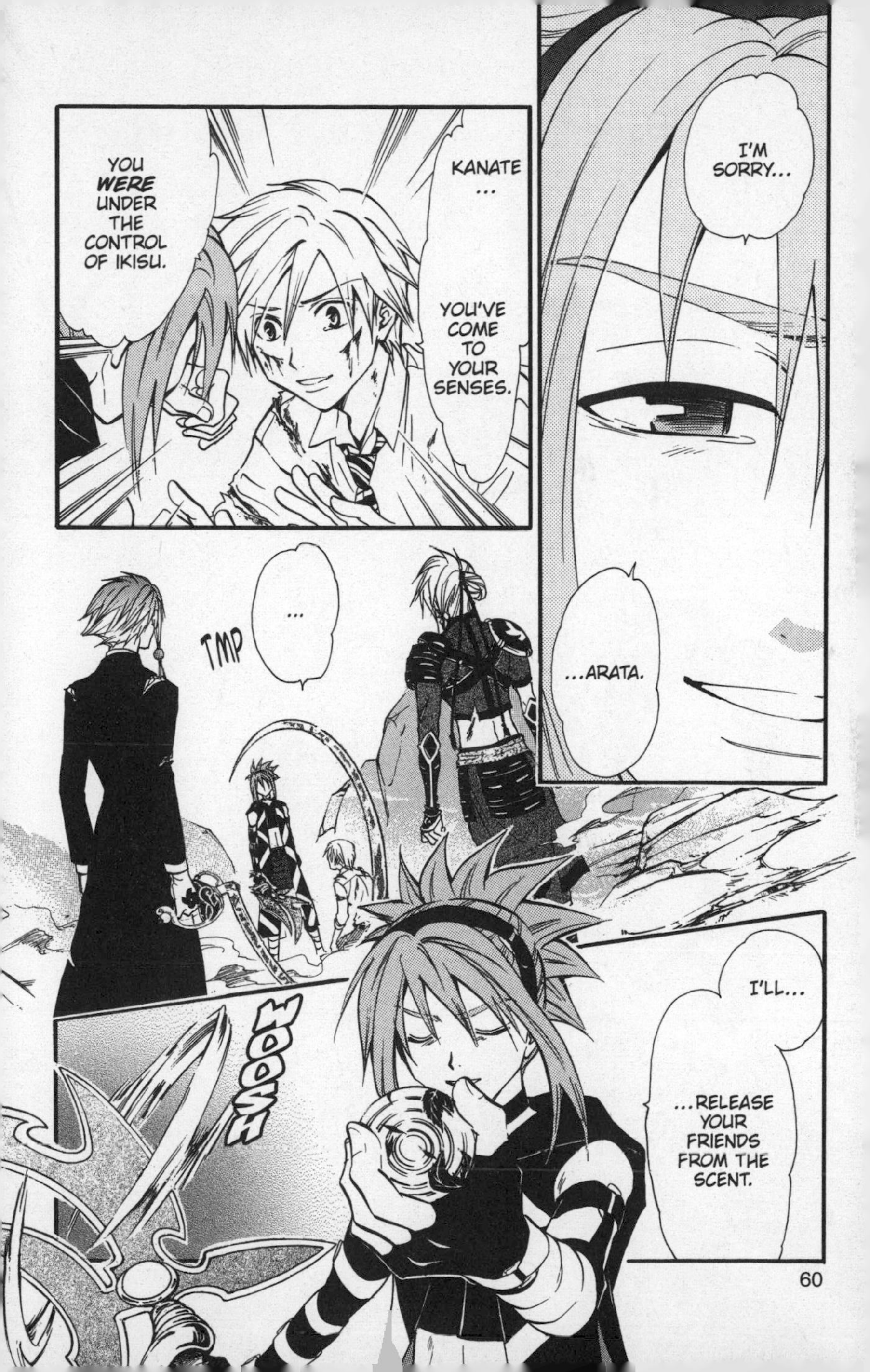
I'M SORRY...
...ARATA.
KANATE ...
YOU'VE COME TO YOUR SENSES.
YOU **WERE** UNDER THE CONTROL OF IKISU.
...
TMP
I'LL...
...RELEASE YOUR FRIENDS FROM THE SCENT.
WHOOSH

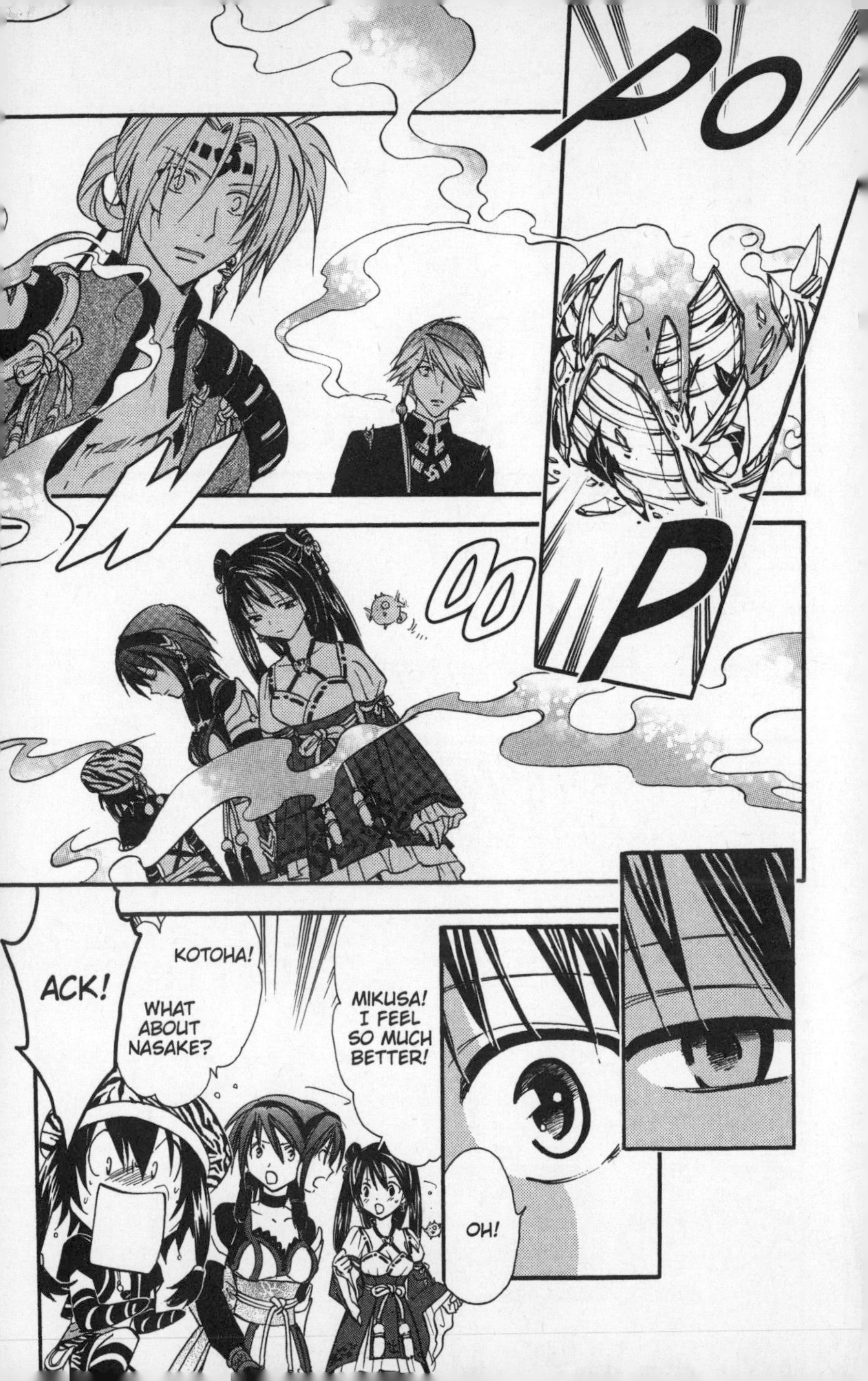
PO
OOP
OH!
MIKUSA! I FEEL SO MUCH BETTER!
KOTOHA! WHAT ABOUT NASAKE?
ACK!

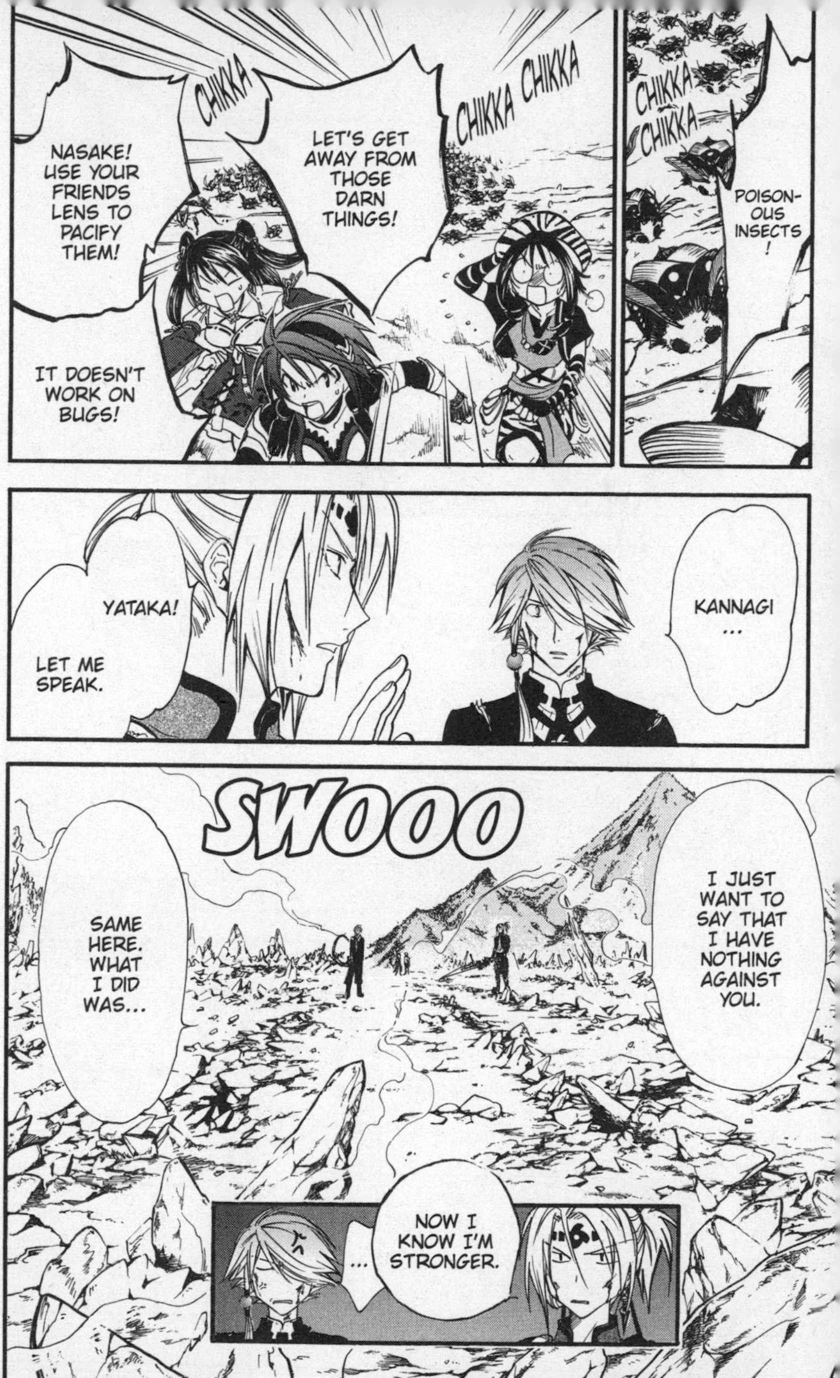
CHIKKA CHIKKA
POISON-OUS INSECTS!
CHIKKA CHIKKA
LET'S GET AWAY FROM THOSE DARN THINGS!
CHIKKA
NASAKE! USE YOUR FRIENDS LENS TO PACIFY THEM!
IT DOESN'T WORK ON BUGS!
KANNAGI ...
YATAKA!
LET ME SPEAK.
I JUST WANT TO SAY THAT I HAVE NOTHING AGAINST YOU.
SWOOO
SAME HERE. WHAT I DID WAS...
NOW I KNOW I'M STRONGER.
...

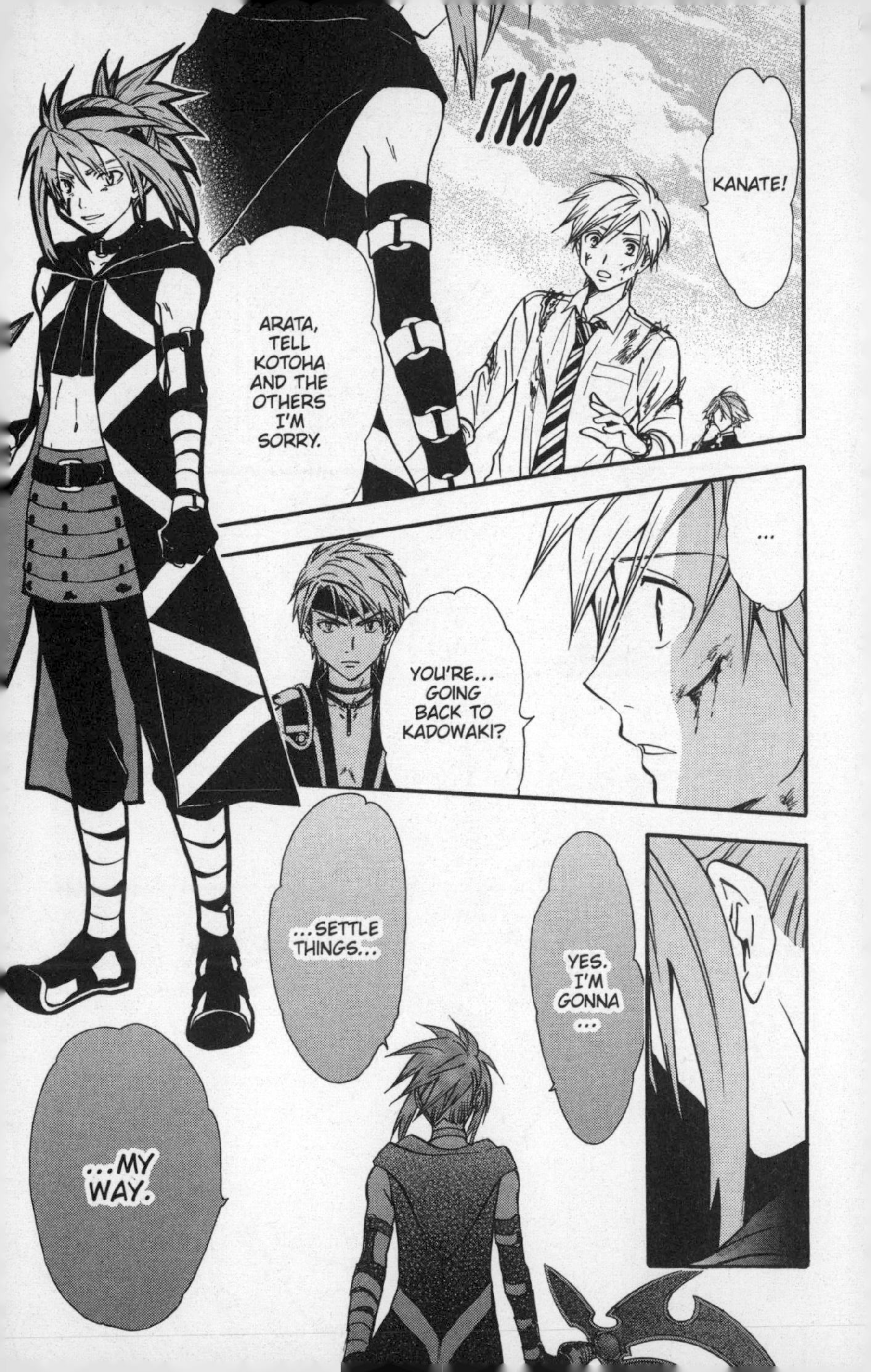
TMP
KANATE!
ARATA, TELL KOTOHA AND THE OTHERS I'M SORRY.
...
YOU'RE... GOING BACK TO KADOWAKI?
YES. I'M GONNA...
...SETTLE THINGS...
...MY WAY.

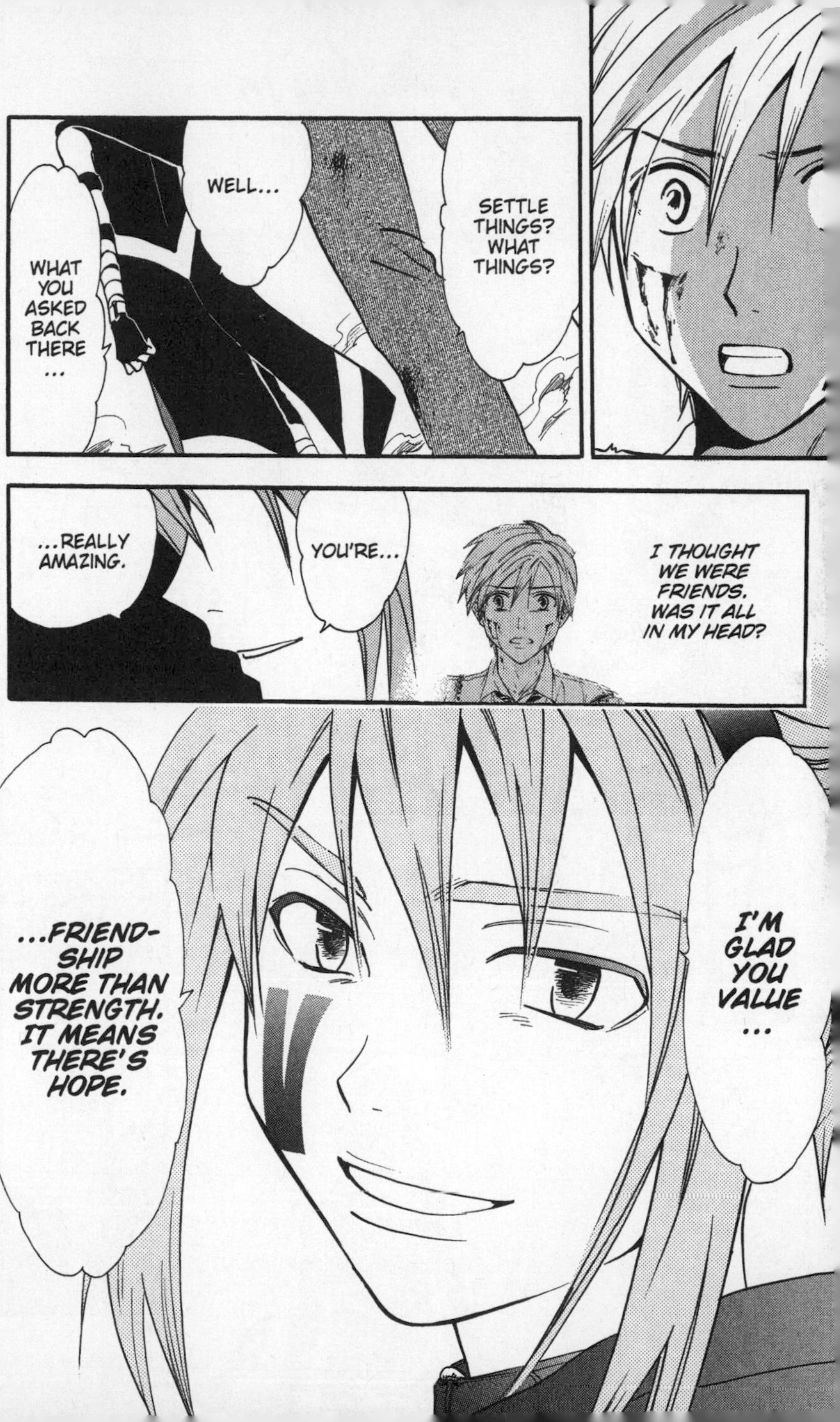
SETTLE THINGS? WHAT THINGS?
WELL...
WHAT YOU ASKED BACK THERE...
I THOUGHT WE WERE FRIENDS. WAS IT ALL IN MY HEAD?
YOU'RE...
...REALLY AMAZING.
I'M GLAD YOU VALUE...
...FRIEND-SHIP MORE THAN STRENGTH. IT MEANS THERE'S HOPE.

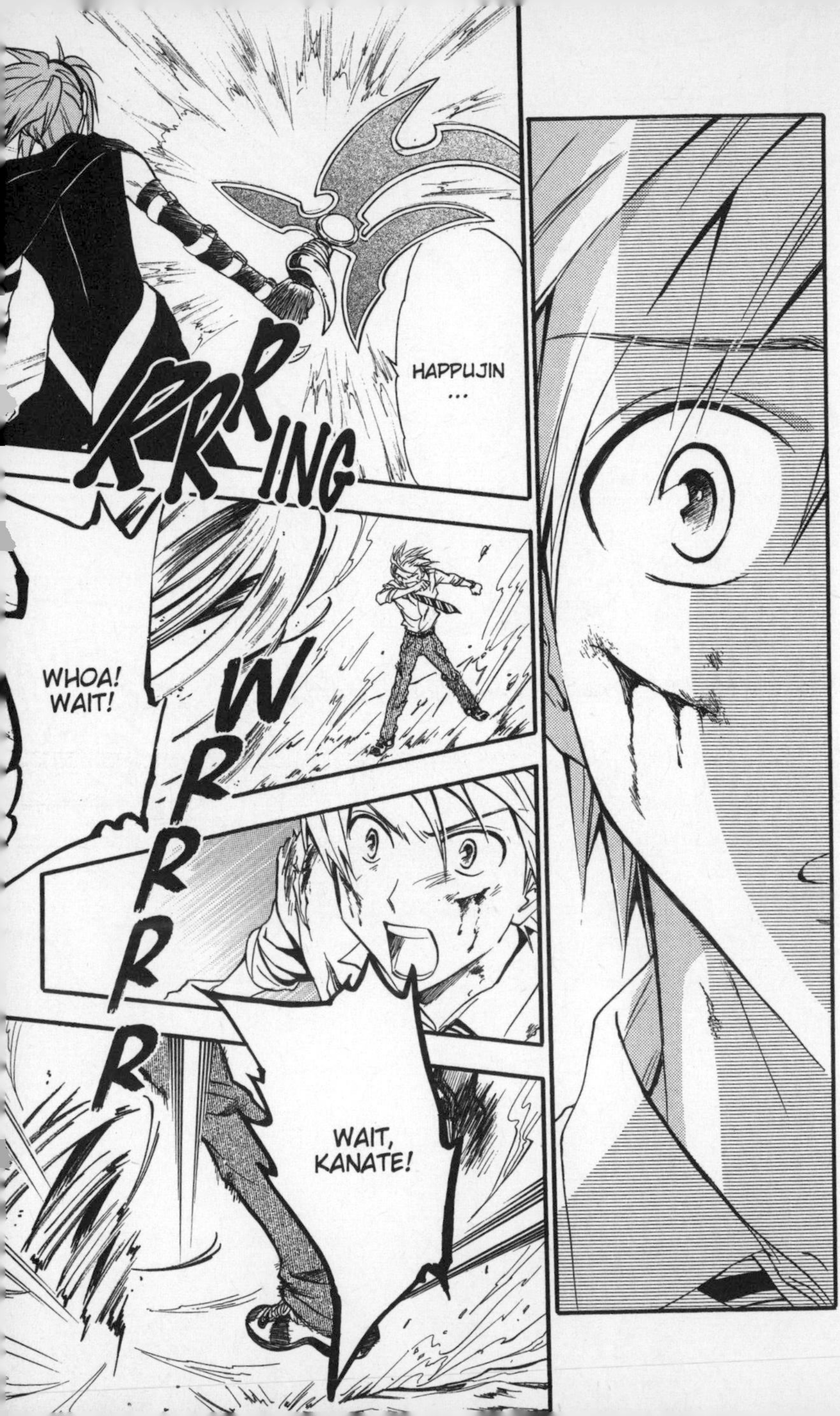
HAPPUJIN
...
KRRRING
WHOA! WAIT!
WRRRRR
WAIT, KANATE!

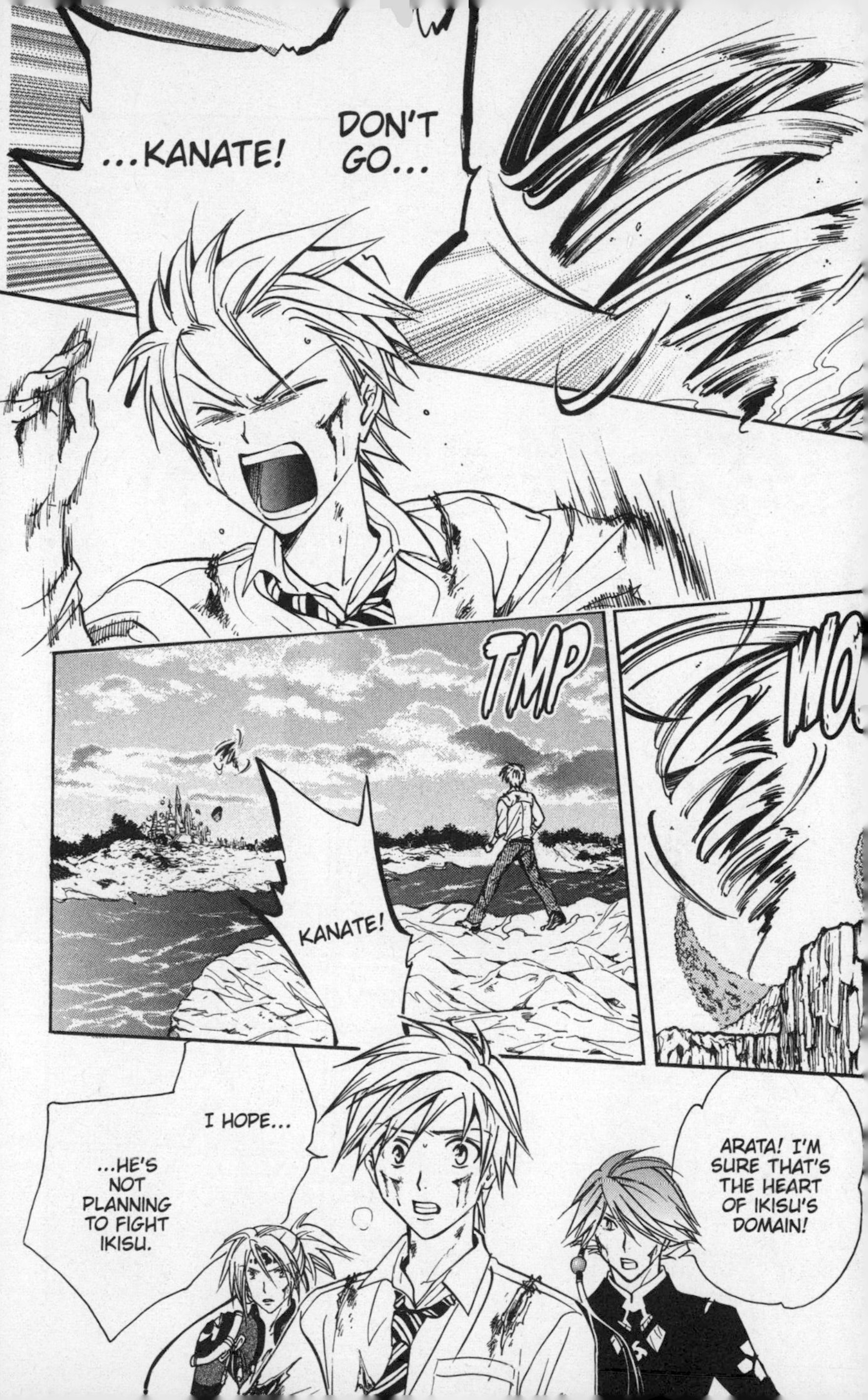
DON'T GO...
...KANATE!
WO
TMP
KANATE!
ARATA! I'M SURE THAT'S THE HEART OF IKISU'S DOMAIN!
I HOPE...
...HE'S NOT PLANNING TO FIGHT IKISU.

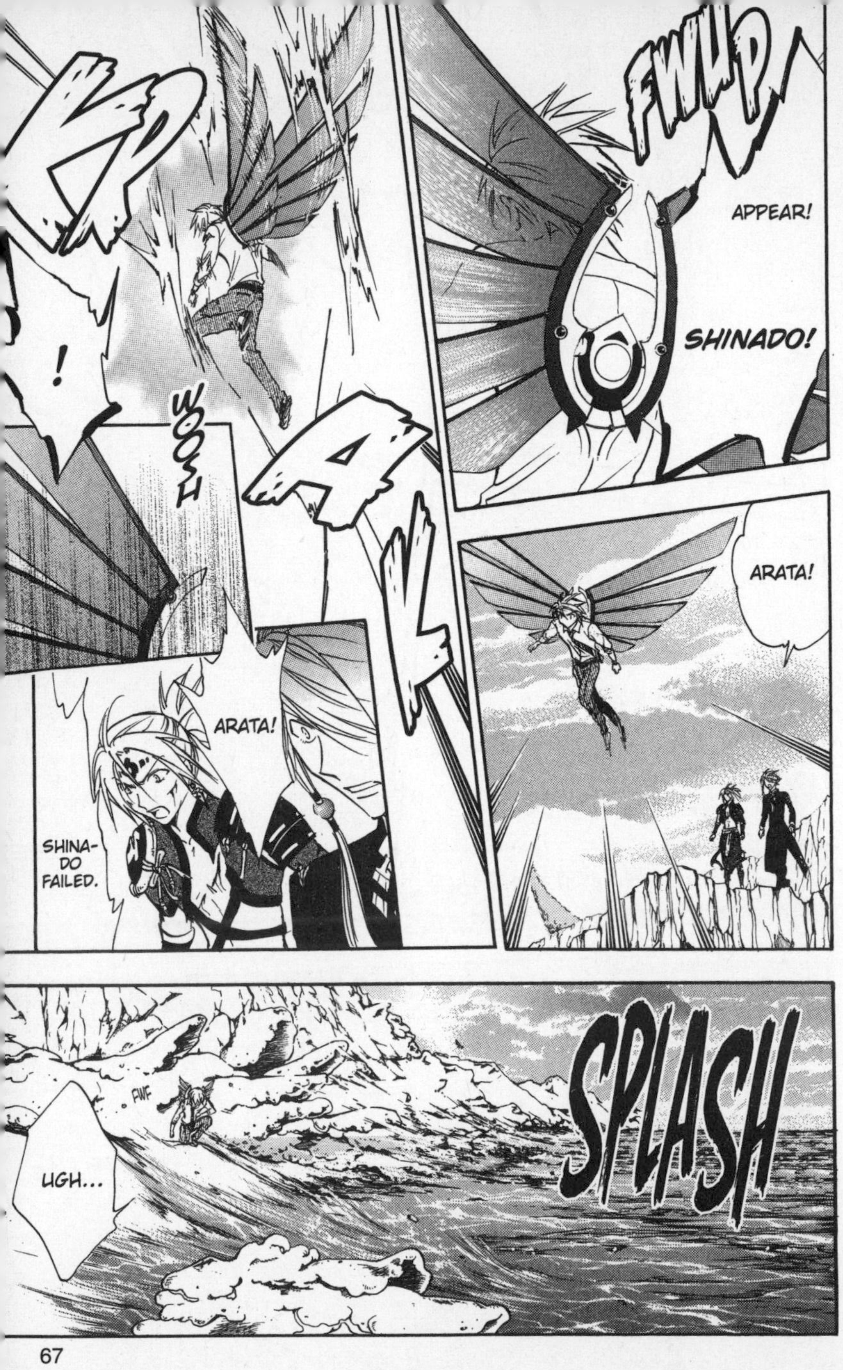
FWUD
APPEAR!
SHINADO!
!
WOOSH
ARATA!
ARATA!
SHINA-DO FAILED.
SPLASH
FWF
UGH...

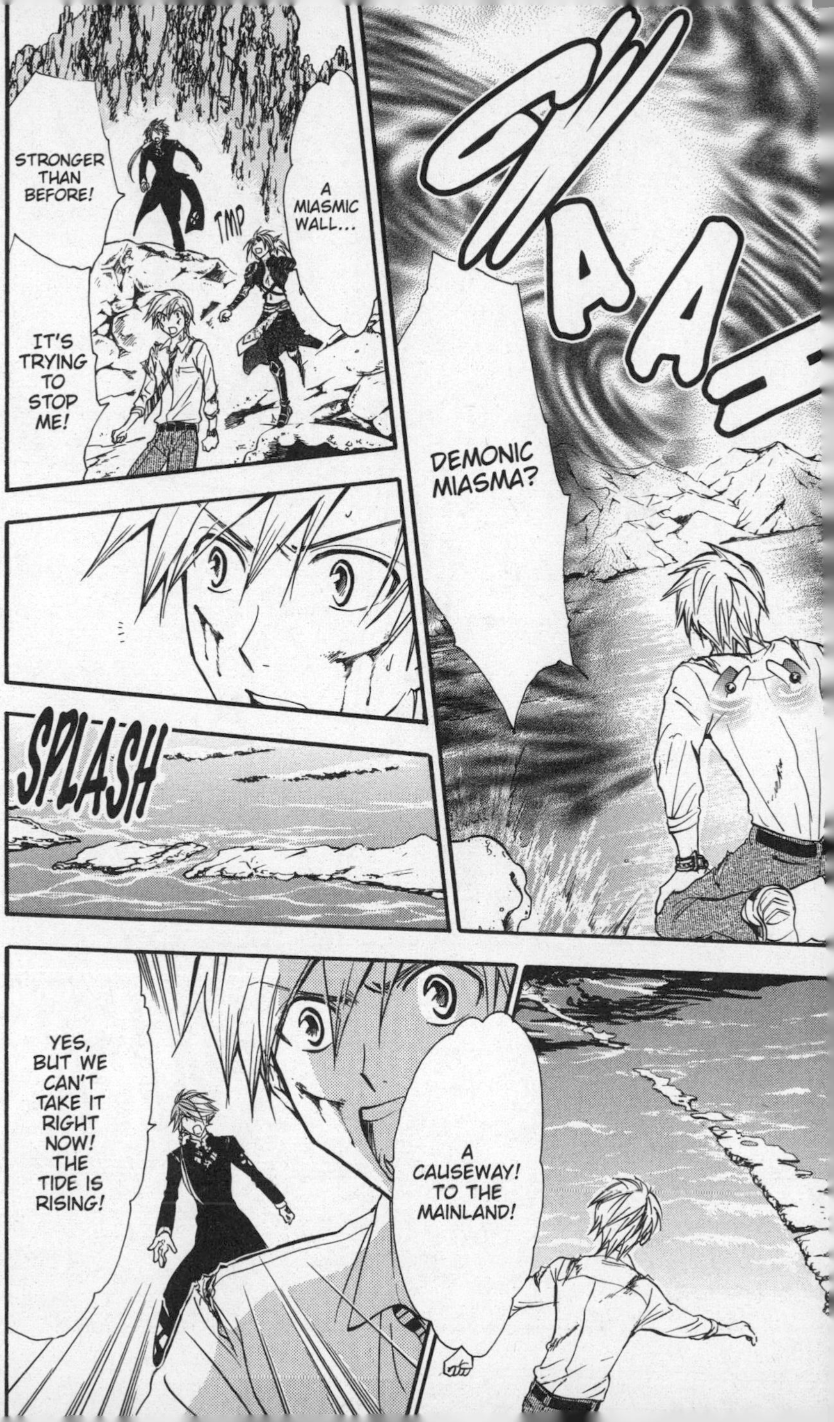
GYAAA
DEMONIC MIASMA?
A MIASMIC WALL...
TMP
STRONGER THAN BEFORE!
IT'S TRYING TO STOP ME!
SPLASH
A CAUSEWAY! TO THE MAINLAND!
YES, BUT WE CAN'T TAKE IT RIGHT NOW! THE TIDE IS RISING!

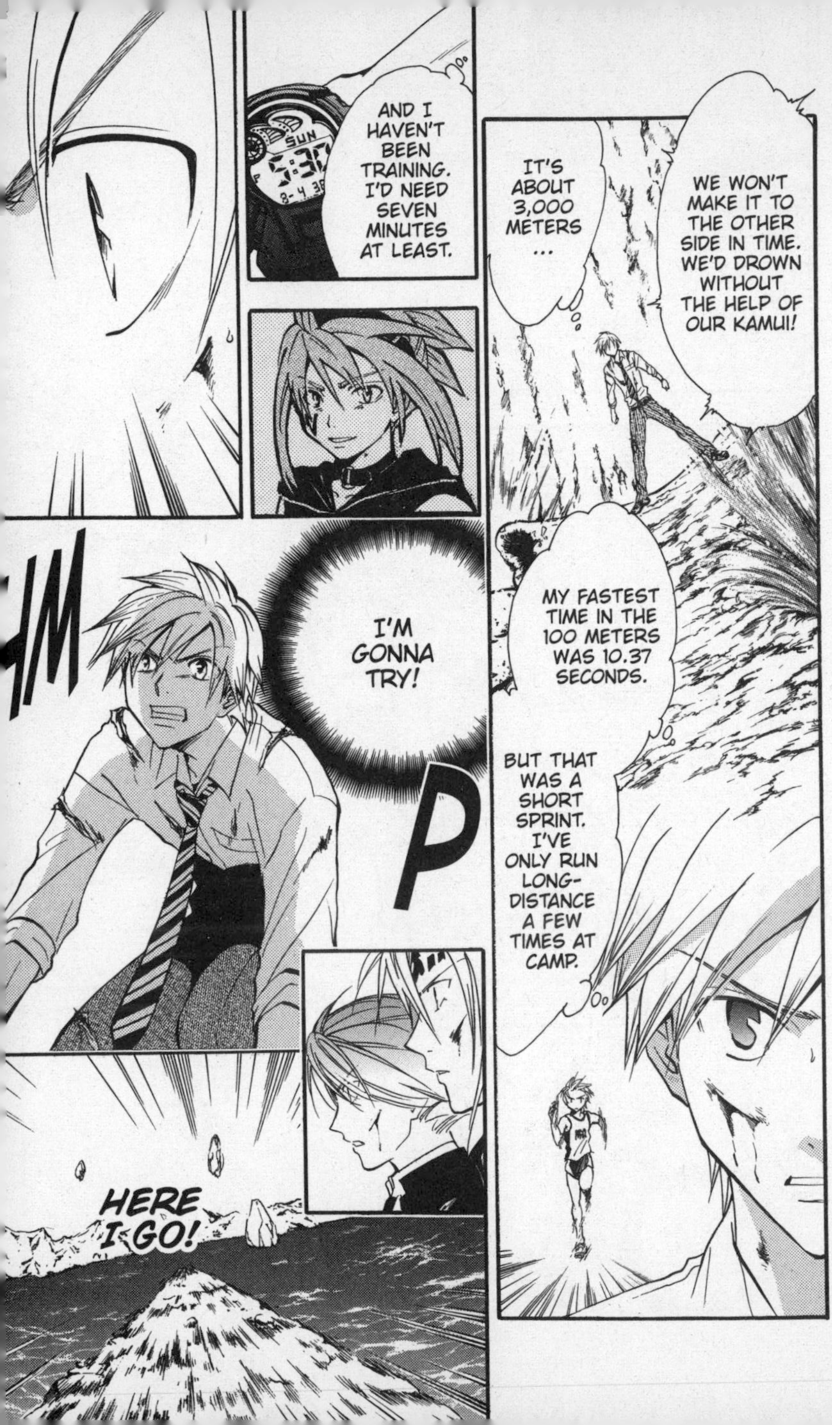
WE WON'T MAKE IT TO THE OTHER SIDE IN TIME. WE'D DROWN WITHOUT THE HELP OF OUR KAMUI!
IT'S ABOUT 3,000 METERS...
MY FASTEST TIME IN THE 100 METERS WAS 10.37 SECONDS.
BUT THAT WAS A SHORT SPRINT. I'VE ONLY RUN LONG-DISTANCE A FEW TIMES AT CAMP.
AND I HAVEN'T BEEN TRAINING. I'D NEED SEVEN MINUTES AT LEAST.
I'M GONNA TRY!
HERE I GO!

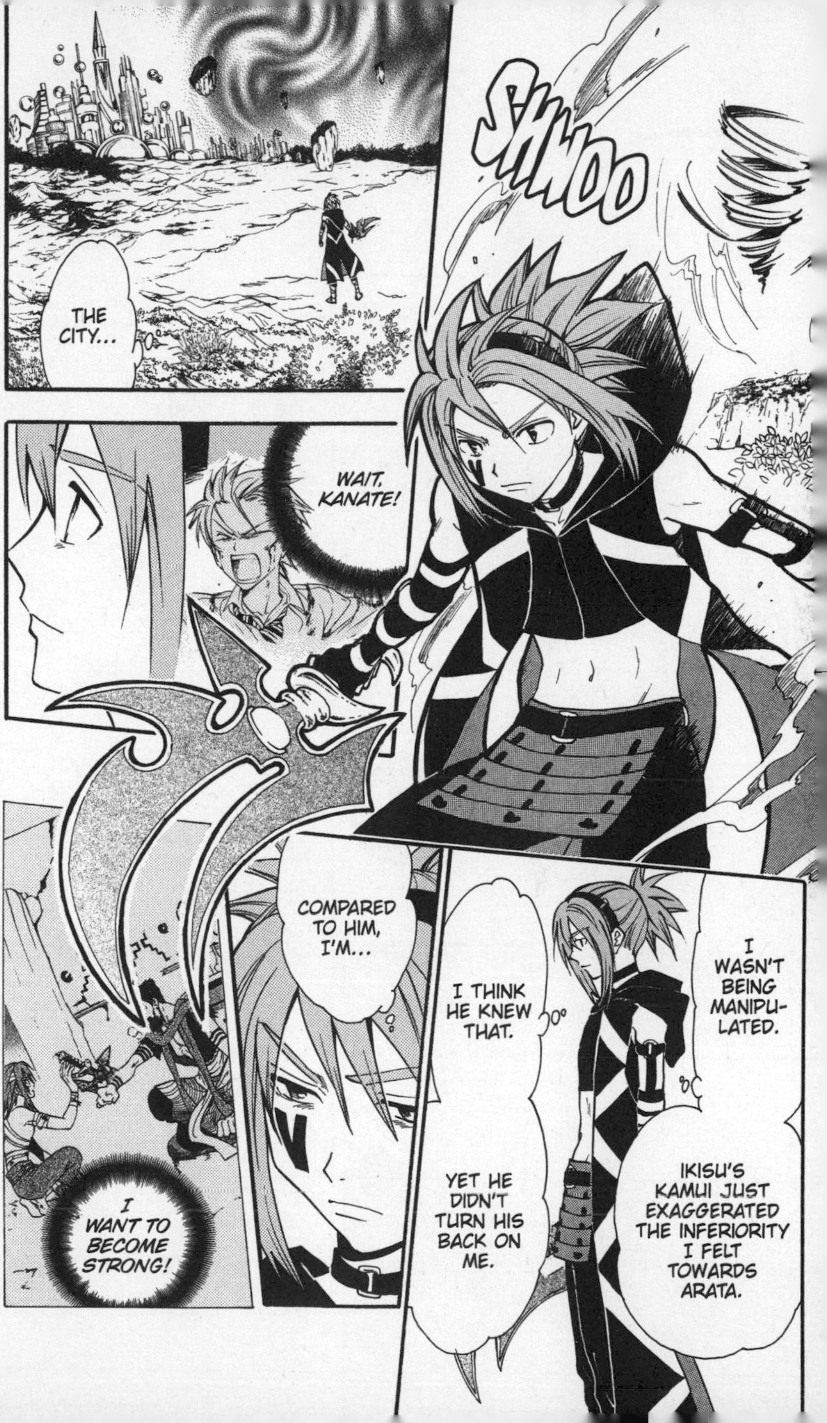
SHWOO
THE CITY...
WAIT, KANATE!
I WASN'T BEING MANIPU-LATED.
I THINK HE KNEW THAT.
IKISU'S KAMUI JUST EXAGGERATED THE INFERIORITY I FELT TOWARDS ARATA.
YET HE DIDN'T TURN HIS BACK ON ME.
COMPARED TO HIM, I'M...
I WANT TO BECOME STRONG!

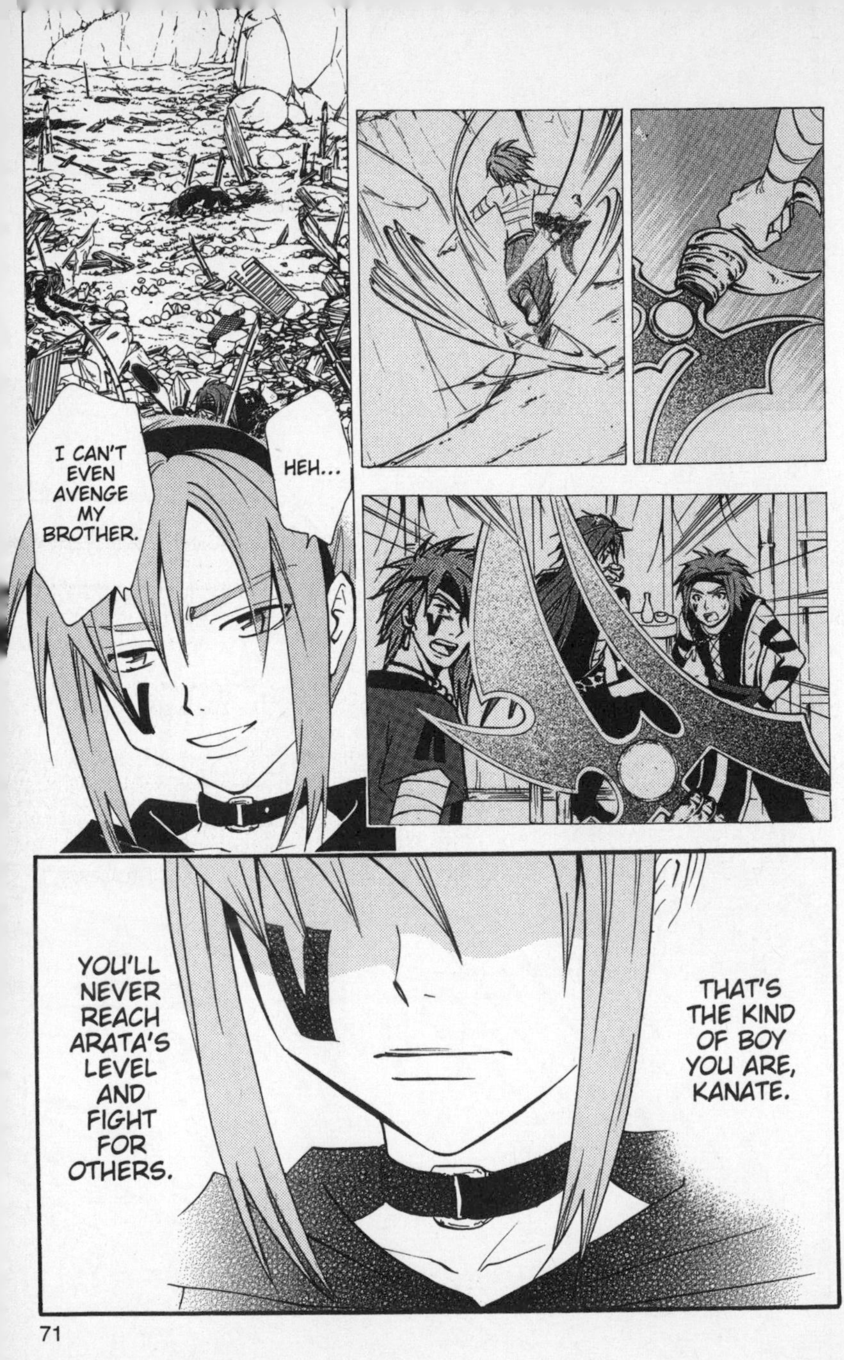
HEH...
I CAN'T EVEN AVENGE MY BROTHER.
THAT'S THE KIND OF BOY YOU ARE, KANATE.
YOU'LL NEVER REACH ARATA'S LEVEL AND FIGHT FOR OTHERS.

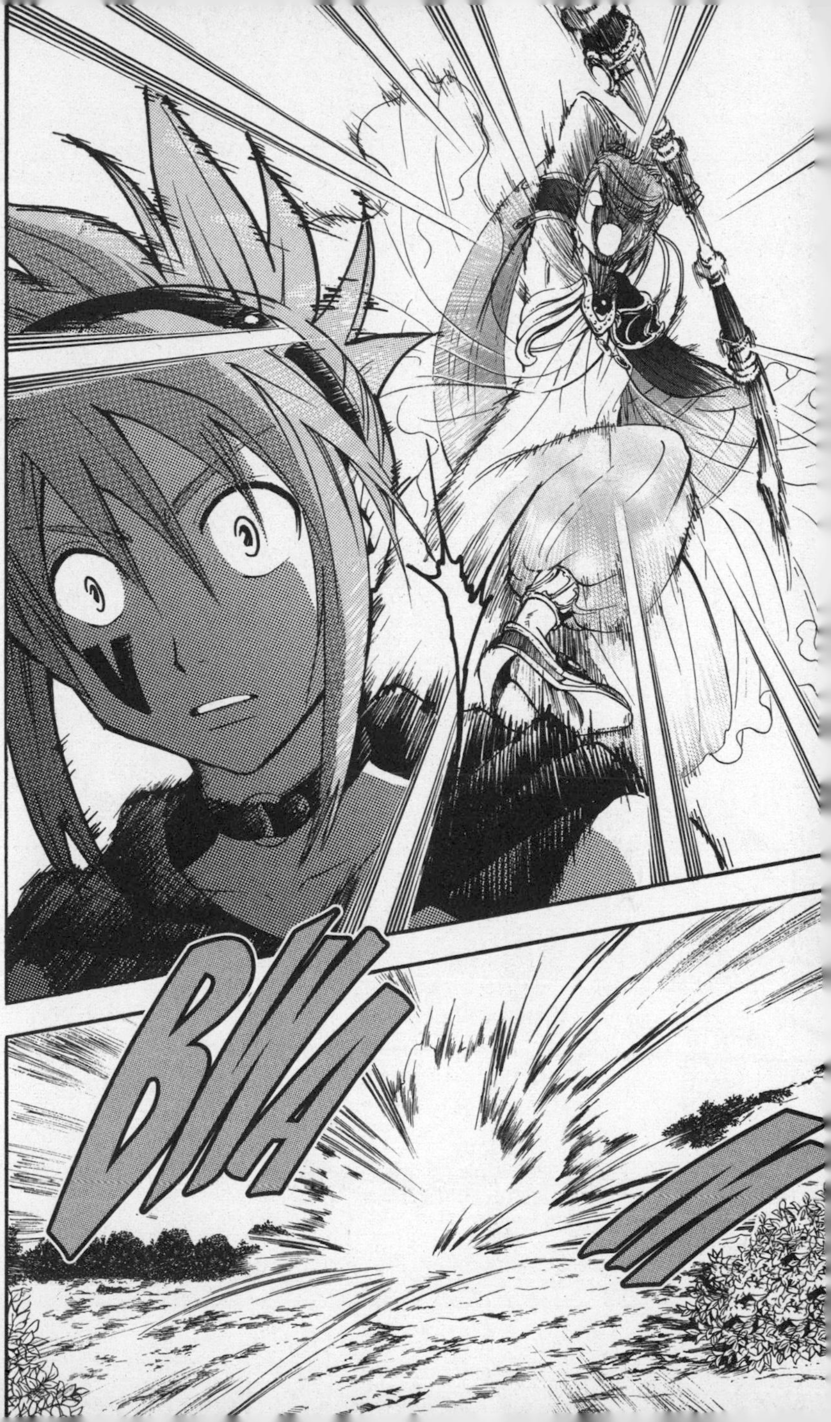

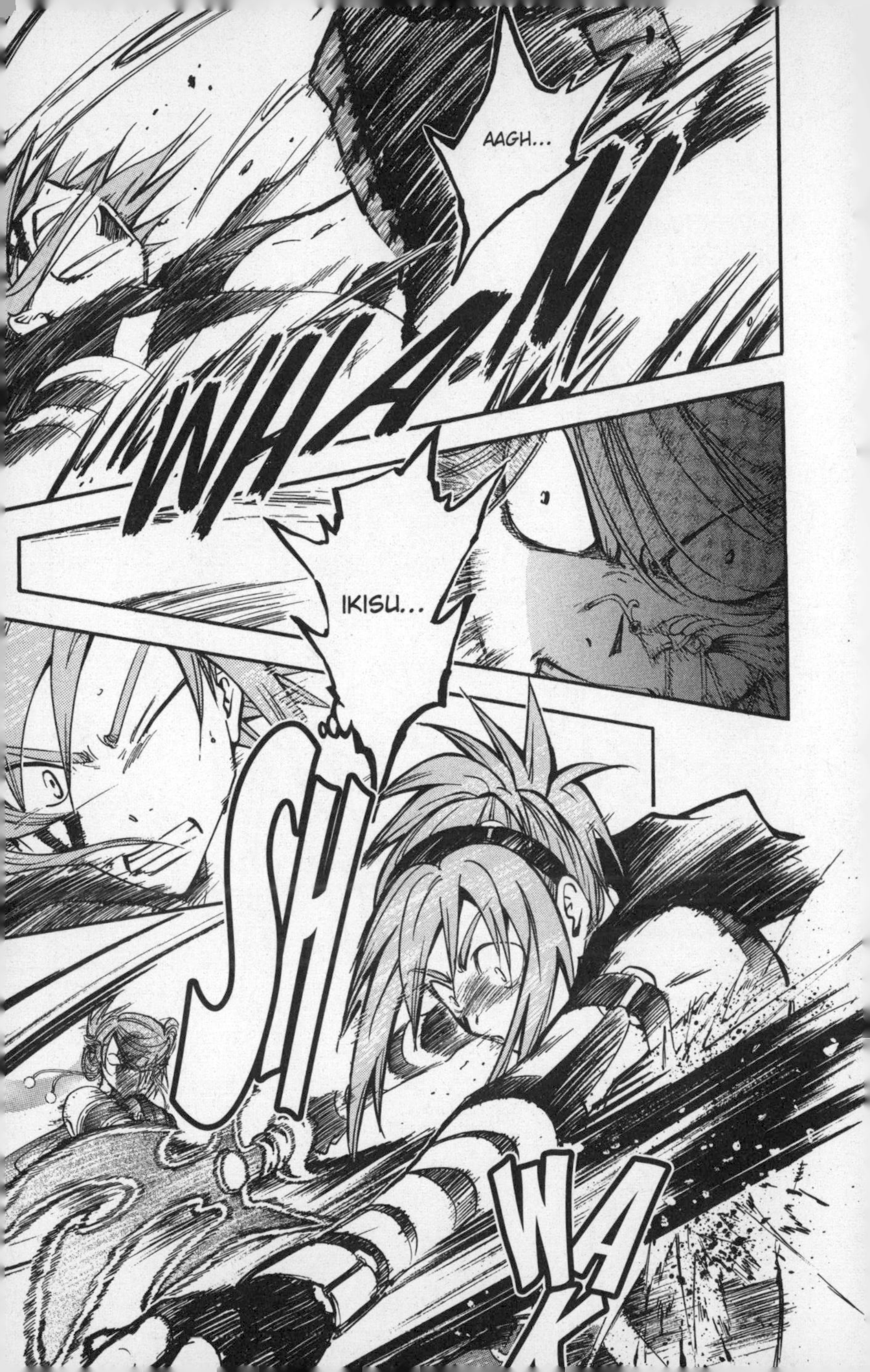
AAGH...
WHAAM
IKISU...
SH
WA

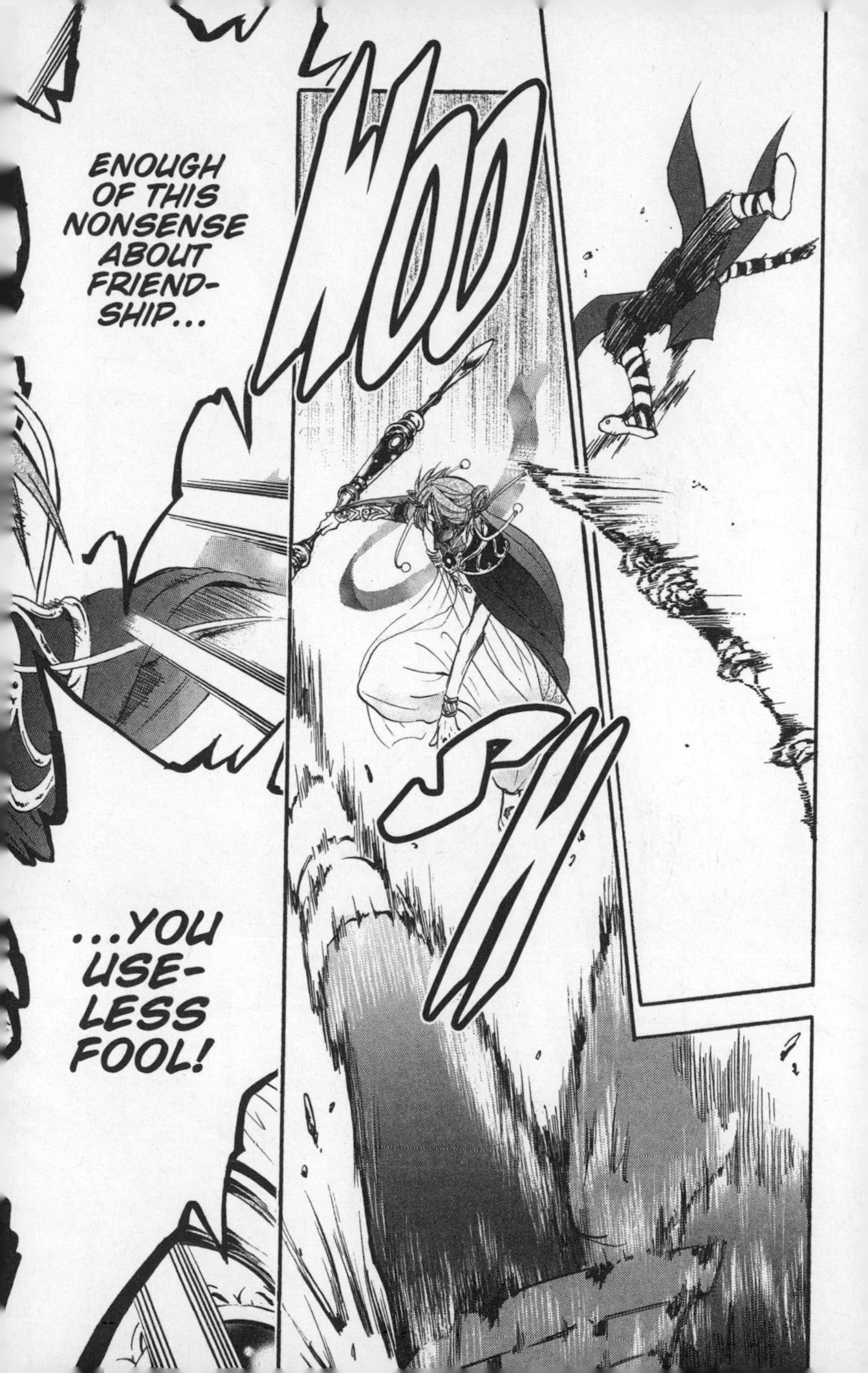
ENOUGH OF THIS NONSENSE ABOUT FRIEND-SHIP...
...YOU USE-LESS FOOL!

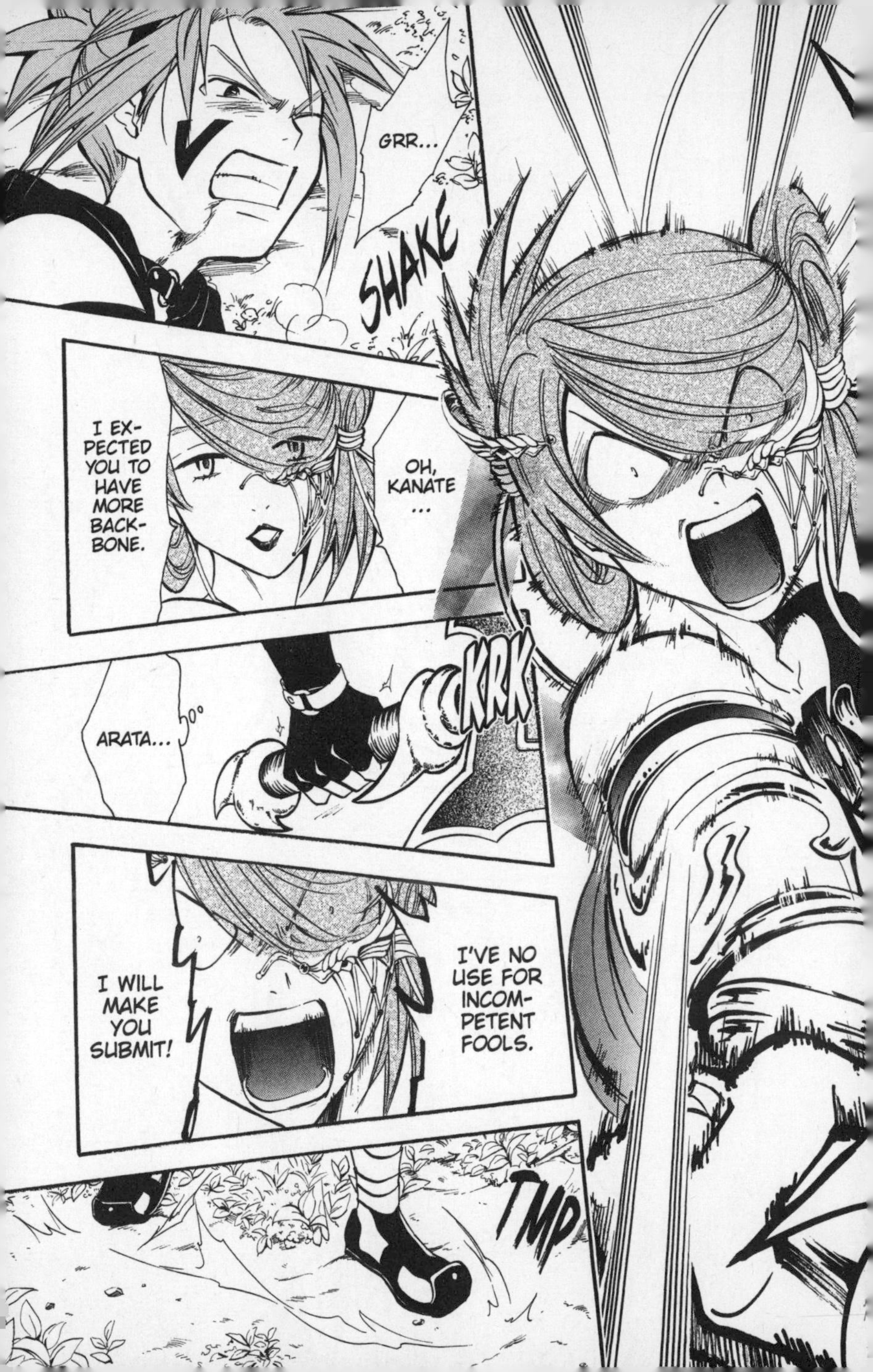

GRR...
SHAKE
OH, KANATE...
I EX-PECTED YOU TO HAVE MORE BACK-BONE.
KRK
ARATA...
I'VE NO USE FOR INCOM-PETENT FOOLS.
I WILL MAKE YOU SUBMIT!
TMP

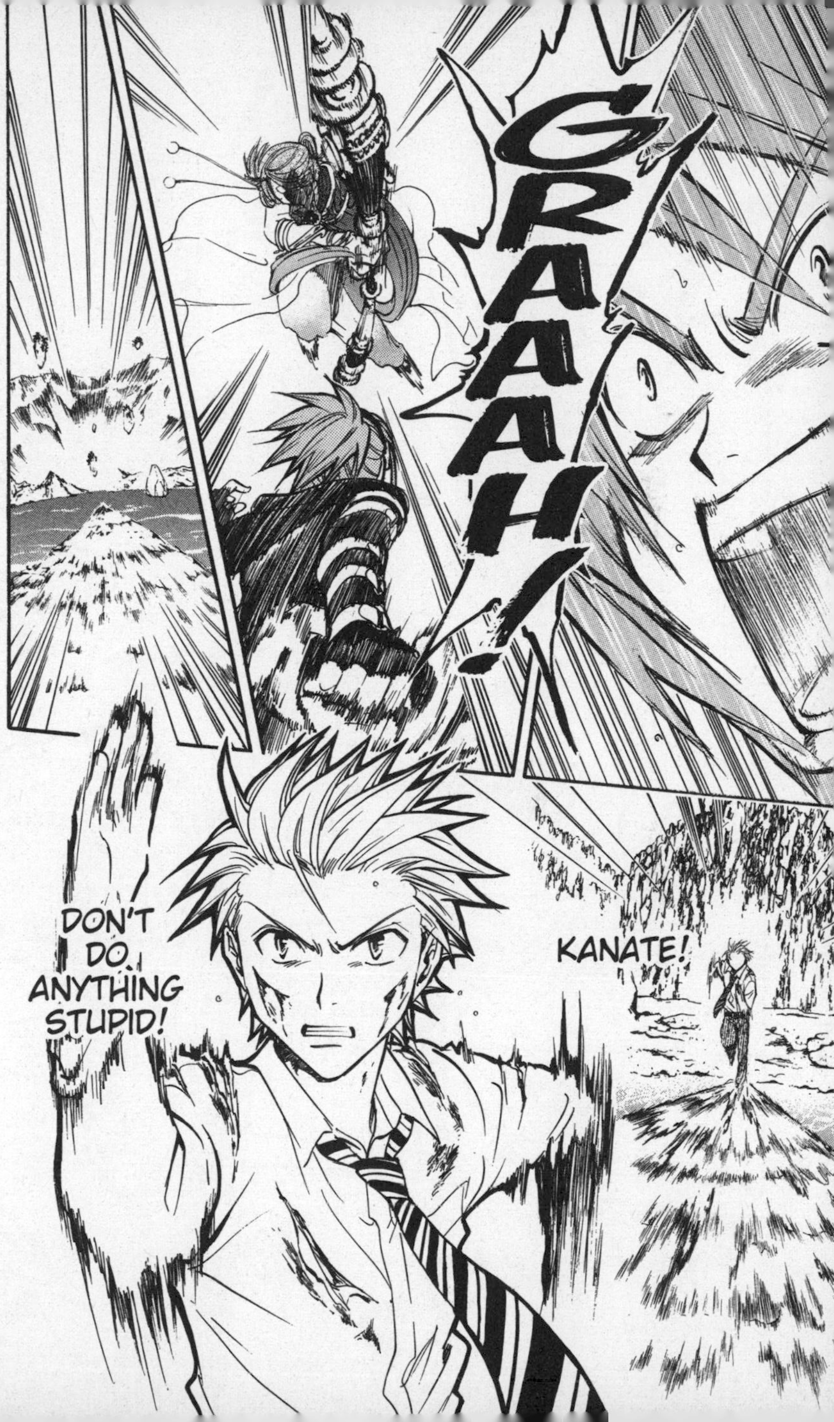
GRAAAH!!
KANATE!
DON'T DO ANYTHING STUPID!

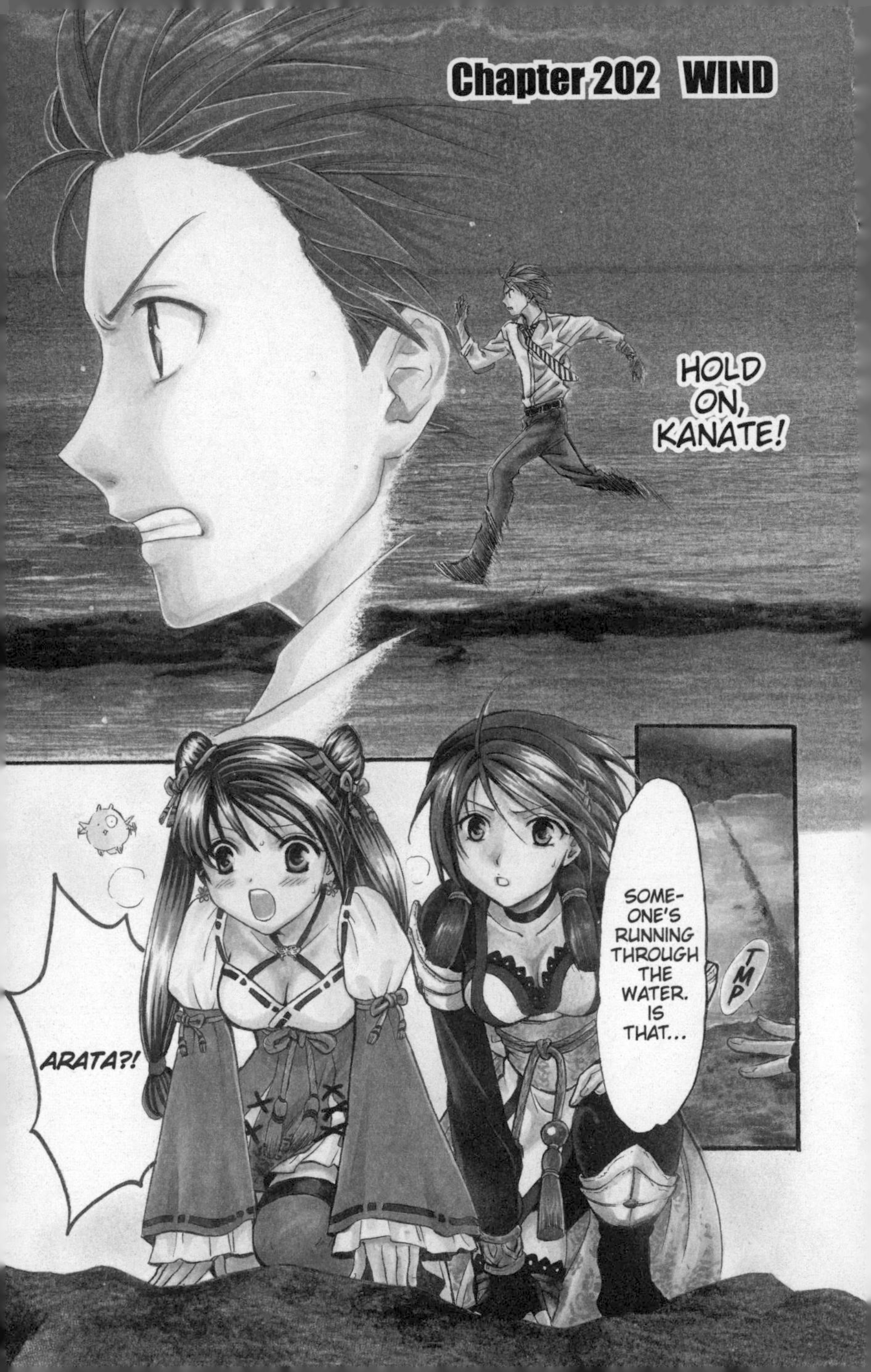
Chapter 202 WIND
HOLD ON, KANATE!
TMP
SOME-ONE'S RUNNING THROUGH THE WATER. IS THAT...
ARATA?!

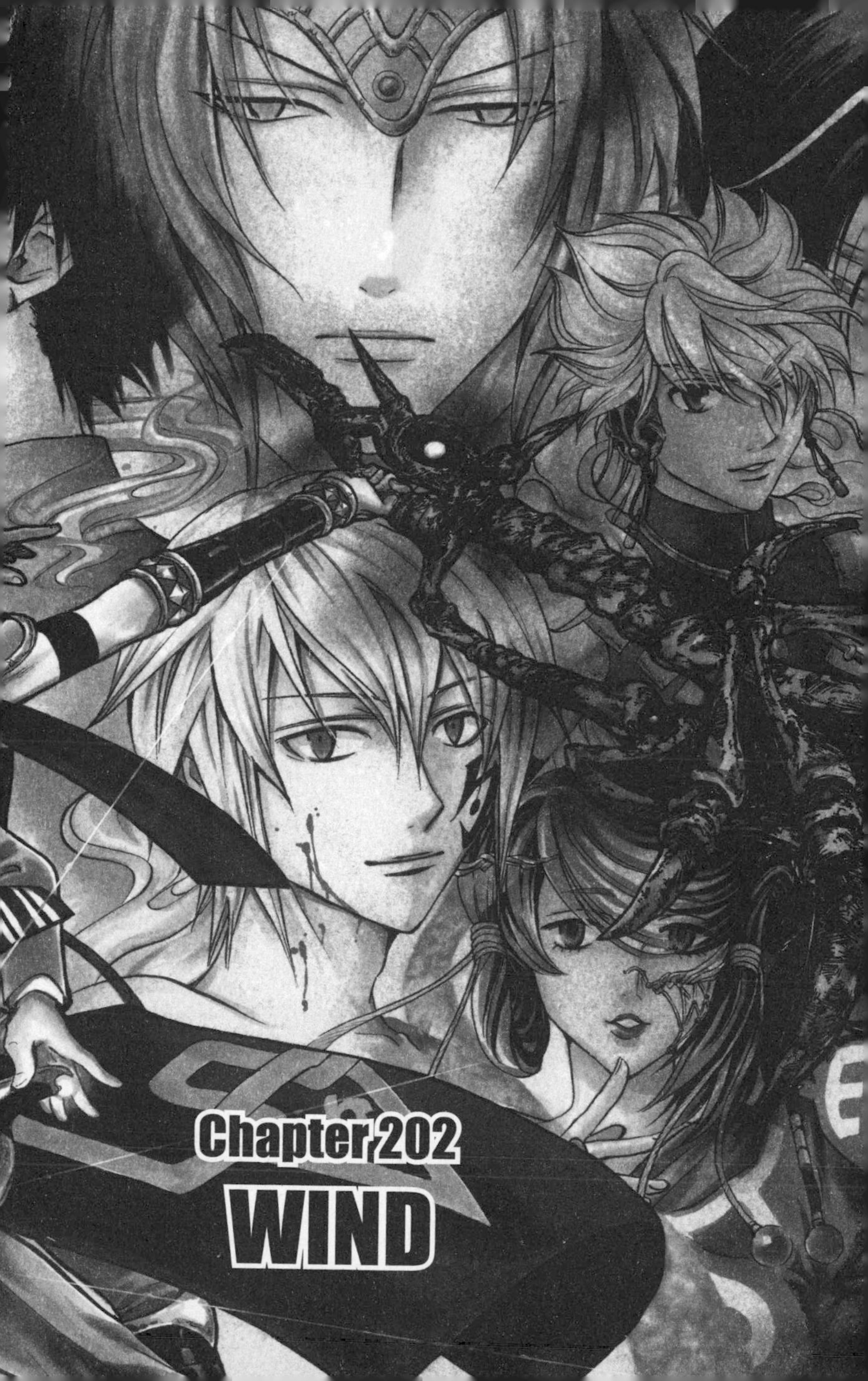
Chapter 202
WIND

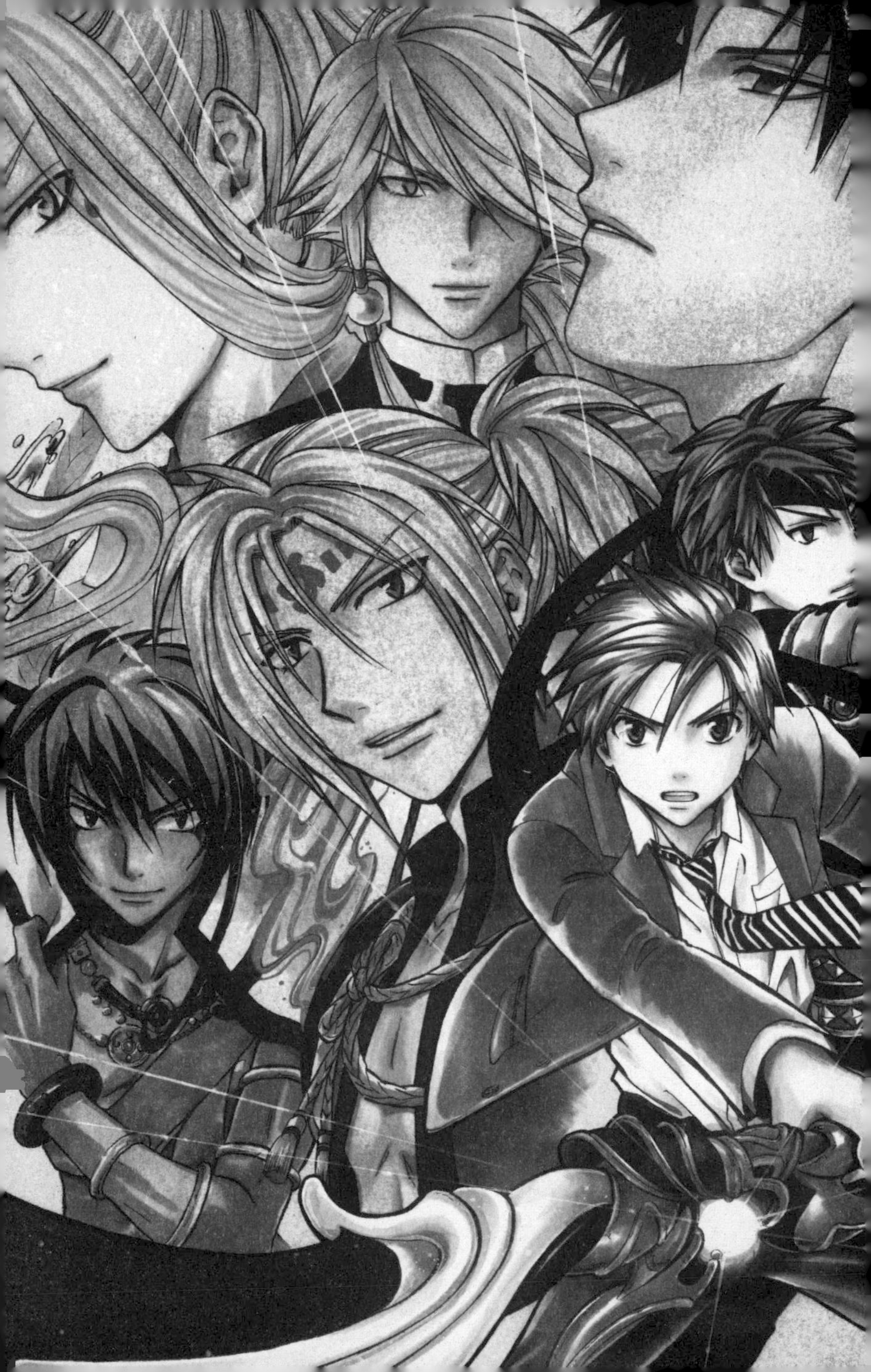

Arata
THE LEGEND

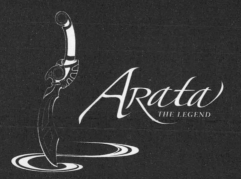

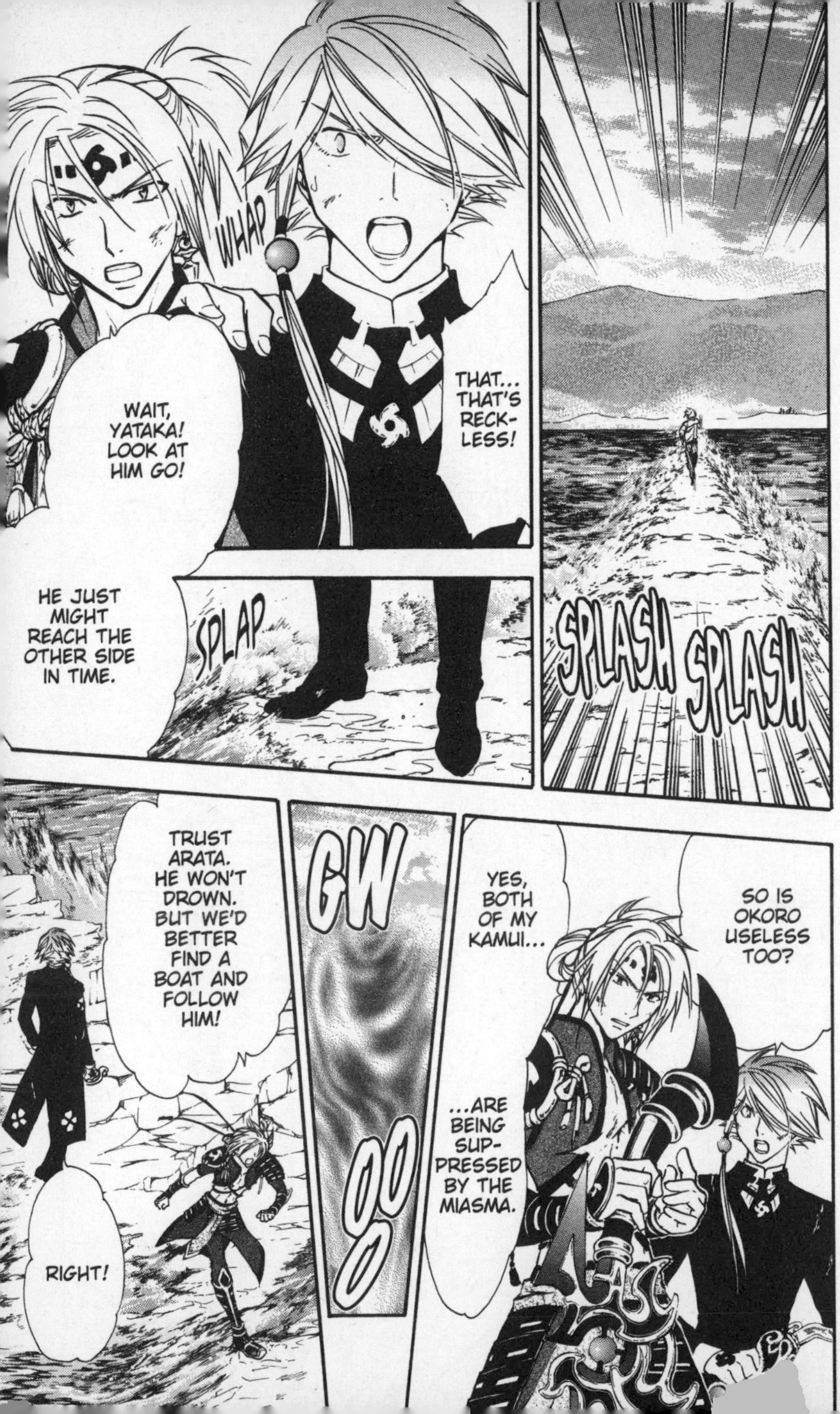
SPLASH SPLASH
THAT... THAT'S RECK-LESS!
WHAP
WAIT, YATAKA! LOOK AT HIM GO!
HE JUST MIGHT REACH THE OTHER SIDE IN TIME.
SPLAP
SO IS OKORO USELESS TOO?
YES, BOTH OF MY KAMUI...
...ARE BEING SUP-PRESSED BY THE MIASMA.
GW
OO
TRUST ARATA. HE WON'T DROWN. BUT WE'D BETTER FIND A BOAT AND FOLLOW HIM!
RIGHT!

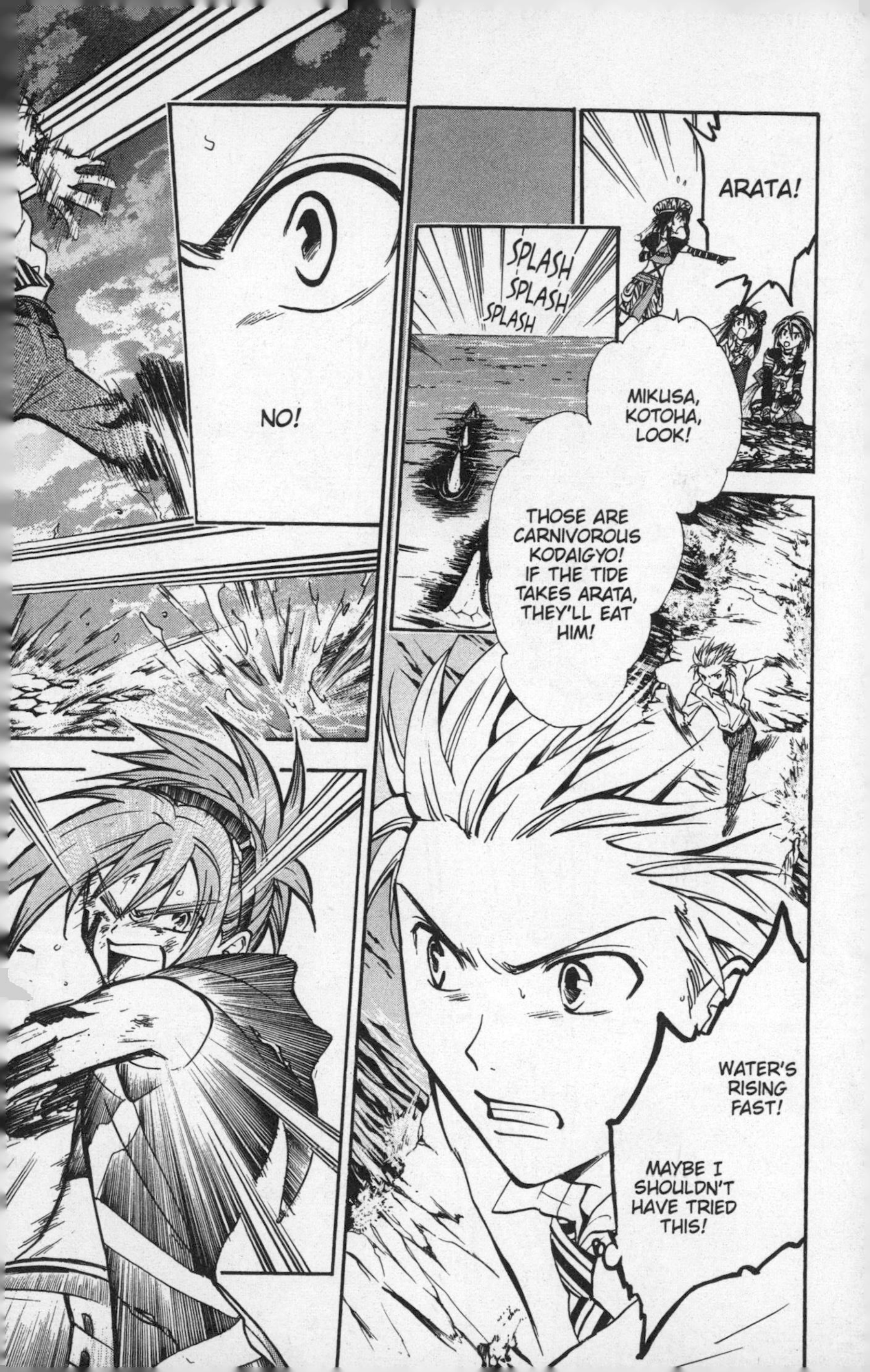
ARATA!
SPLASH
SPLASH
SPLASH
MIKUSA, KOTOHA, LOOK!
THOSE ARE CARNIVOROUS KODAIGYO! IF THE TIDE TAKES ARATA, THEY'LL EAT HIM!
NO!
WATER'S RISING FAST!
MAYBE I SHOULDN'T HAVE TRIED THIS!

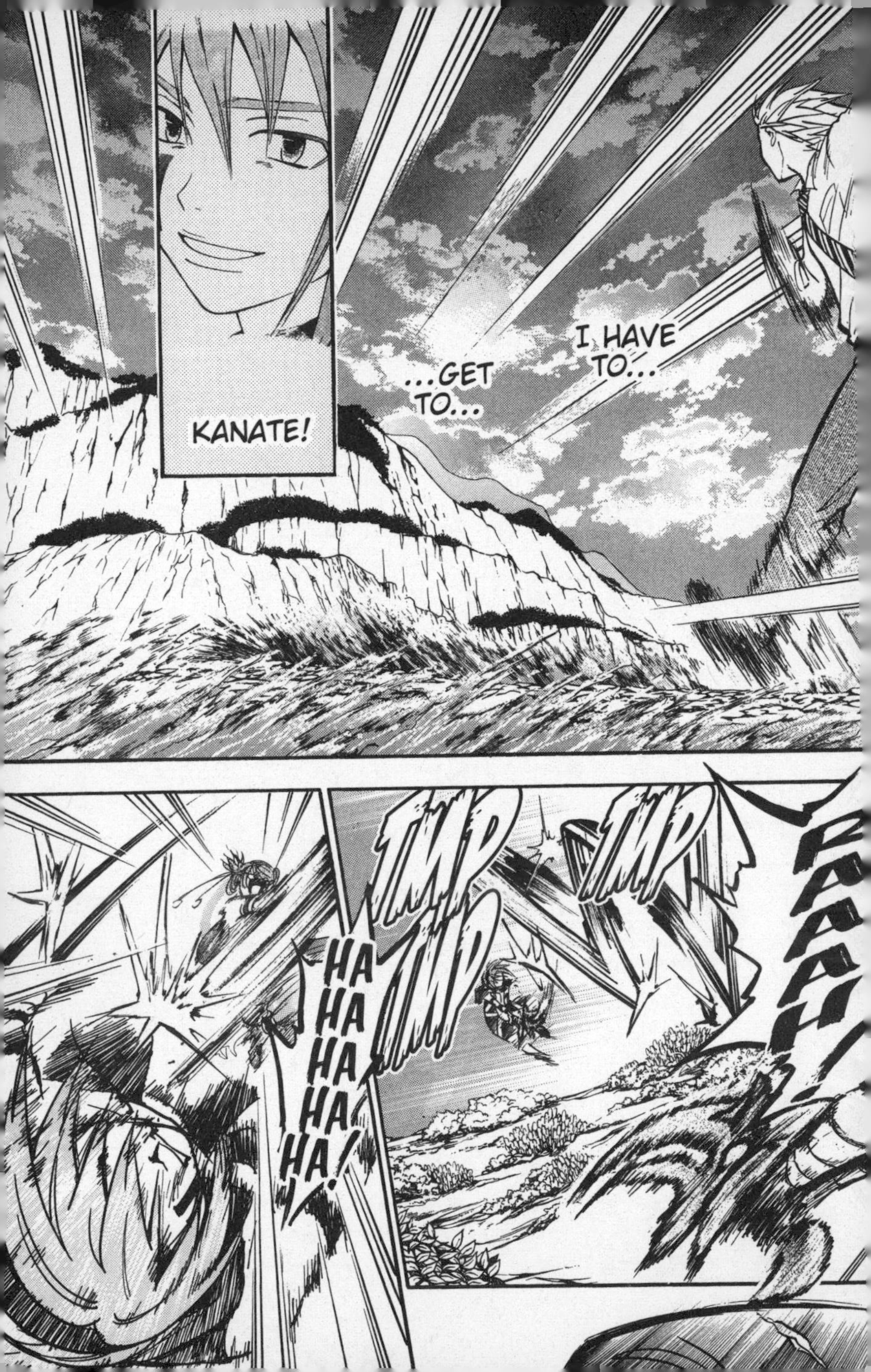
I HAVE TO...
...GET TO...
KANATE!
AAAAH!!
TMP TMP
TMP TMP
HA HA HA HA HA HA!

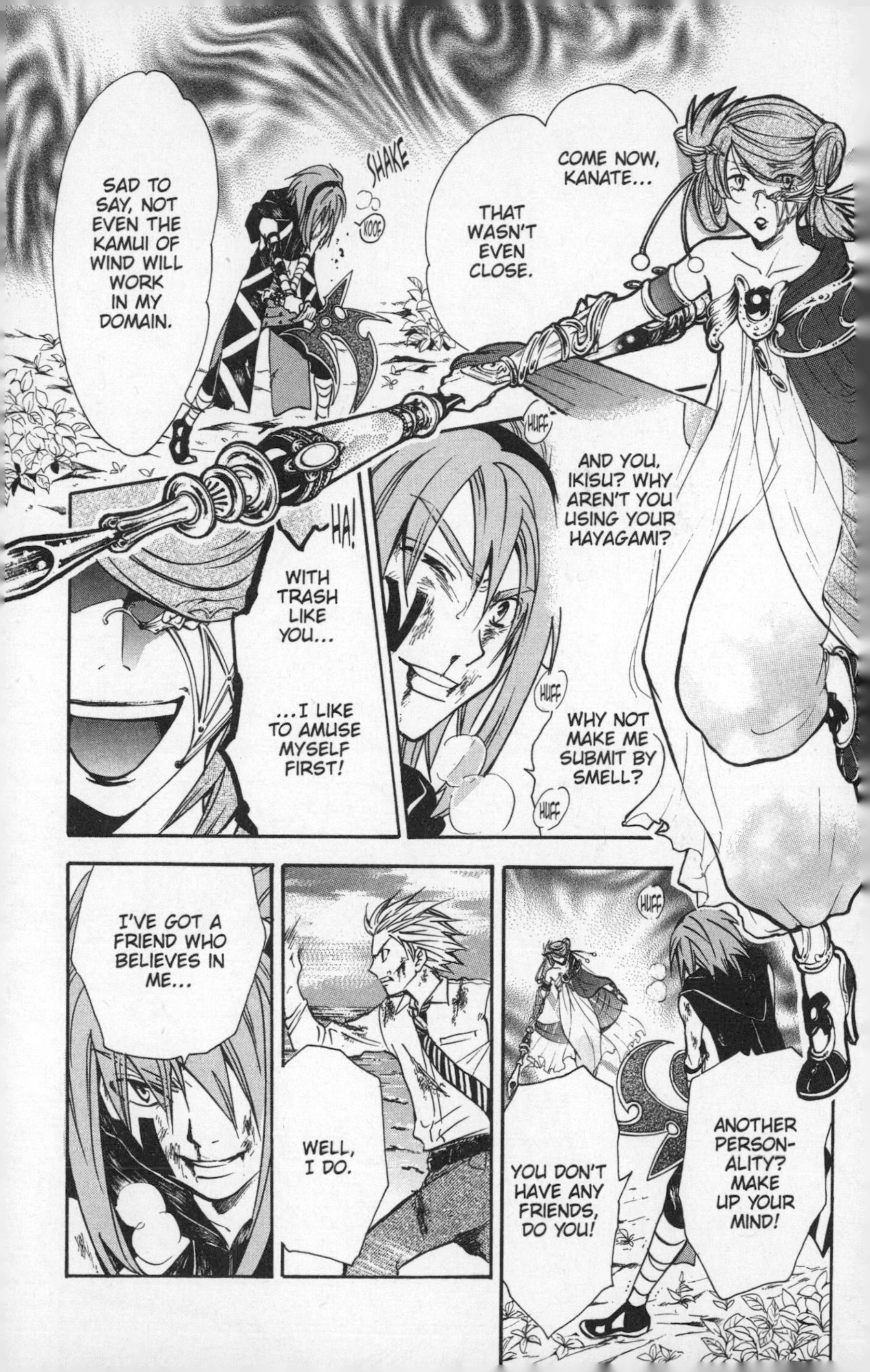
COME NOW, KANATE...
THAT WASN'T EVEN CLOSE.
SHAKE
KOOF
SAD TO SAY, NOT EVEN THE KAMUI OF WIND WILL WORK IN MY DOMAIN.
HUFF
AND YOU, IKISU? WHY AREN'T YOU USING YOUR HAYAGAMI?
HUFF
WHY NOT MAKE ME SUBMIT BY SMELL?
HUFF
HA!
WITH TRASH LIKE YOU...
...I LIKE TO AMUSE MYSELF FIRST!
HUFF
ANOTHER PERSONALITY? MAKE UP YOUR MIND!
YOU DON'T HAVE ANY FRIENDS, DO YOU!
WELL, I DO.
I'VE GOT A FRIEND WHO BELIEVES IN ME...

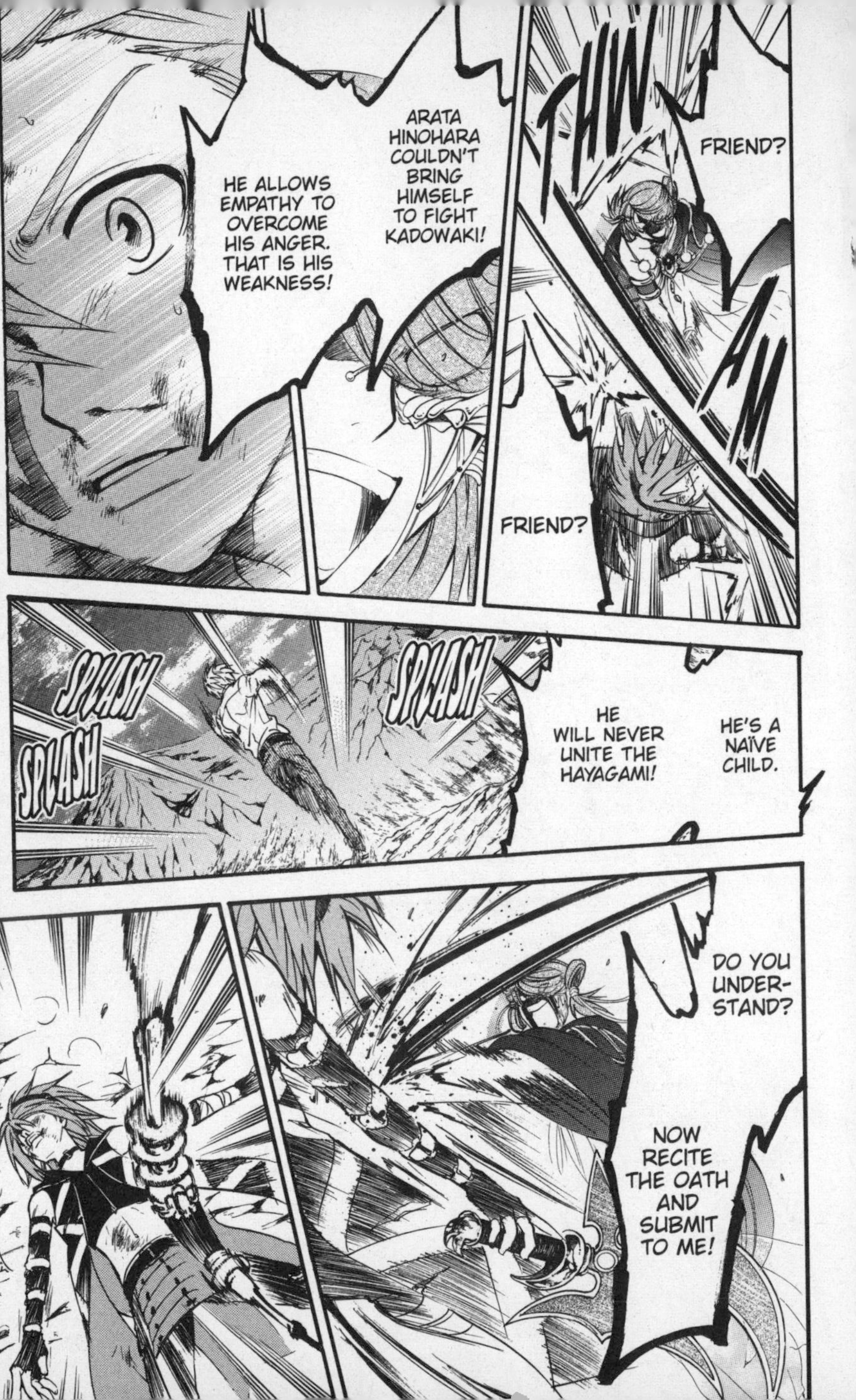
THWAM
FRIEND?
FRIEND?
ARATA HINOHARA COULDN'T BRING HIMSELF TO FIGHT KADOWAKI!
HE ALLOWS EMPATHY TO OVERCOME HIS ANGER. THAT IS HIS WEAKNESS!
HE'S A NAÏVE CHILD.
HE WILL NEVER UNITE THE HAYAGAMI!
SPLASH
SPLASH
SPLASH
DO YOU UNDER-STAND?
NOW RECITE THE OATH AND SUBMIT TO ME!

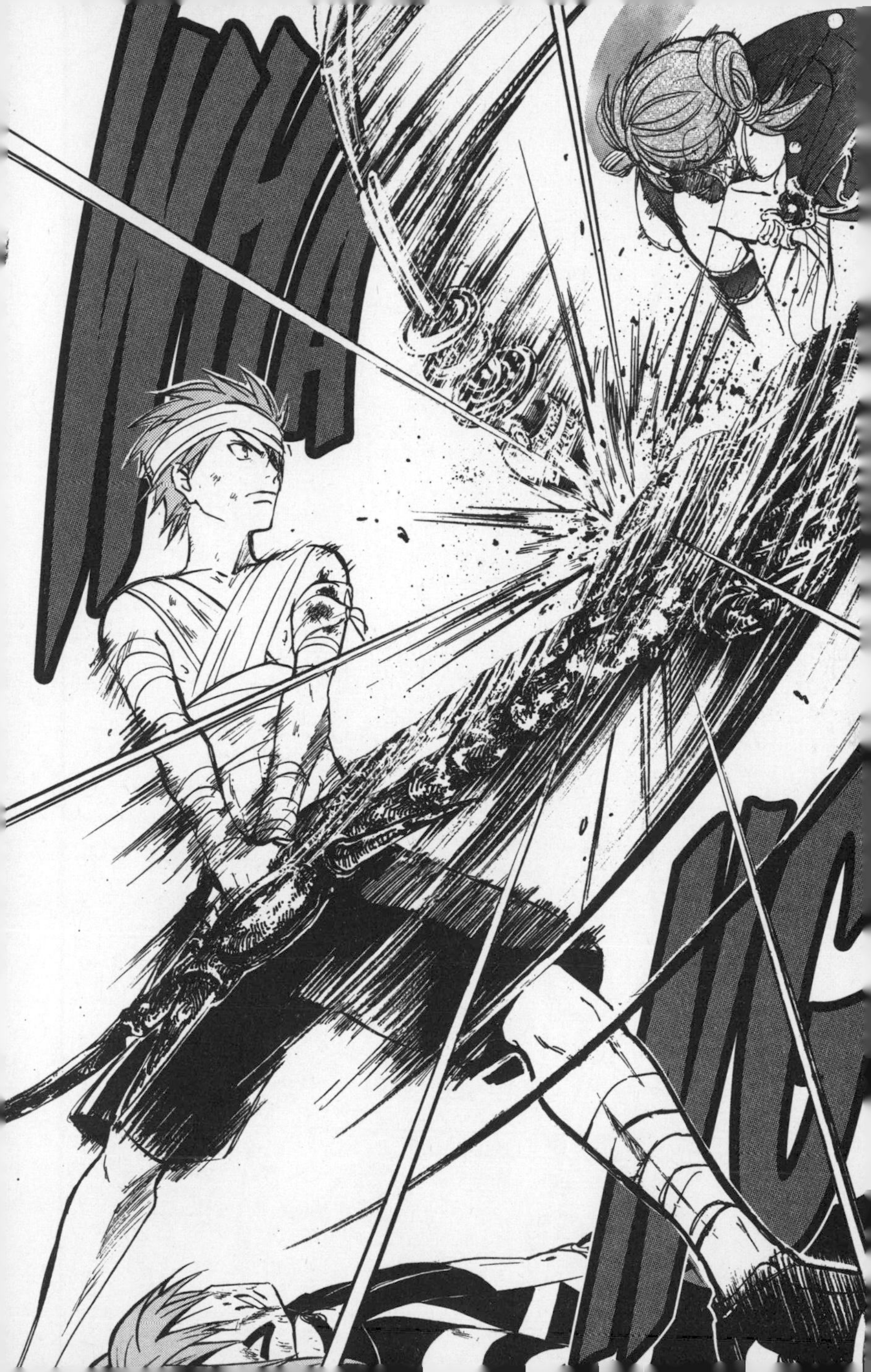

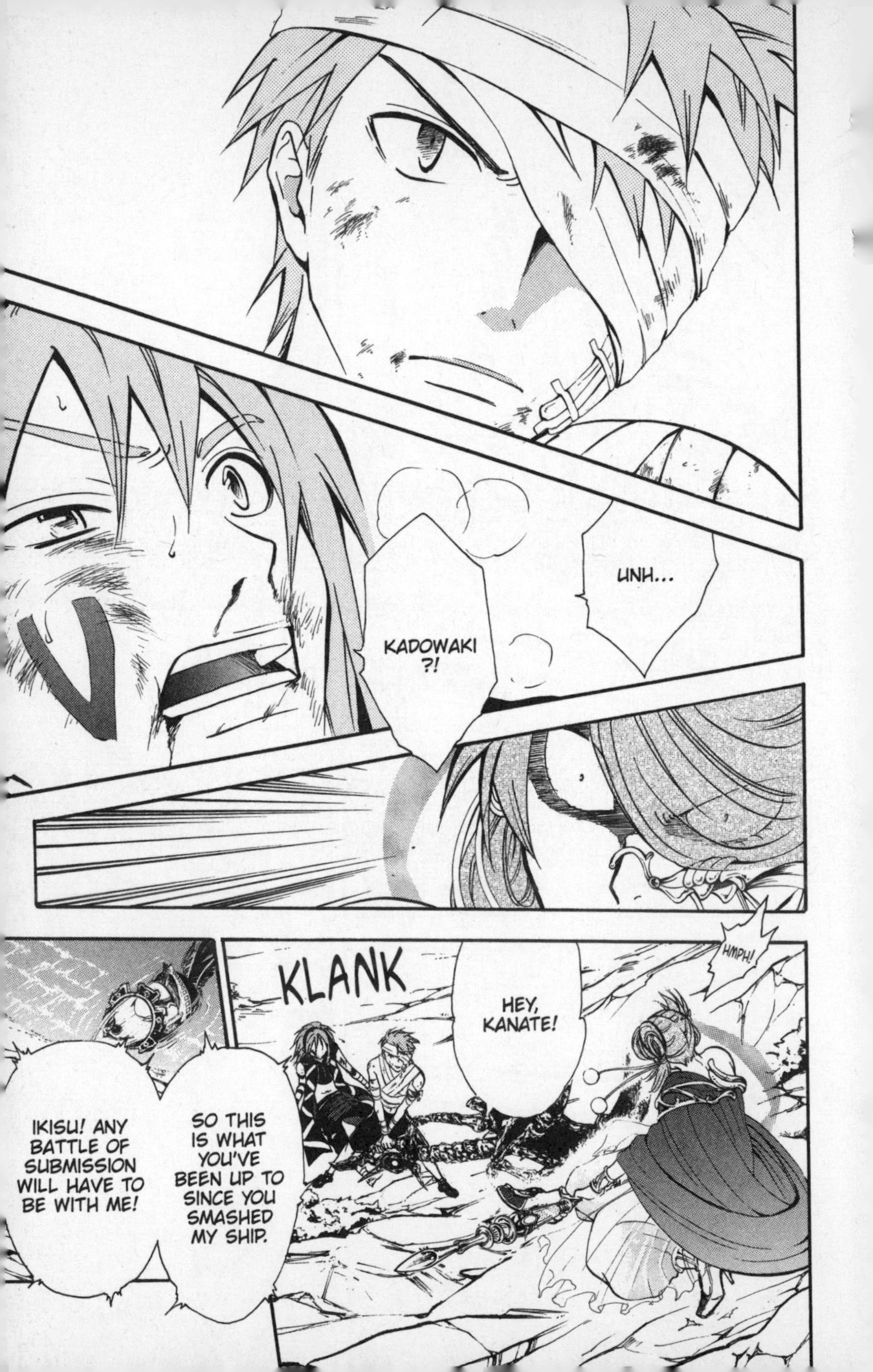
UNH...
KADOWAKI ?!
HMPH!
HEY, KANATE!
KLANK
SO THIS IS WHAT YOU'VE BEEN UP TO SINCE YOU SMASHED MY SHIP.
IKISU! ANY BATTLE OF SUBMISSION WILL HAVE TO BE WITH ME!

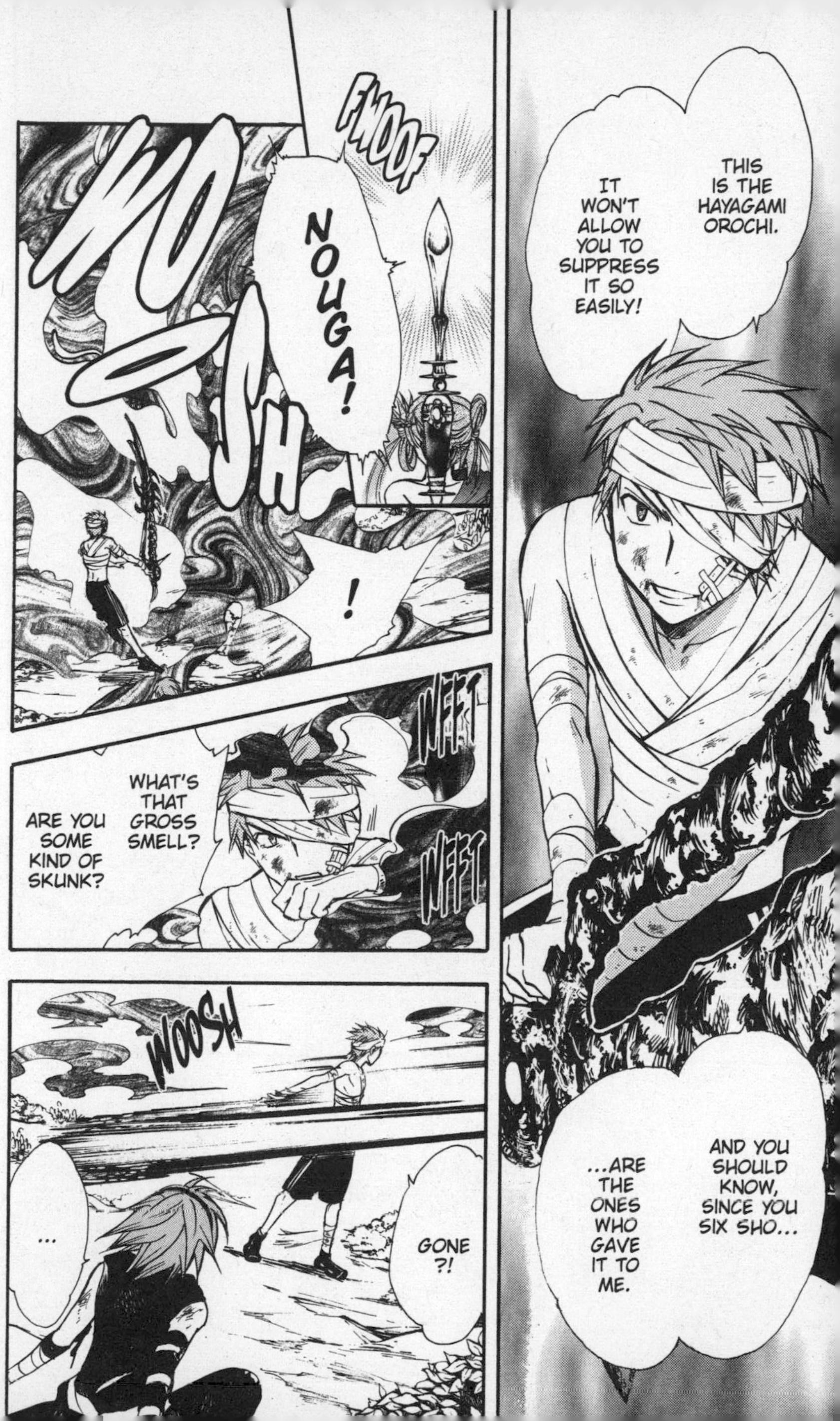
THIS IS THE HAYAGAMI OROCHI.
IT WON'T ALLOW YOU TO SUPPRESS IT SO EASILY!
AND YOU SHOULD KNOW, SINCE YOU SIX SHO...
...ARE THE ONES WHO GAVE IT TO ME.
FWOOF
NOUGA!
WOOSH
!
WFFT
WFFT
WHAT'S THAT GROSS SMELL?
ARE YOU SOME KIND OF SKUNK?
WOOSH
GONE?!
...

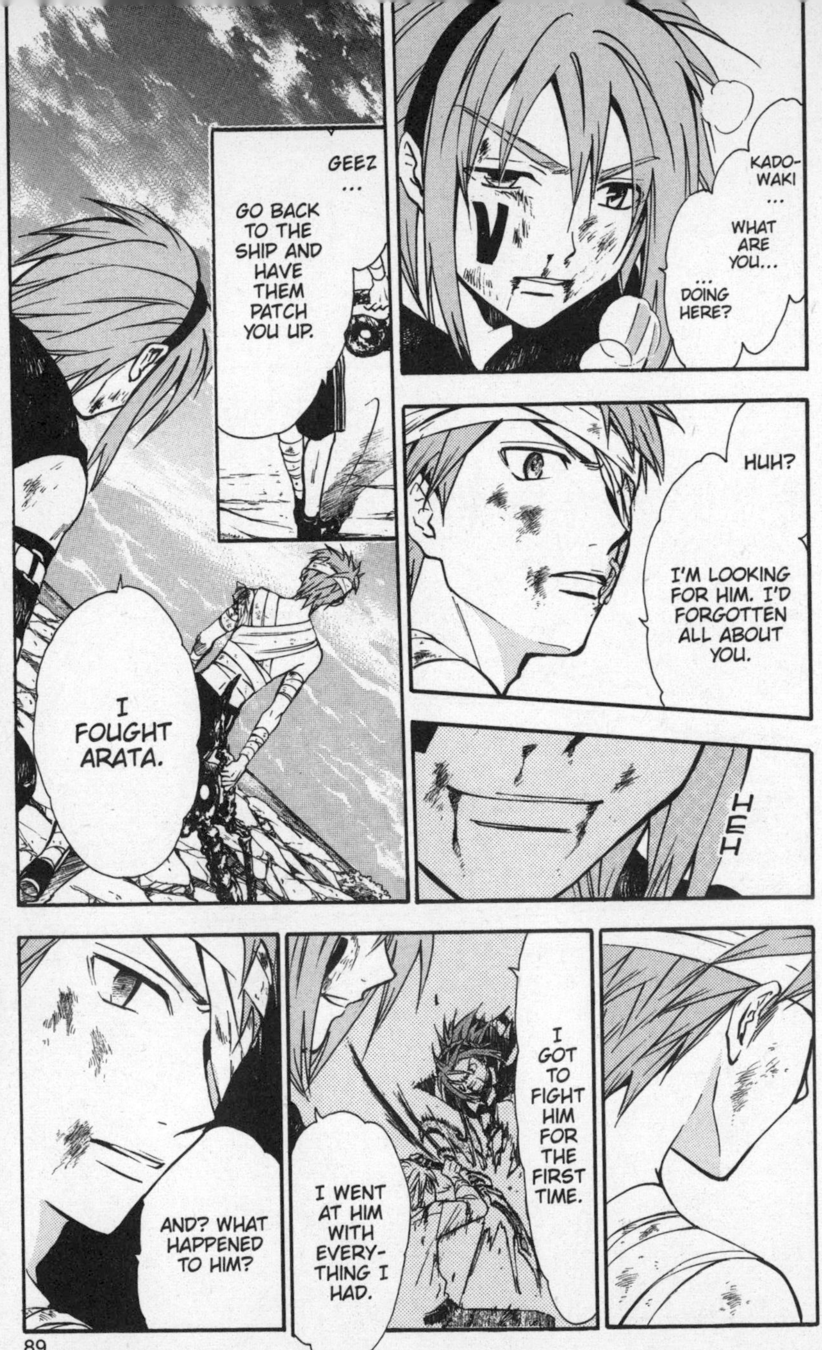
KADO-WAKI ... WHAT ARE YOU... ...DOING HERE?
HUH?
I'M LOOKING FOR HIM. I'D FORGOTTEN ALL ABOUT YOU.
HEH
GEEZ ...
GO BACK TO THE SHIP AND HAVE THEM PATCH YOU UP.
I FOUGHT ARATA.
I GOT TO FIGHT HIM FOR THE FIRST TIME.
I WENT AT HIM WITH EVERY-THING I HAD.
AND? WHAT HAPPENED TO HIM?

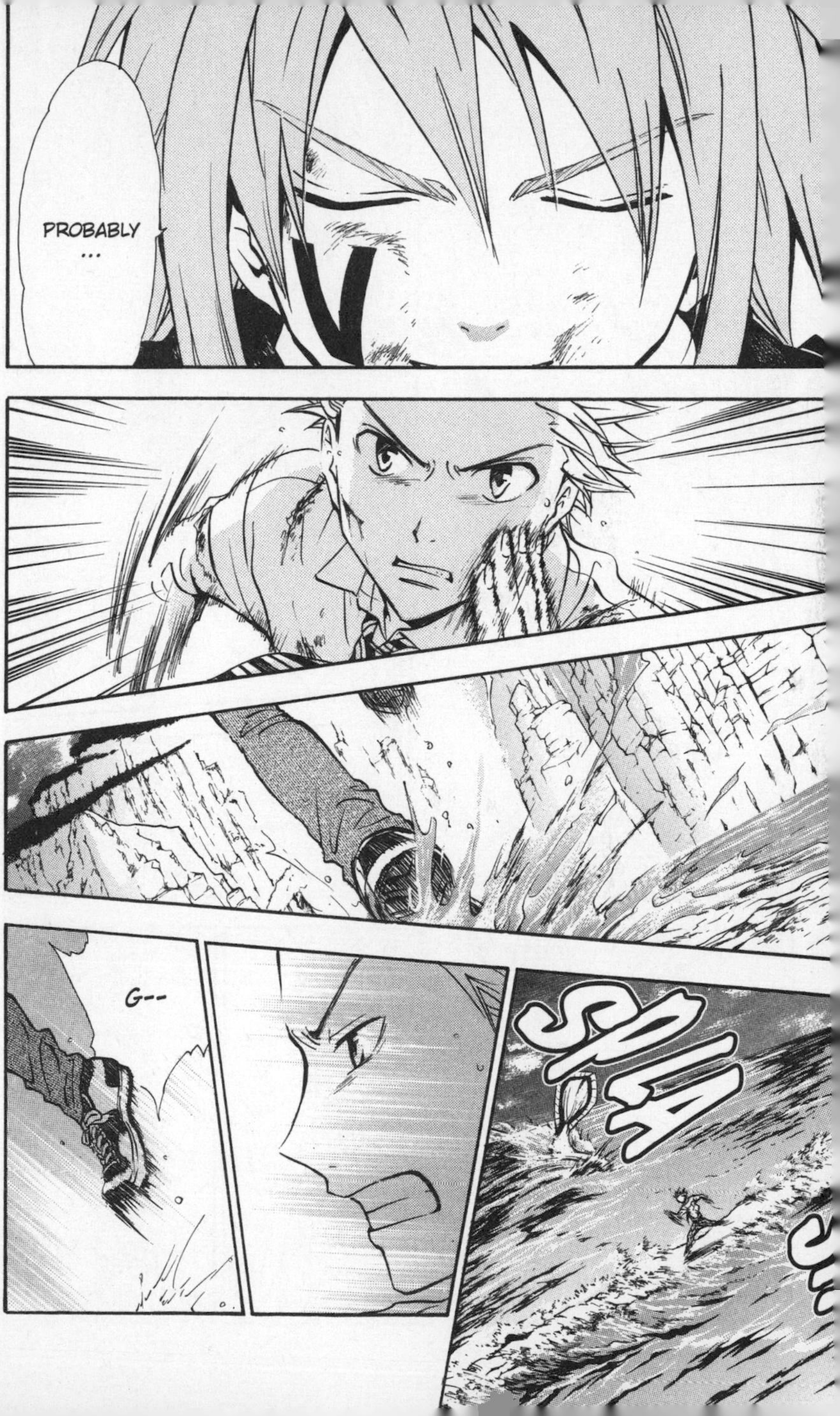
PROBABLY
...
SPLA
G--

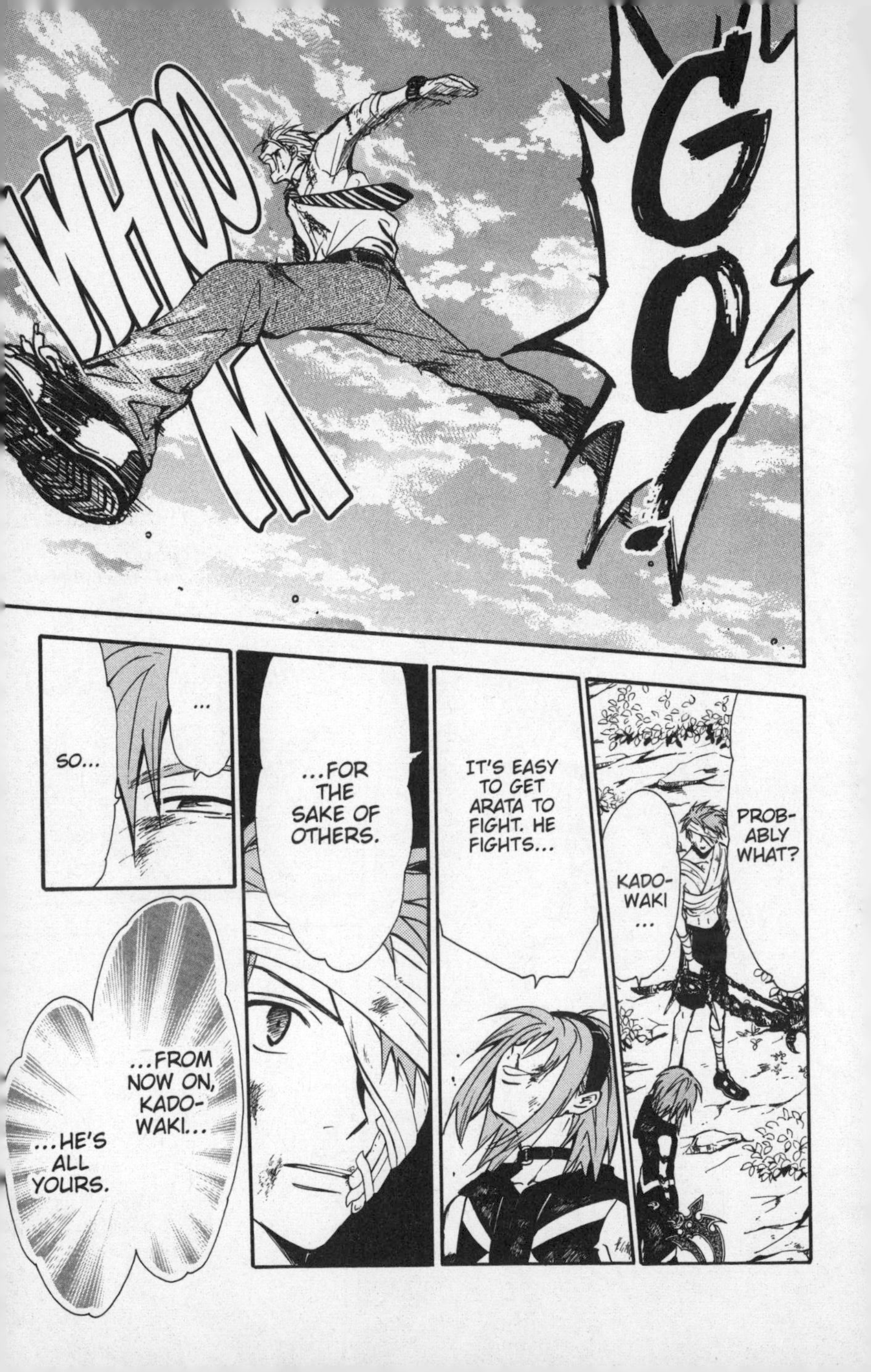
GO!
WHOOM
PROBABLY WHAT?
KADOWAKI...
IT'S EASY TO GET ARATA TO FIGHT. HE FIGHTS...
...FOR THE SAKE OF OTHERS.
...
SO...
...FROM NOW ON, KADOWAKI...
...HE'S ALL YOURS.

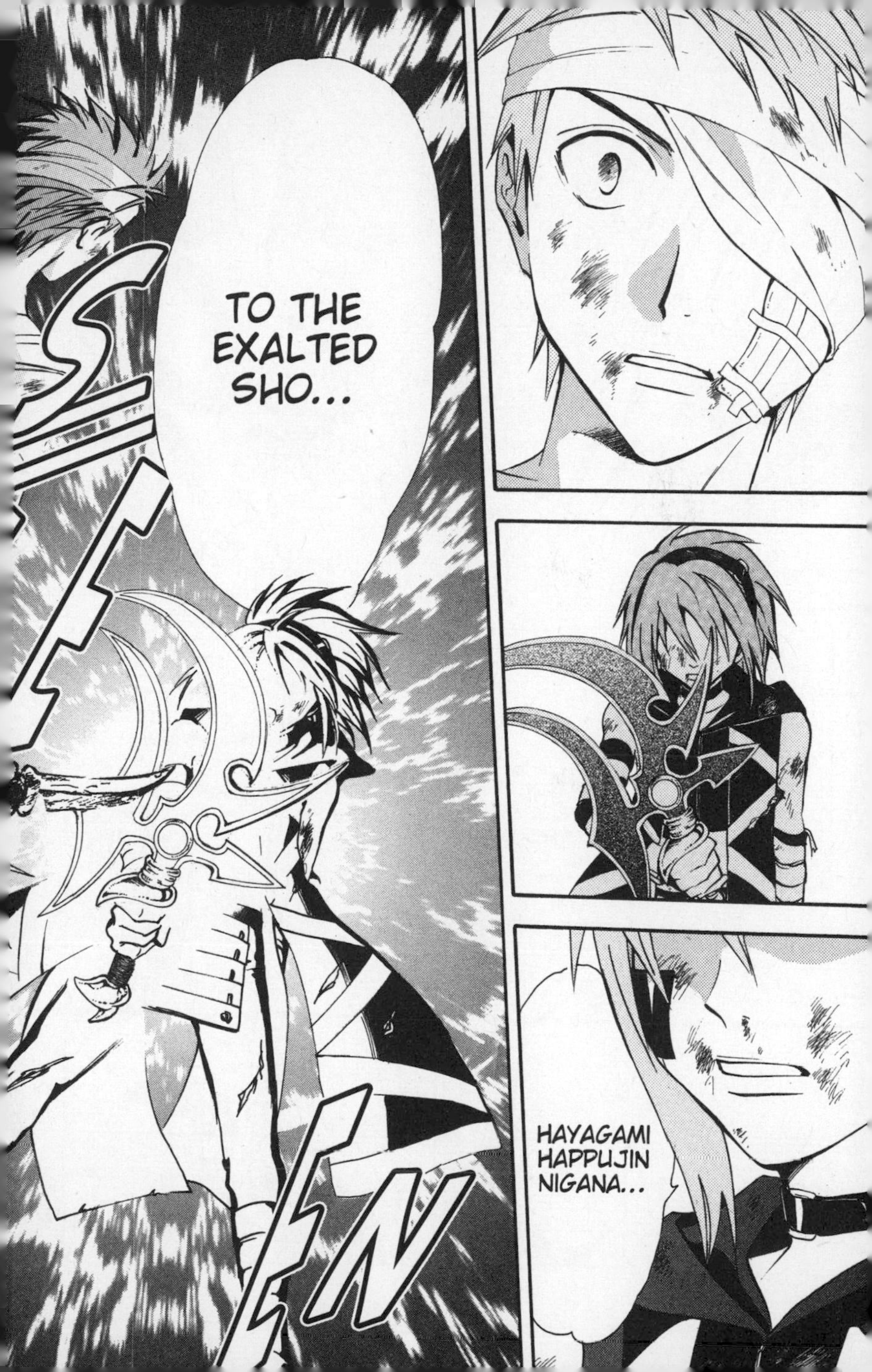
HAYAGAMI HAPPUJIN NIGANA...
TO THE EXALTED SHO...

KADOWAKI,
YOU'RE
STRONG
ENOUGH
TO GO
HEAD TO
HEAD WITH
ARATA.

YOU CAN
DO...WHAT I
COULD NOT.

KANATE...

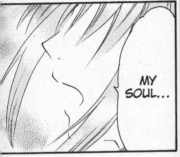

MY
SOUL...

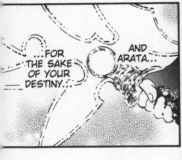

...FOR
THE SAKE
OF YOUR
DESTINY...

AND
ARATA...

...GET
STRONGER.

THIS IS
ALL I CAN
DO FOR
YOU.

YOU...

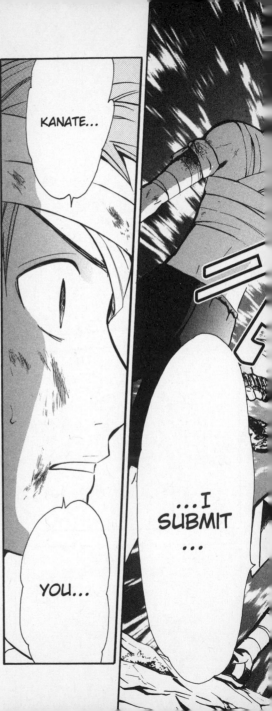

...I
SUBMIT
...

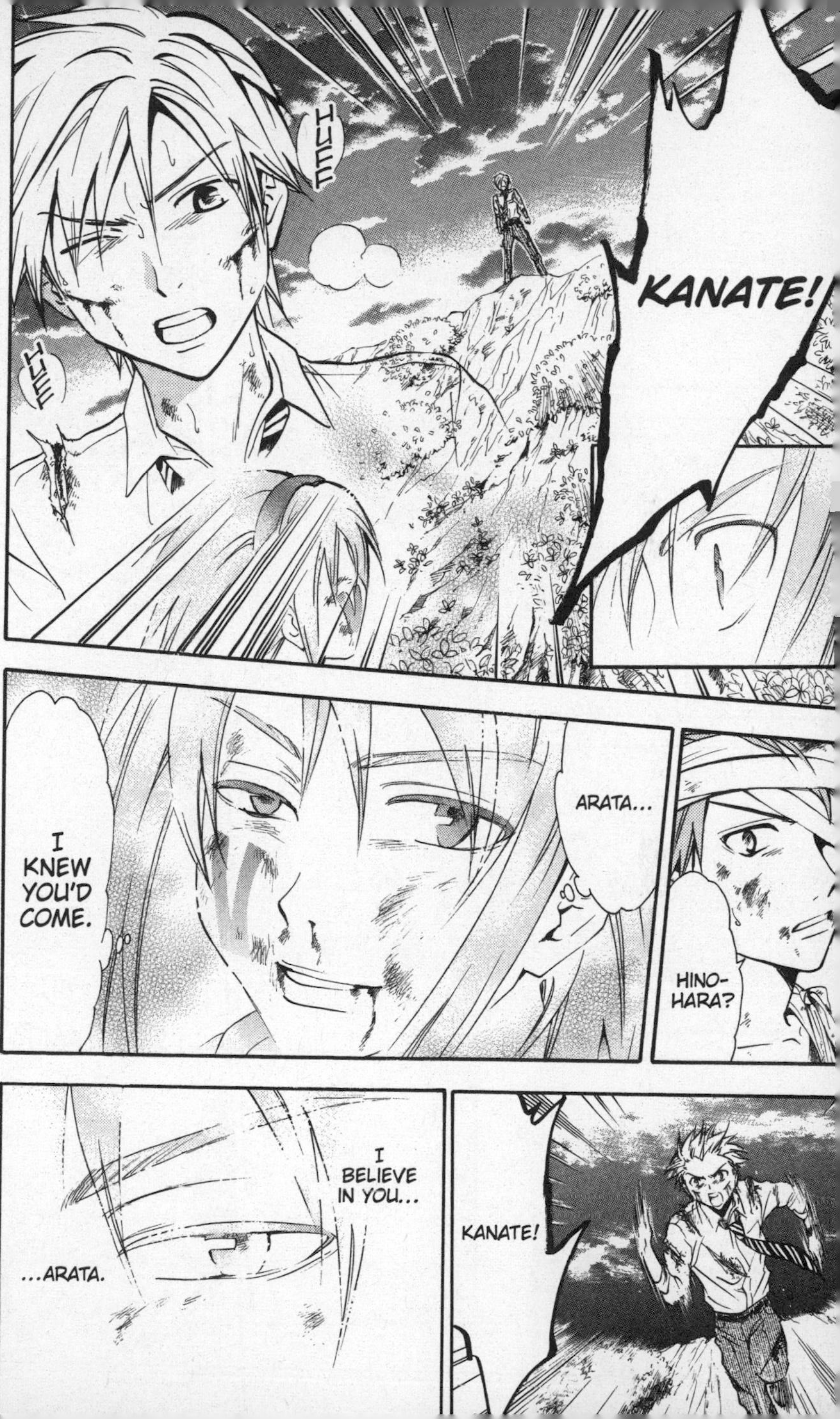
KANATE!
HUFF
HUFF
HINO-HARA?
ARATA...
I KNEW YOU'D COME.
KANATE!
I BELIEVE IN YOU...
...ARATA.

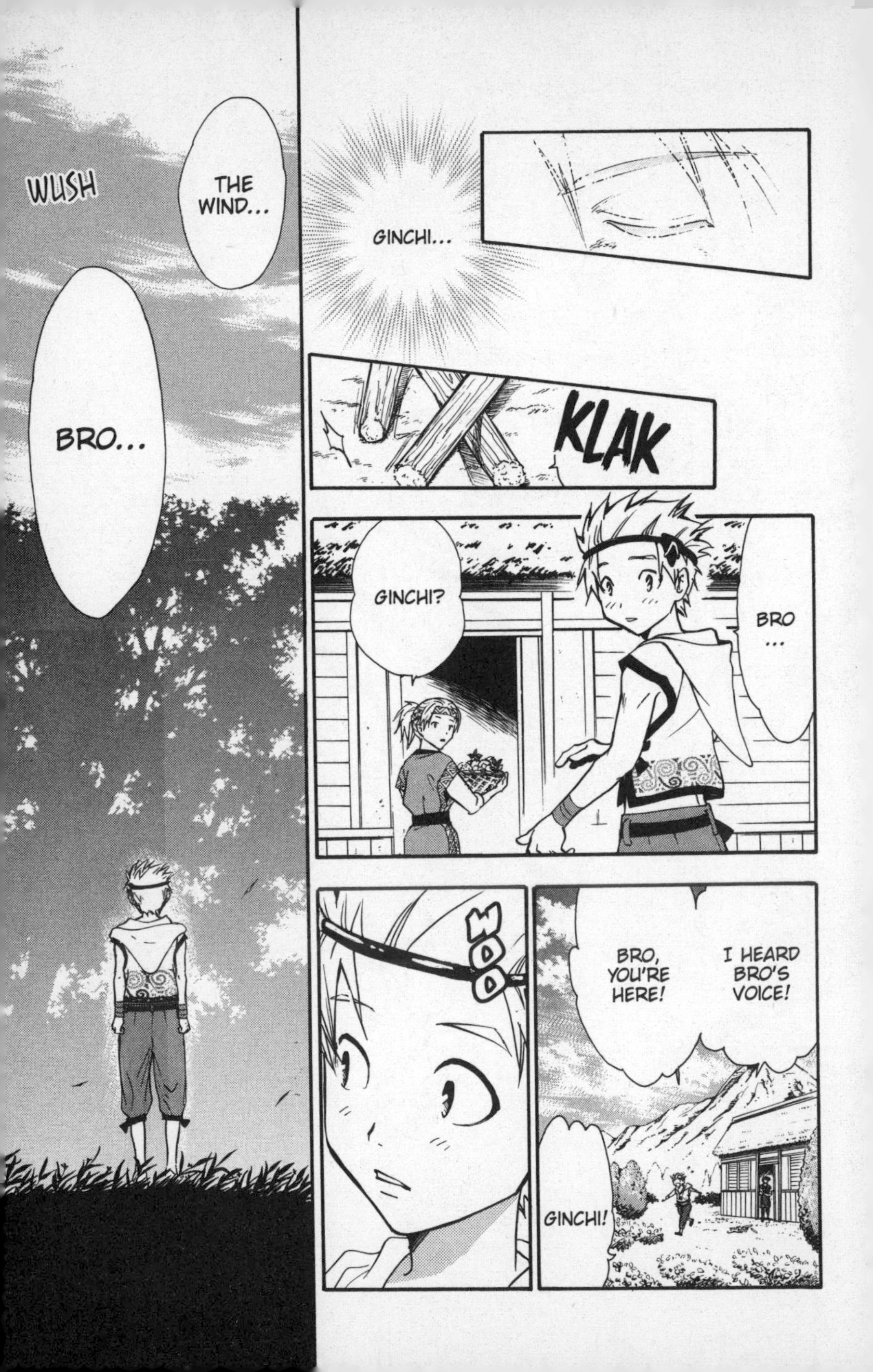
GINCHI...
KLAK
BRO
...
GINCHI?
I HEARD BRO'S VOICE!
BRO, YOU'RE HERE!
GINCHI!
WOO
THE WIND...
BRO...
WUSH

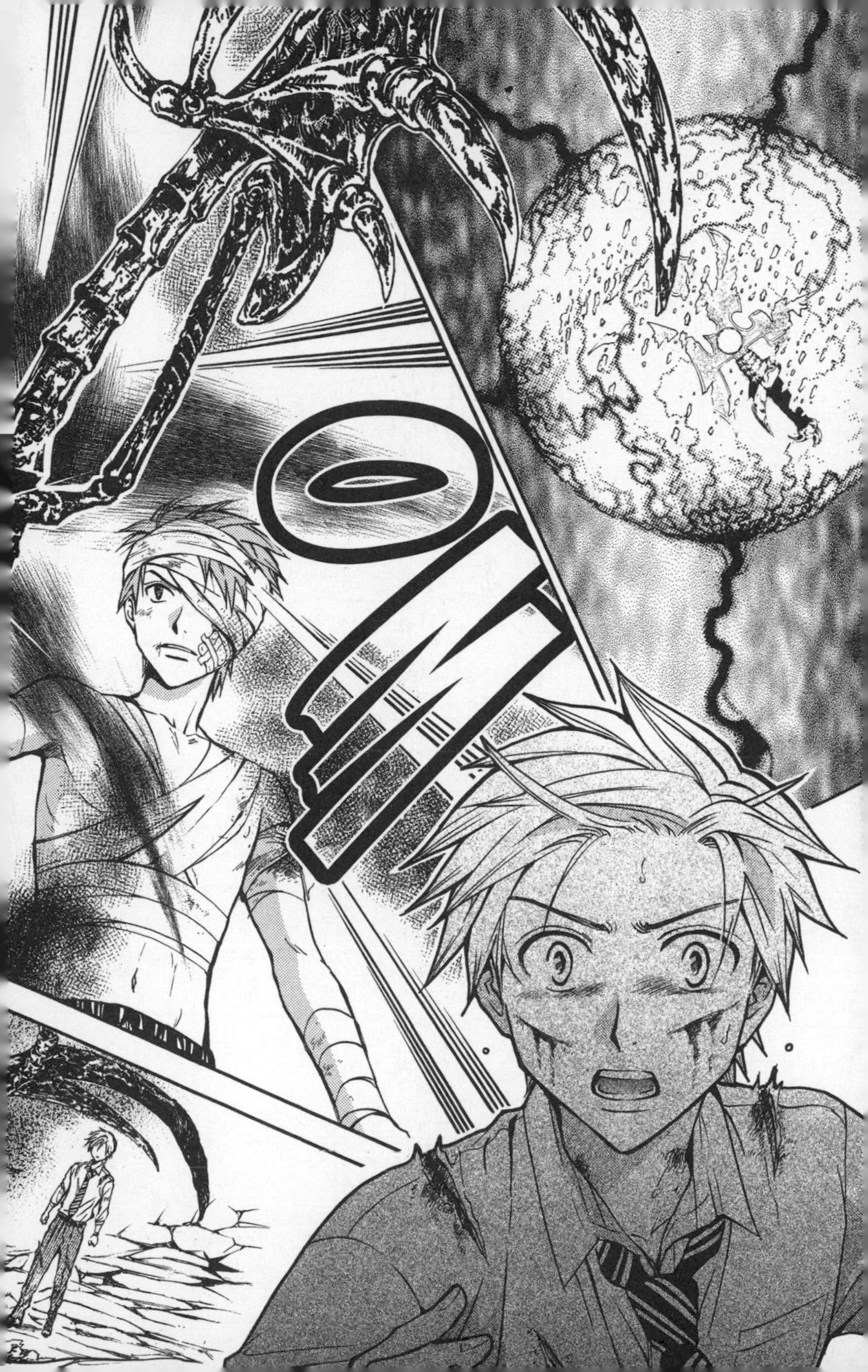

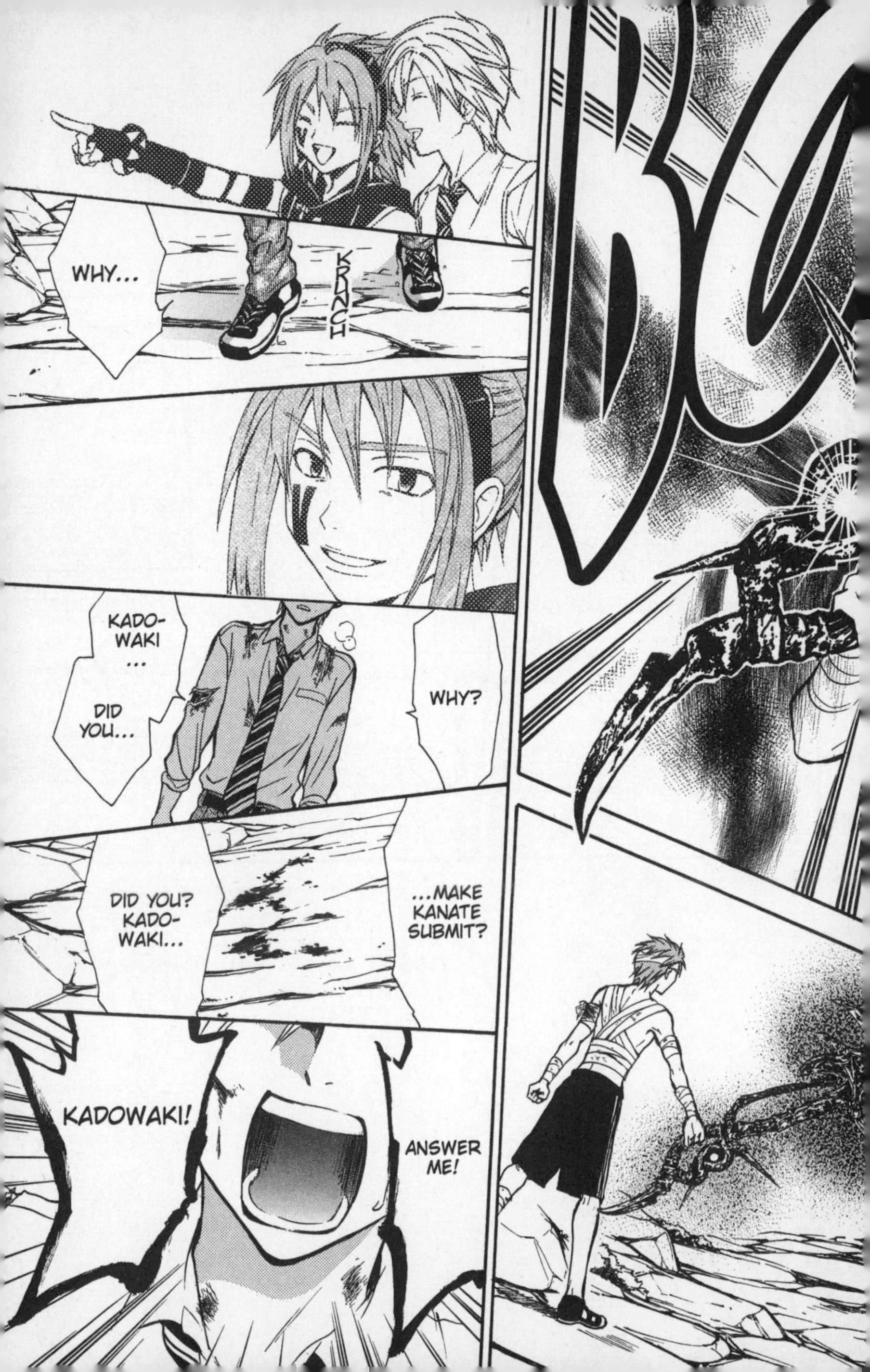
WHY...
KRUNCH
KADO-WAKI ... DID YOU...
WHY?
DID YOU? KADO-WAKI...
...MAKE KANATE SUBMIT?
KADOWAKI!
ANSWER ME!
BO

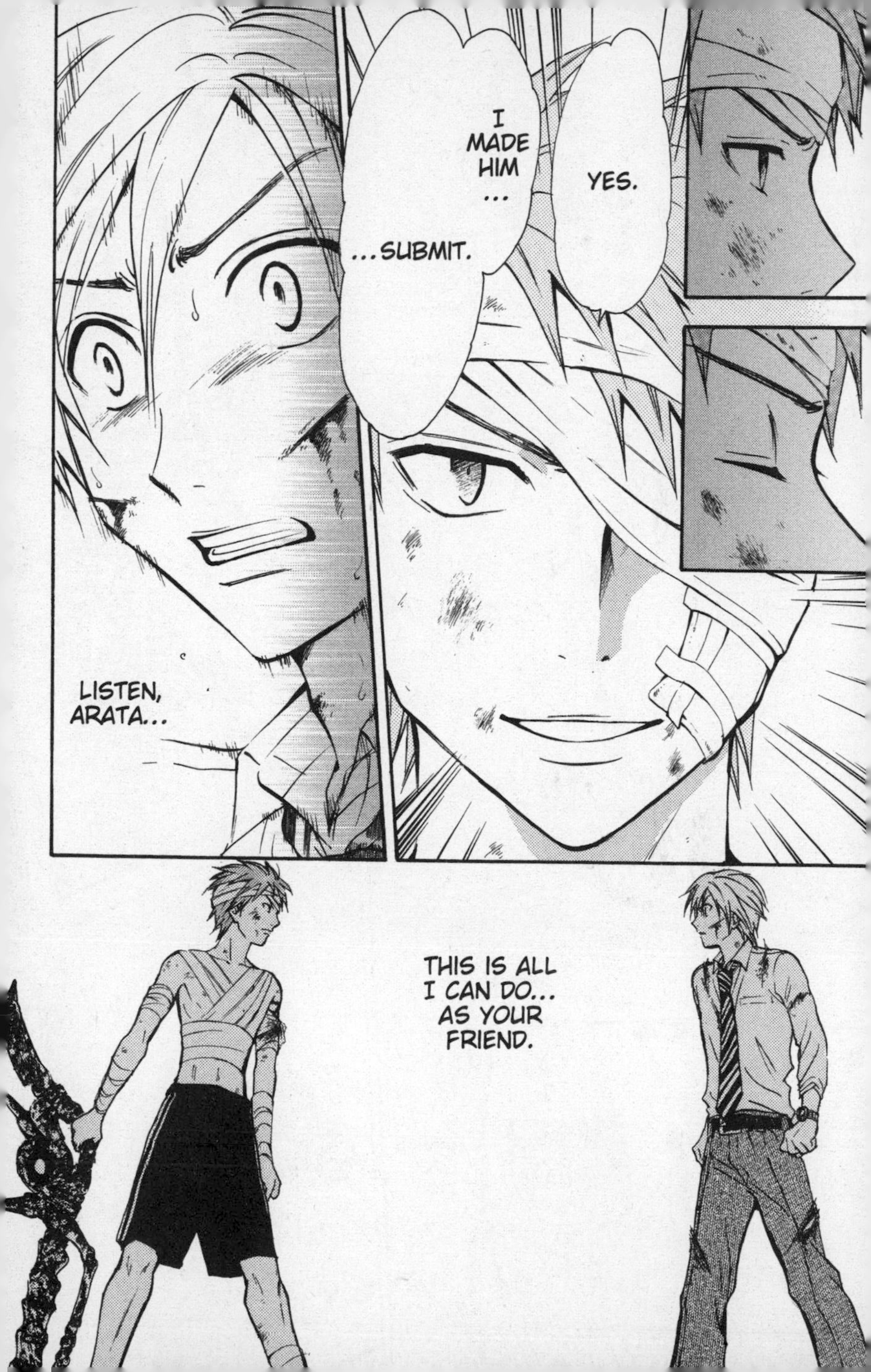
I MADE HIM ...
...SUBMIT.
YES.
LISTEN, ARATA...
THIS IS ALL I CAN DO... AS YOUR FRIEND.

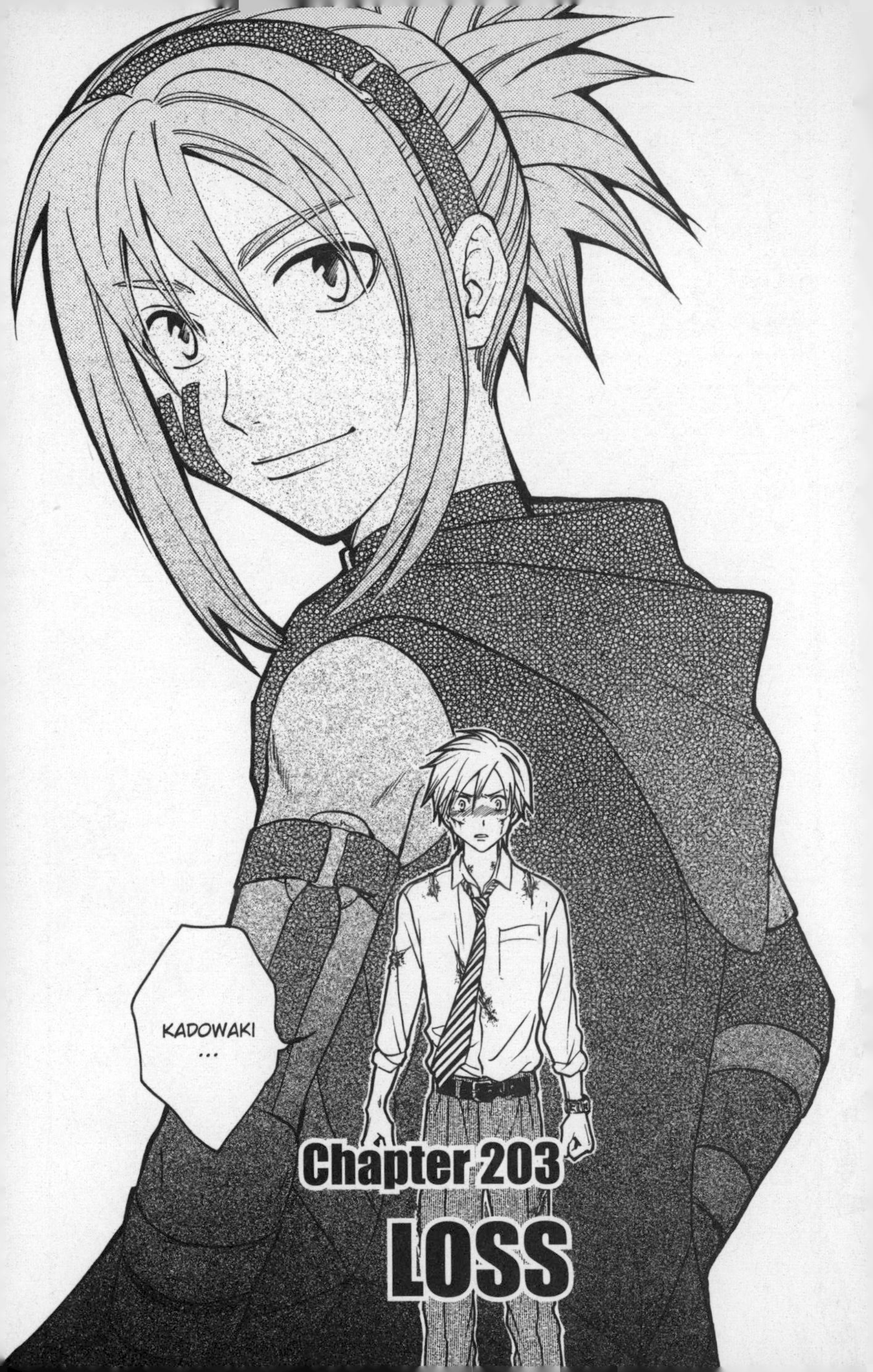
KADOWAKI ...
Chapter 203
LOSS

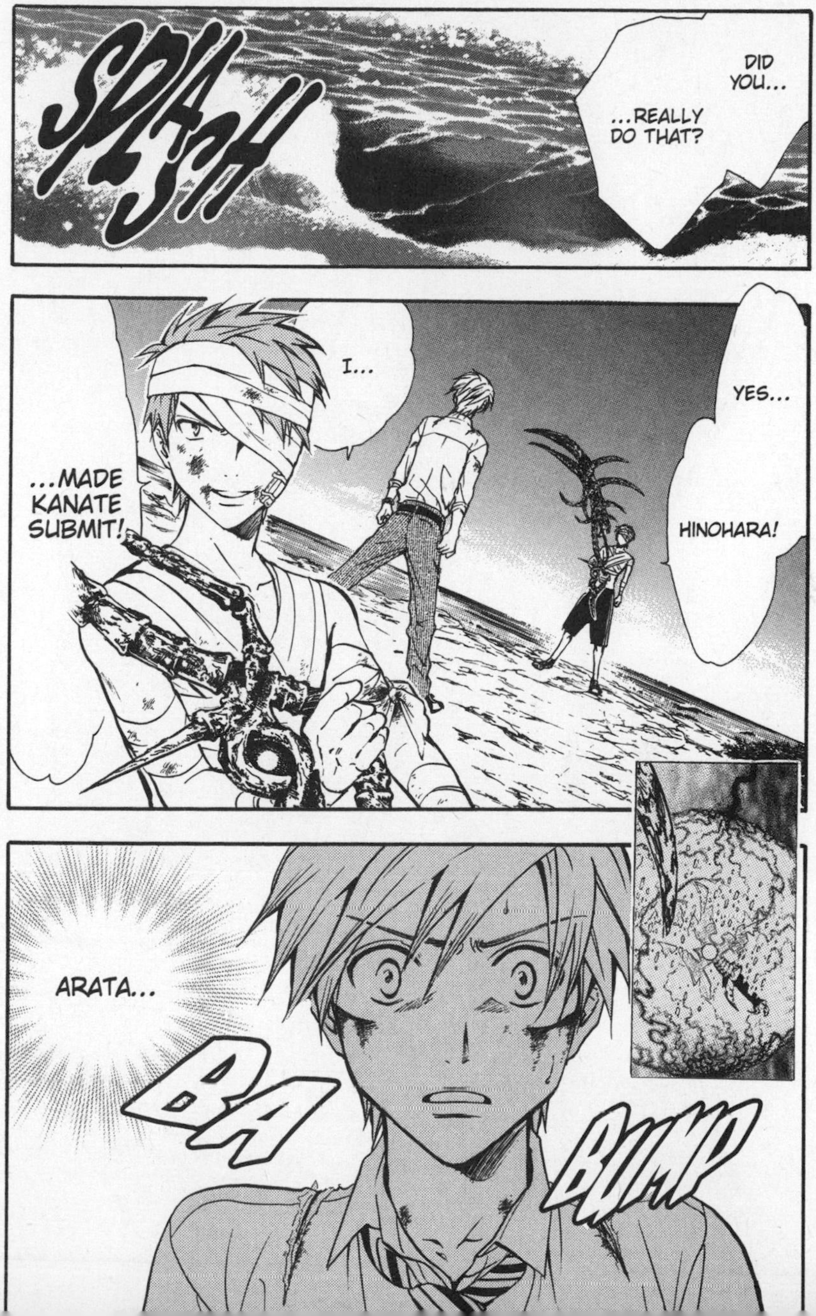
DID YOU...
...REALLY DO THAT?
SPLASH
YES...
HINOHARA!
I...
...MADE KANATE SUBMIT!
ARATA...
BA
BUMP

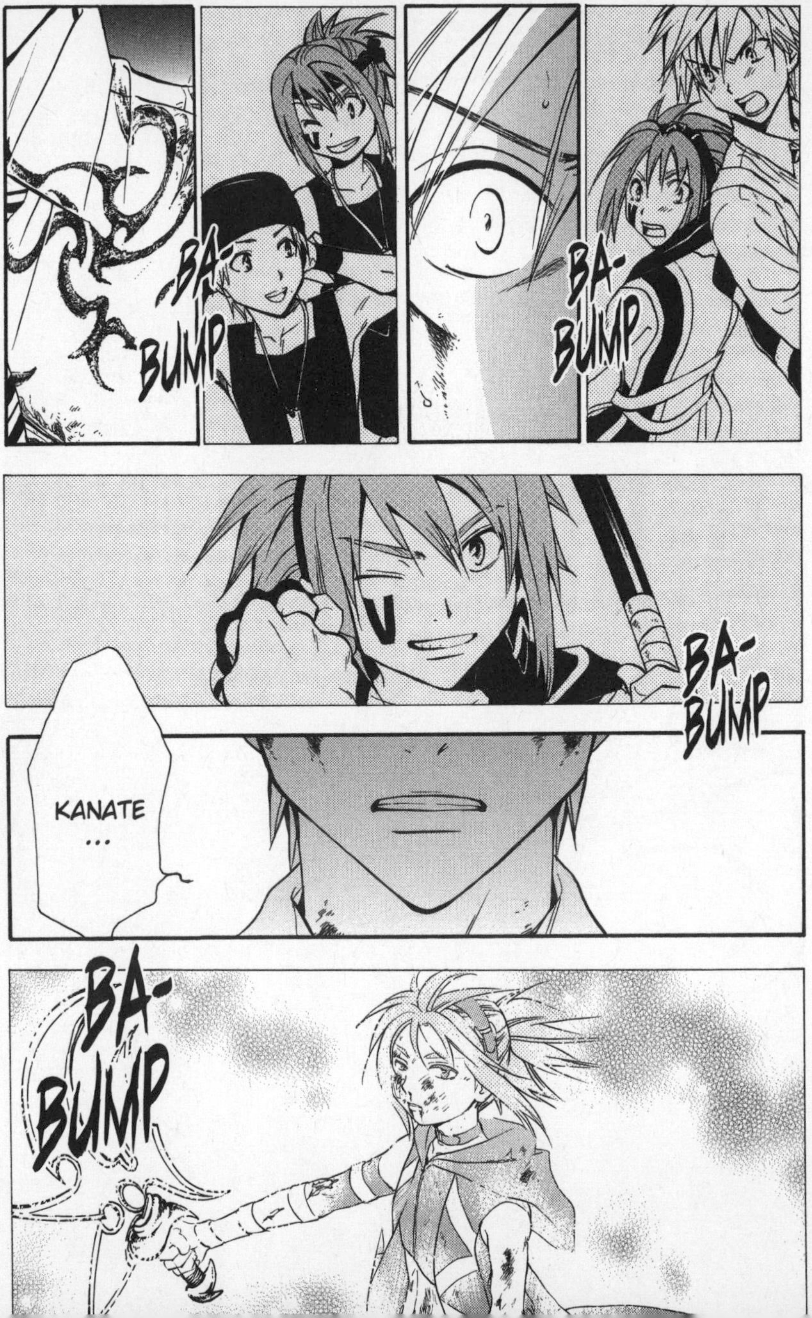
BA-BUMP
BA-BUMP
BA-BUMP
KANATE ...
BA-BUMP

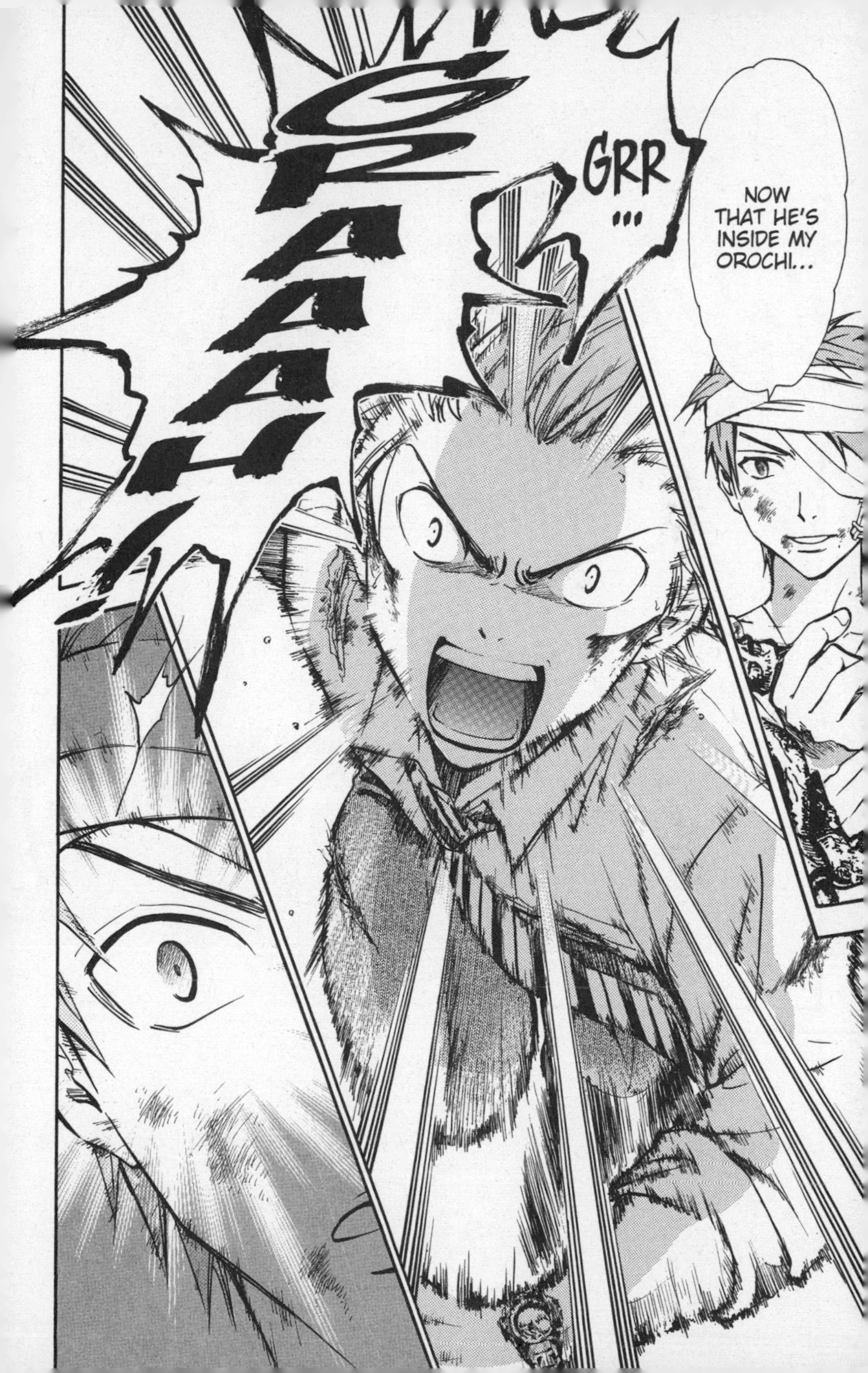
NOW THAT HE'S INSIDE MY OROCHI...
GRR...
GRAAAH!!

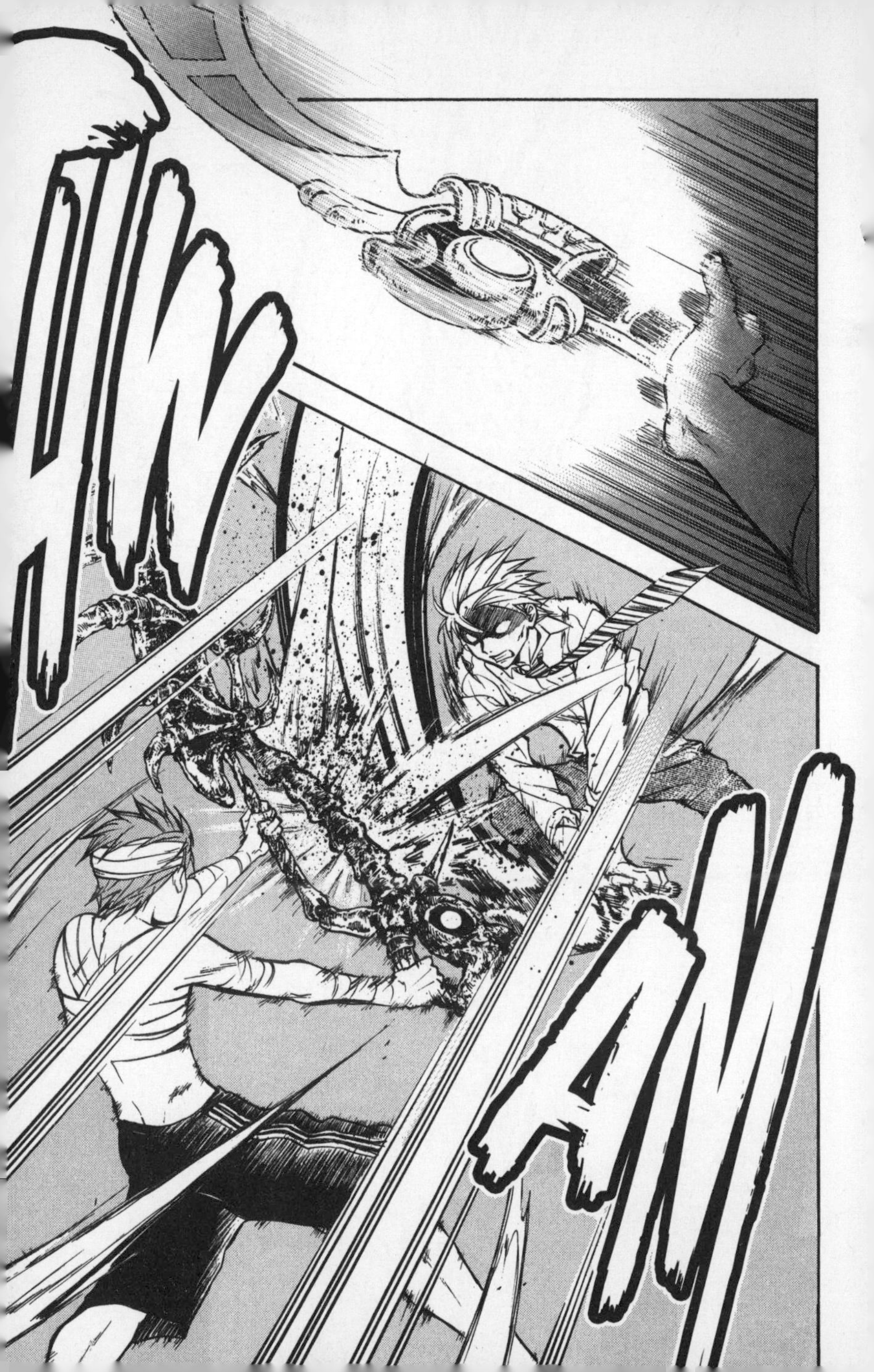
SHW
AM

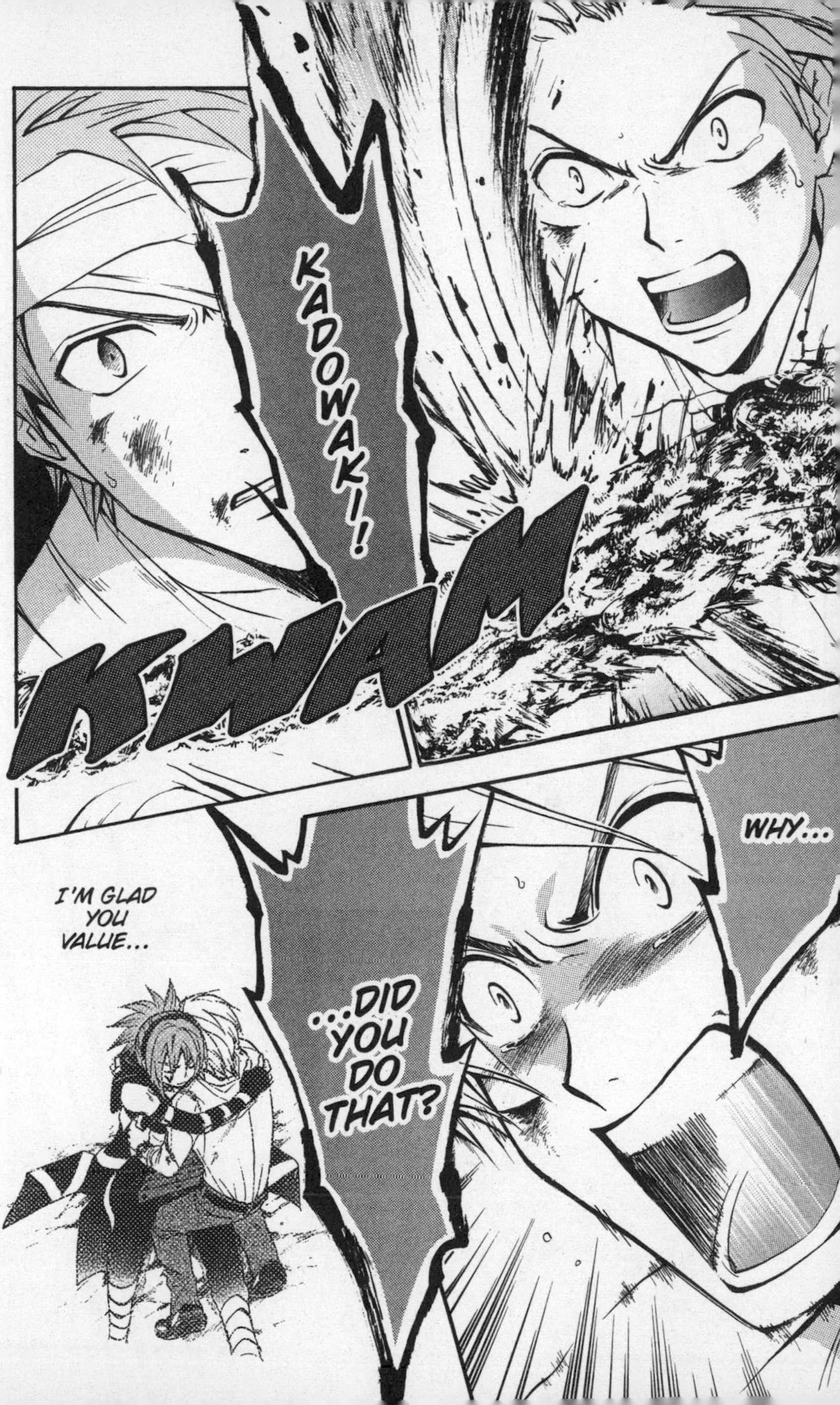
KADOWAKI!
KWAM
WHY...
...DID YOU DO THAT?
I'M GLAD YOU VALUE...

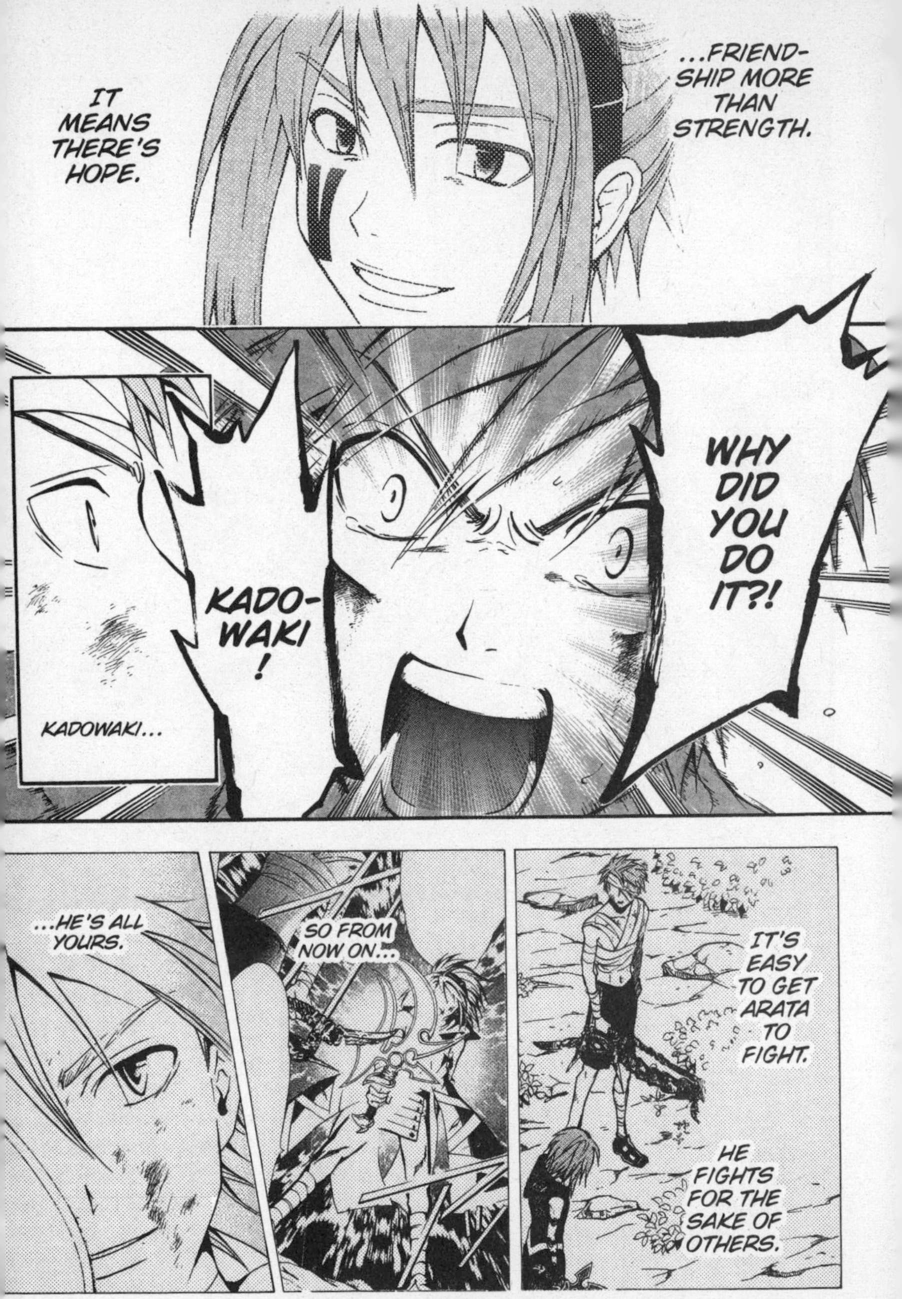
...FRIEND-SHIP MORE THAN STRENGTH.
IT MEANS THERE'S HOPE.
WHY DID YOU DO IT?!
KADO-WAKI!
KADOWAKI...
IT'S EASY TO GET ARATA TO FIGHT.
HE FIGHTS FOR THE SAKE OF OTHERS.
SO FROM NOW ON...
...HE'S ALL YOURS.

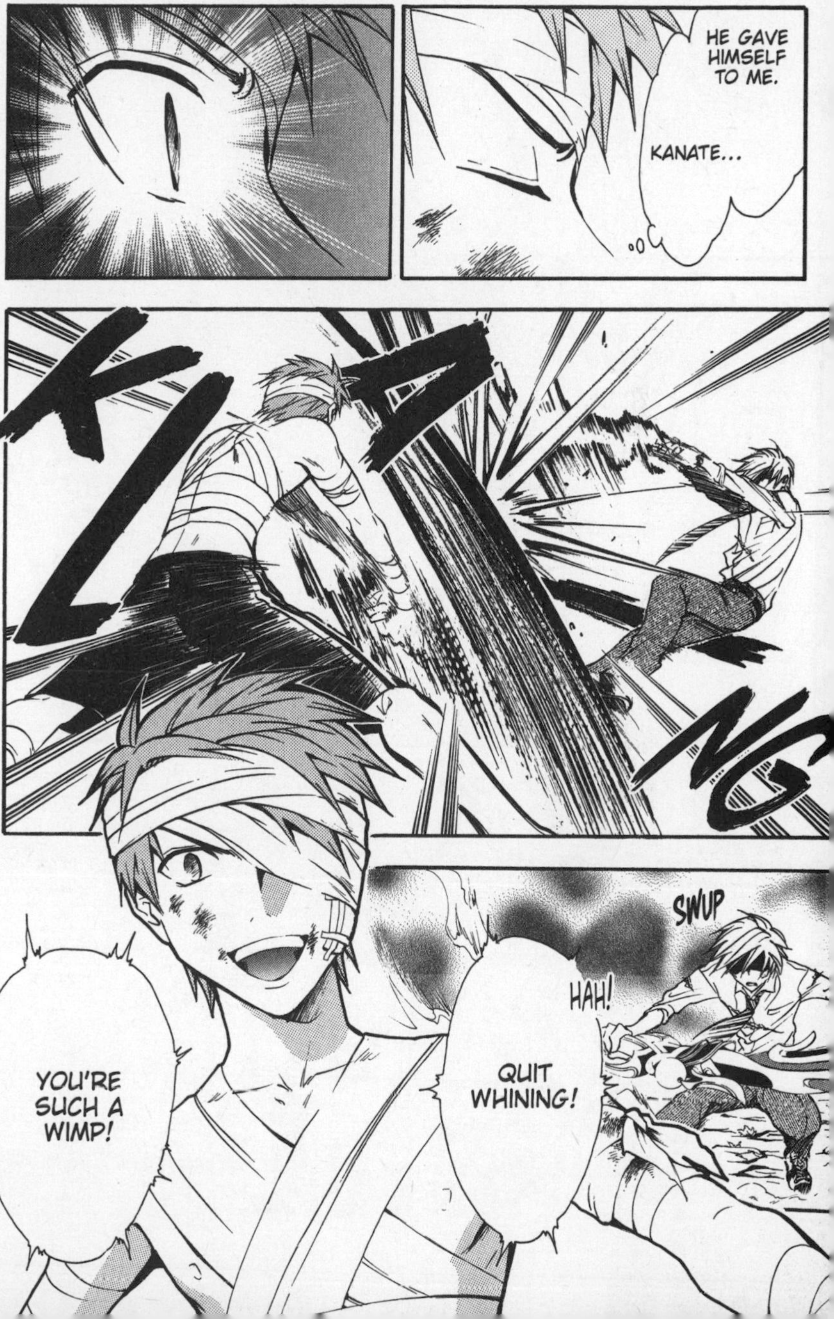
HE GAVE HIMSELF TO ME.
KANATE...
KANG
SWUP
HAH!
QUIT WHINING!
YOU'RE SUCH A WIMP!

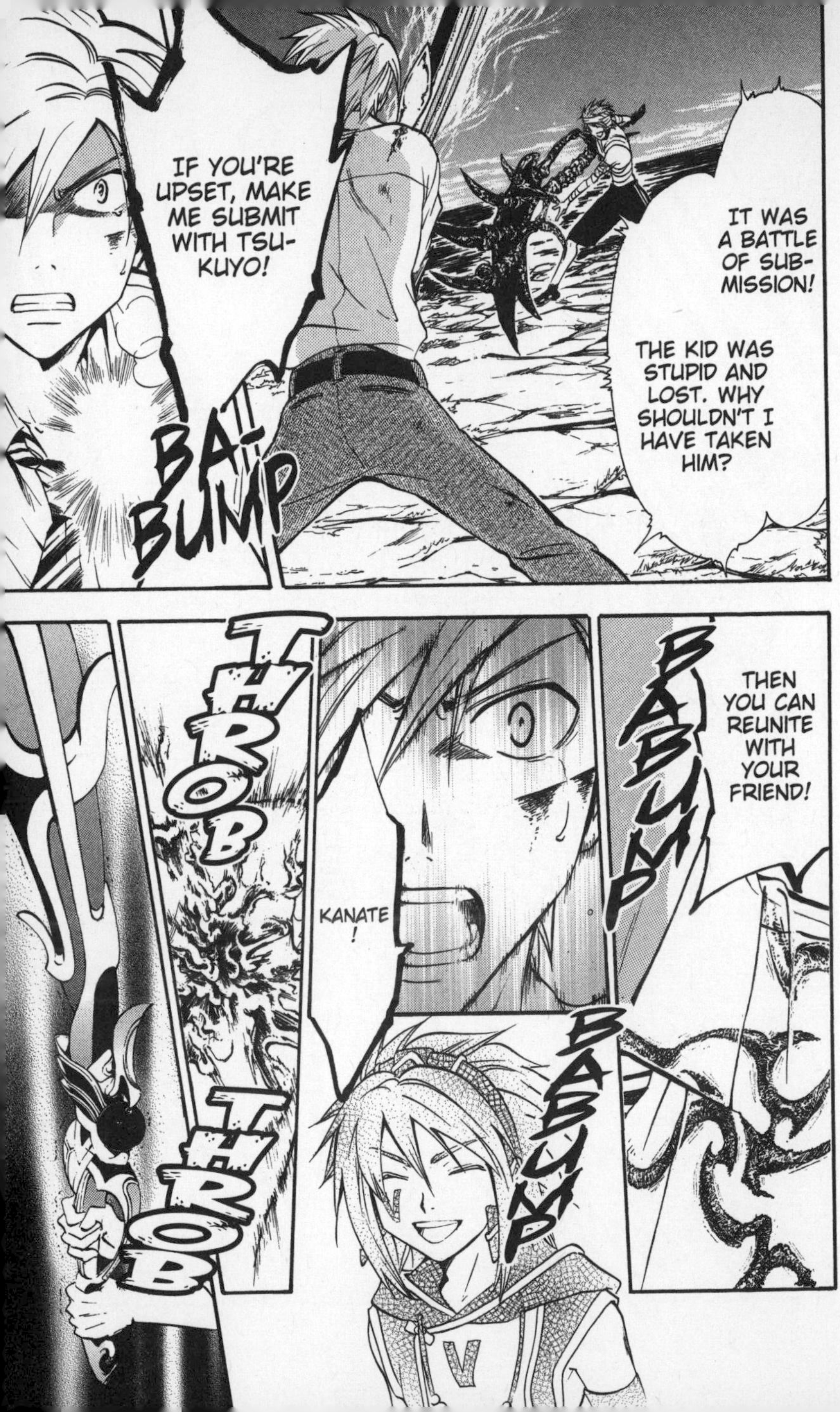
IT WAS A BATTLE OF SUB-MISSION!
THE KID WAS STUPID AND LOST. WHY SHOULDN'T I HAVE TAKEN HIM?
IF YOU'RE UPSET, MAKE ME SUBMIT WITH TSU-KUYO!
BA-BUMP
THEN YOU CAN REUNITE WITH YOUR FRIEND!
BA-BUMP
KANATE!
BA-BUMP
THROB
THROB

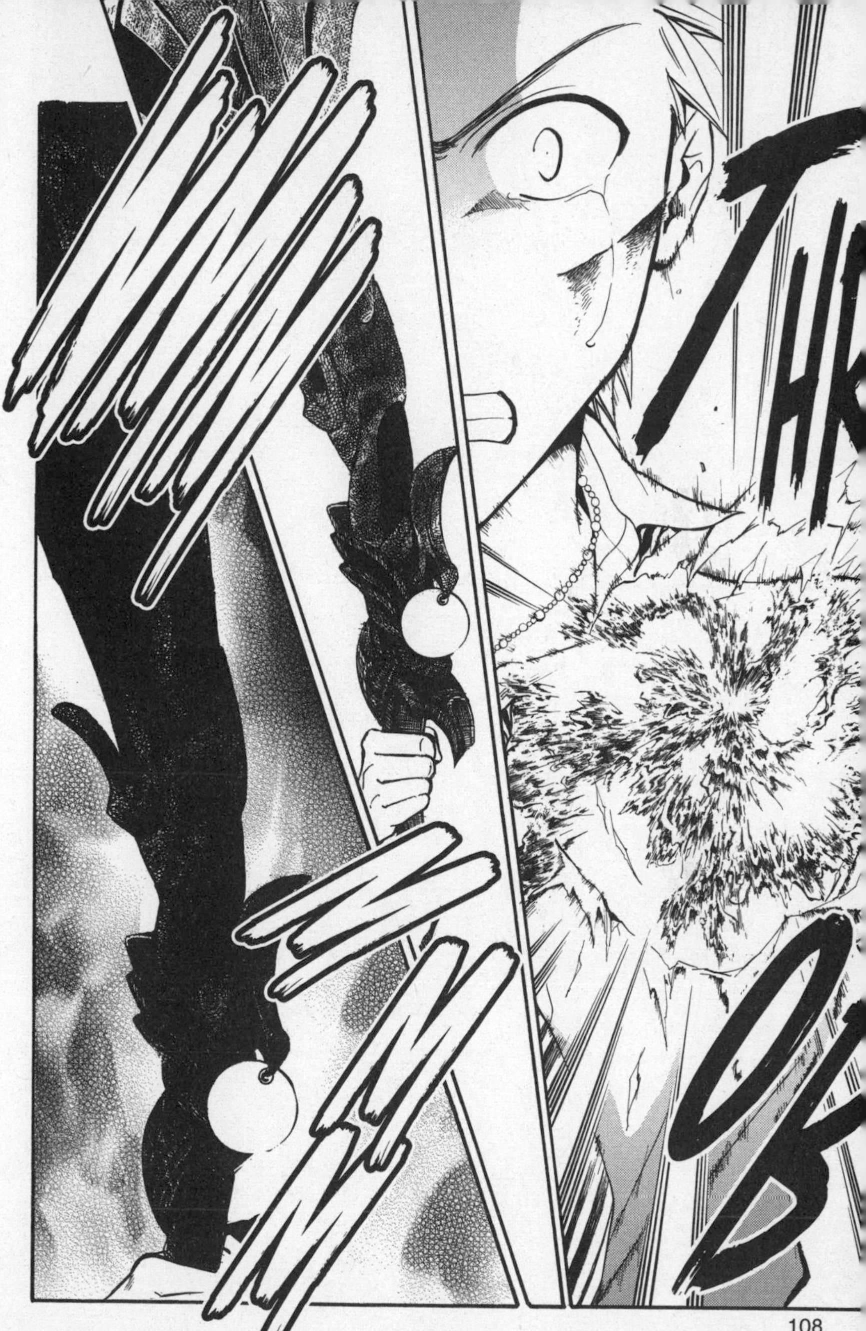

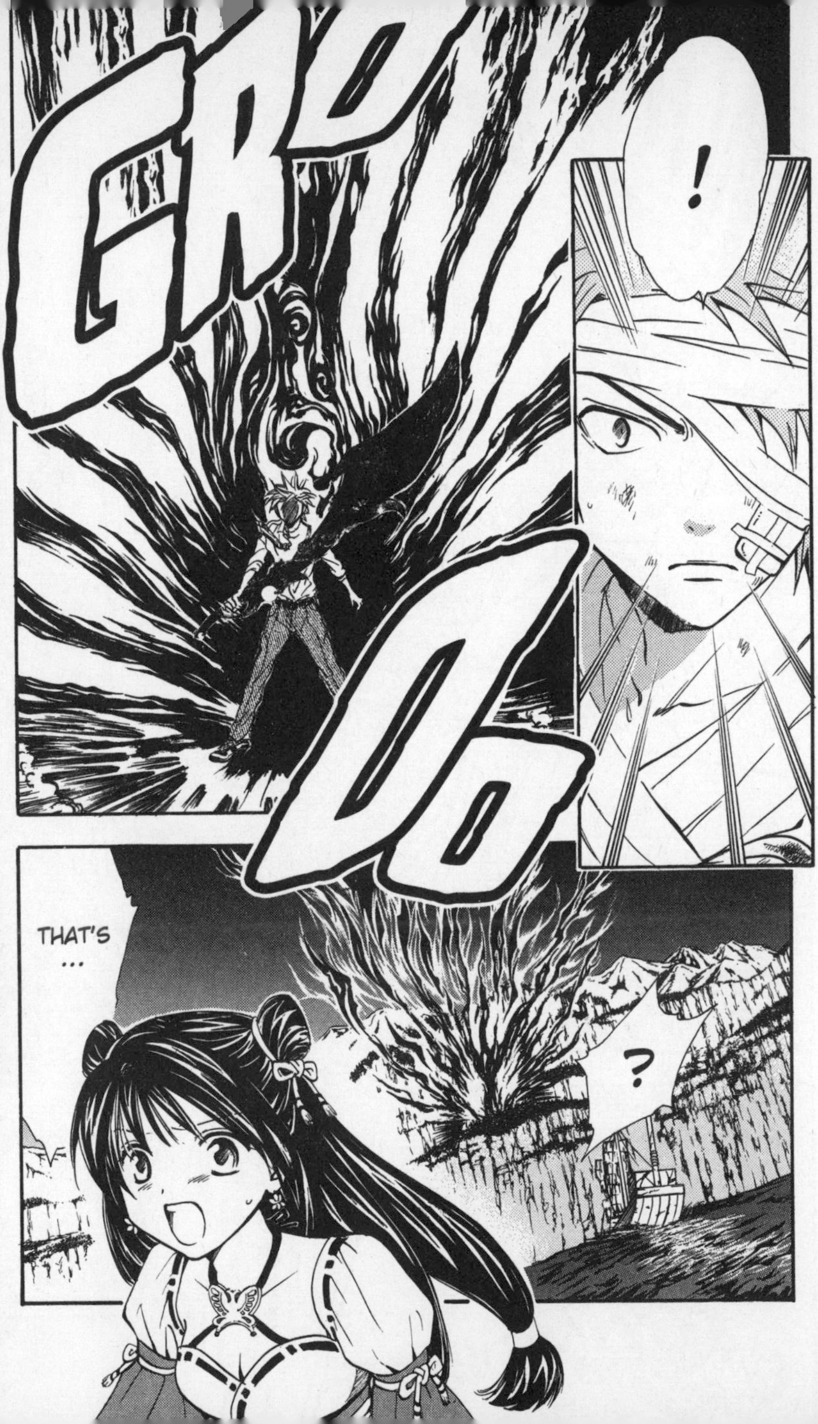
!
THAT'S ...
?

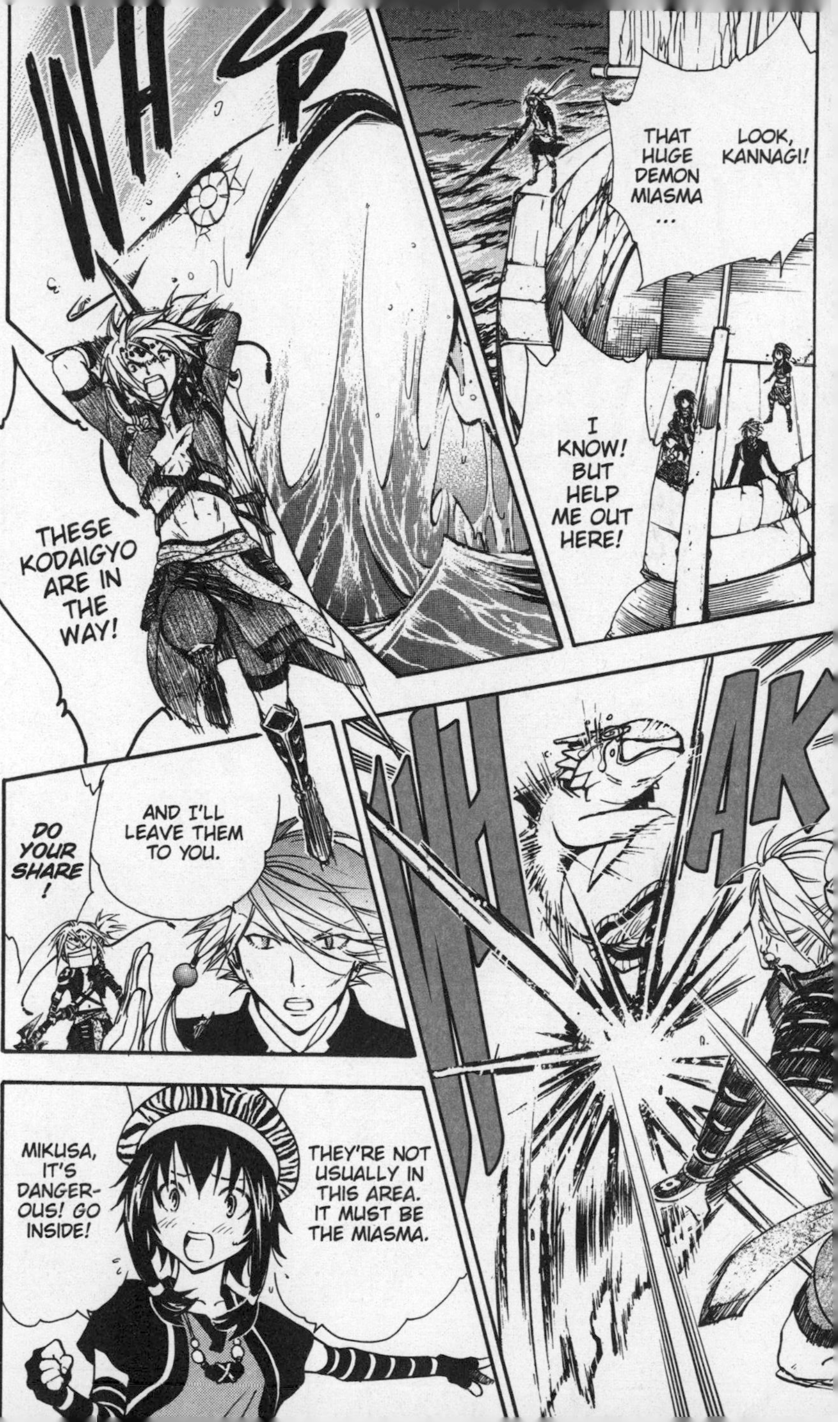
LOOK, KANNAGI!
THAT HUGE DEMON MIASMA ...
I KNOW! BUT HELP ME OUT HERE!
WHUP
THESE KODAIGYO ARE IN THE WAY!
WHAK
AND I'LL LEAVE THEM TO YOU.
DO YOUR SHARE!
THEY'RE NOT USUALLY IN THIS AREA. IT MUST BE THE MIASMA.
MIKUSA, IT'S DANGER-OUS! GO INSIDE!

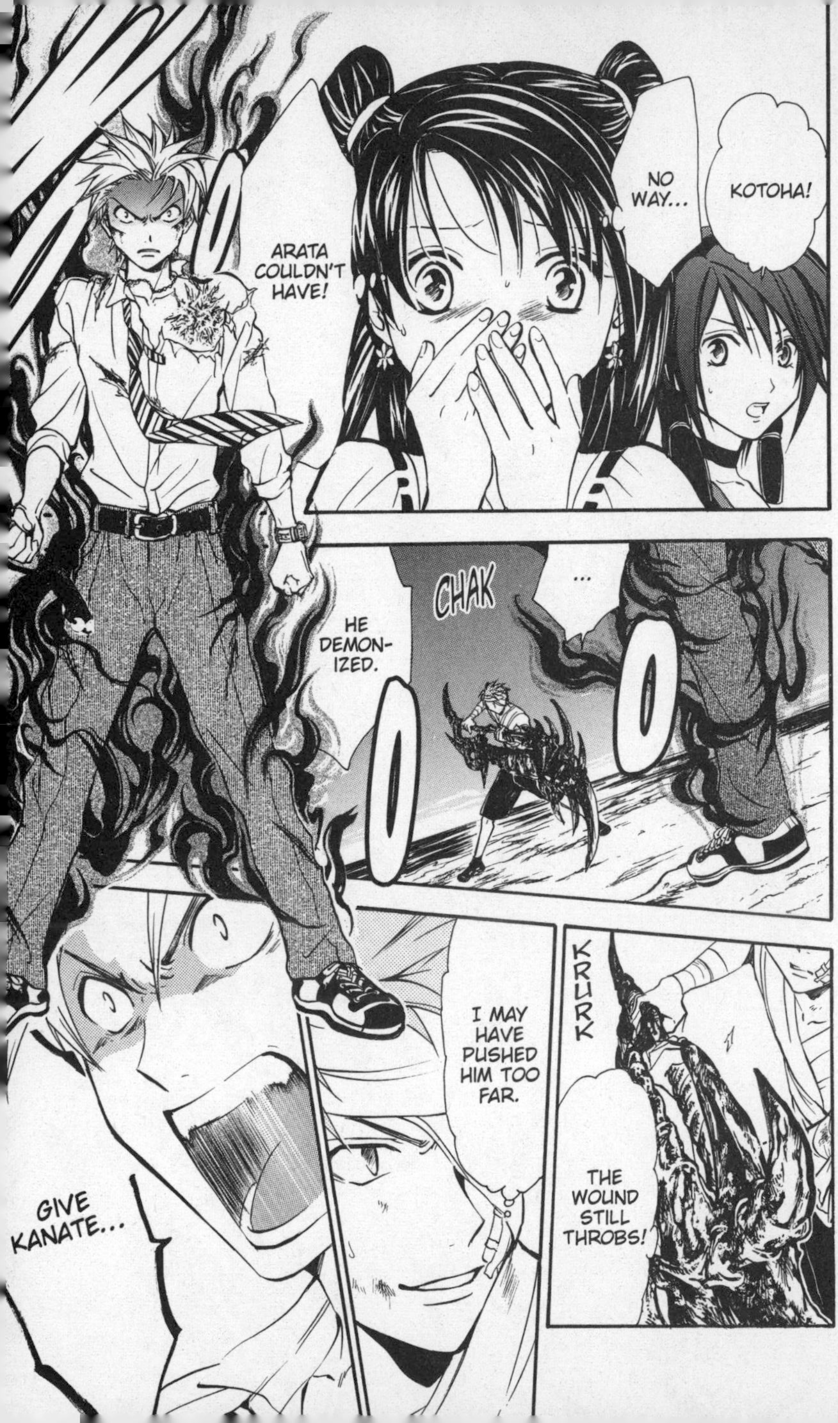
KOTOHA!
NO WAY...
ARATA COULDN'T HAVE!
...
CHAK
HE DEMONIZED.
KRURK
THE WOUND STILL THROBS!
I MAY HAVE PUSHED HIM TOO FAR.
GIVE KANATE...

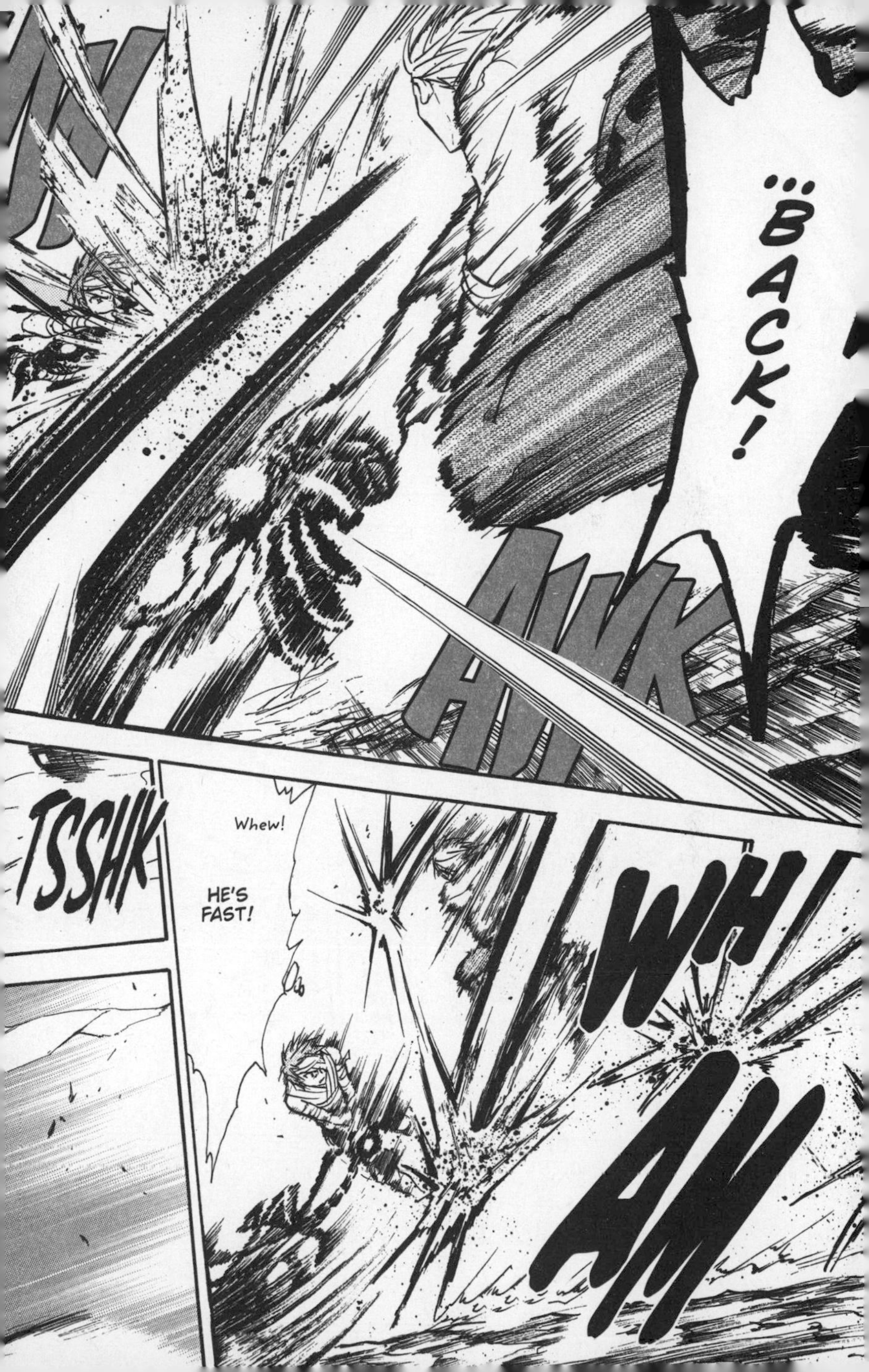
BACK!
Whew!
HE'S FAST!
TSSHK

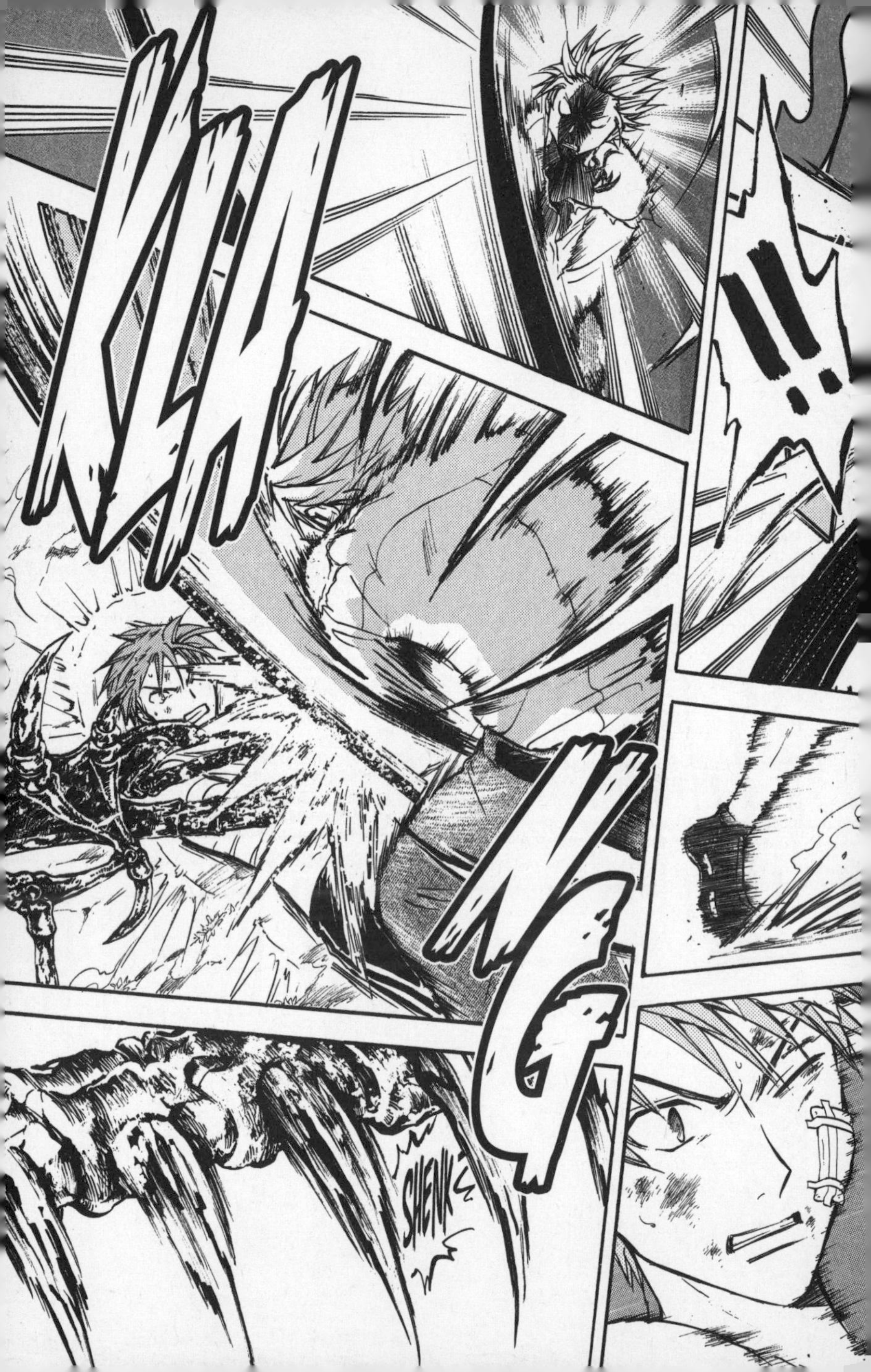
!!
SHENK

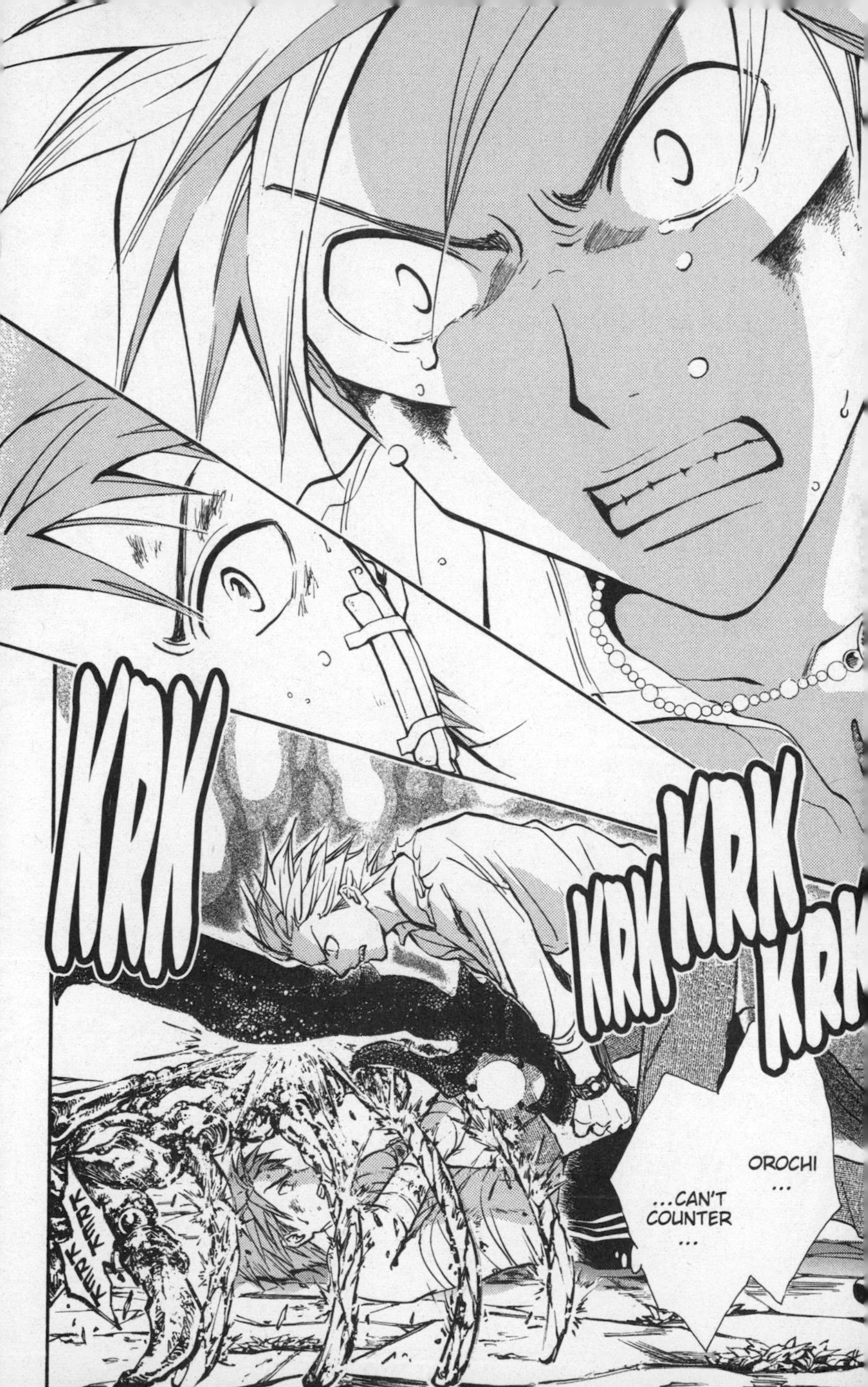
KRK KRK KRK
KRK
OROCHI ...
...CAN'T COUNTER ...
KRK KRK

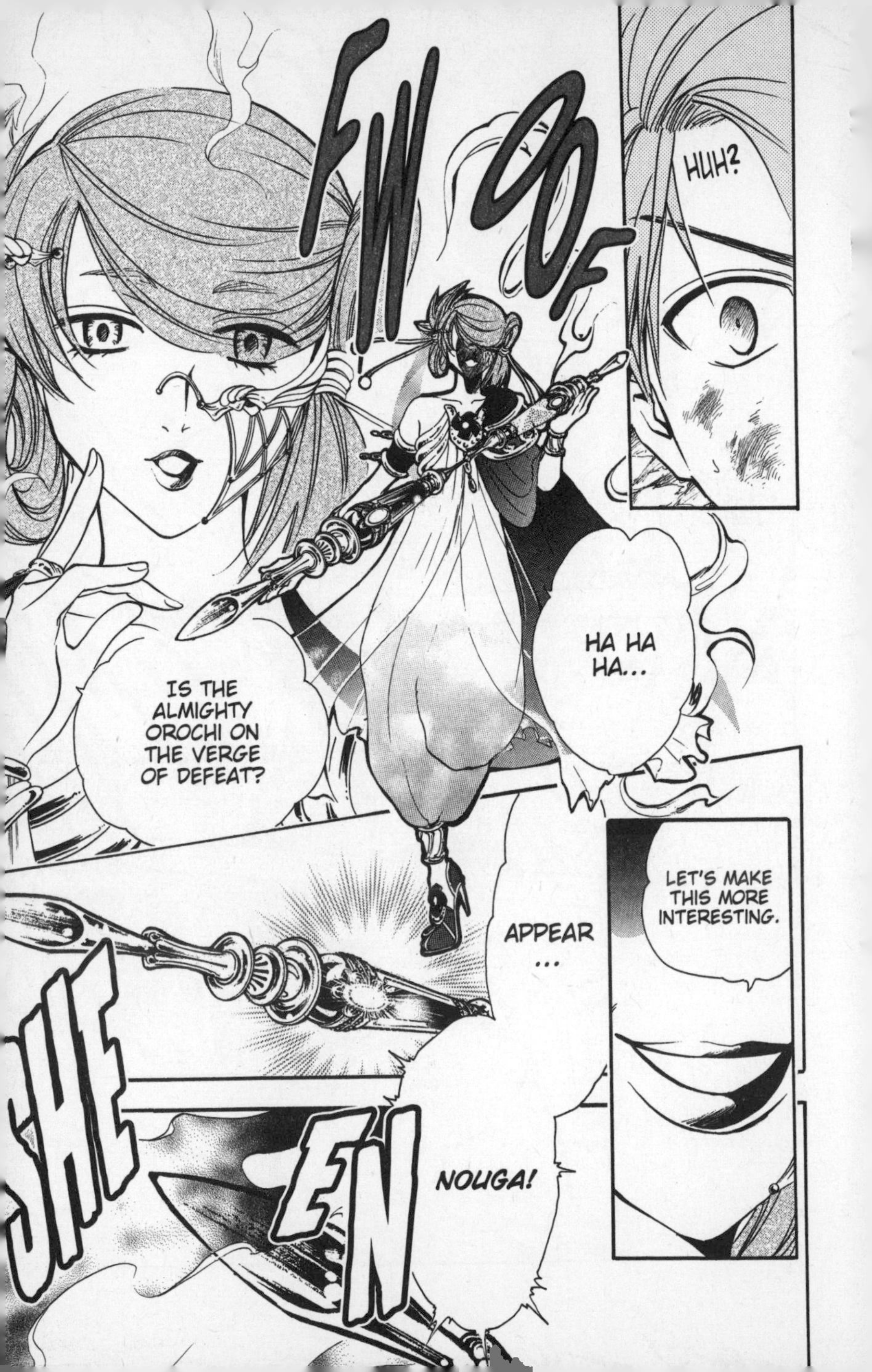
HUH?
FWOOF
HA HA HA...
IS THE ALMIGHTY OROCHI ON THE VERGE OF DEFEAT?
LET'S MAKE THIS MORE INTERESTING.
APPEAR...
NOUGA!
SHEEN

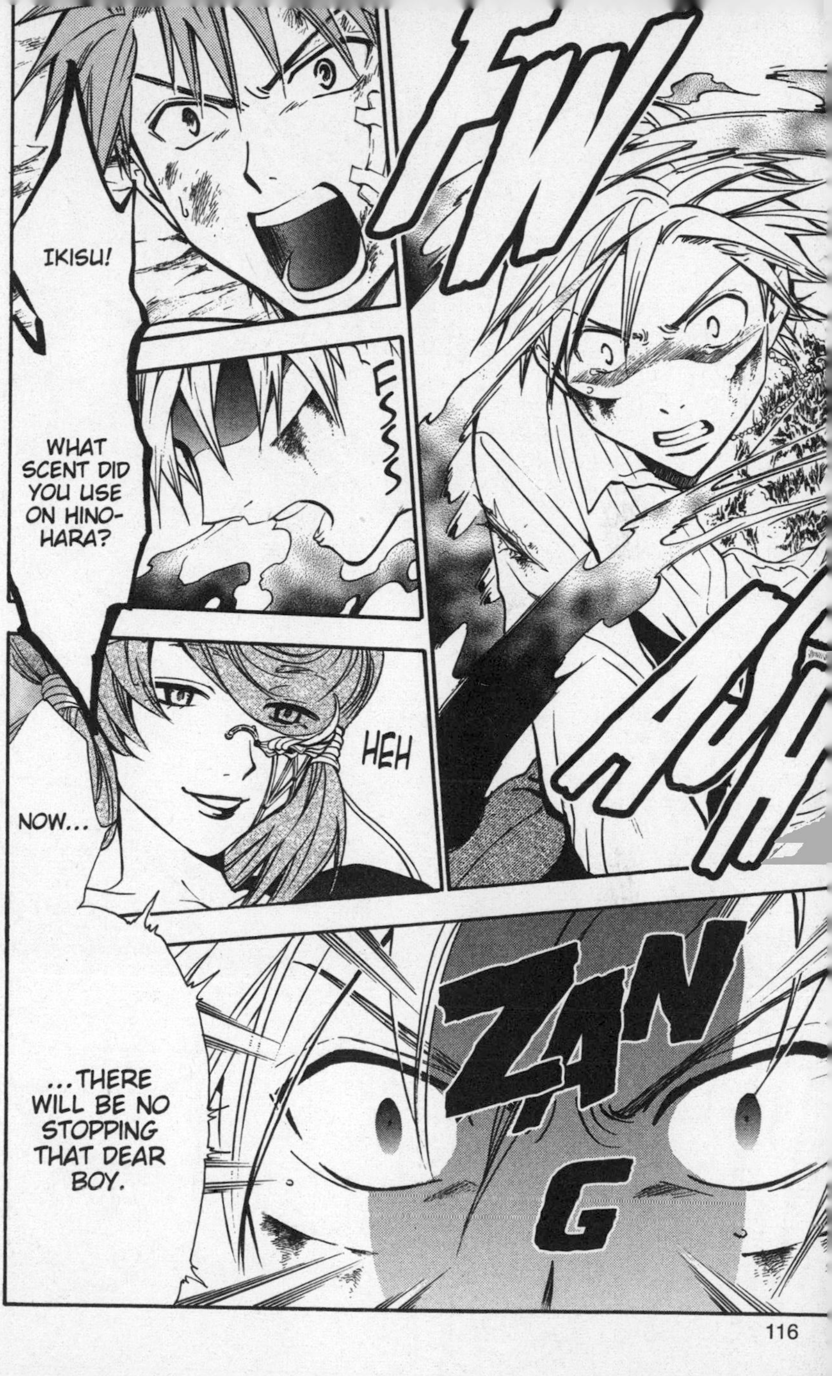
IKISU!
WHAT SCENT DID YOU USE ON HINO-HARA?
HEH
NOW...
ZAN G
...THERE WILL BE NO STOPPING THAT DEAR BOY.

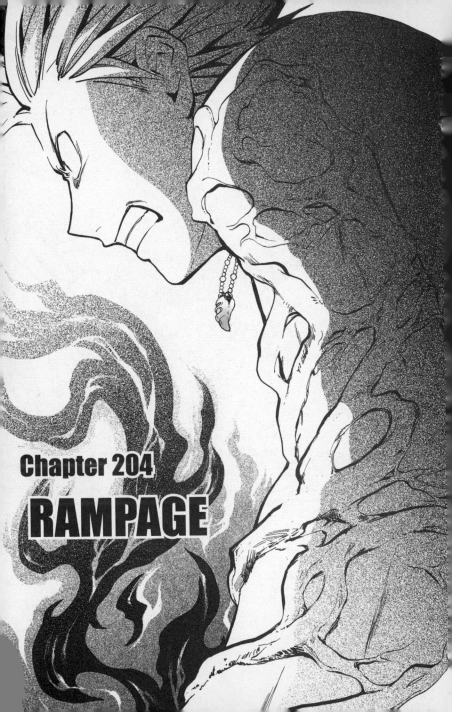

Chapter 204

RAMPAGE

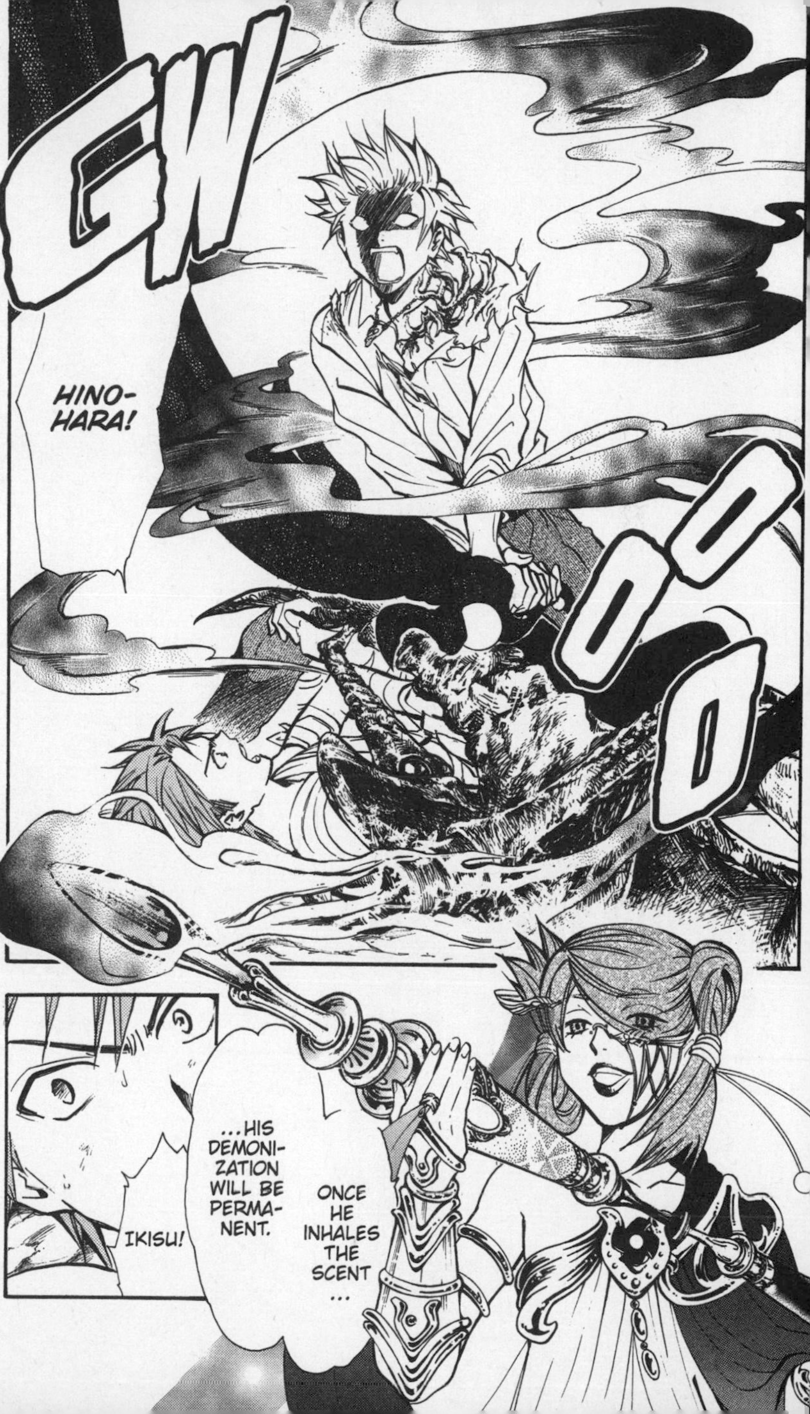
GW
HINO-HARA!
ONCE HE INHALES THE SCENT ...
...HIS DEMONIZATION WILL BE PERMANENT.
IKISU!

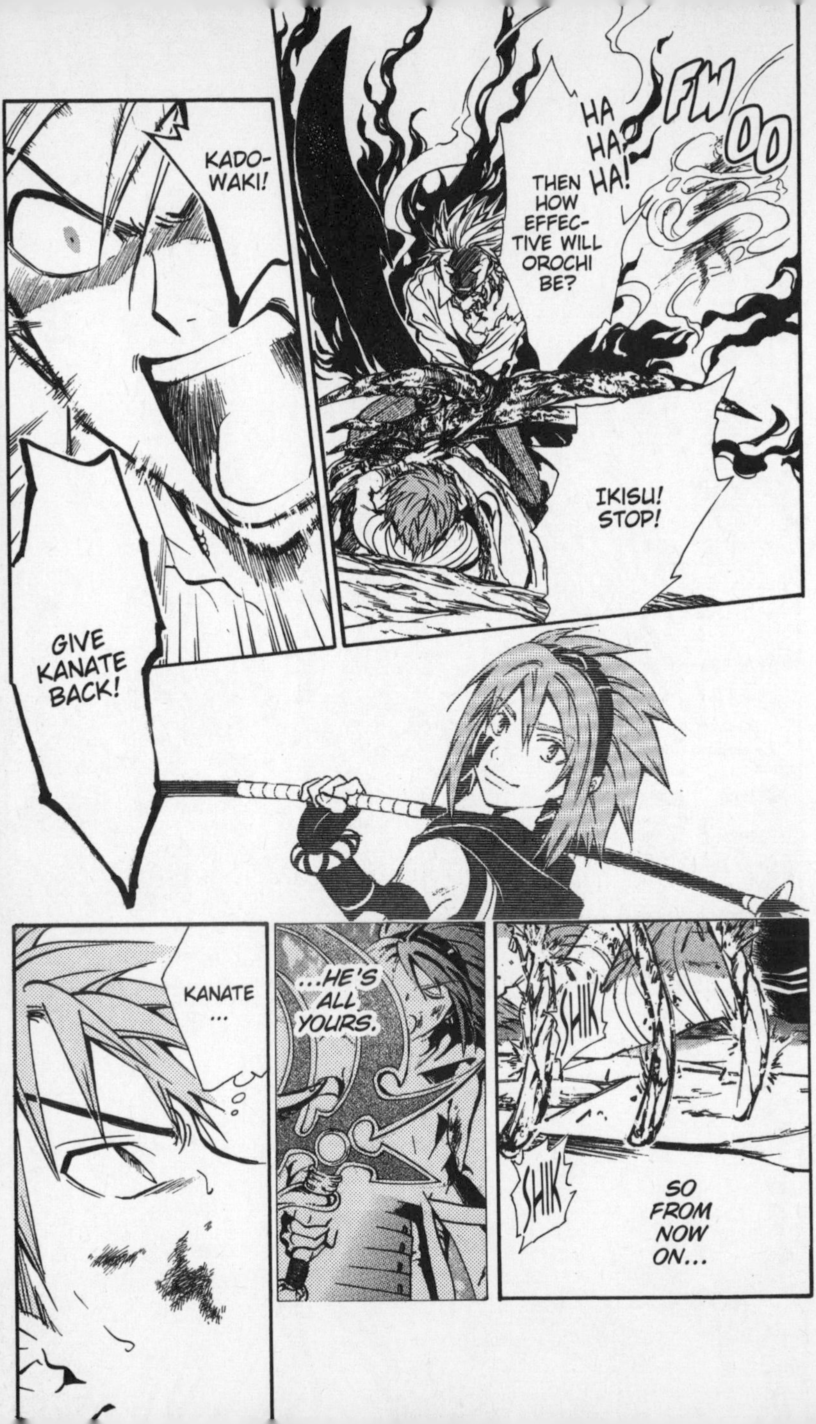
FWOO
HA HA! HA!
THEN HOW EFFECTIVE WILL OROCHI BE?
IKISU! STOP!
KADO-WAKI!
GIVE KANATE BACK!
SHIK
SHIK
SO FROM NOW ON...
...HE'S ALL YOURS.
KANATE ...

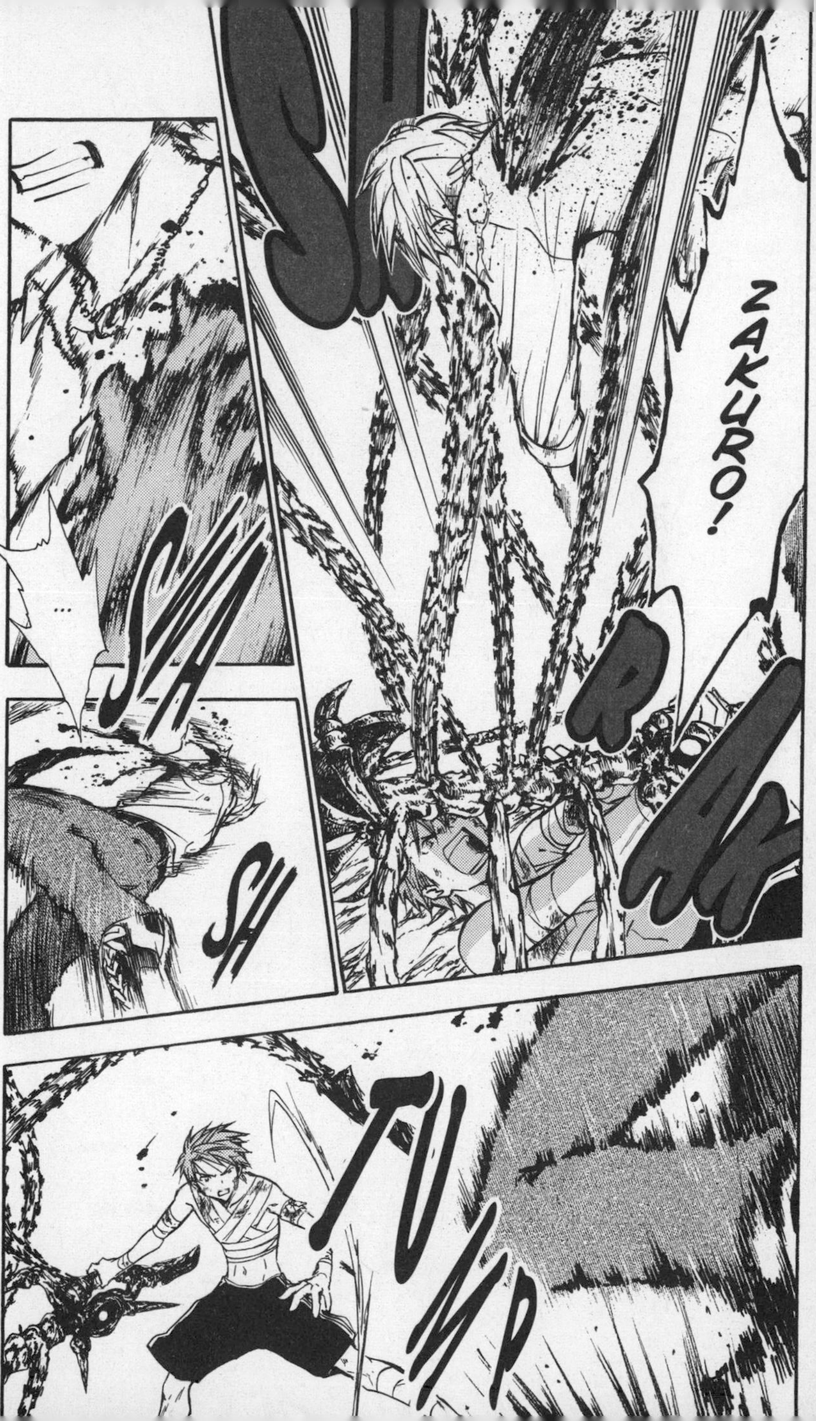
SH
ZAKURO!
RAH
SHA
...
SH
TUMP

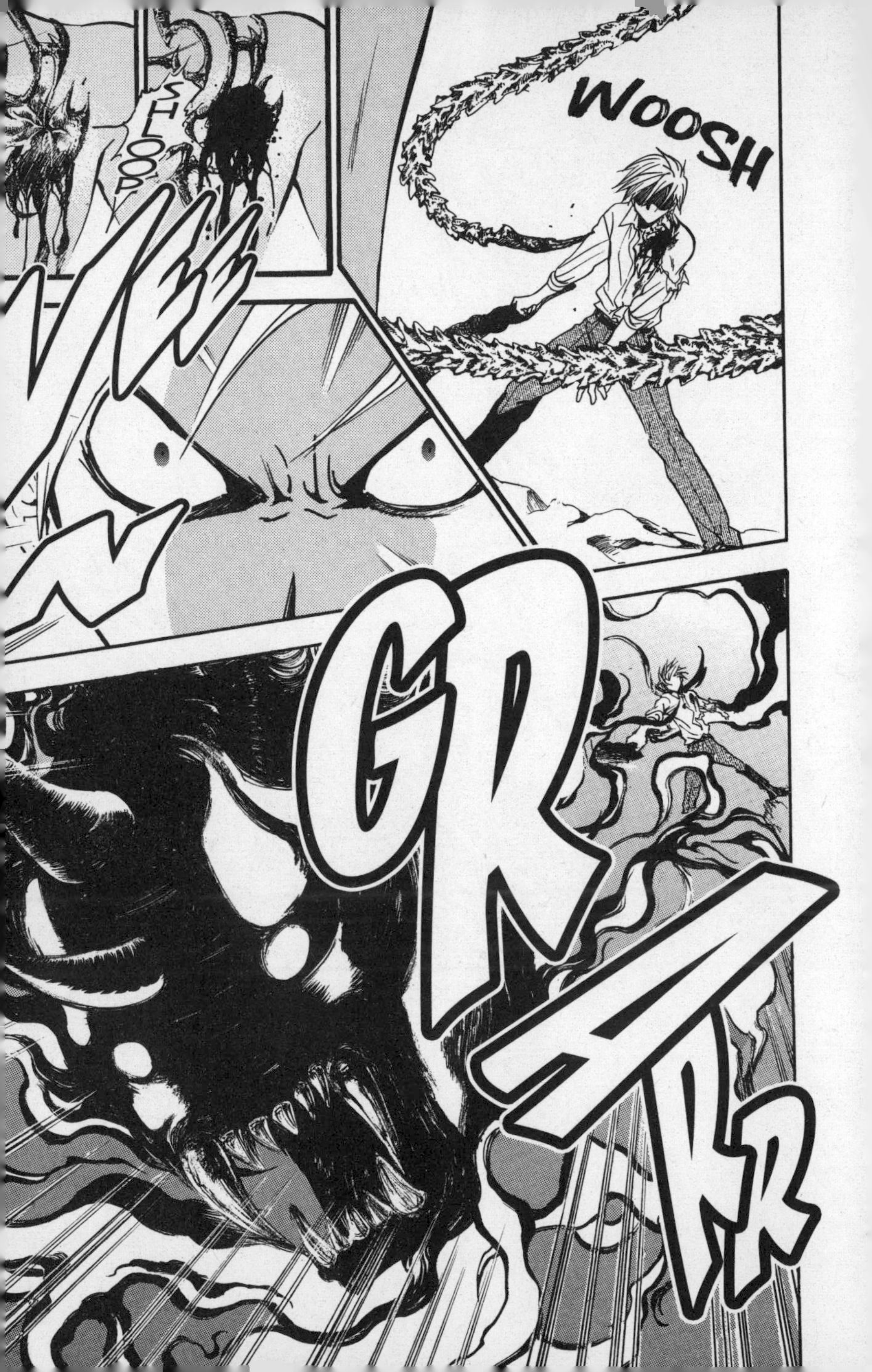
WOOSH
SHLOOP
GRAAR

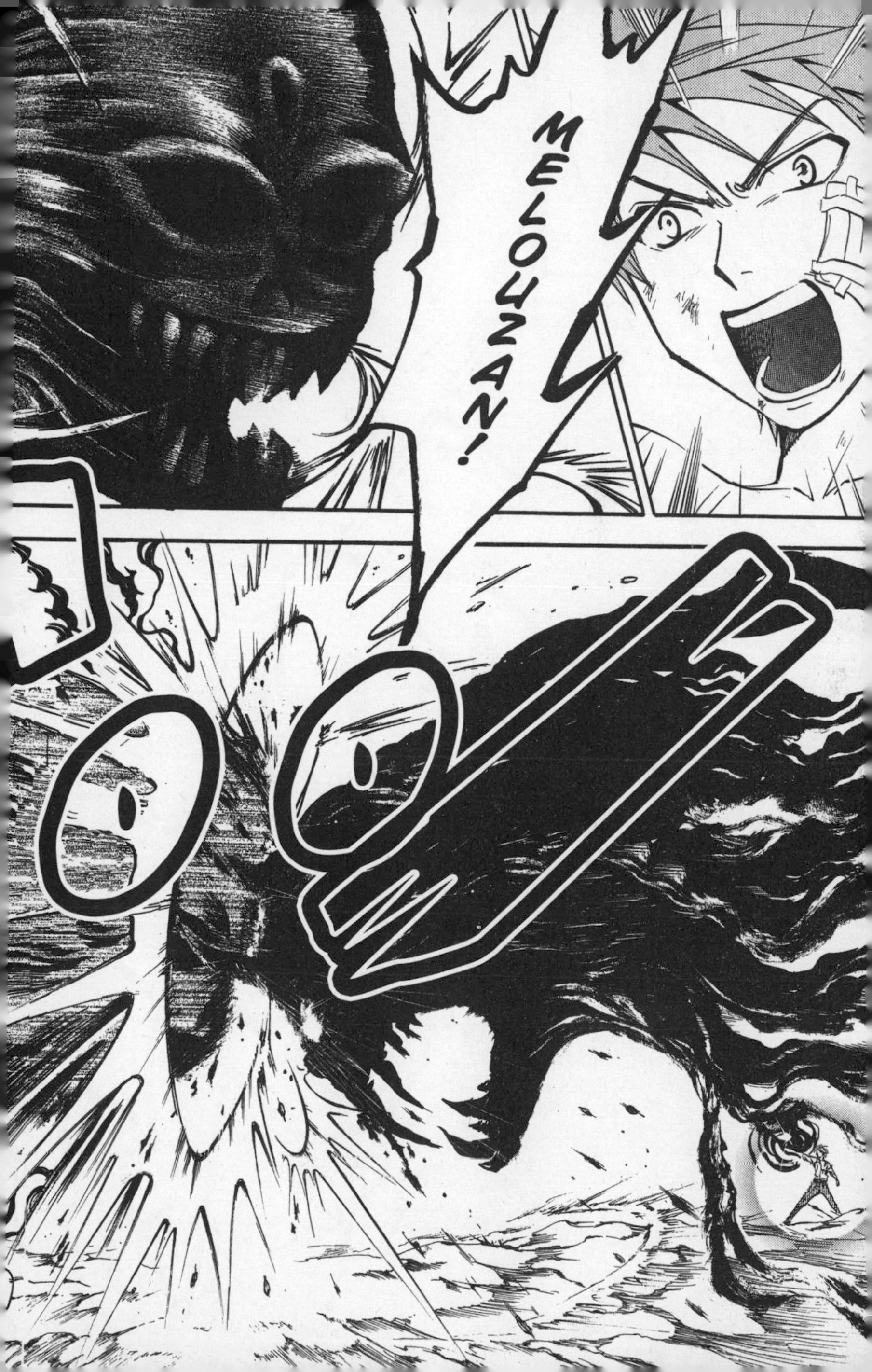
MELOUZAN!

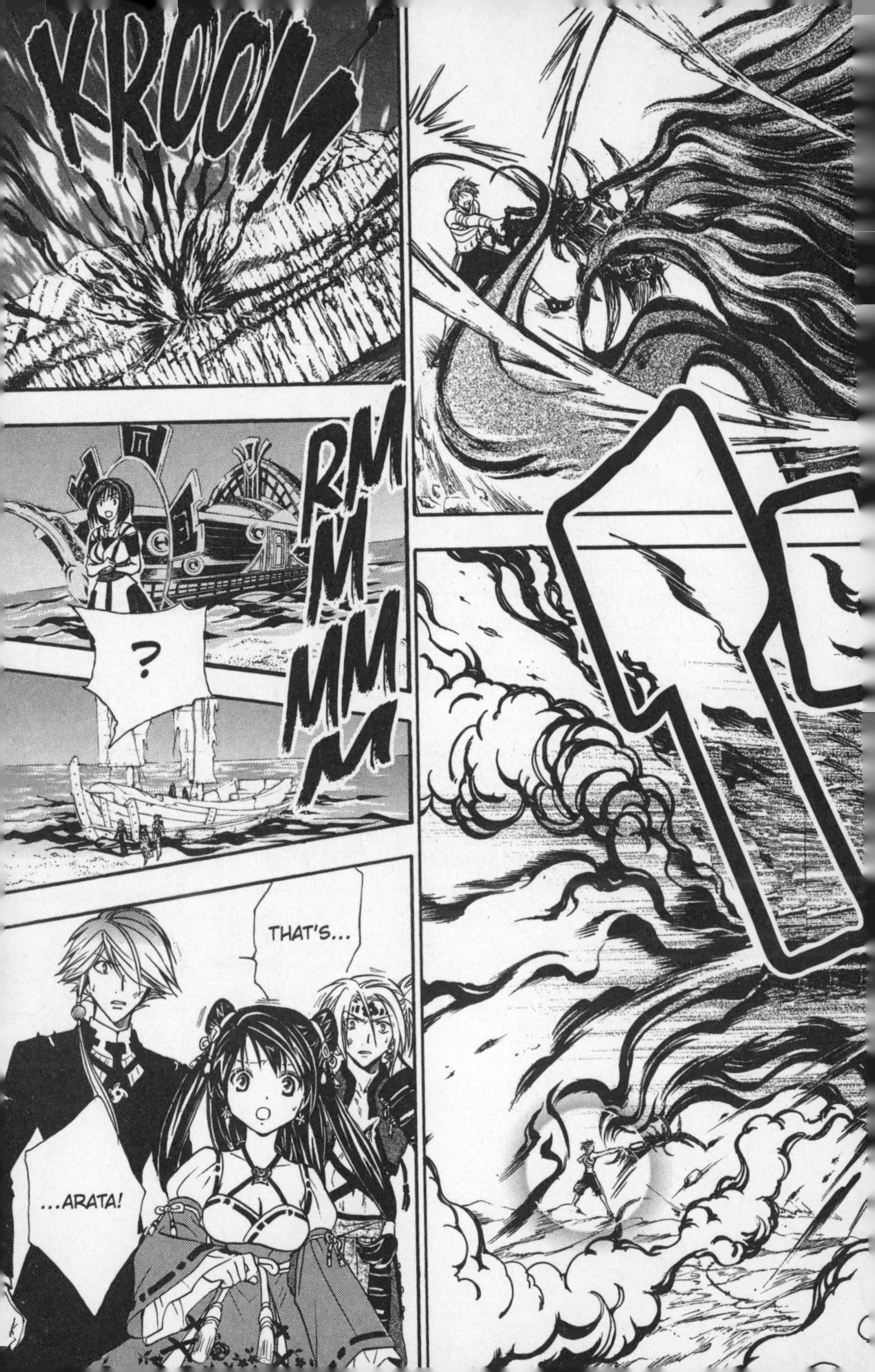
KROOM
RMMMMM
?
THAT'S...
...ARATA!

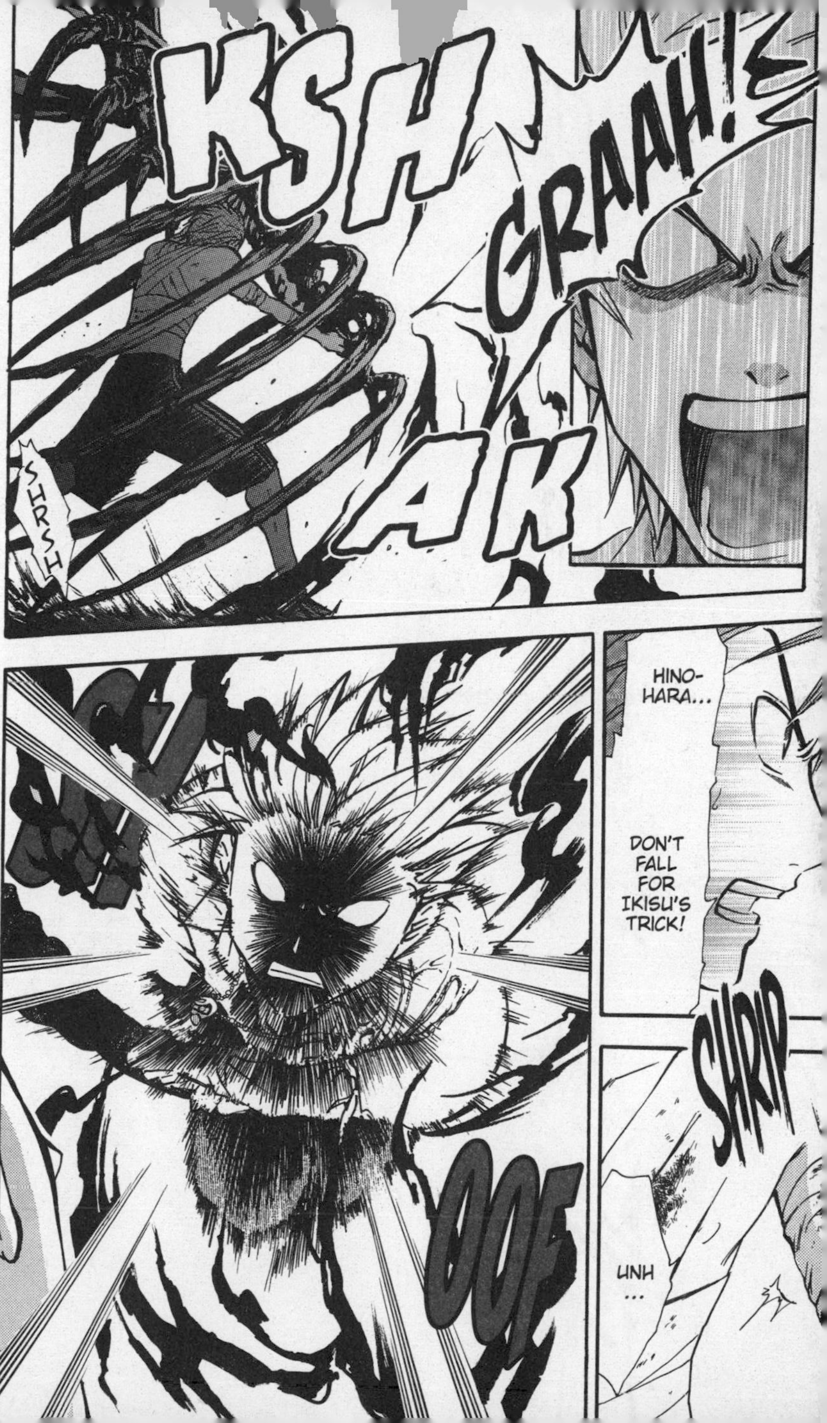
GRAAH!
KSHAK
SHRSH
HINO-HARA...
DON'T FALL FOR IKISU'S TRICK!
SHRIP
UNH ...
OOF

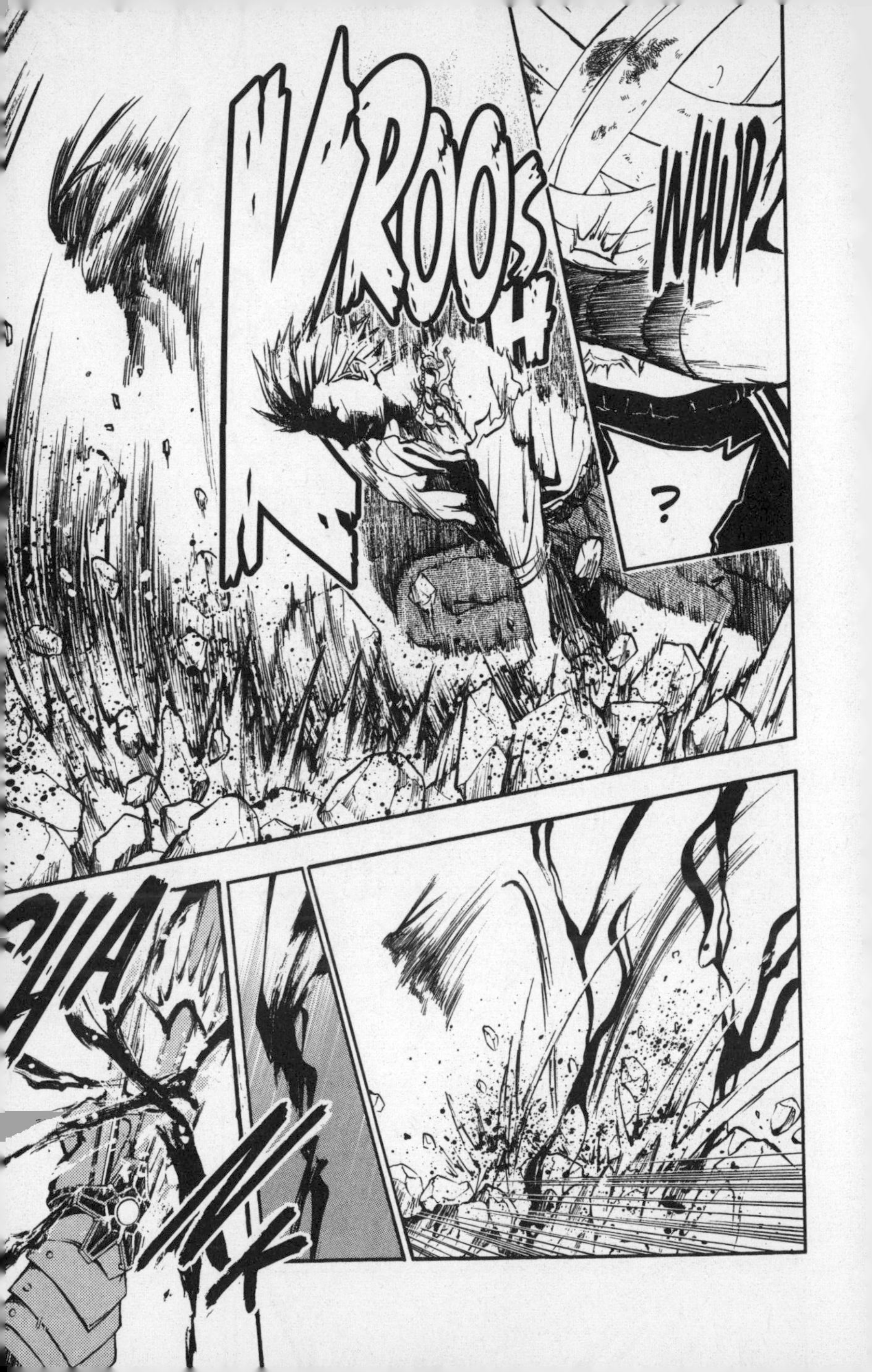
WHUP
?
WROOSH

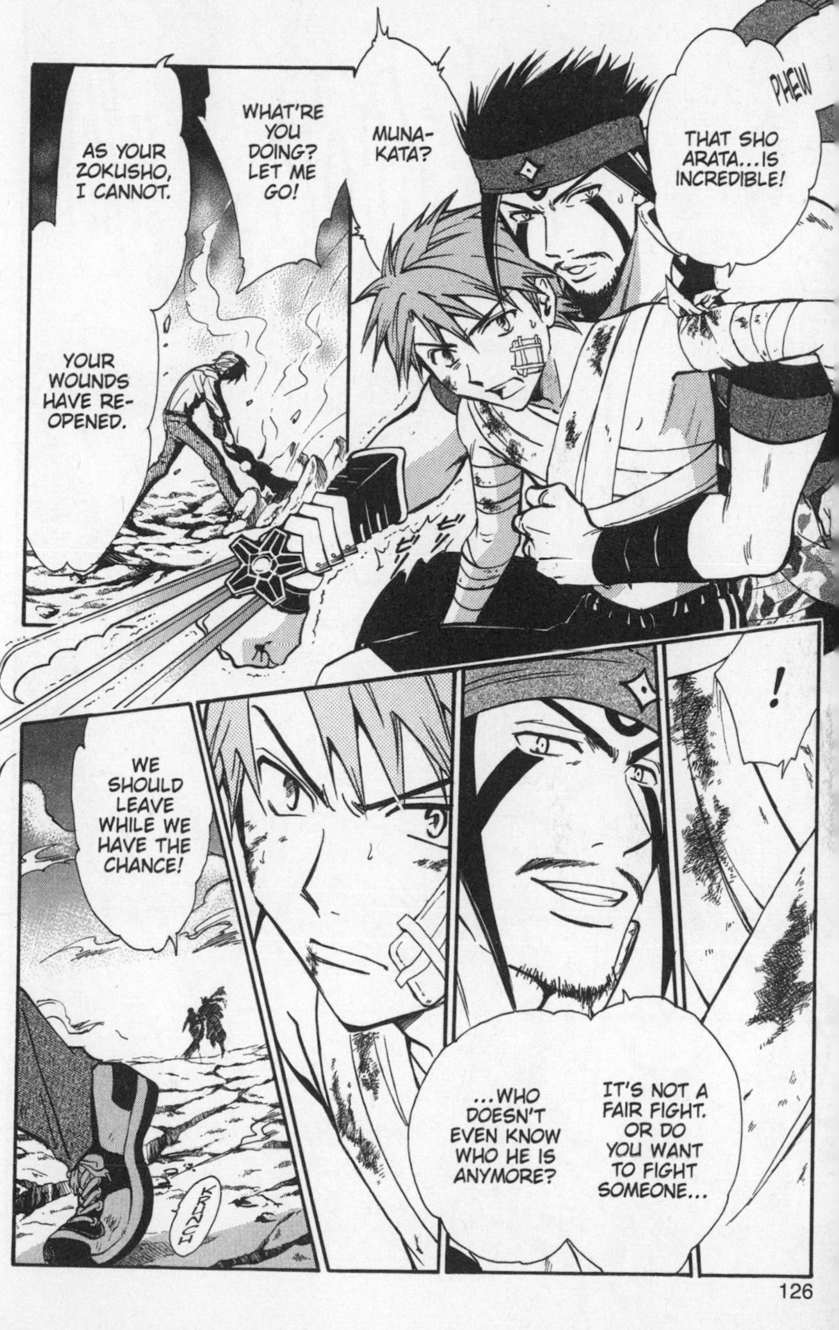
PHEW
THAT SHO ARATA...IS INCREDIBLE!
MUNA-KATA?
WHAT'RE YOU DOING? LET ME GO!
AS YOUR ZOKUSHO, I CANNOT.
YOUR WOUNDS HAVE RE-OPENED.
!
IT'S NOT A FAIR FIGHT. OR DO YOU WANT TO FIGHT SOMEONE...
...WHO DOESN'T EVEN KNOW WHO HE IS ANYMORE?
WE SHOULD LEAVE WHILE WE HAVE THE CHANCE!
KRUNCH

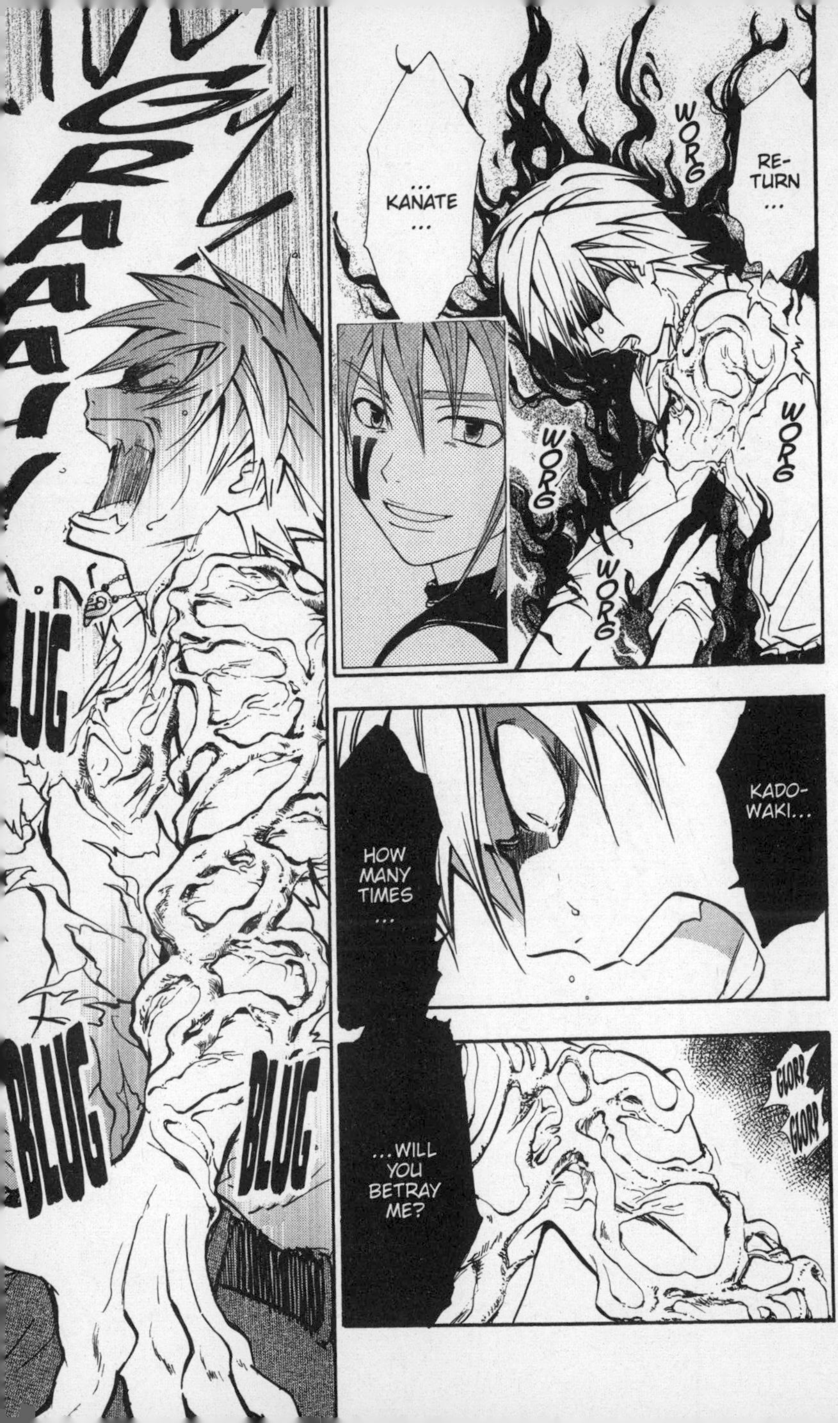
RE-TURN...
WORG
WORG
WORG
WORG
...KANATE...
KADO-WAKI...
HOW MANY TIMES...
GLORP GLORP
...WILL YOU BETRAY ME?
GRAAAA
BLUG
BLUG
BLUG

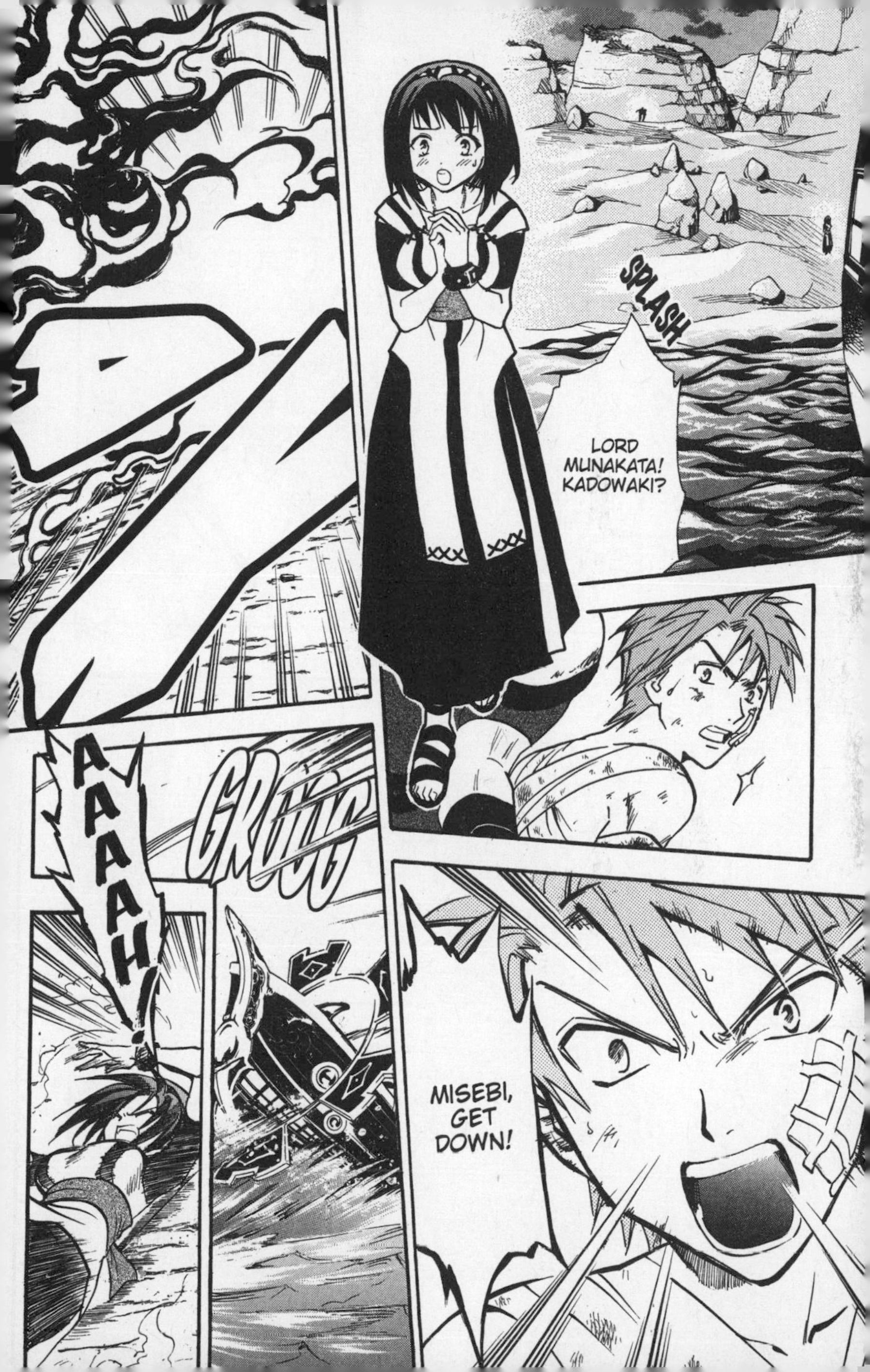
SPLASH
LORD MUNAKATA! KADOWAKI?
MISEBI, GET DOWN!
GROOO
AAAAH!

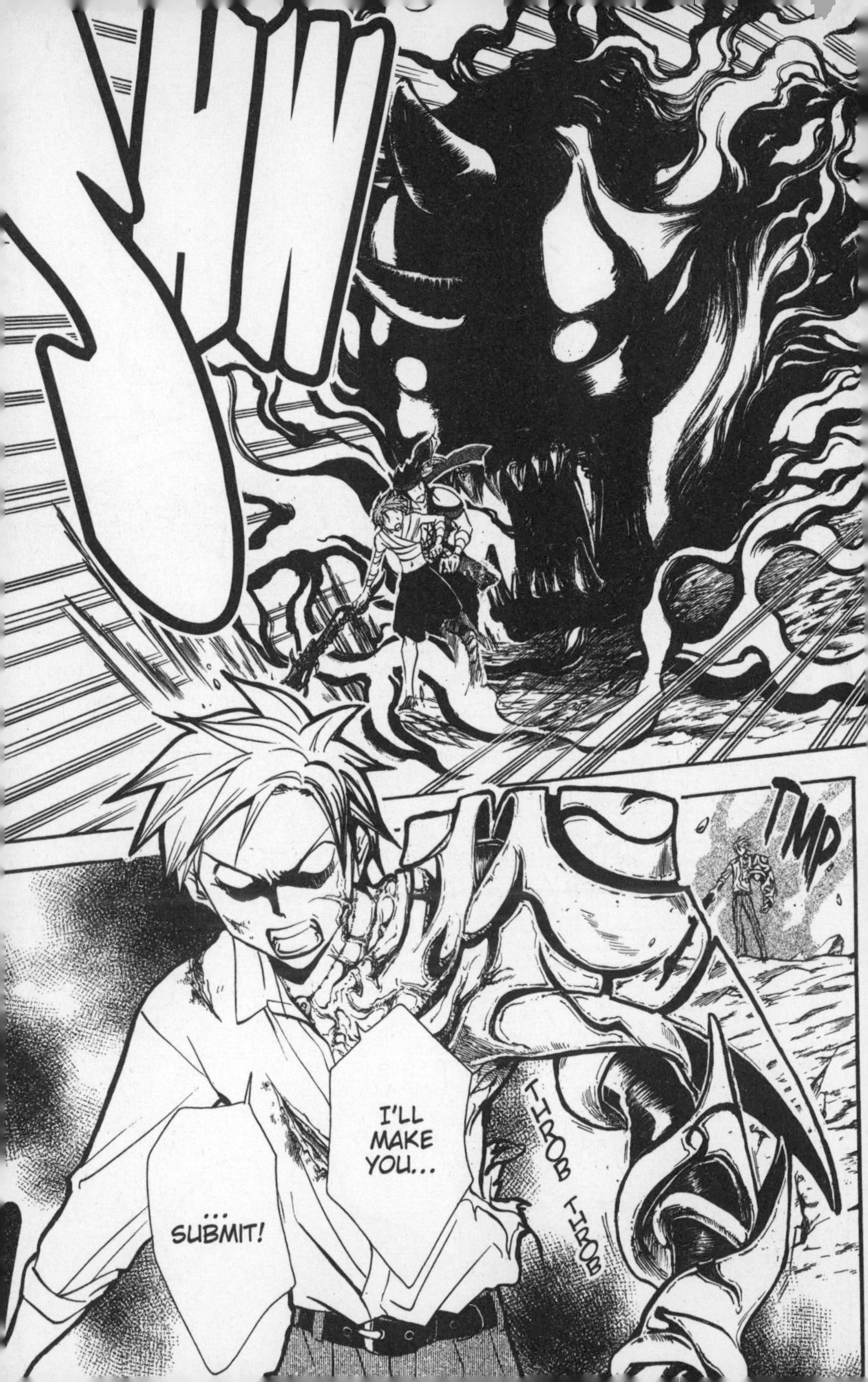
TMP
THROB THROB
I'LL MAKE YOU...
...SUBMIT!

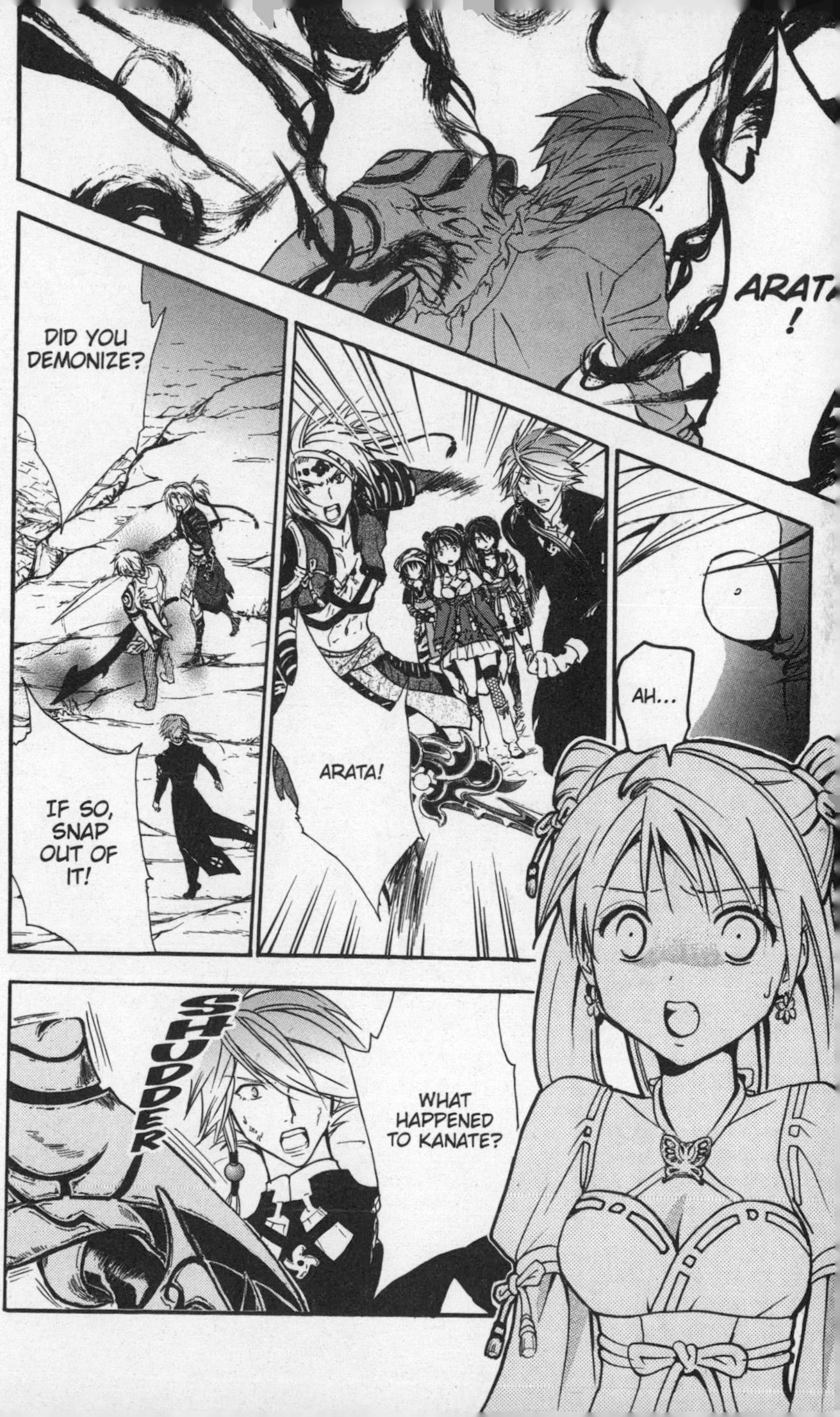
ARATA!
AH...
ARATA!
DID YOU DEMONIZE?
IF SO, SNAP OUT OF IT!
WHAT HAPPENED TO KANATE?
SHUDDER

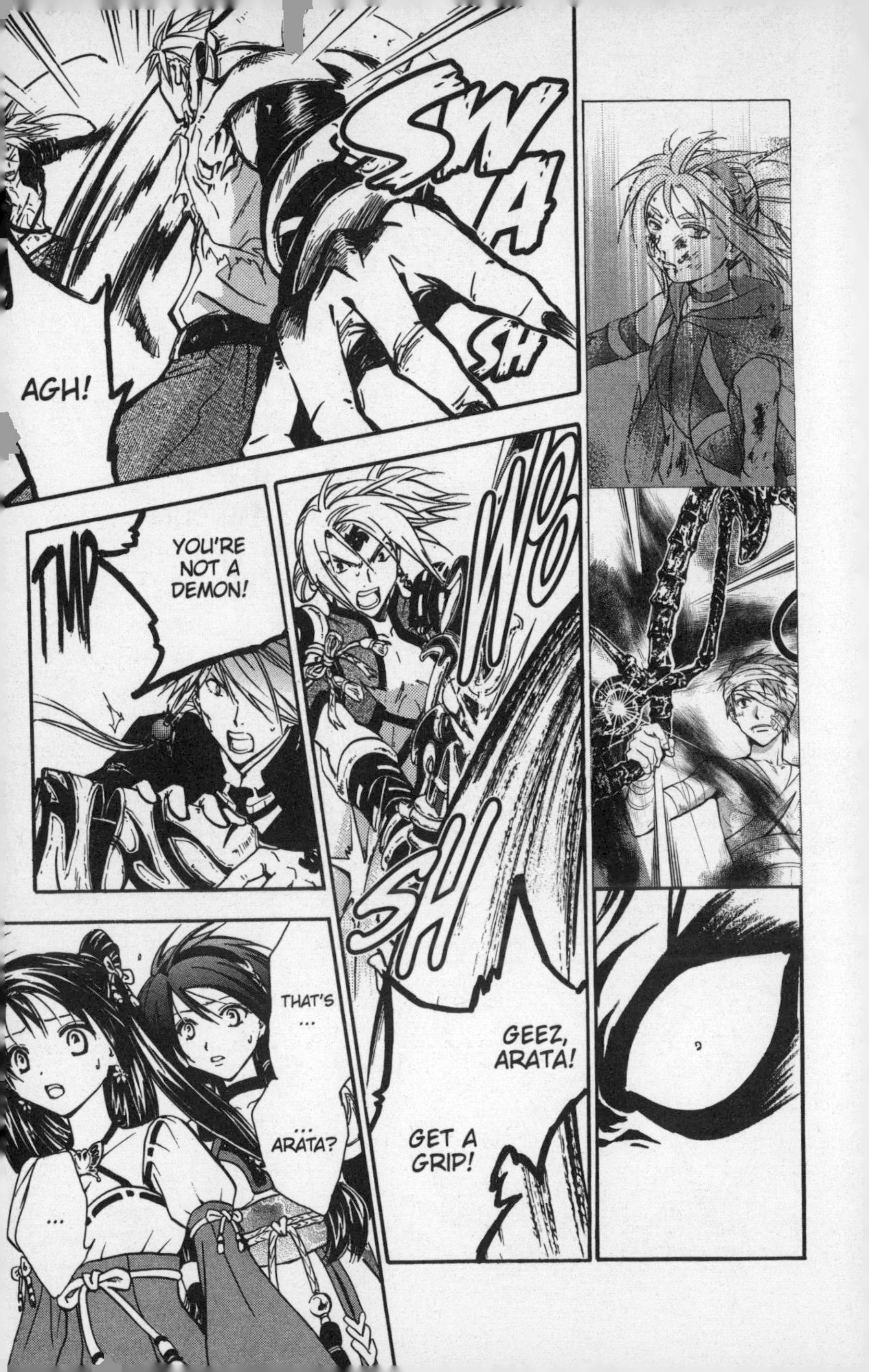
SWA
SH
AGH!
SWO
SH
TMP
YOU'RE NOT A DEMON!
GEEZ, ARATA!
GET A GRIP!
THAT'S ...
... ARATA?
...

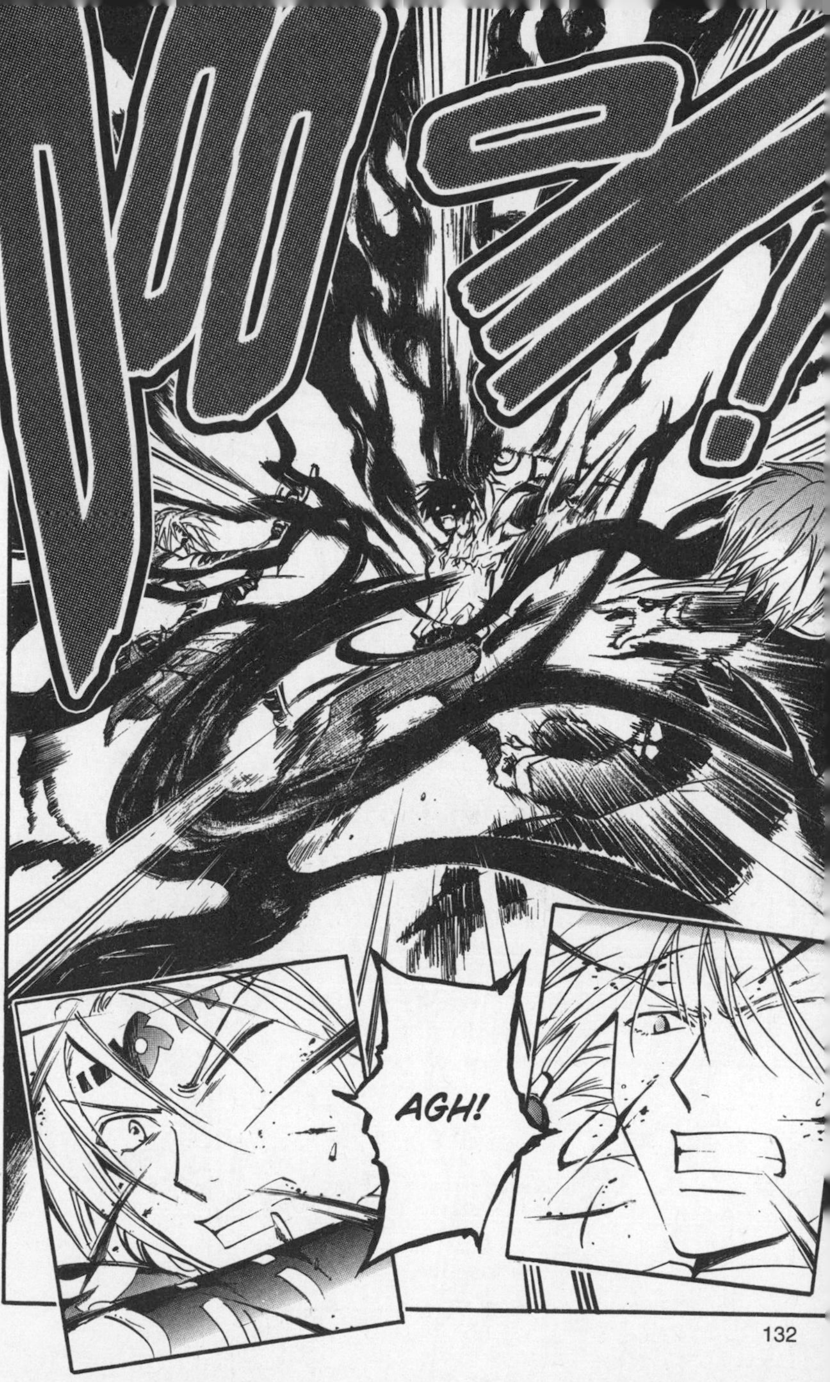
AGH!

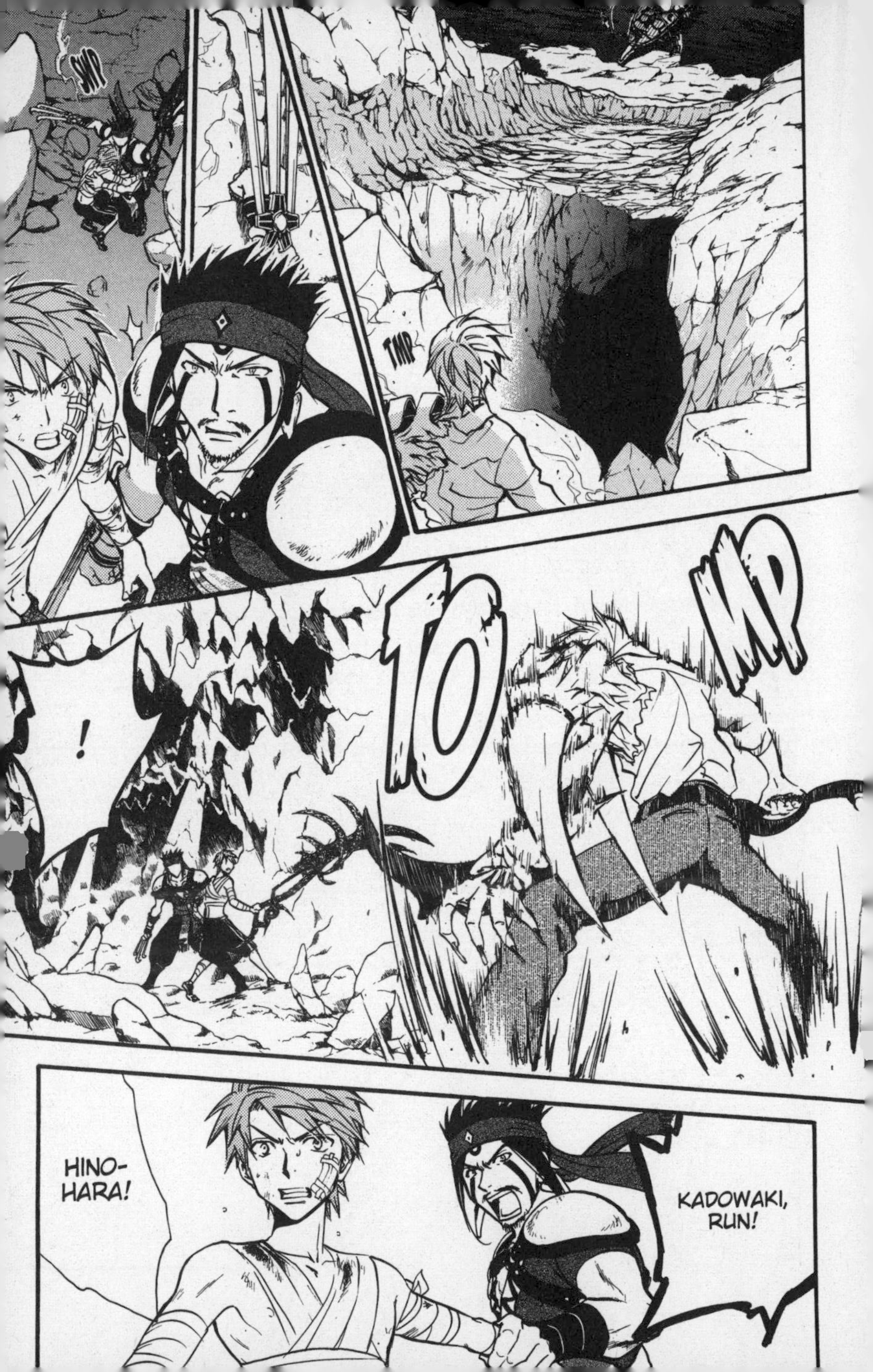
TMP
SWP
TOMP
!
KADOWAKI, RUN!
HINO-HARA!

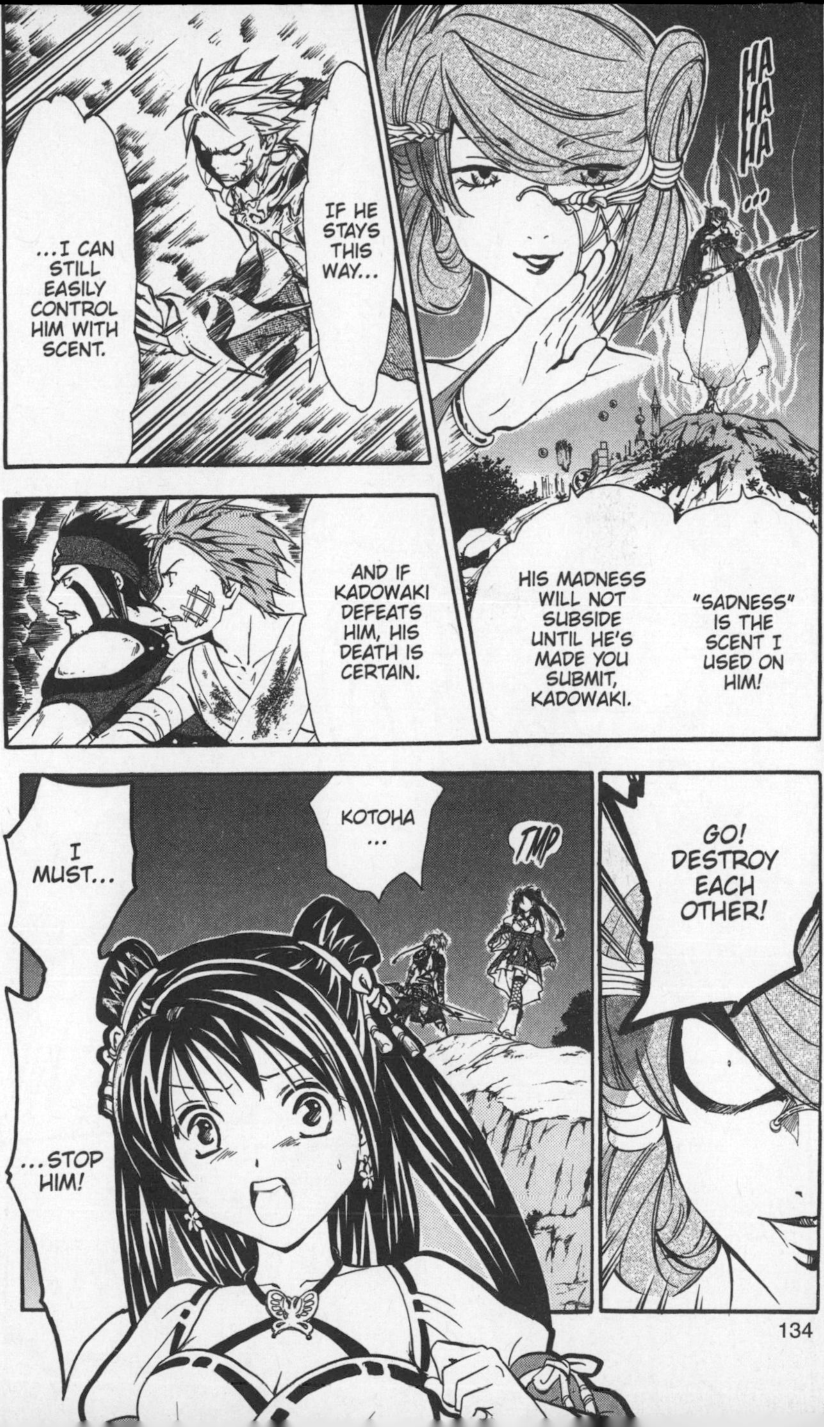
HA HA HA HA...
IF HE STAYS THIS WAY...
...I CAN STILL EASILY CONTROL HIM WITH SCENT.
"SADNESS" IS THE SCENT I USED ON HIM!
HIS MADNESS WILL NOT SUBSIDE UNTIL HE'S MADE YOU SUBMIT, KADOWAKI.
AND IF KADOWAKI DEFEATS HIM, HIS DEATH IS CERTAIN.
GO! DESTROY EACH OTHER!
KOTOHA...
TMP
I MUST...
...STOP HIM!

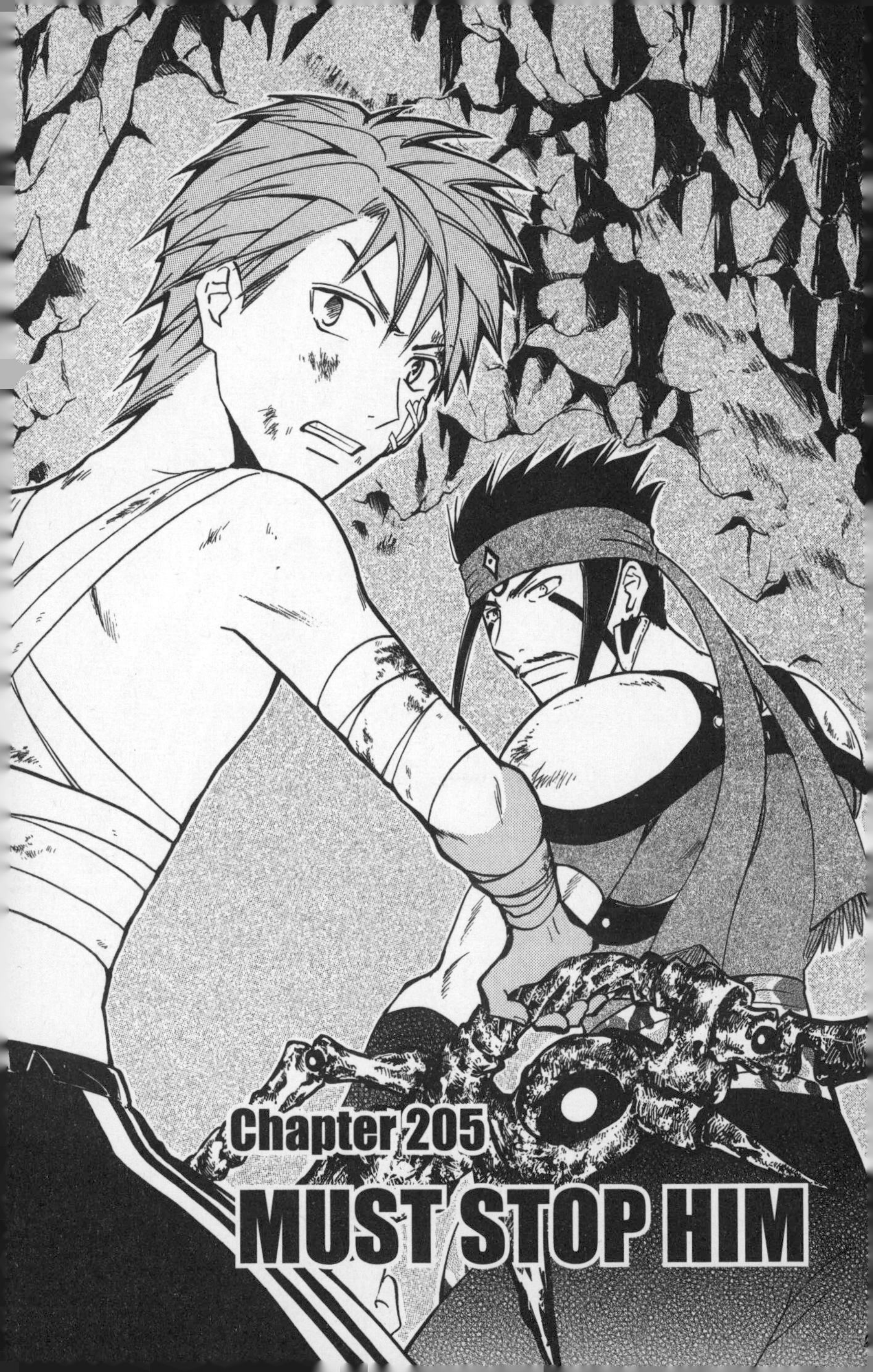
Chapter 205
MUST STOP HIM

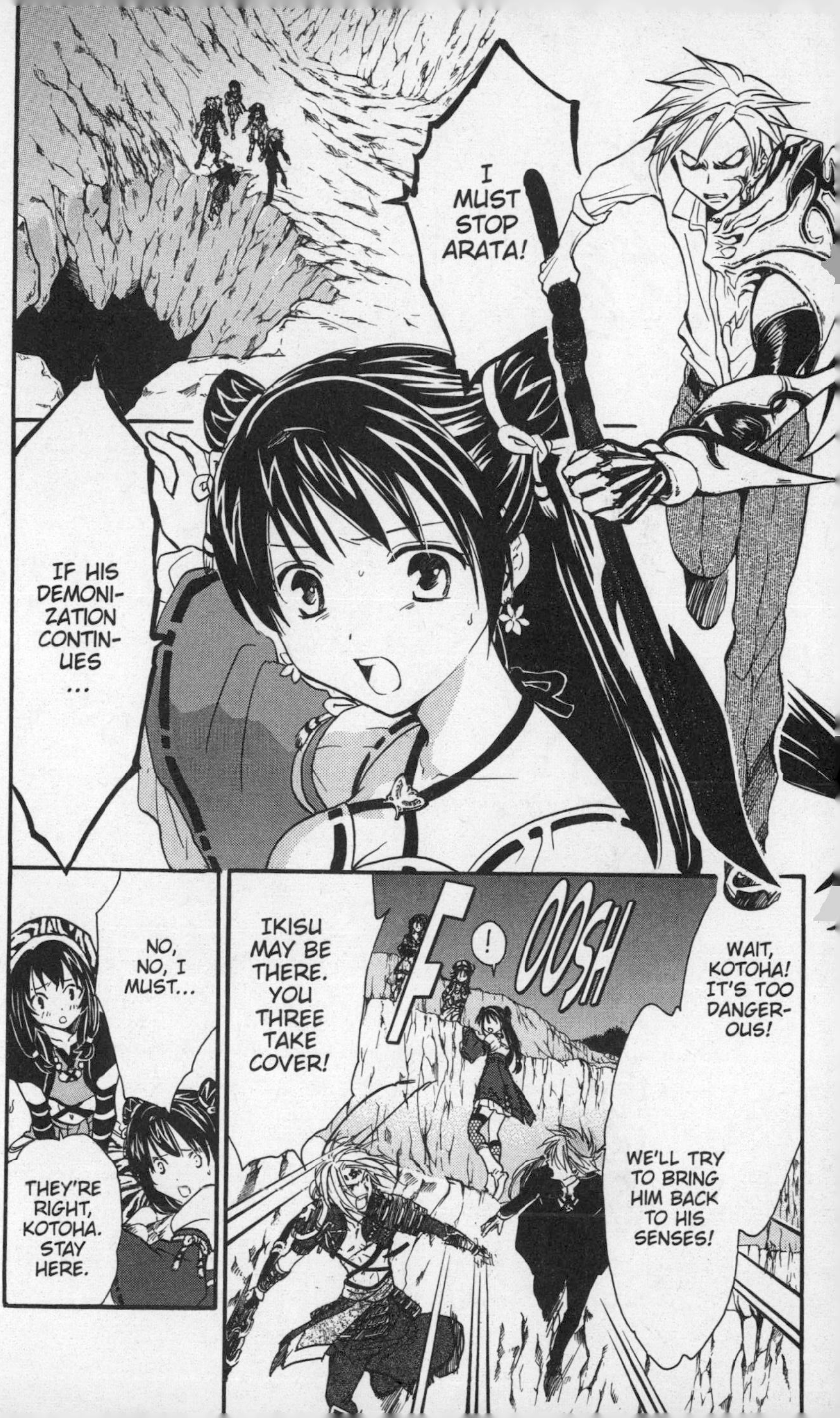
I MUST STOP ARATA!
IF HIS DEMONIZATION CONTINUES...
WAIT, KOTOHA! IT'S TOO DANGEROUS!
WE'LL TRY TO BRING HIM BACK TO HIS SENSES!
FOOSH
!
IKISU MAY BE THERE. YOU THREE TAKE COVER!
NO, NO, I MUST...
THEY'RE RIGHT, KOTOHA. STAY HERE.

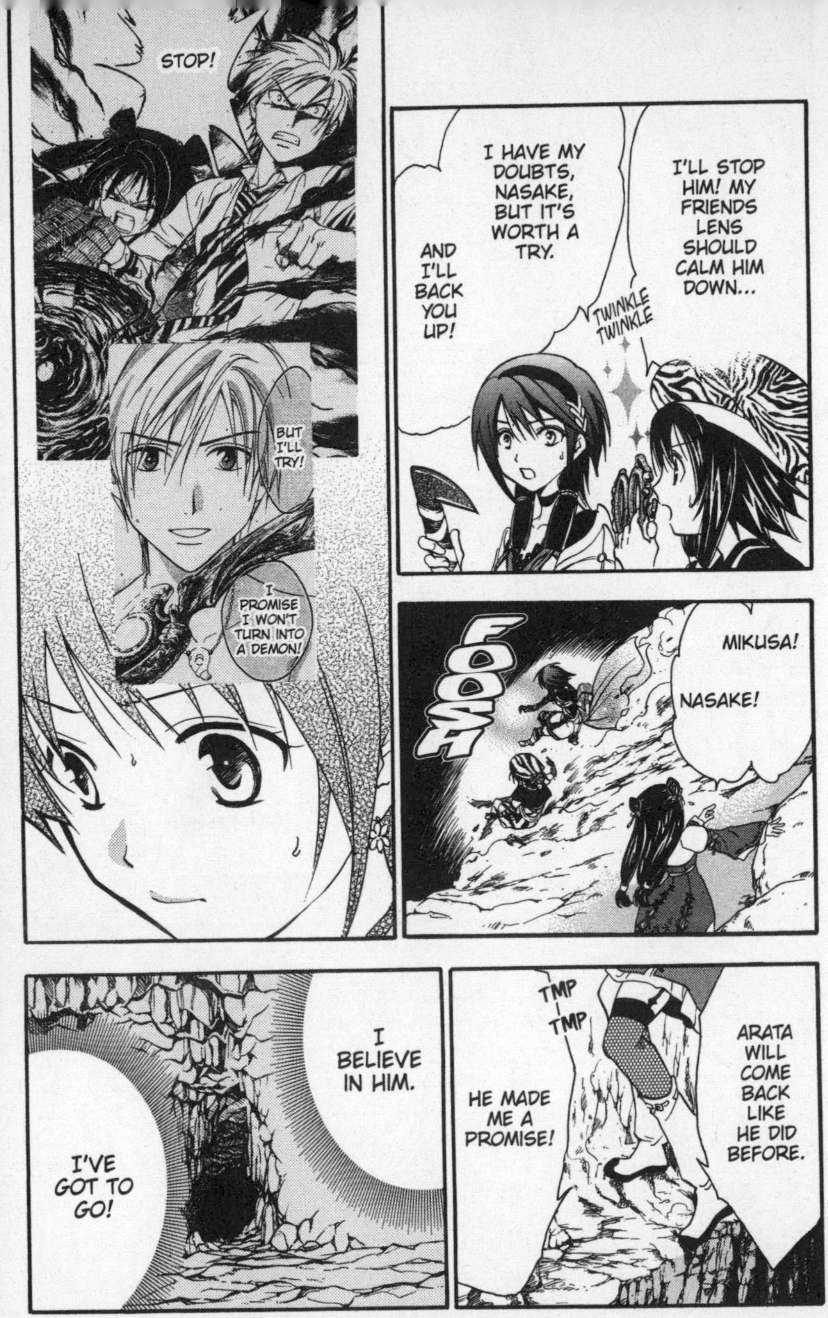
I'LL STOP HIM! MY FRIENDS LENS SHOULD CALM HIM DOWN...
TWINKLE TWINKLE
I HAVE MY DOUBTS, NASAKE, BUT IT'S WORTH A TRY.
AND I'LL BACK YOU UP!
MIKUSA!
NASAKE!
FOOSH
STOP!
BUT I'LL TRY!
I PROMISE I WON'T TURN INTO A DEMON!
ARATA WILL COME BACK LIKE HE DID BEFORE.
TMP TMP
HE MADE ME A PROMISE!
I BELIEVE IN HIM.
I'VE GOT TO GO!

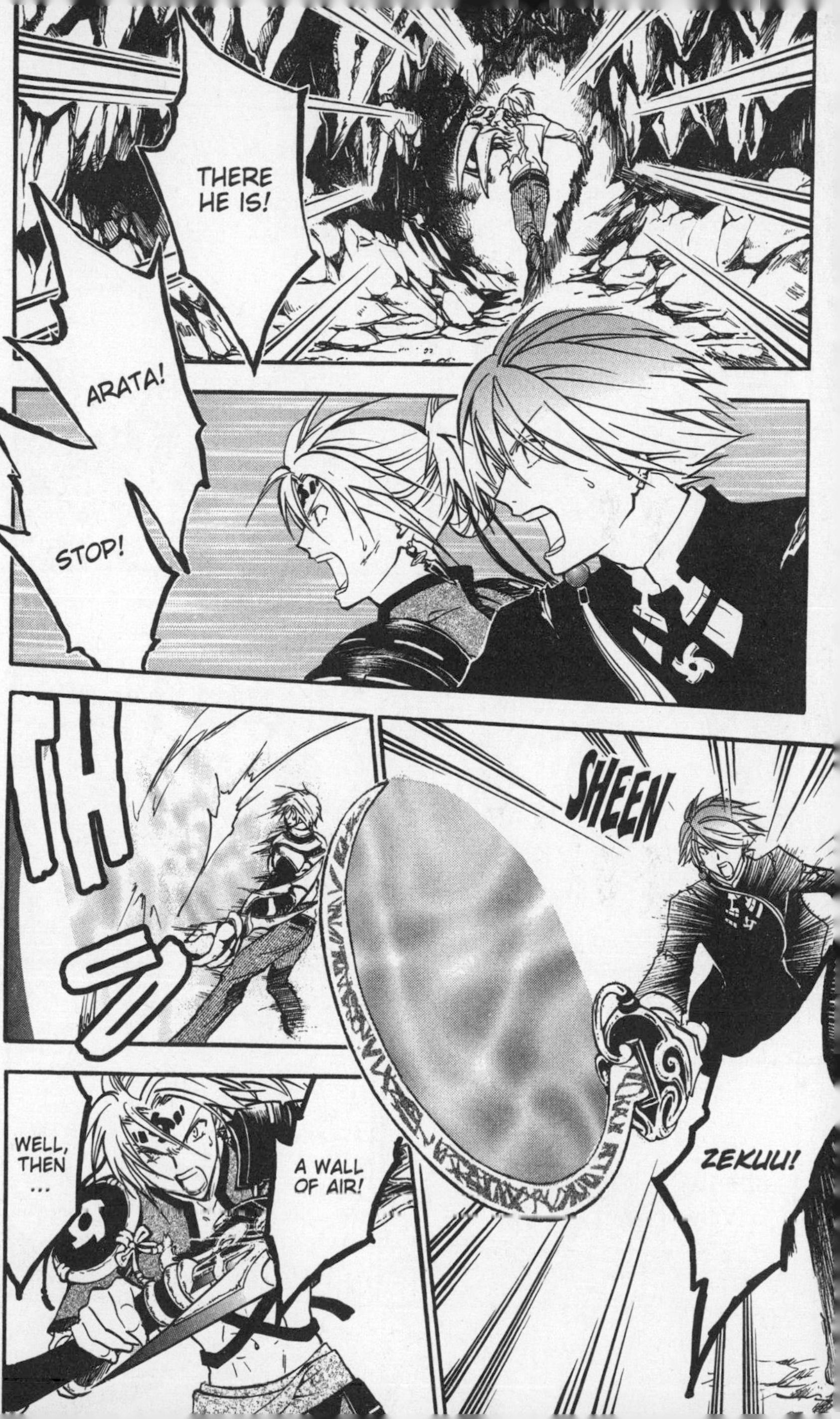
THERE HE IS!
ARATA!
STOP!
SHEEN
ZEKUU!
A WALL OF AIR!
WELL, THEN ...

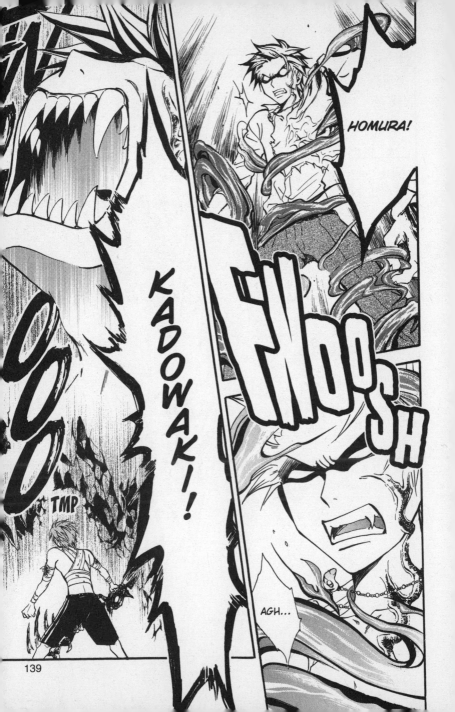

HOMURA!

KADOWAKI!!

FWOOSH

OOO

TMP

AGH...

139

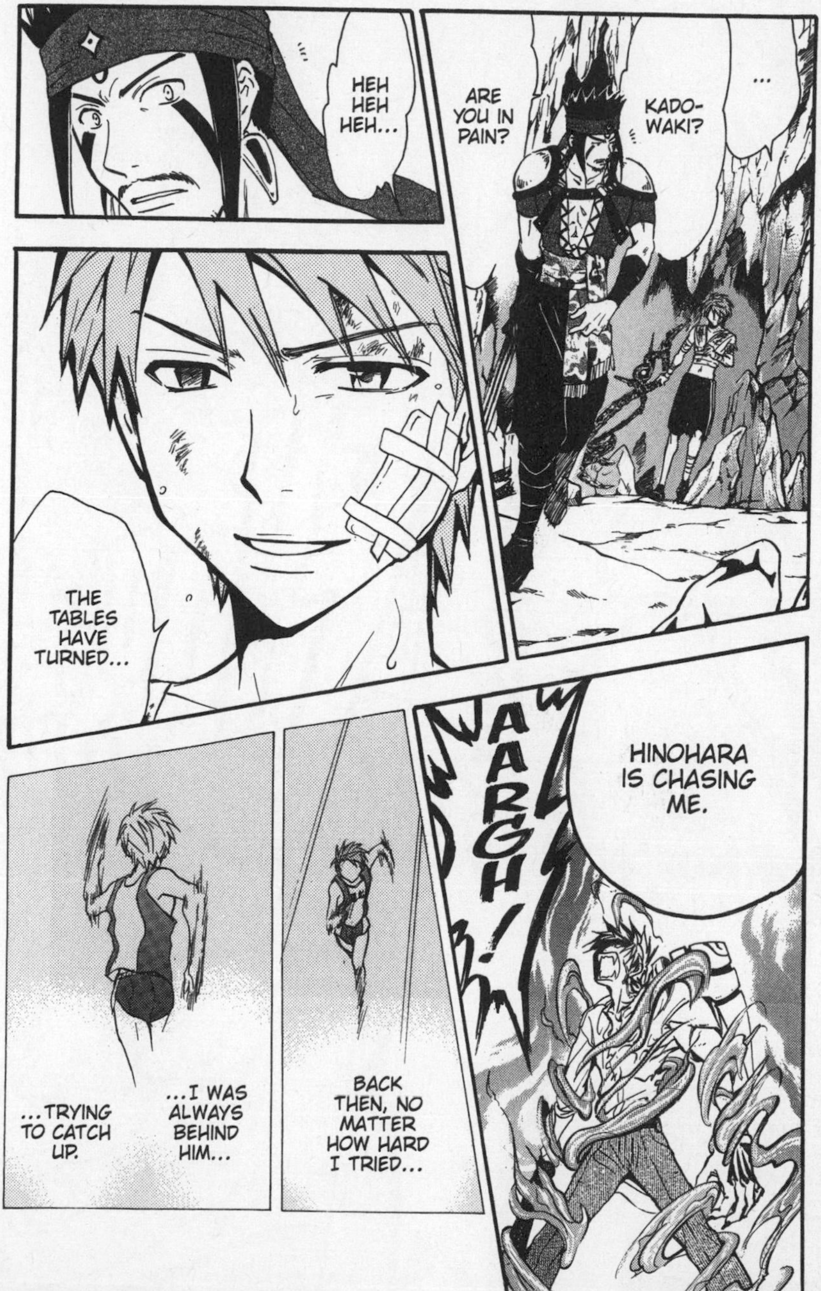
...
KADO-WAKI?
ARE YOU IN PAIN?
HEH HEH HEH...
THE TABLES HAVE TURNED...
HINOHARA IS CHASING ME.
AARGH!
BACK THEN, NO MATTER HOW HARD I TRIED...
...I WAS ALWAYS BEHIND HIM...
...TRYING TO CATCH UP.

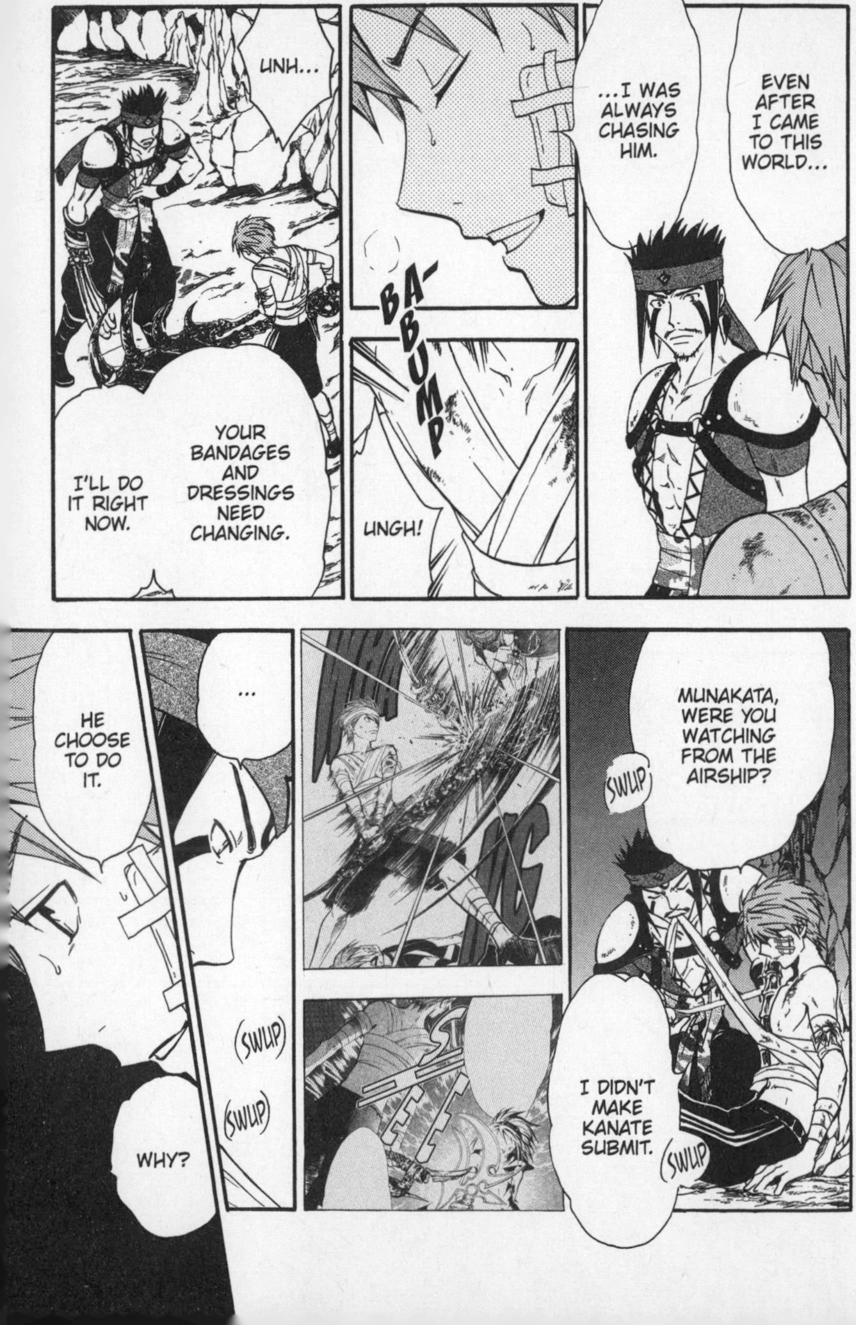
EVEN AFTER I CAME TO THIS WORLD...
...I WAS ALWAYS CHASING HIM.
BA-BUMP
UNGH!
UNH...
YOUR BANDAGES AND DRESSINGS NEED CHANGING.
I'LL DO IT RIGHT NOW.
MUNAKATA, WERE YOU WATCHING FROM THE AIRSHIP?
SWUP
I DIDN'T MAKE KANATE SUBMIT.
SWUP
...
(SWUP)
(SWUP)
HE CHOOSE TO DO IT.
WHY?

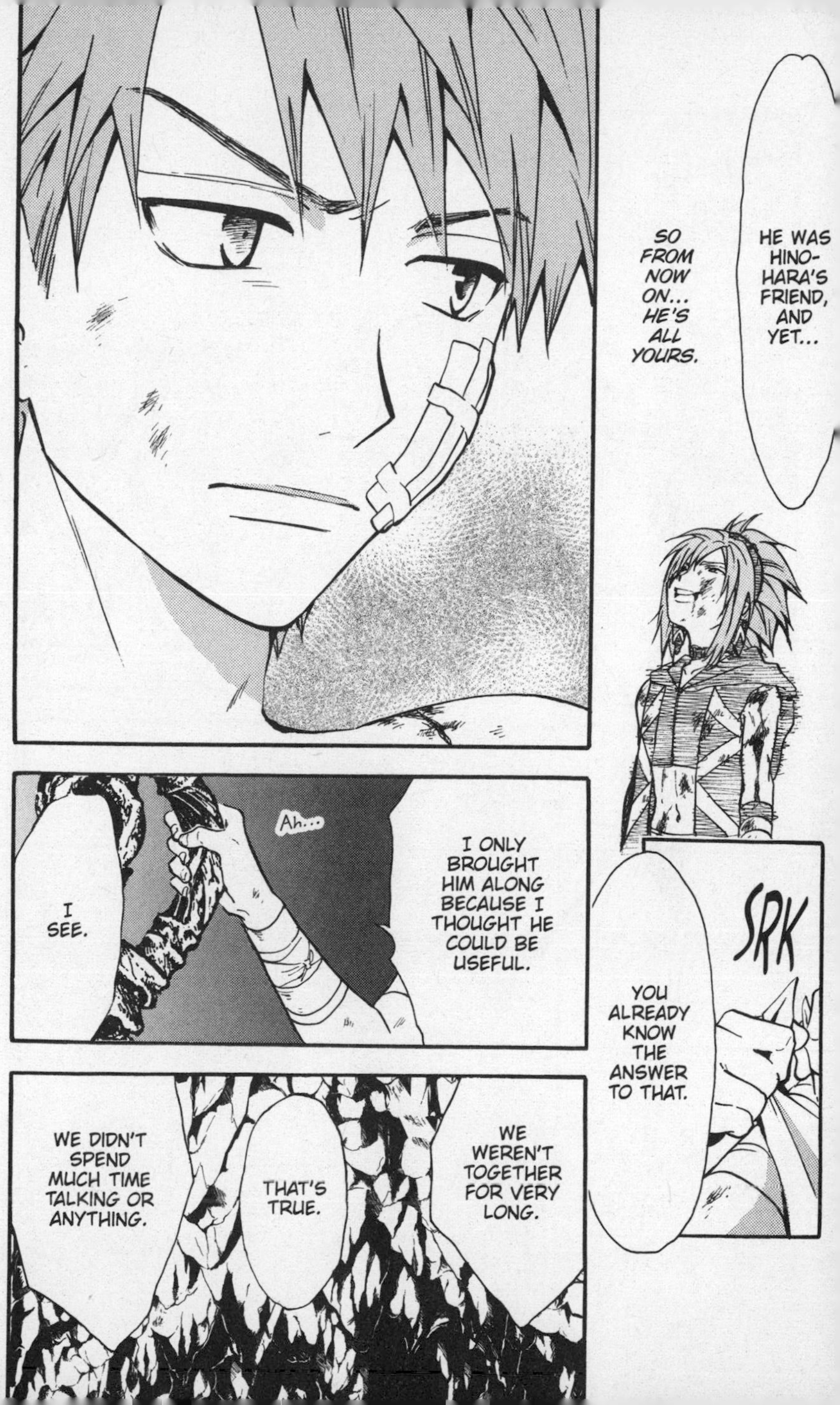
HE WAS HINO-HARA'S FRIEND, AND YET...
SO FROM NOW ON... HE'S ALL YOURS.
SRK
YOU ALREADY KNOW THE ANSWER TO THAT.
I ONLY BROUGHT HIM ALONG BECAUSE I THOUGHT HE COULD BE USEFUL.
Ah...
I SEE.
WE WEREN'T TOGETHER FOR VERY LONG.
THAT'S TRUE.
WE DIDN'T SPEND MUCH TIME TALKING OR ANYTHING.

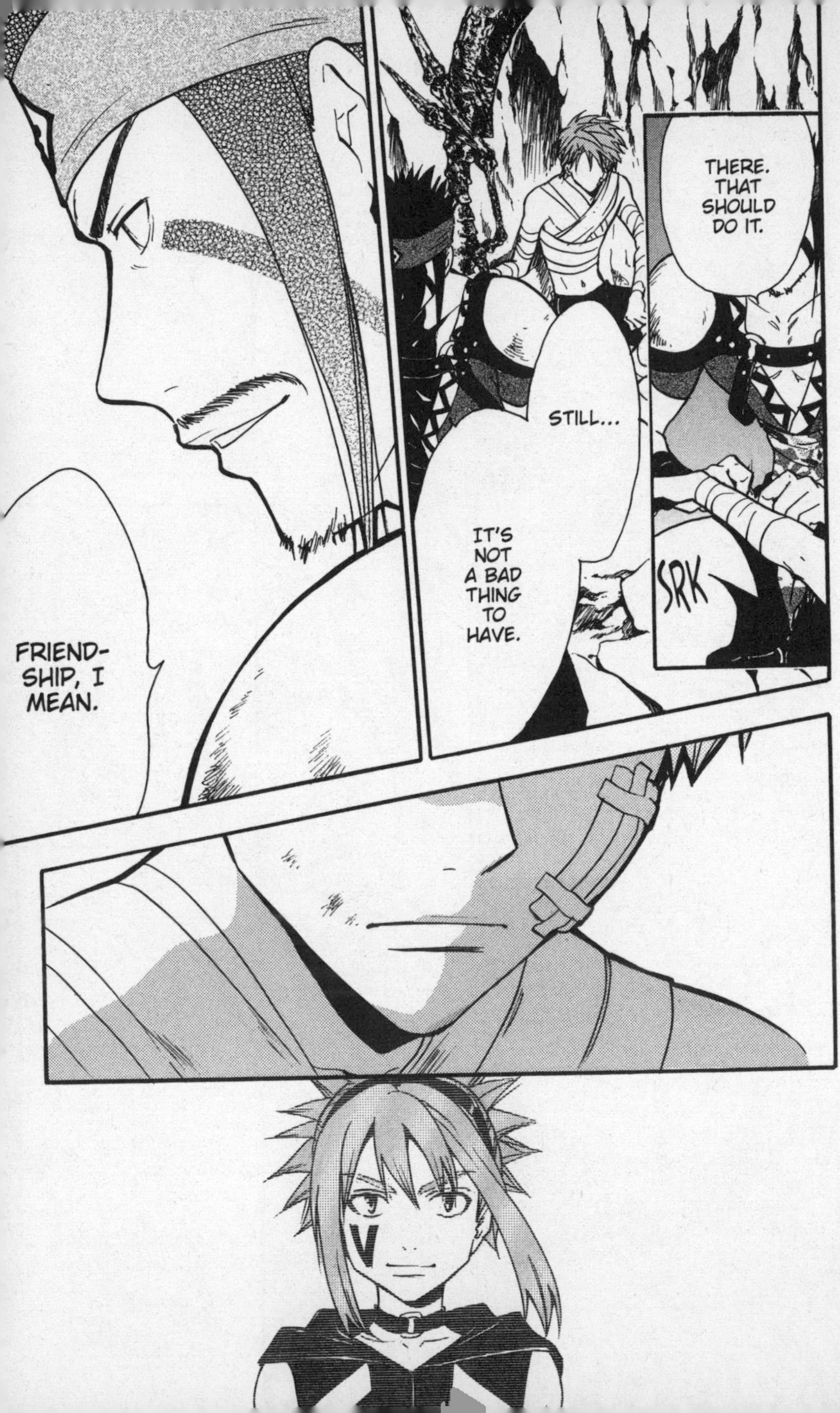
THERE. THAT SHOULD DO IT.
SRK
STILL...
IT'S NOT A BAD THING TO HAVE.
FRIEND-SHIP, I MEAN.

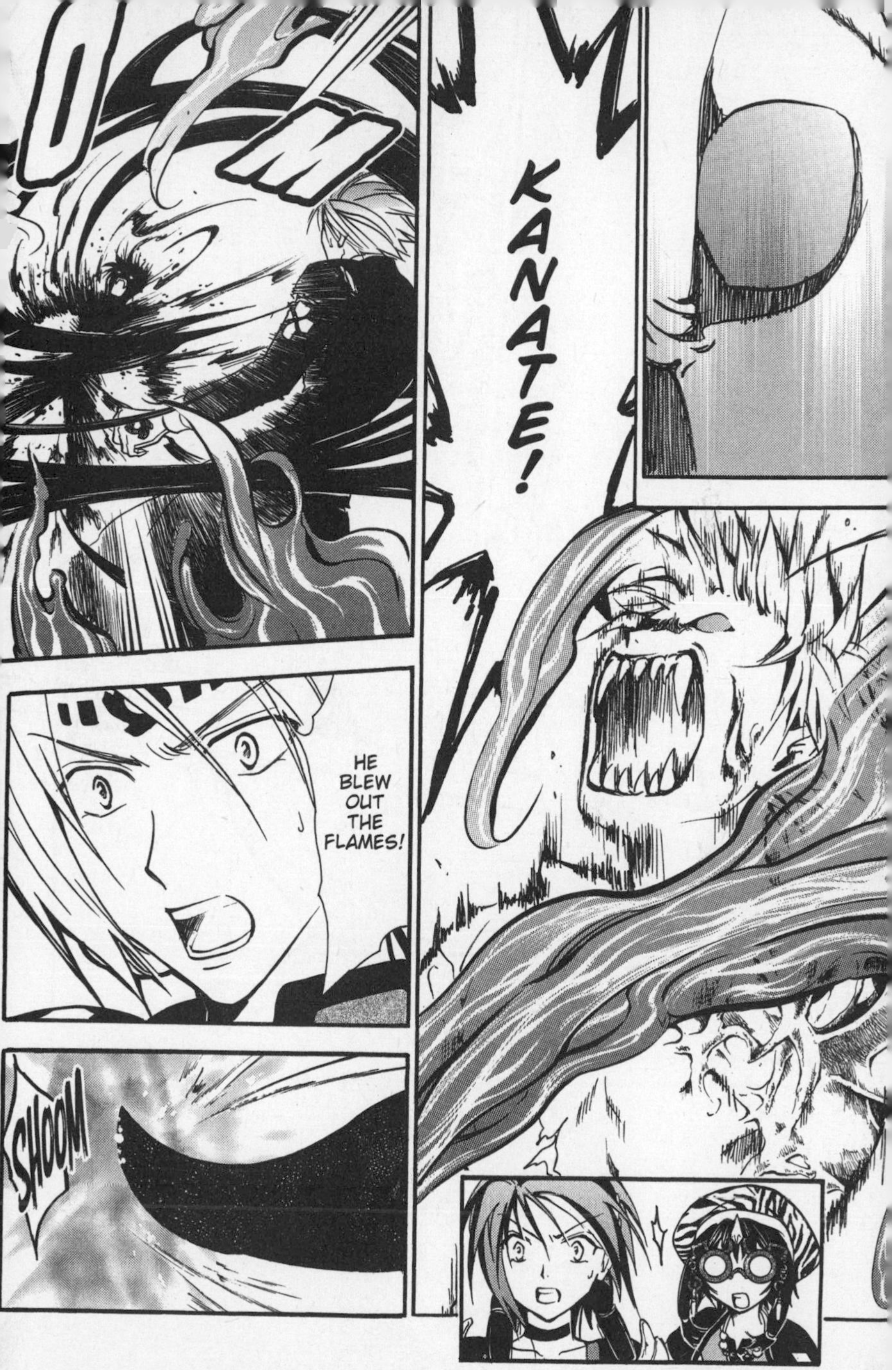
KANATE!
HE BLEW OUT THE FLAMES!
SHOOM

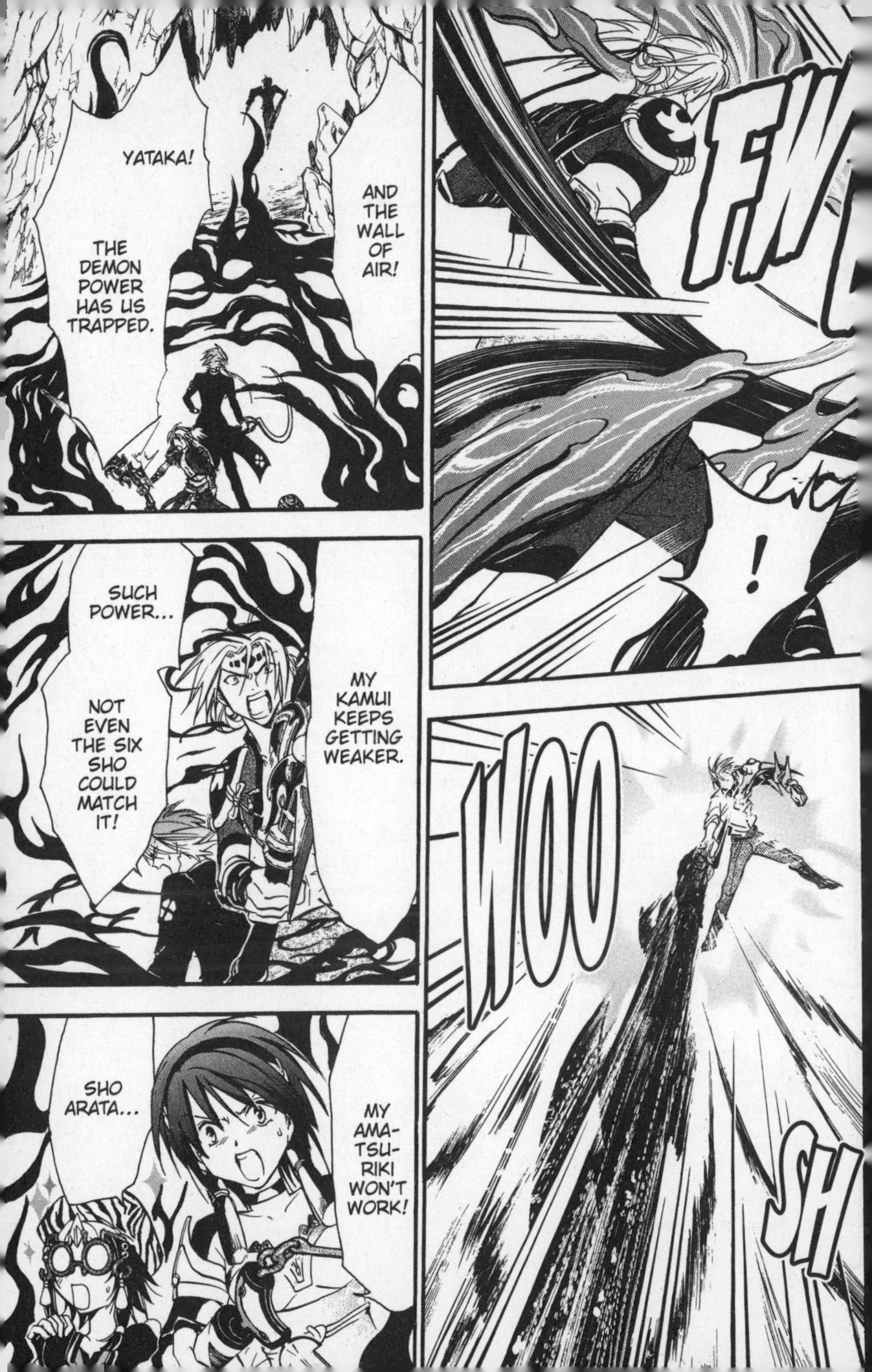
FW
!
WOO
SH
YATAKA!
THE DEMON POWER HAS US TRAPPED.
AND THE WALL OF AIR!
MY KAMUI KEEPS GETTING WEAKER.
SUCH POWER...
NOT EVEN THE SIX SHO COULD MATCH IT!
MY AMATSURIKI WON'T WORK!
SHO ARATA...

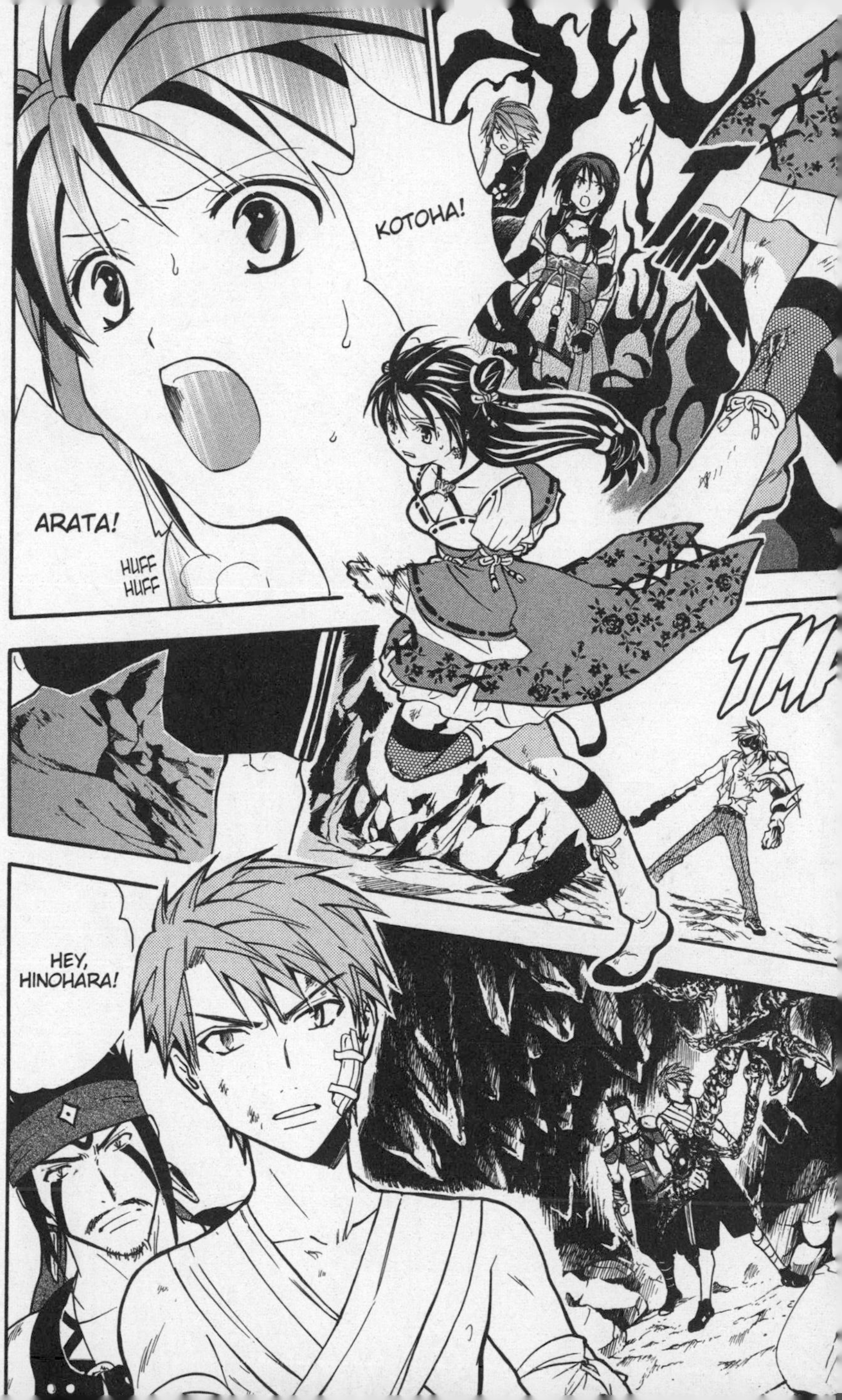
KOTOHA!
ARATA!
HUFF
HUFF
HEY, HINOHARA!

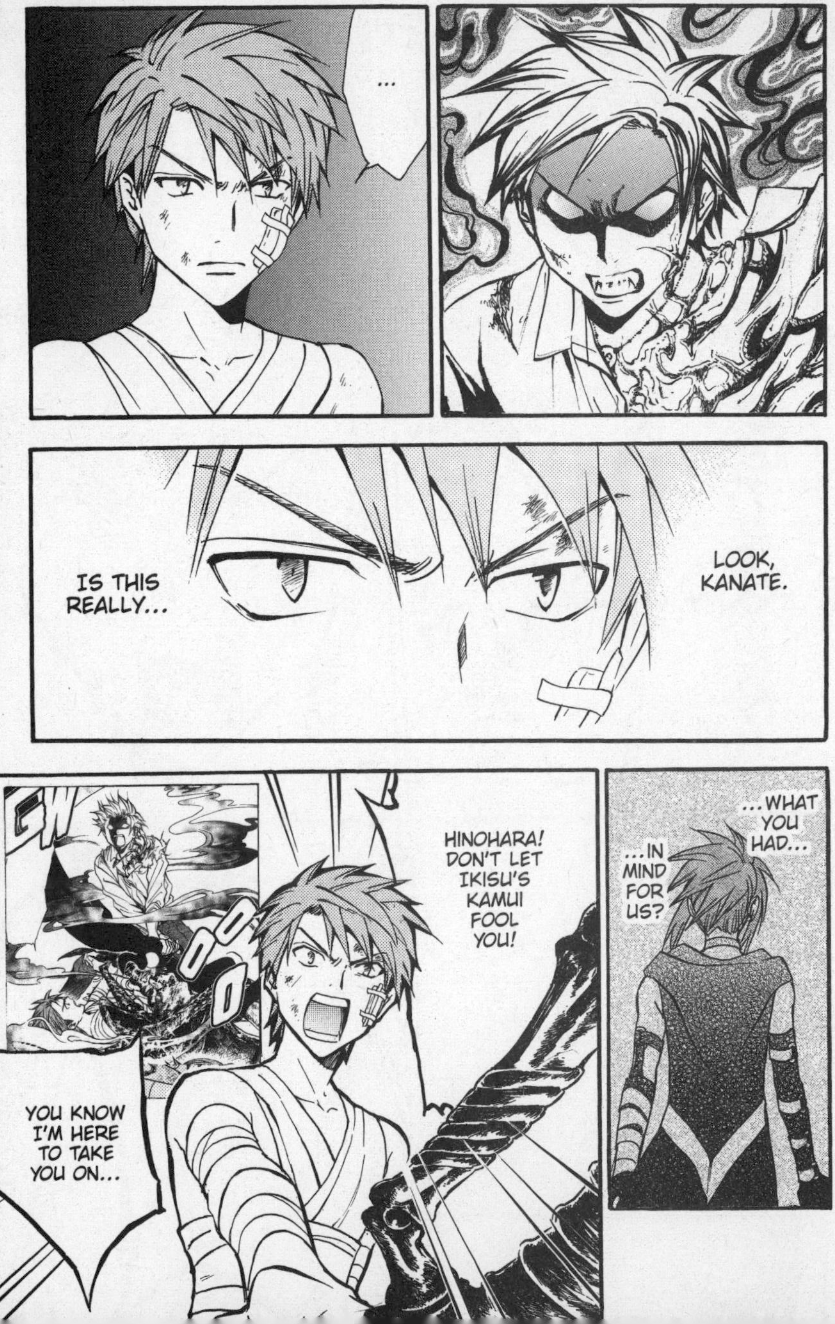
...
LOOK, KANATE.
IS THIS REALLY...
...WHAT YOU HAD...
...IN MIND FOR US?
HINOHARA! DON'T LET IKISU'S KAMUI FOOL YOU!
GWOOOO
YOU KNOW I'M HERE TO TAKE YOU ON...

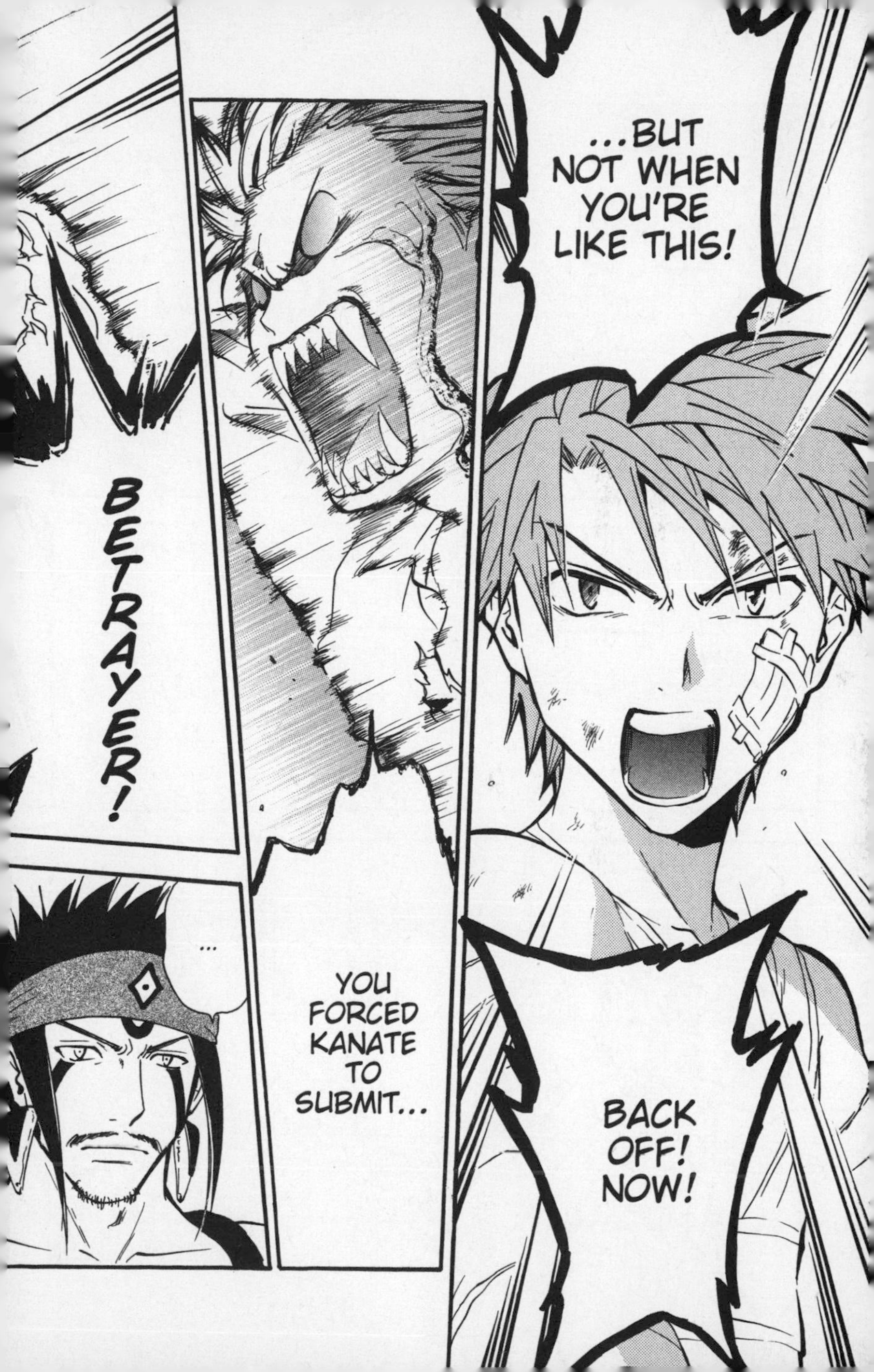
...BUT NOT WHEN YOU'RE LIKE THIS!
BACK OFF! NOW!
YOU FORCED KANATE TO SUBMIT...
BETRAYER!
...

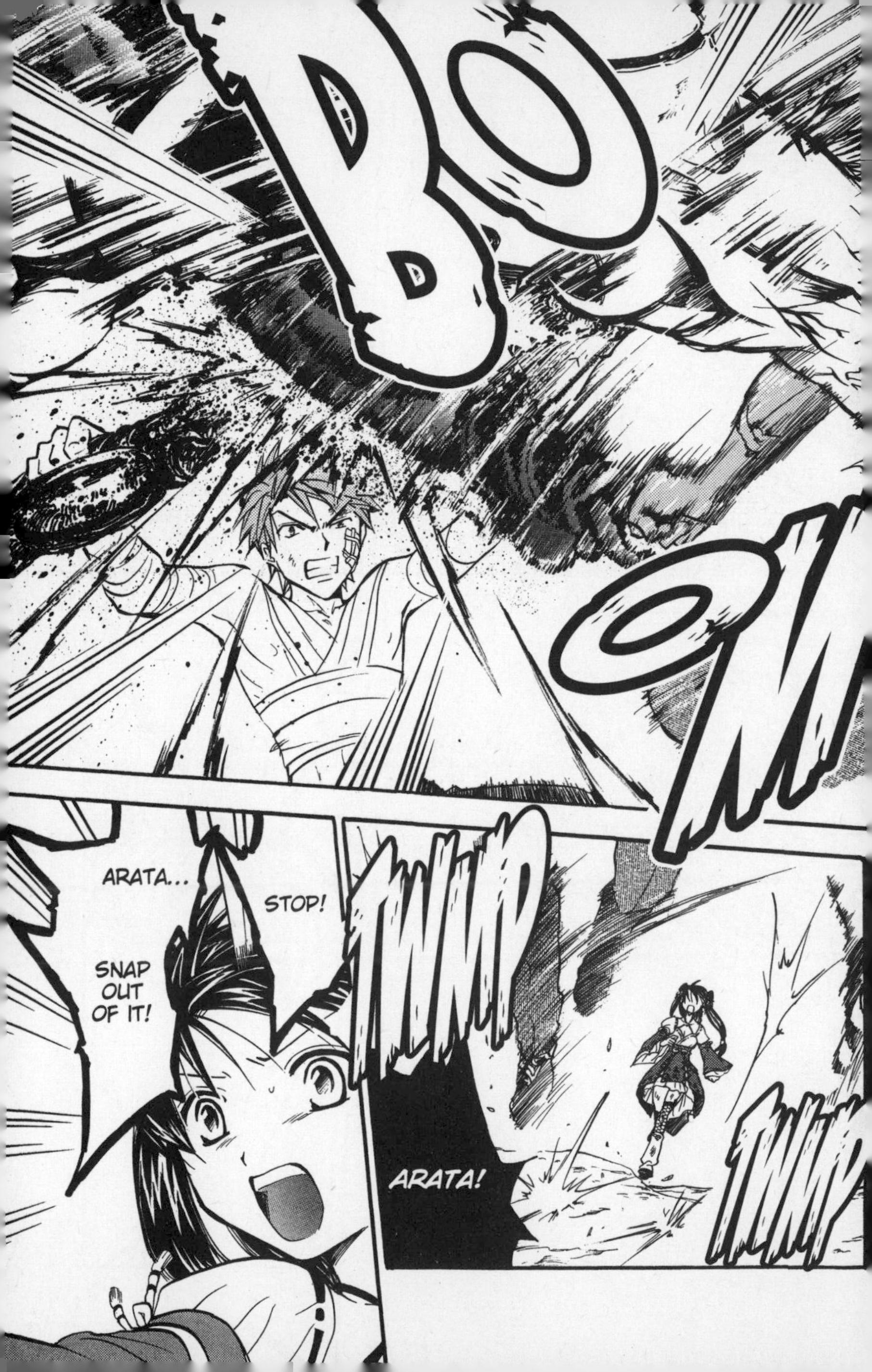
BOOM
THMP
ARATA!
THMP
ARATA...
STOP!
SNAP OUT OF IT!

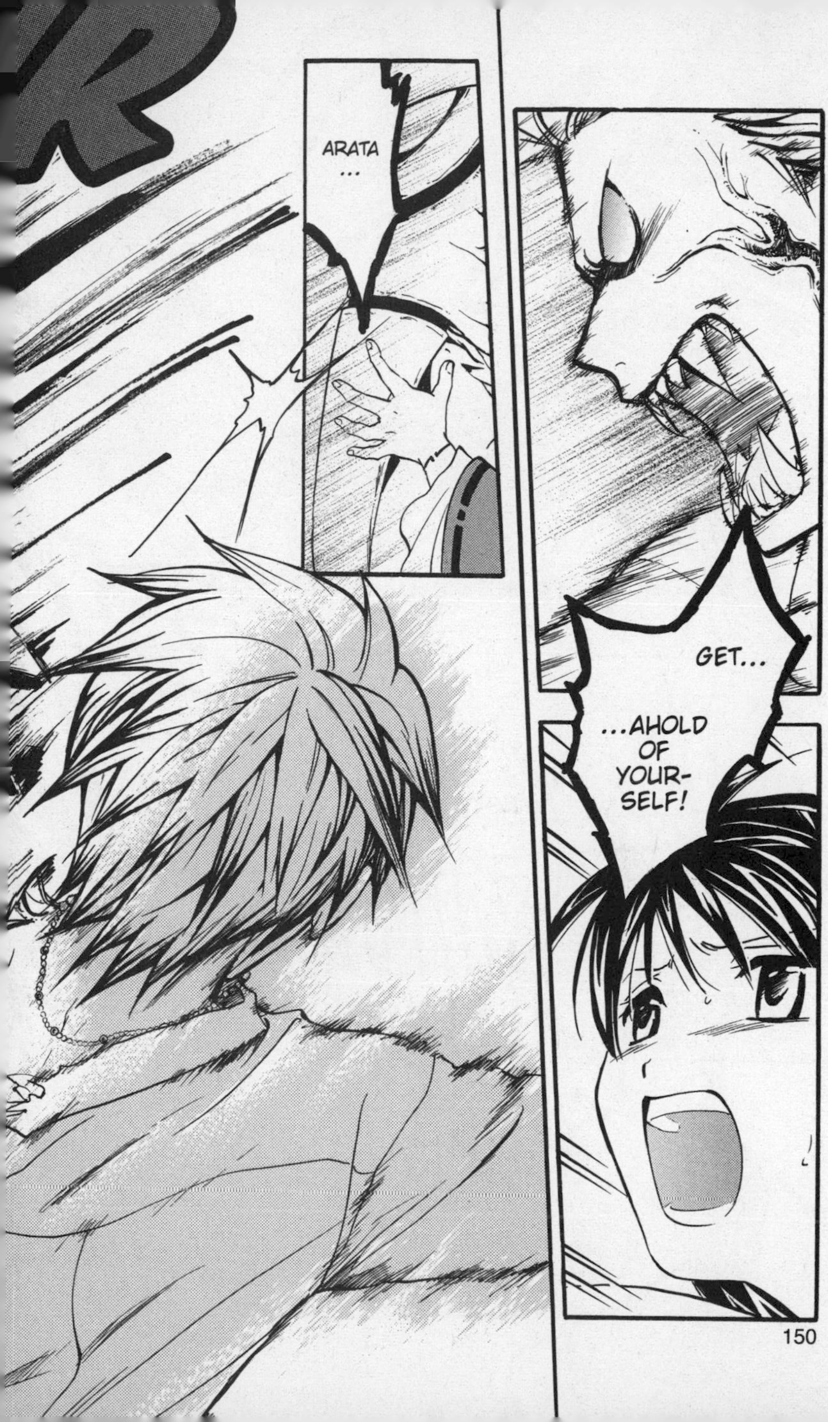
GET...
...AHOLD OF YOURSELF!
ARATA ...

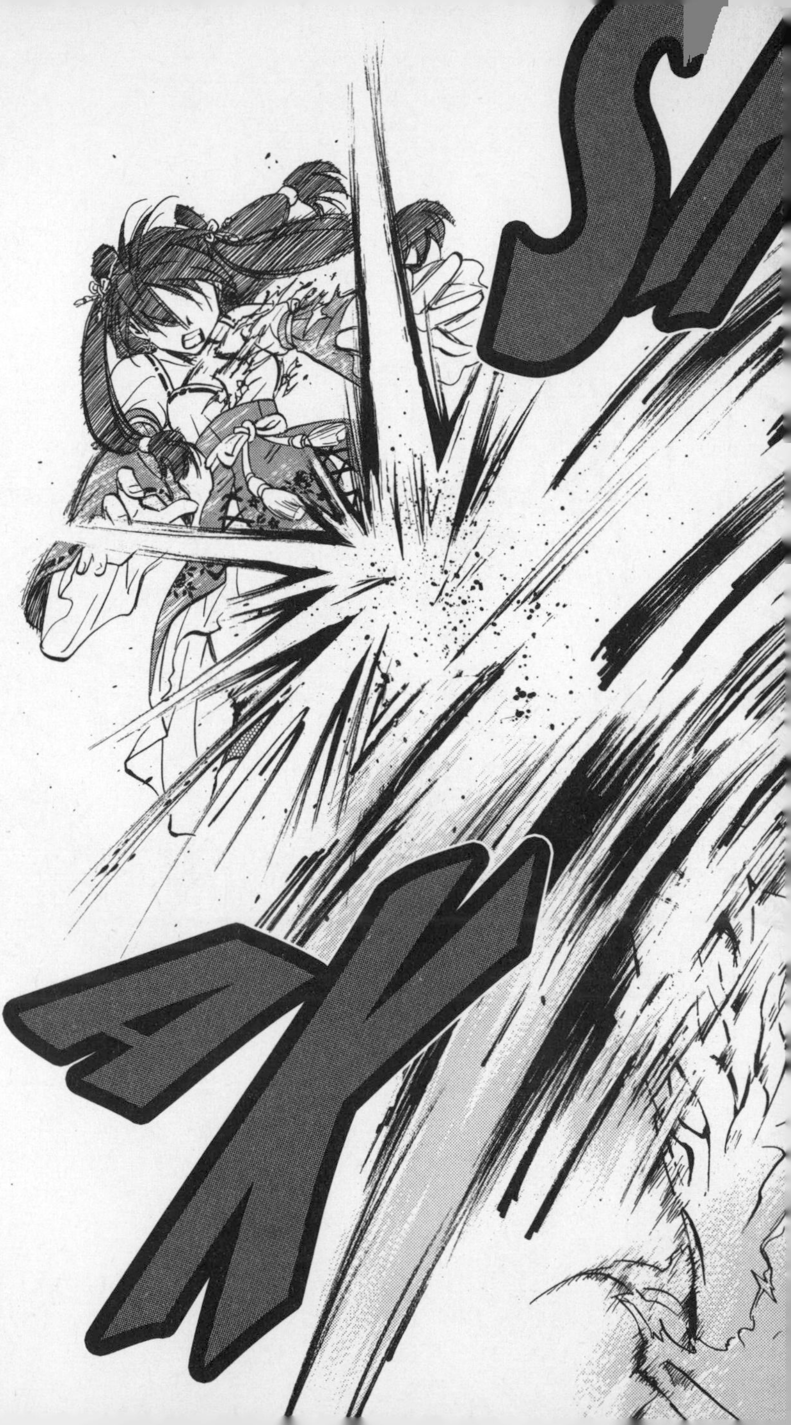

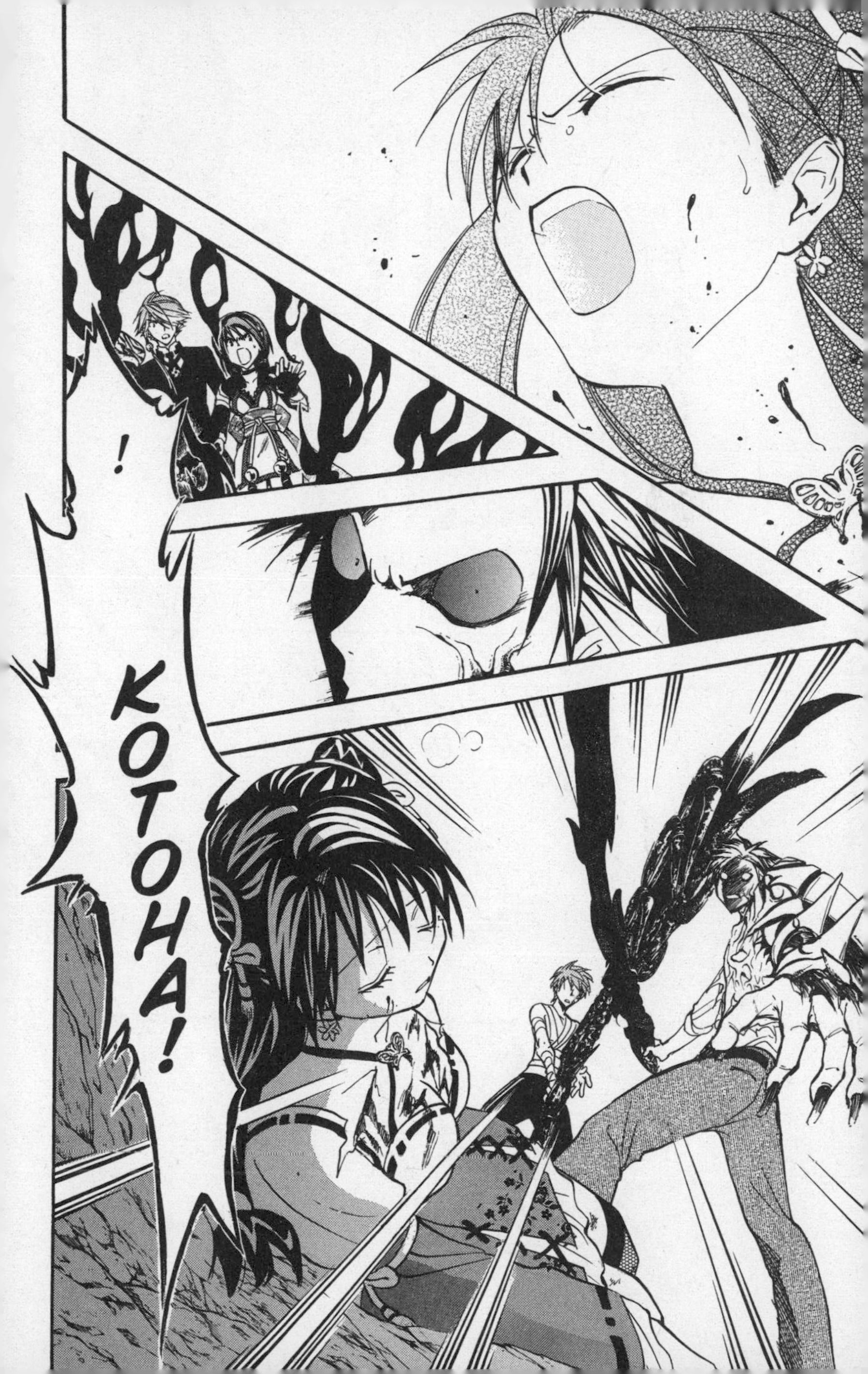
!
KOTOHA!

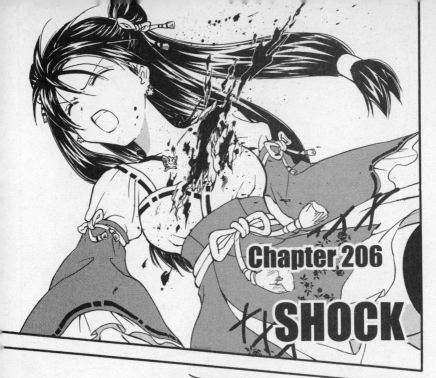

Chapter 206

SHOCK

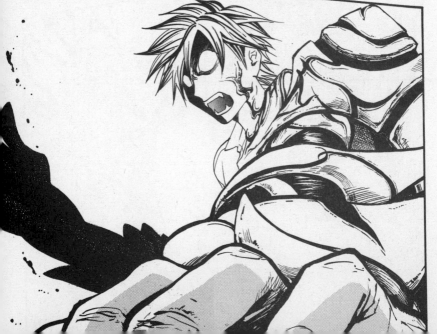

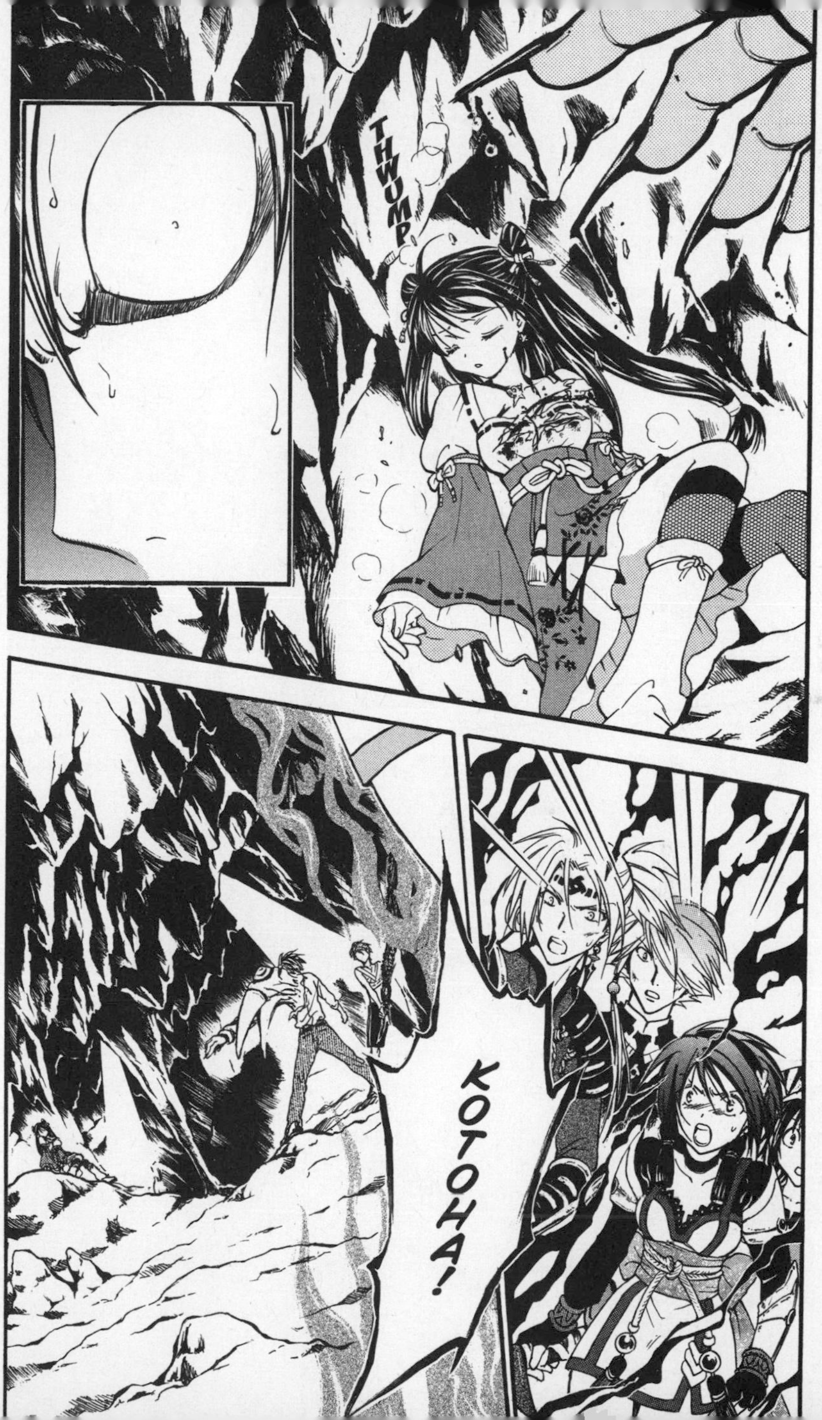
THWUMP
KOTOHA!

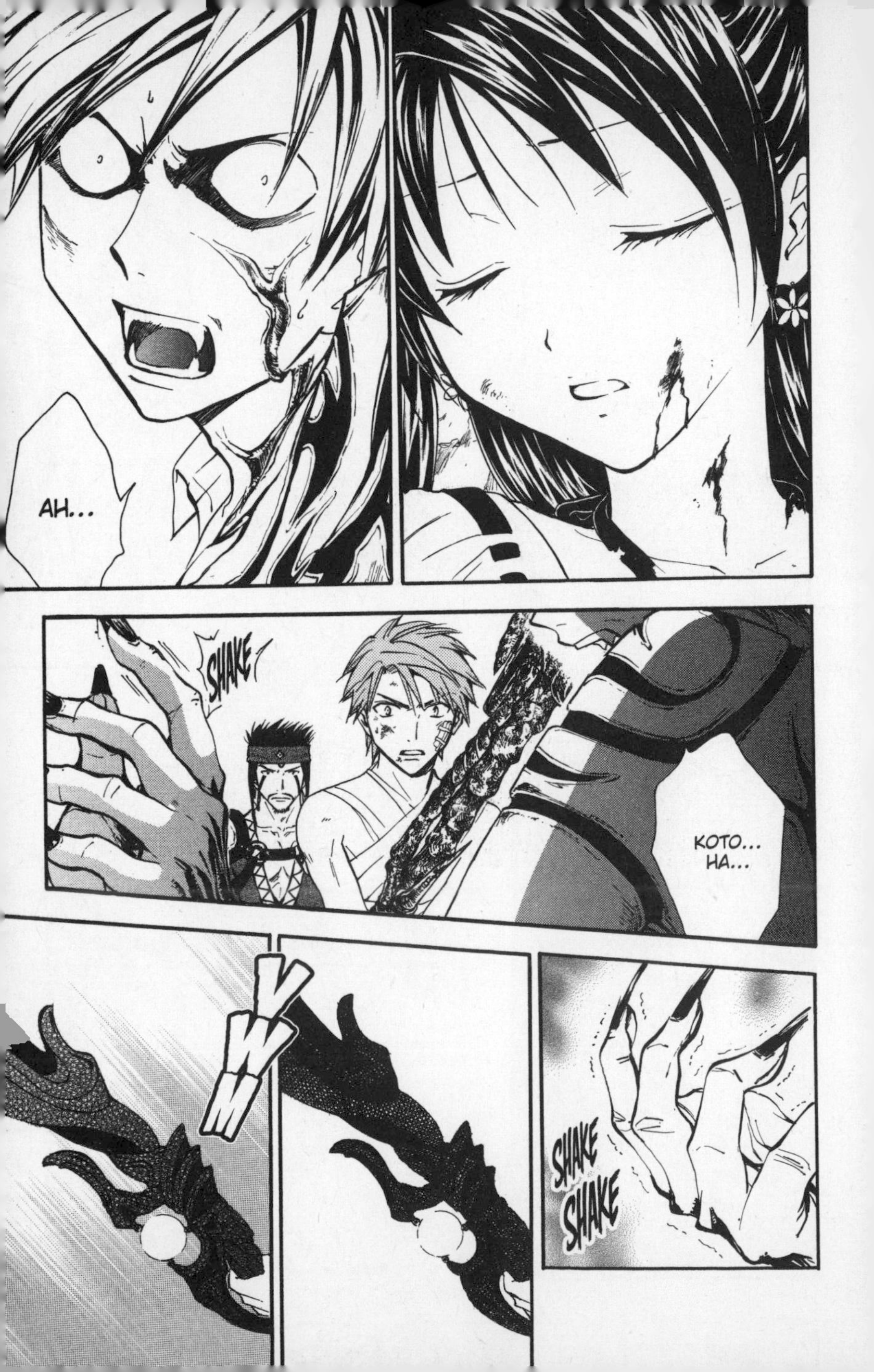
AH...
KOTO... HA...
SHAKE
SHAKE SHAKE

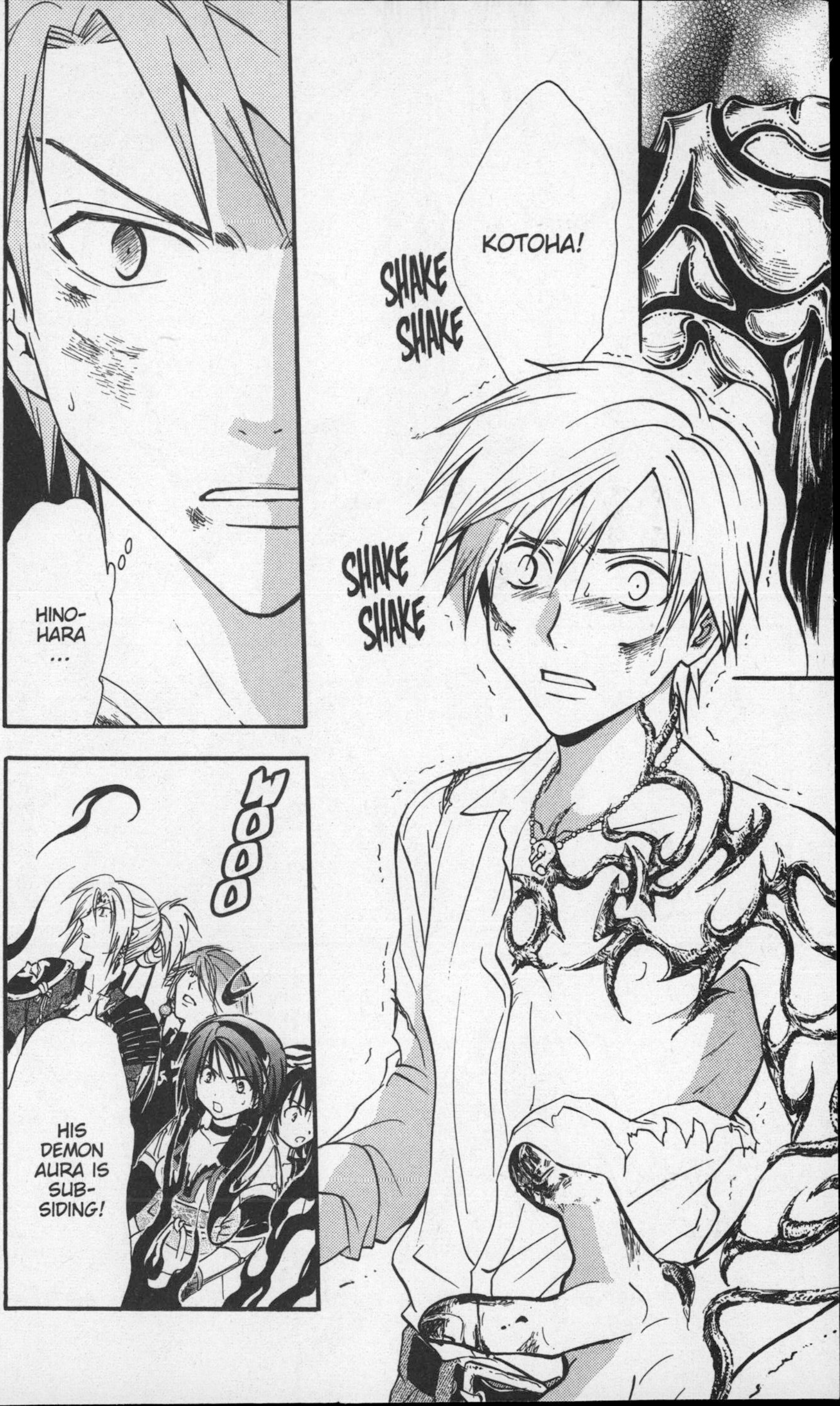

KOTOHA!
SHAKE SHAKE
SHAKE SHAKE
HINO-HARA ...
WOOOO
HIS DEMON AURA IS SUB-SIDING!

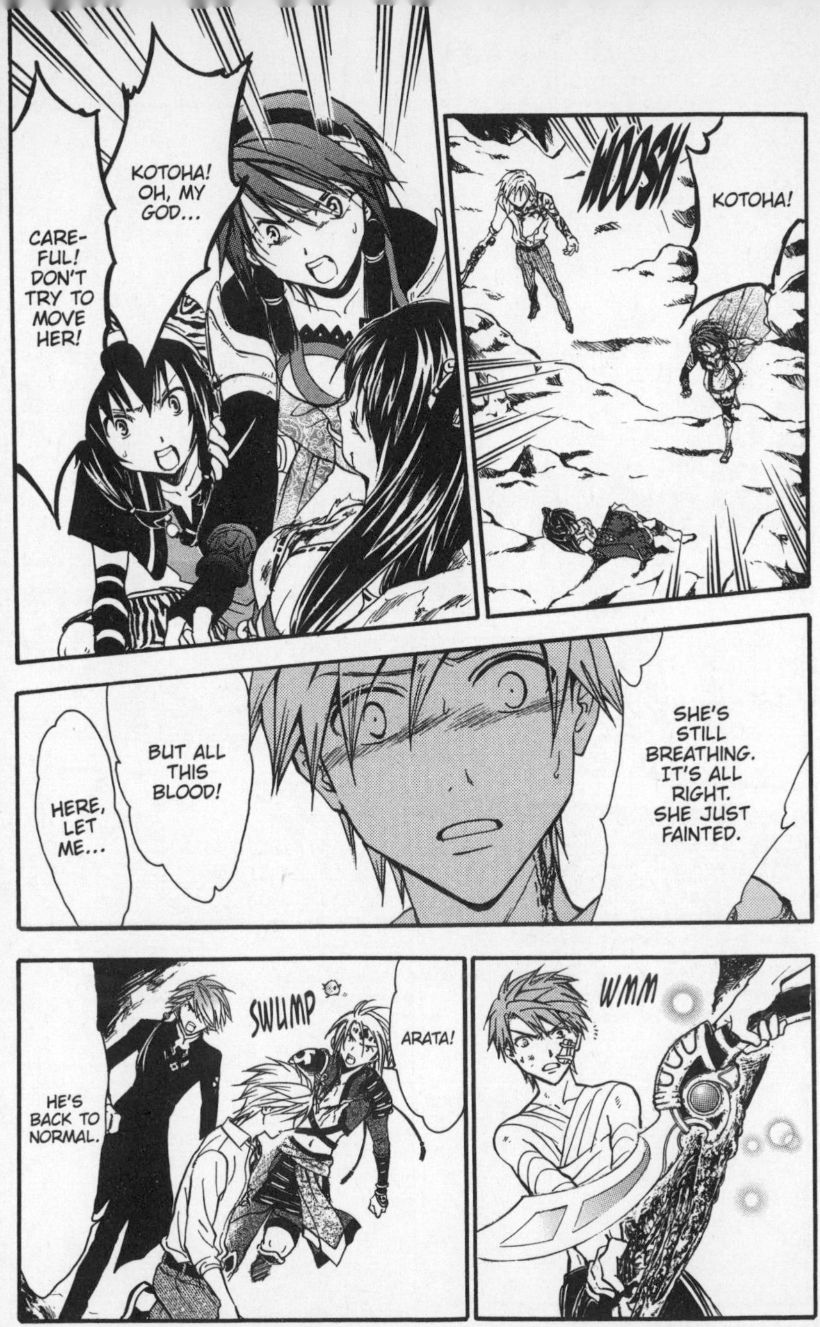
WHOOSH
KOTOHA!
KOTOHA! OH, MY GOD...
CARE-FUL! DON'T TRY TO MOVE HER!
SHE'S STILL BREATHING. IT'S ALL RIGHT. SHE JUST FAINTED.
BUT ALL THIS BLOOD!
HERE, LET ME...
WMM
SWUMP
ARATA!
HE'S BACK TO NORMAL.

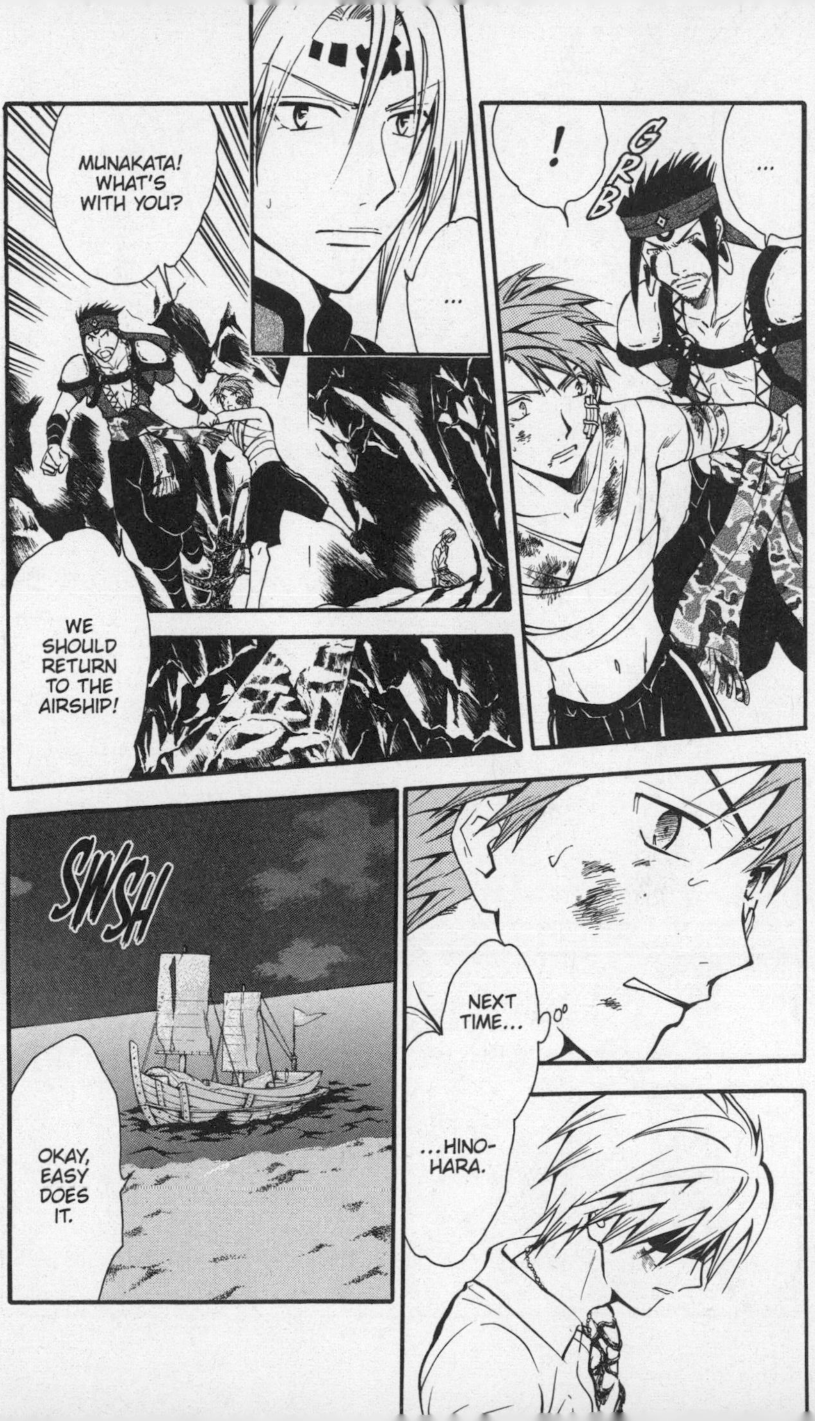
...
GRB
!
...
MUNAKATA! WHAT'S WITH YOU?
WE SHOULD RETURN TO THE AIRSHIP!
NEXT TIME...
...HINO-HARA.
SWSH
OKAY, EASY DOES IT.

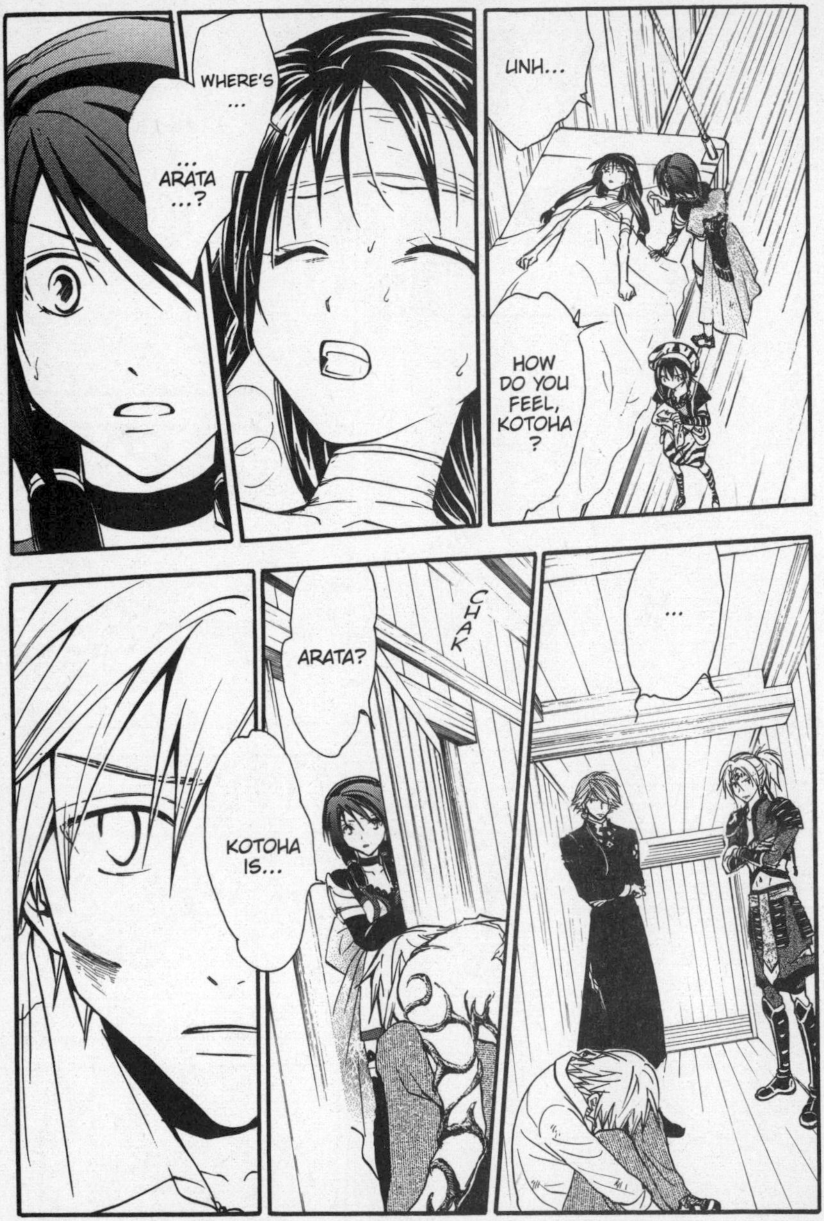
UNH...
HOW DO YOU FEEL, KOTOHA?
WHERE'S ...
... ARATA ...?
...
CHAK
ARATA?
KOTOHA IS...

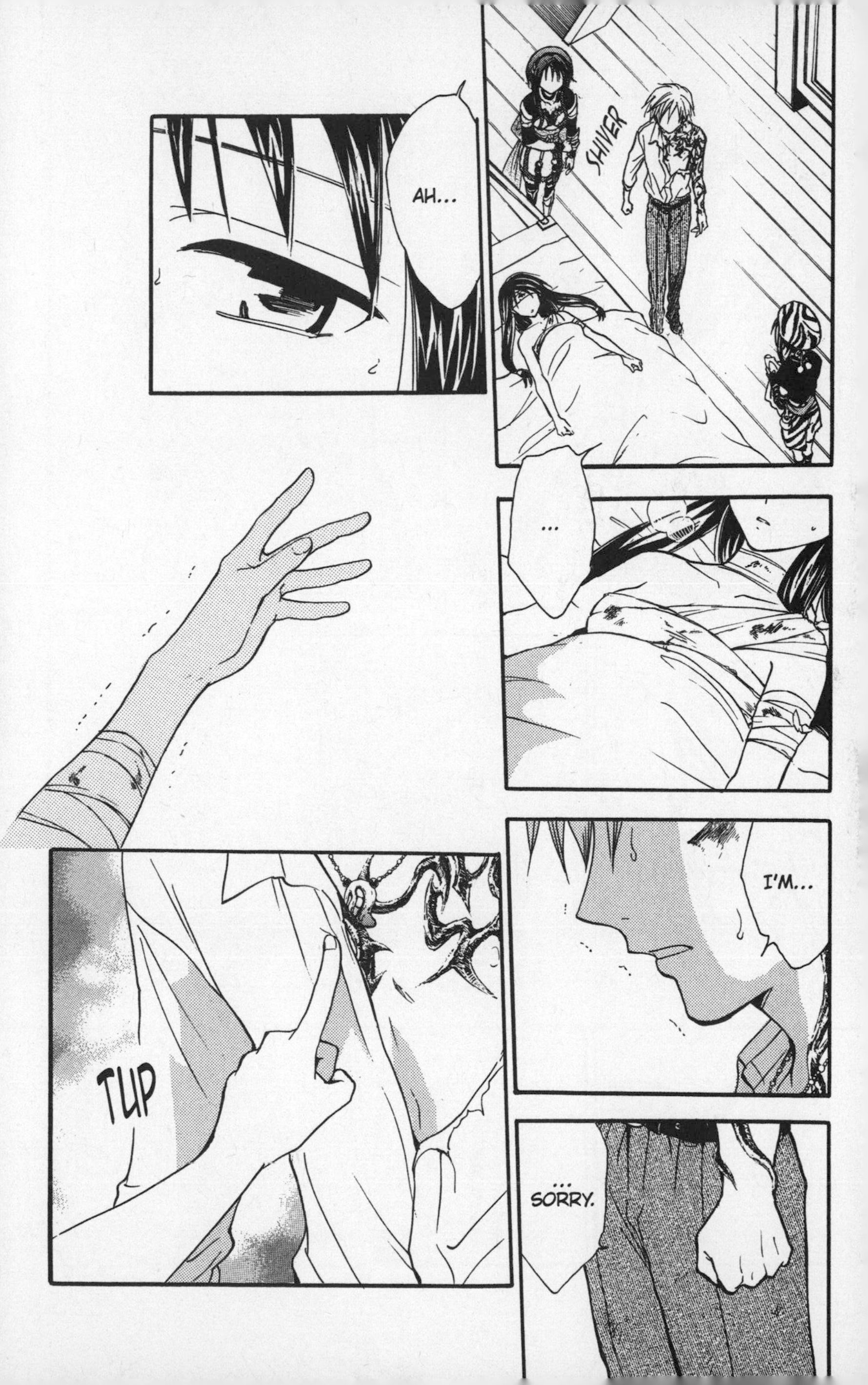
SHIVER
AH...
...
I'M...
TUP
...SORRY.

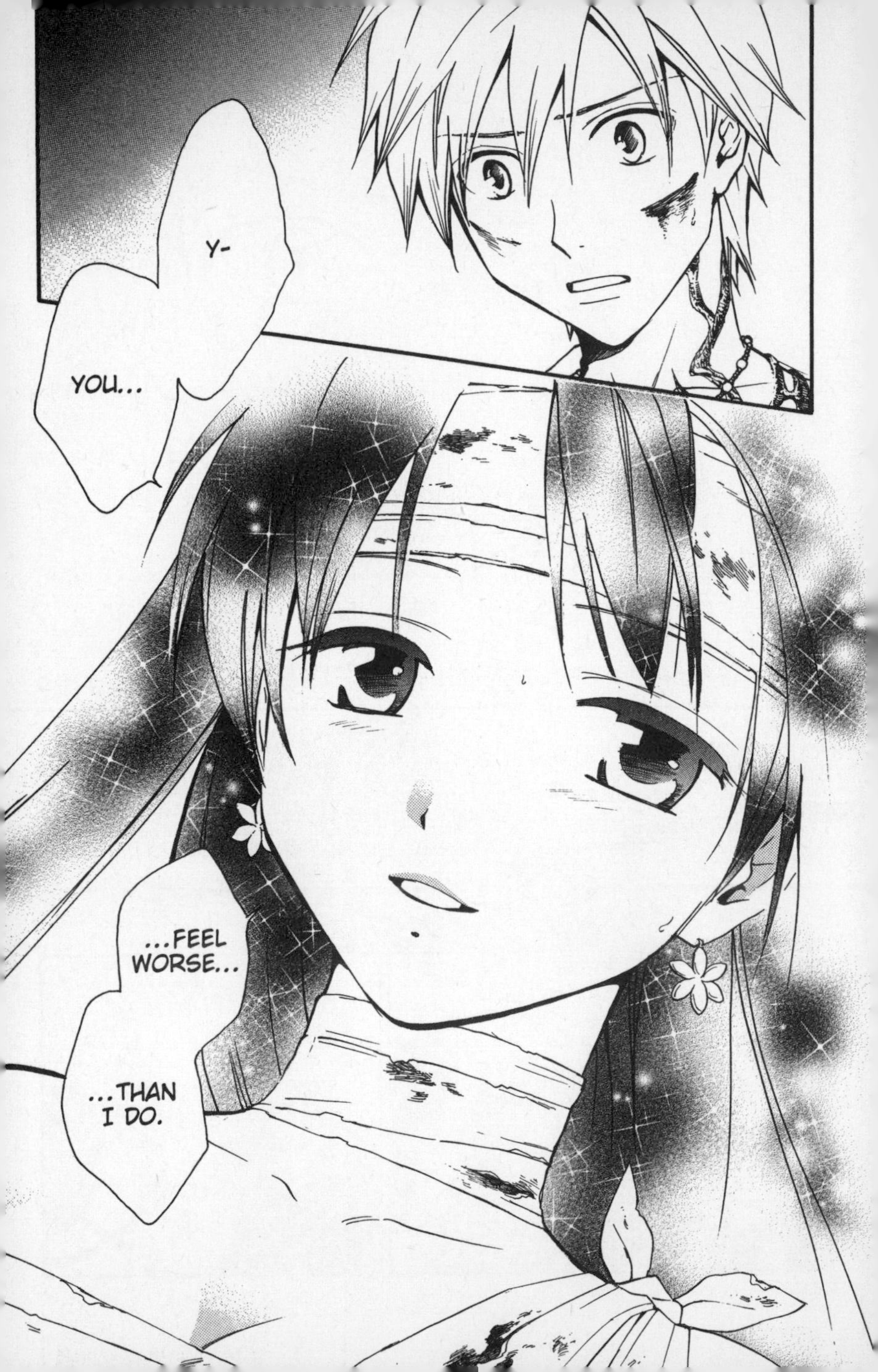
Y-
YOU...
...FEEL WORSE...
...THAN I DO.

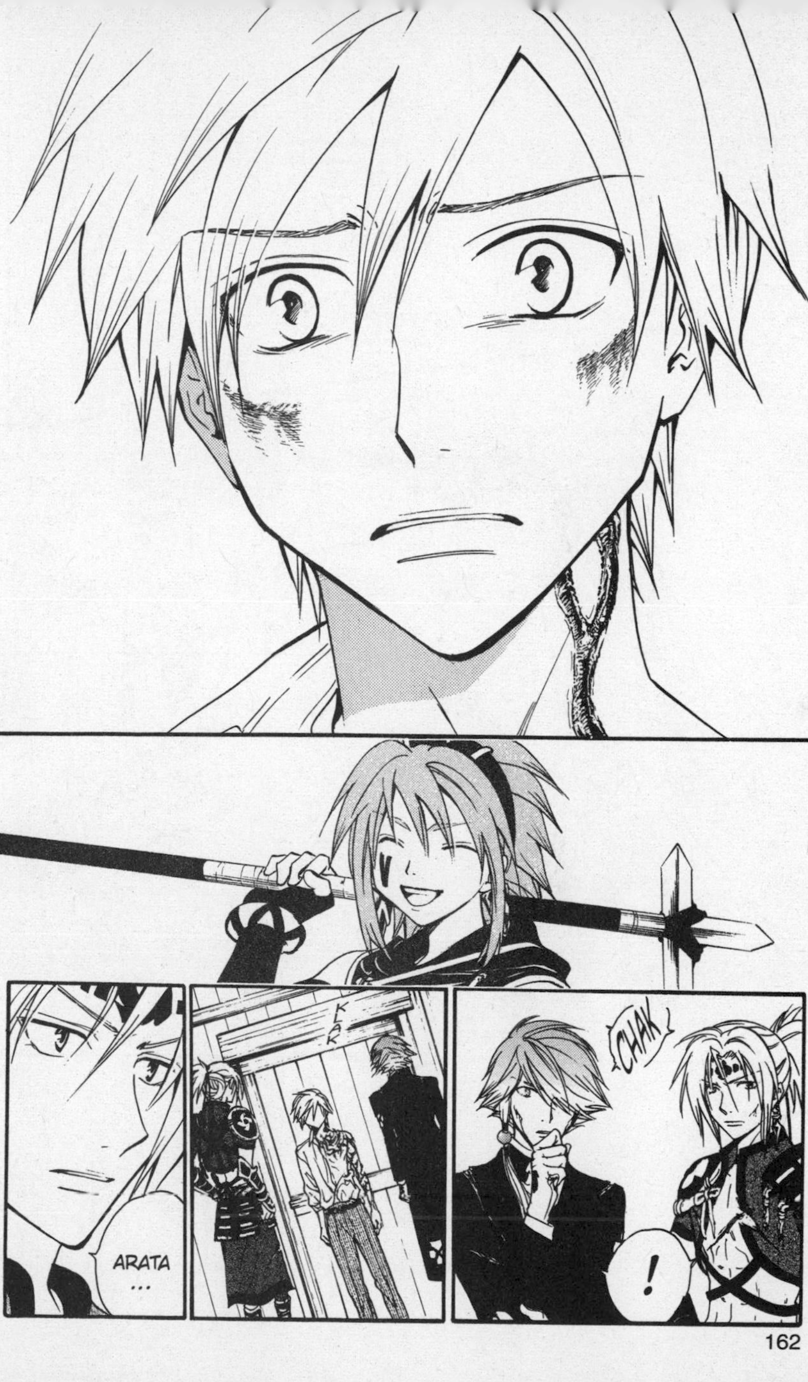
CHAK
!
KLAK
ARATA ...

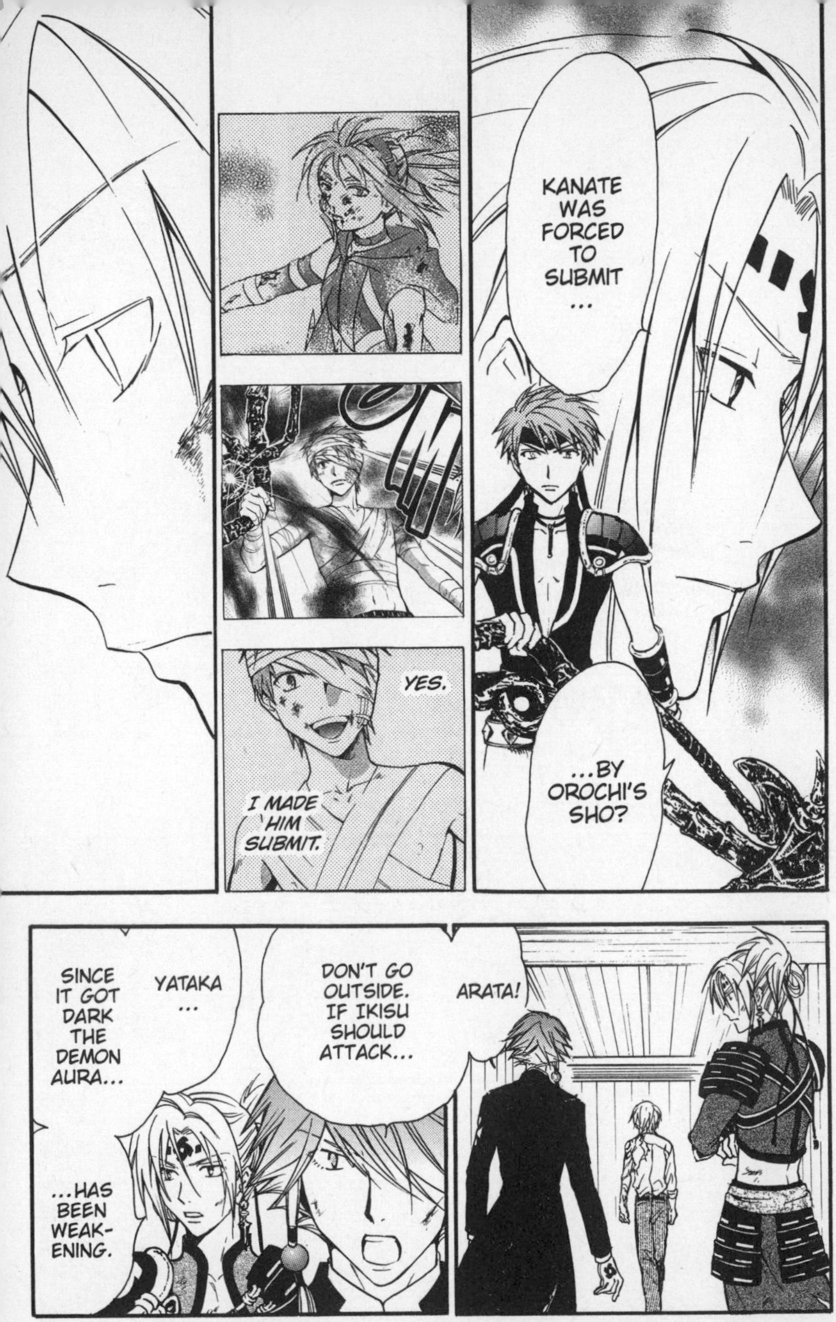
KANATE WAS FORCED TO SUBMIT ...
...BY OROCHI'S SHO?
YES.
I MADE HIM SUBMIT.
ARATA!
DON'T GO OUTSIDE. IF IKISU SHOULD ATTACK...
YATAKA ...
SINCE IT GOT DARK THE DEMON AURA...
...HAS BEEN WEAKENING.

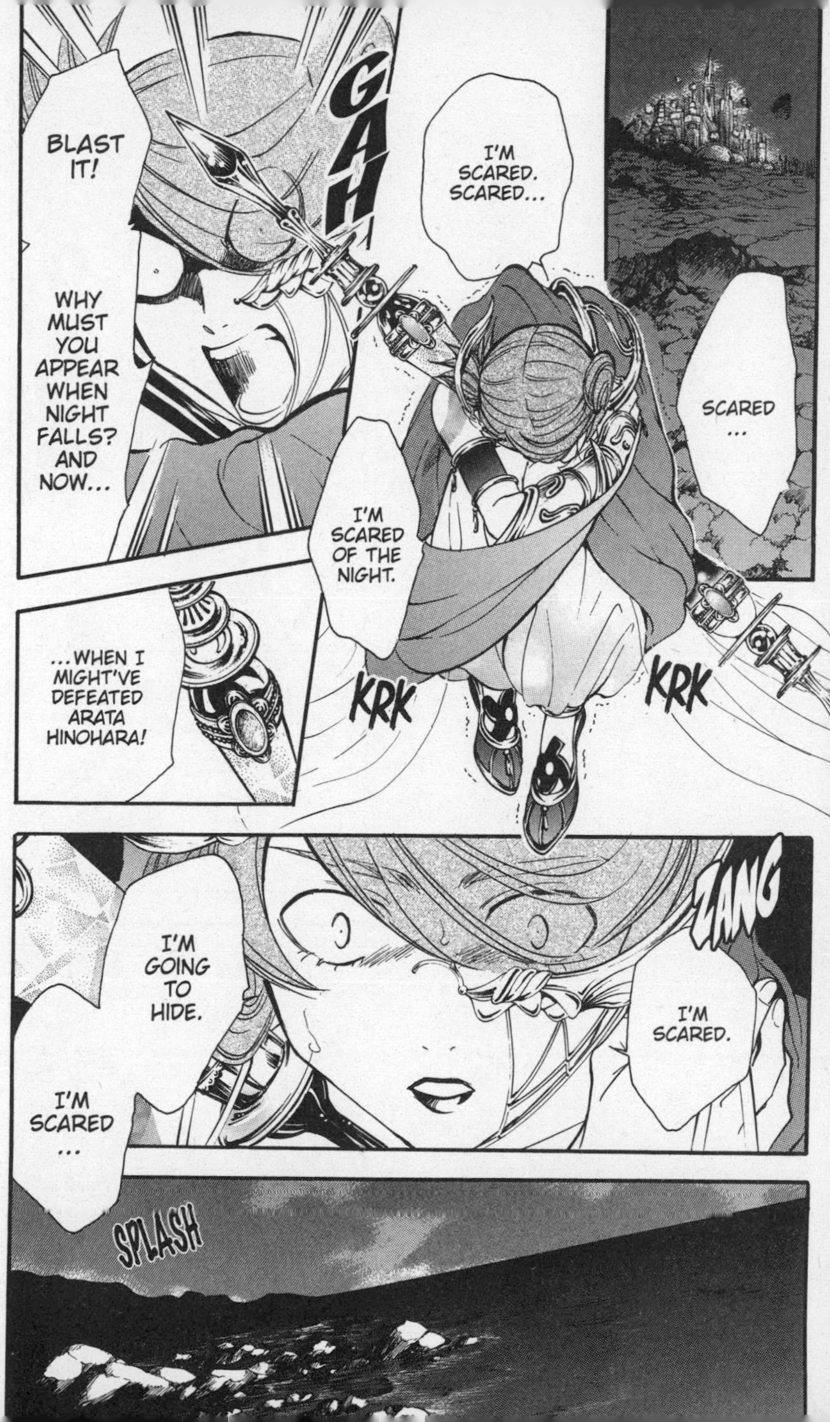
I'M SCARED. SCARED...
SCARED ...
I'M SCARED OF THE NIGHT.
GAH
BLAST IT!
WHY MUST YOU APPEAR WHEN NIGHT FALLS? AND NOW...
...WHEN I MIGHT'VE DEFEATED ARATA HINOHARA!
KRK
KRK
ZANG
I'M SCARED.
I'M GOING TO HIDE.
I'M SCARED ...
SPLASH

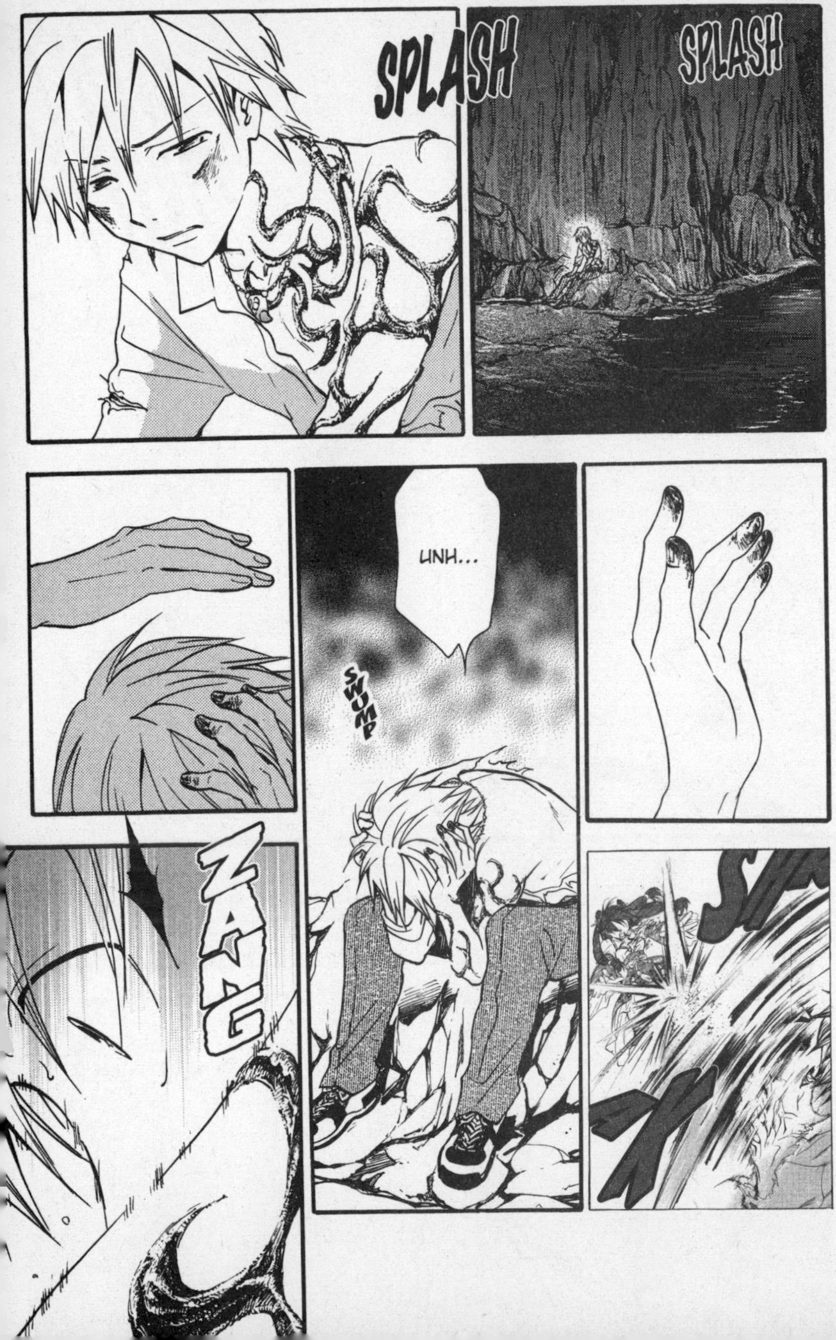
SPLASH
SPLASH
UNH...
SWUMP
ZANG

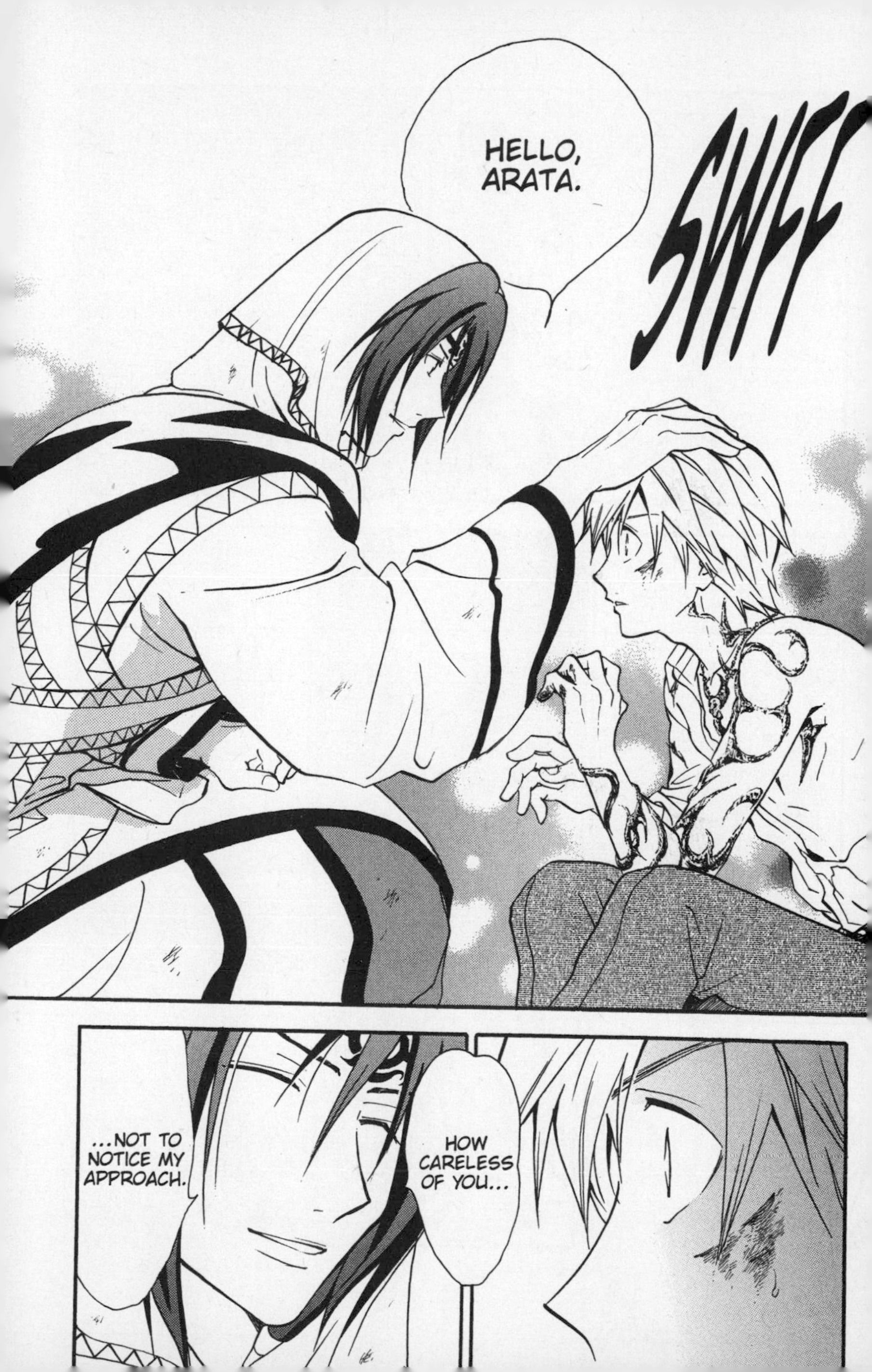
SWFF
HELLO, ARATA.
HOW CARELESS OF YOU...
...NOT TO NOTICE MY APPROACH.

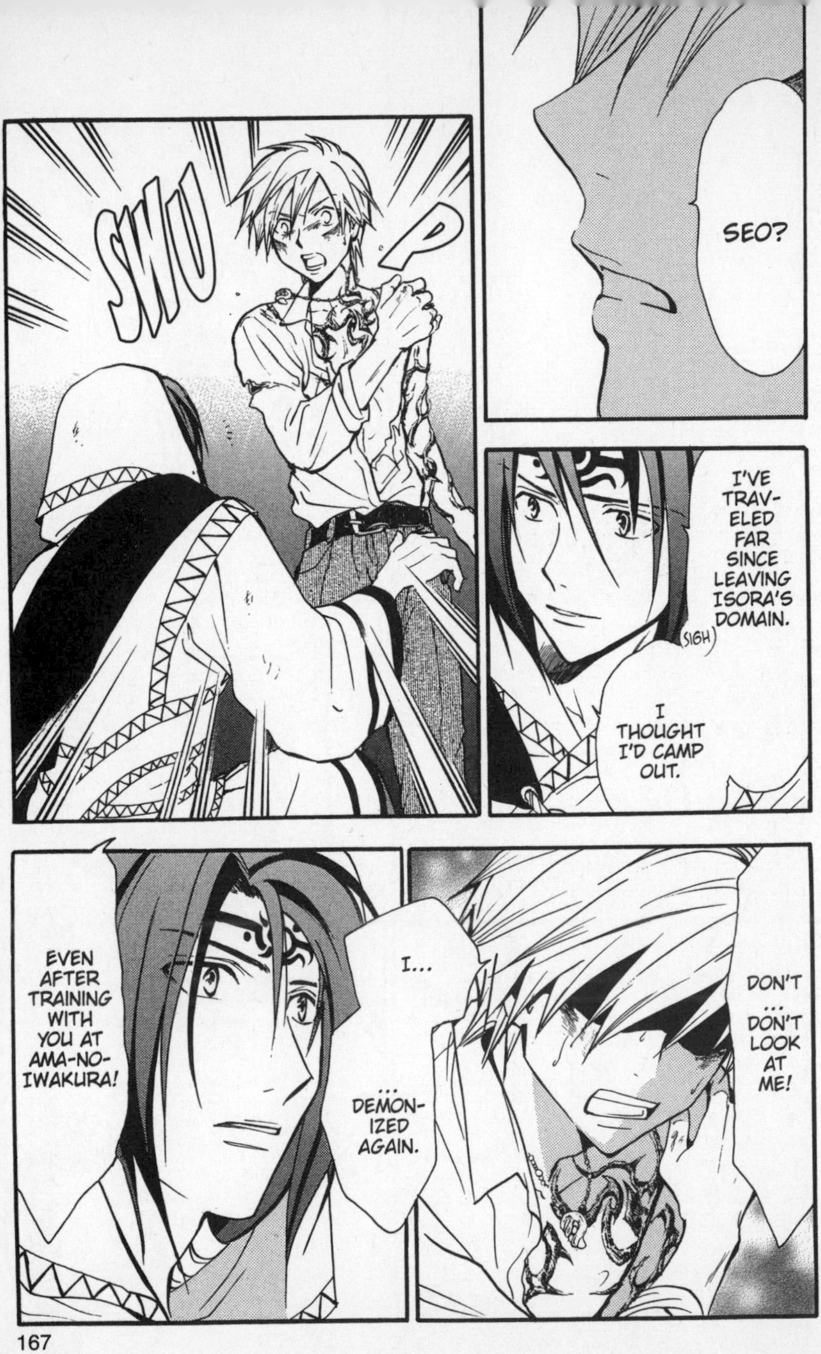
SEO?
I'VE TRAV-ELED FAR SINCE LEAVING ISORA'S DOMAIN.
(SIGH)
I THOUGHT I'D CAMP OUT.
SWOOP
DON'T ... DON'T LOOK AT ME!
I...
... DEMON-IZED AGAIN.
EVEN AFTER TRAINING WITH YOU AT AMA-NO-IWAKURA!

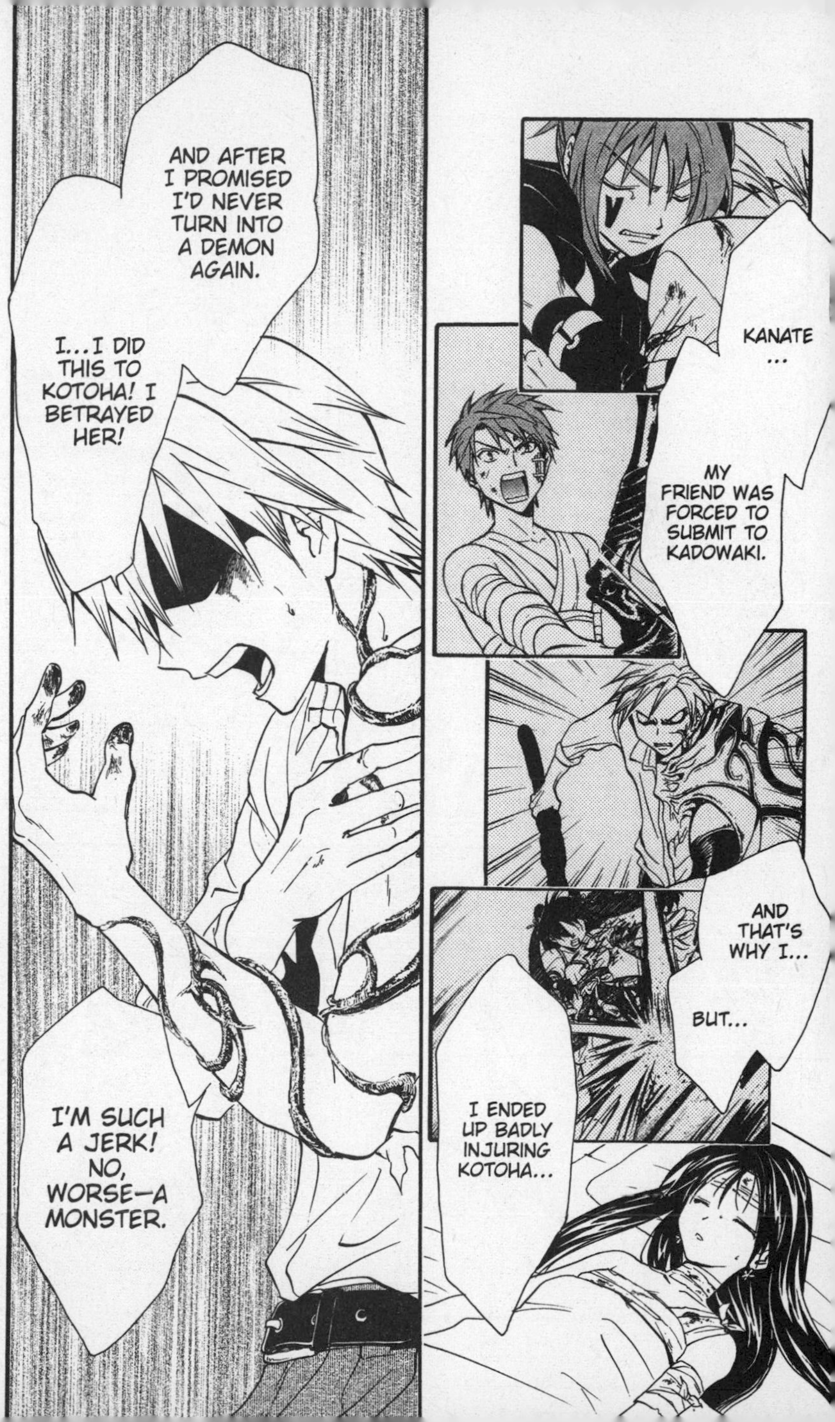
KANATE …
MY FRIEND WAS FORCED TO SUBMIT TO KADOWAKI.
AND THAT'S WHY I…
BUT…
I ENDED UP BADLY INJURING KOTOHA…
AND AFTER I PROMISED I'D NEVER TURN INTO A DEMON AGAIN.
I…I DID THIS TO KOTOHA! I BETRAYED HER!
I'M SUCH A JERK! NO, WORSE—A MONSTER.

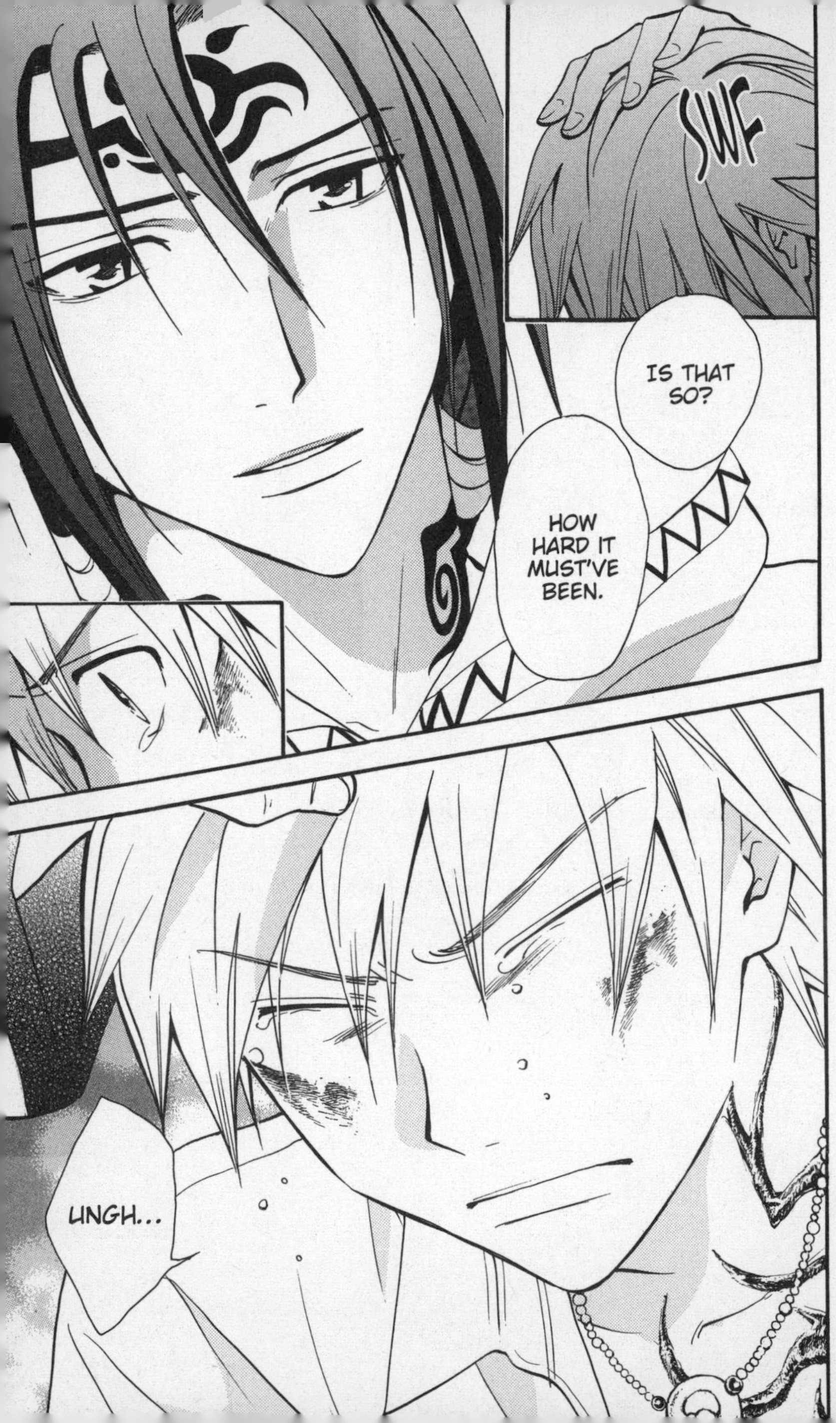
SWF
IS THAT SO?
HOW HARD IT MUST'VE BEEN.
UNGH...

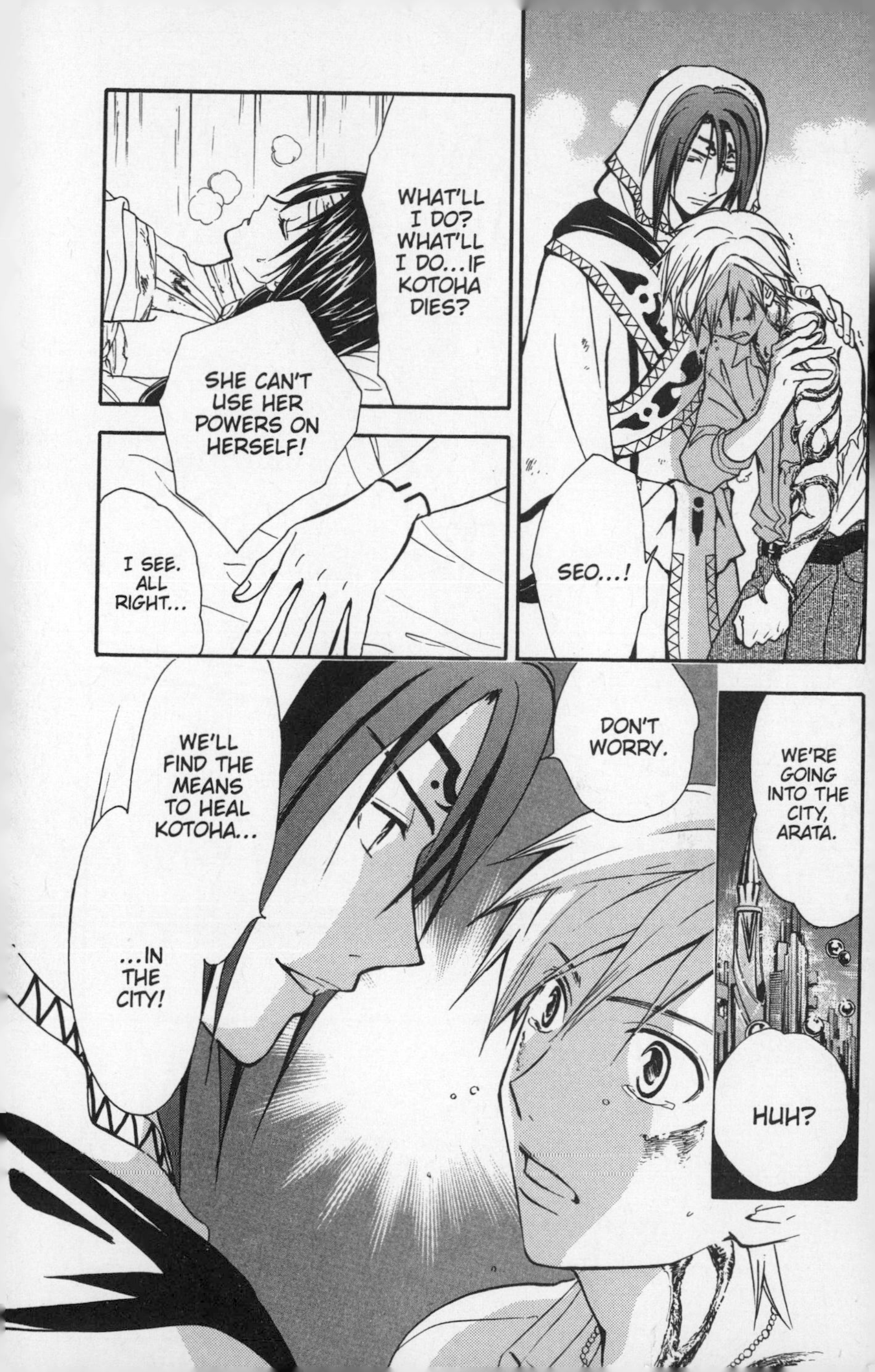
SEO...!
WHAT'LL I DO? WHAT'LL I DO...IF KOTOHA DIES?
SHE CAN'T USE HER POWERS ON HERSELF!
I SEE. ALL RIGHT...
WE'RE GOING INTO THE CITY, ARATA.
HUH?
DON'T WORRY.
WE'LL FIND THE MEANS TO HEAL KOTOHA...
...IN THE CITY!

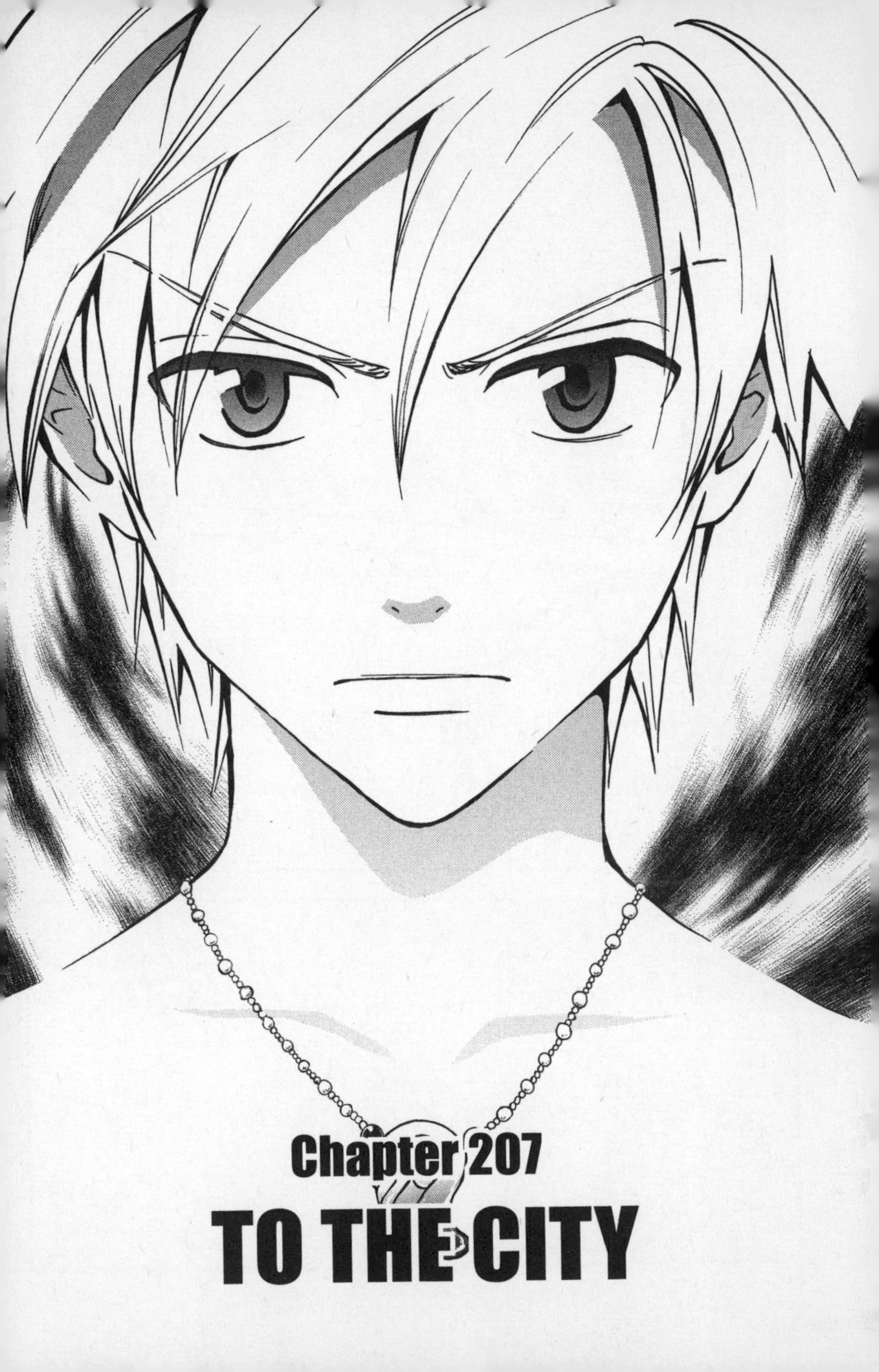
Chapter 207
TO THE CITY

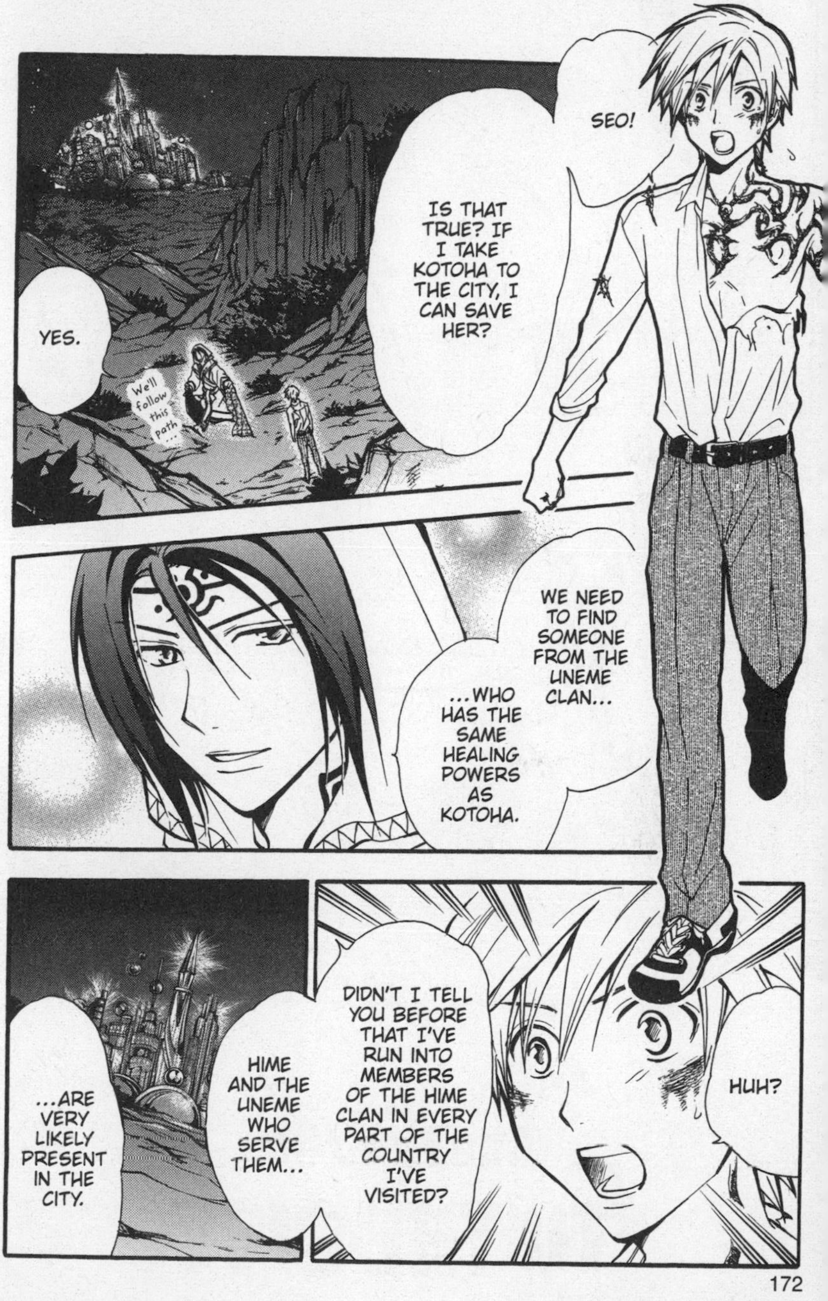
SEO!
IS THAT TRUE? IF I TAKE KOTOHA TO THE CITY, I CAN SAVE HER?
YES.
We'll follow this path...
WE NEED TO FIND SOMEONE FROM THE UNEME CLAN...
...WHO HAS THE SAME HEALING POWERS AS KOTOHA.
HUH?
DIDN'T I TELL YOU BEFORE THAT I'VE RUN INTO MEMBERS OF THE HIME CLAN IN EVERY PART OF THE COUNTRY I'VE VISITED?
HIME AND THE UNEME WHO SERVE THEM...
...ARE VERY LIKELY PRESENT IN THE CITY.

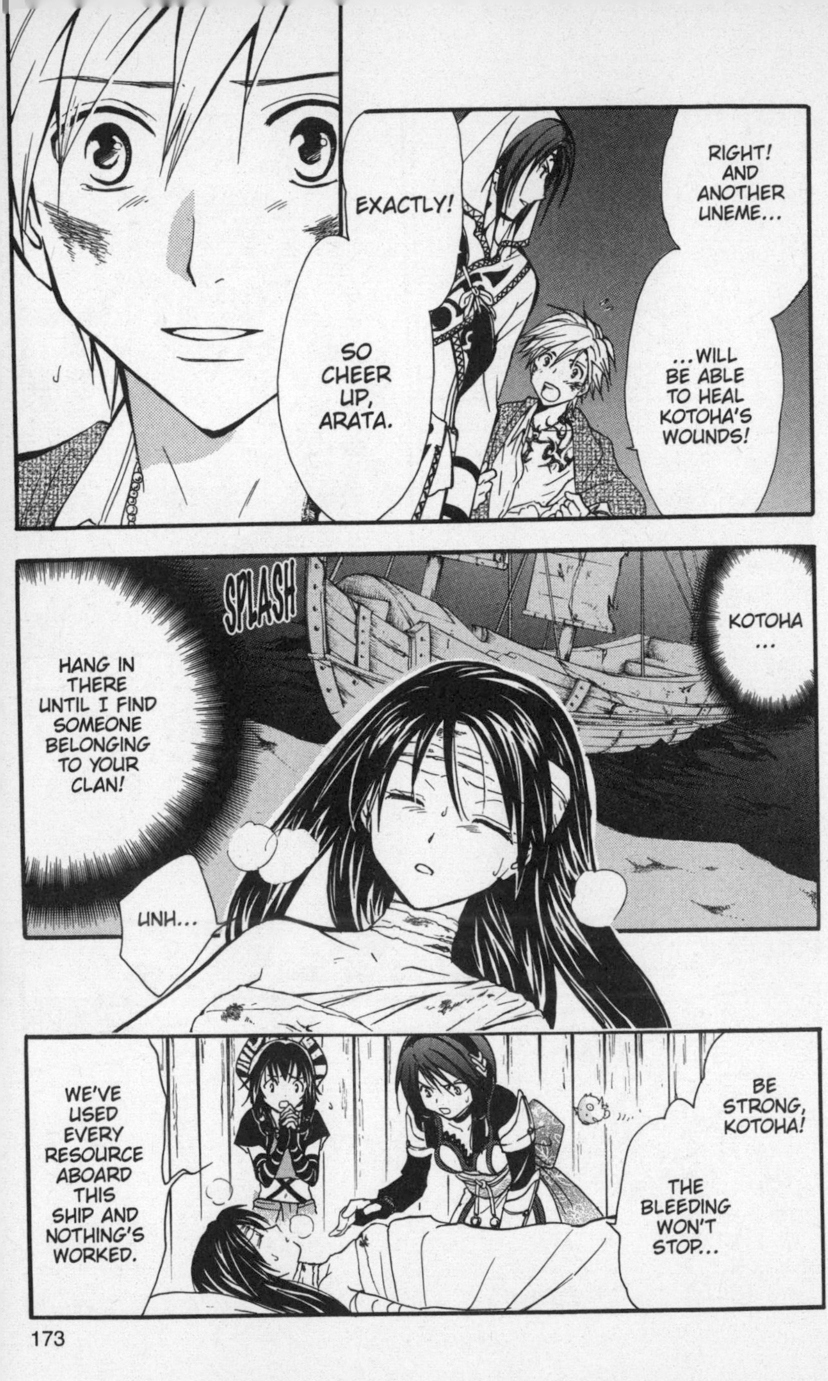
RIGHT! AND ANOTHER UNEME...
...WILL BE ABLE TO HEAL KOTOHA'S WOUNDS!
EXACTLY!
SO CHEER UP, ARATA.
KOTOHA...
SPLASH
HANG IN THERE UNTIL I FIND SOMEONE BELONGING TO YOUR CLAN!
UNH...
BE STRONG, KOTOHA!
THE BLEEDING WON'T STOP...
WE'VE USED EVERY RESOURCE ABOARD THIS SHIP AND NOTHING'S WORKED.

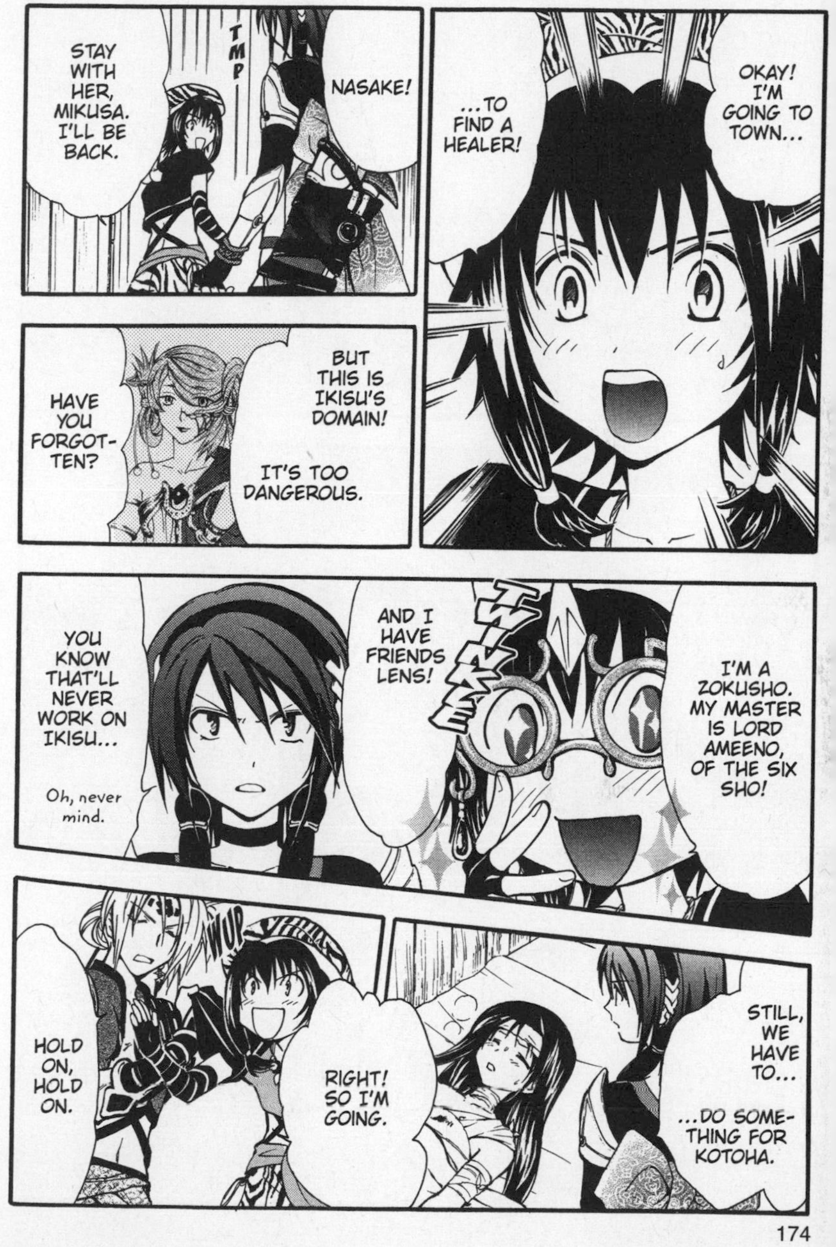
OKAY! I'M GOING TO TOWN...
...TO FIND A HEALER!
NASAKE!
TMP
STAY WITH HER, MIKUSA. I'LL BE BACK.
BUT THIS IS IKISU'S DOMAIN!
IT'S TOO DANGEROUS.
HAVE YOU FORGOTTEN?
I'M A ZOKUSHO. MY MASTER IS LORD AMEENO, OF THE SIX SHO!
AND I HAVE FRIENDS LENS!
TWINKLE
YOU KNOW THAT'LL NEVER WORK ON IKISU...
Oh, never mind.
STILL, WE HAVE TO...
...DO SOMETHING FOR KOTOHA.
RIGHT! SO I'M GOING.
WUP
HOLD ON, HOLD ON.

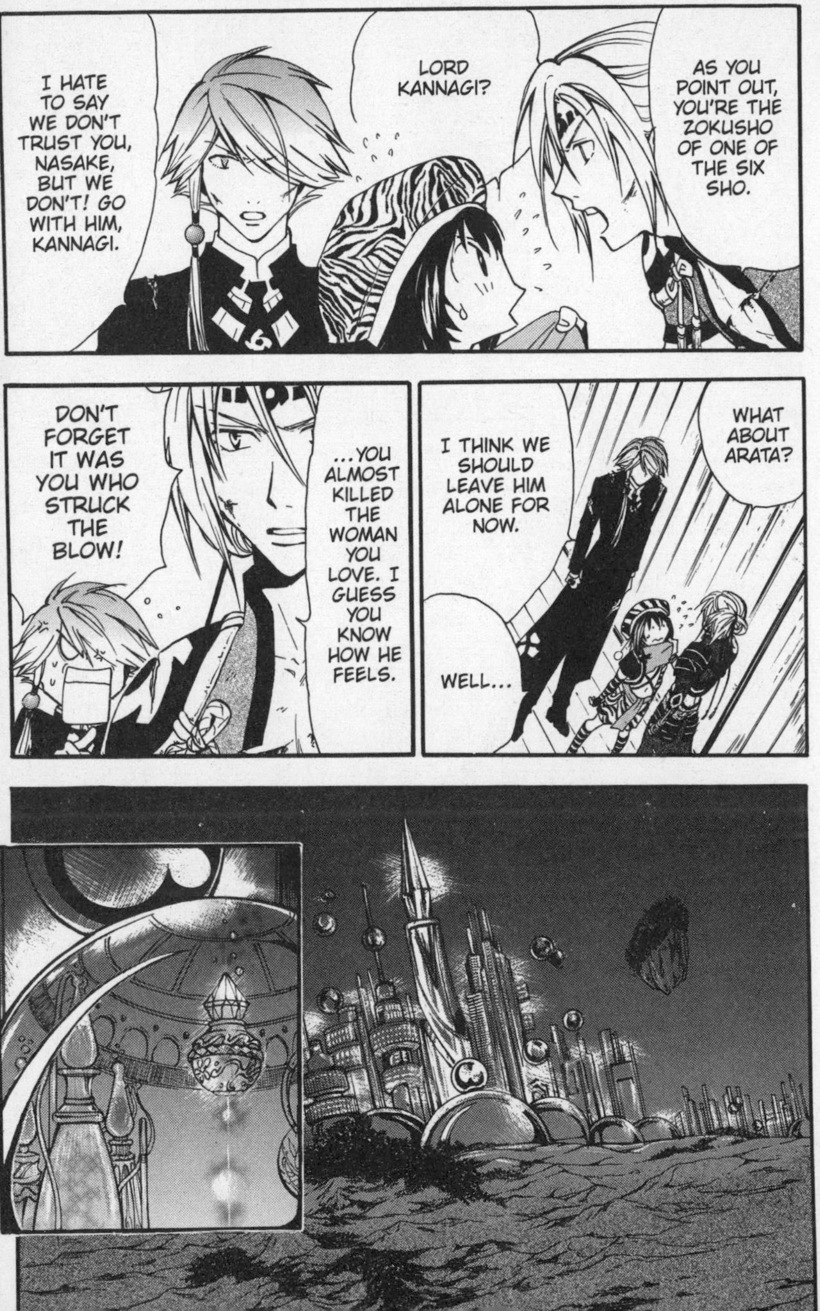
AS YOU POINT OUT, YOU'RE THE ZOKUSHO OF ONE OF THE SIX SHO.
LORD KANNAGI?
I HATE TO SAY WE DON'T TRUST YOU, NASAKE, BUT WE DON'T! GO WITH HIM, KANNAGI.
WHAT ABOUT ARATA?
I THINK WE SHOULD LEAVE HIM ALONE FOR NOW.
WELL...
...YOU ALMOST KILLED THE WOMAN YOU LOVE. I GUESS YOU KNOW HOW HE FEELS.
DON'T FORGET IT WAS YOU WHO STRUCK THE BLOW!

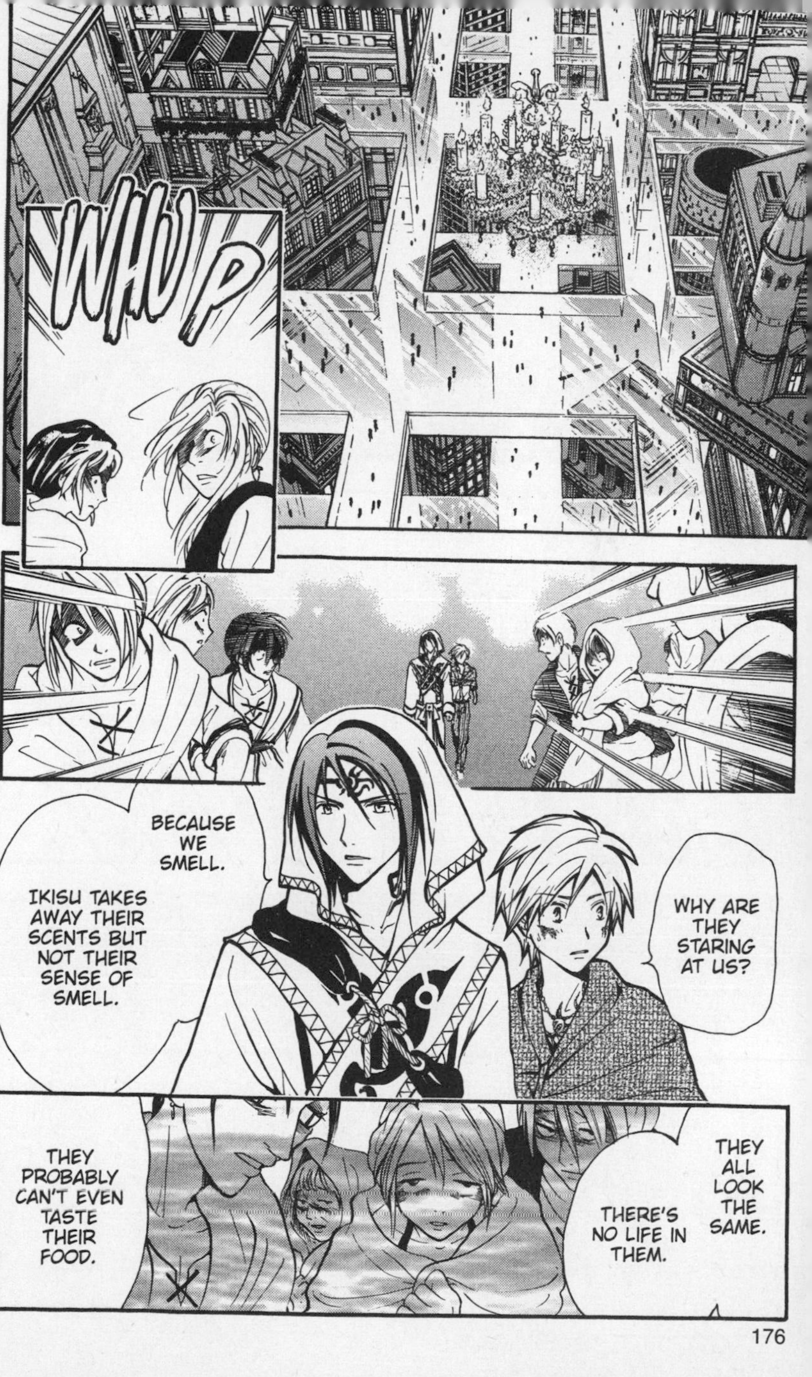
WHUP
WHY ARE THEY STARING AT US?
BECAUSE WE SMELL.
IKISU TAKES AWAY THEIR SCENTS BUT NOT THEIR SENSE OF SMELL.
THEY ALL LOOK THE SAME.
THERE'S NO LIFE IN THEM.
THEY PROBABLY CAN'T EVEN TASTE THEIR FOOD.

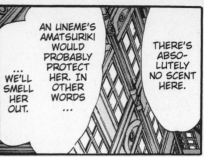

THERE'S ABSOLUTELY NO SCENT HERE.
AN UNEME'S AMATSURIKI WOULD PROBABLY PROTECT HER. IN OTHER WORDS...
...WE'LL SMELL HER OUT.
SO WE'RE LOOKING FOR SOMEONE... ODOROUS?
YES! HOW'S YOUR NOSE, ARATA?
...
ARATA?
SEO...
AREN'T YOU DISAPPOINTED THAT I DEMONIZED?
I FEEL WRETCHED FOR HURTING KOTOHA.
BUT...

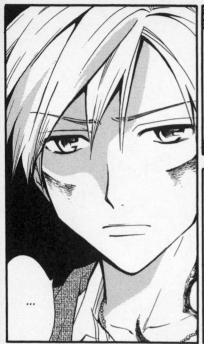

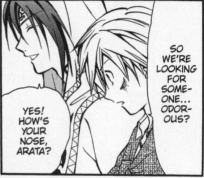

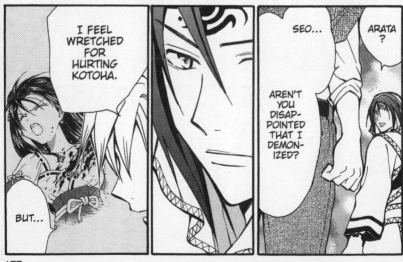

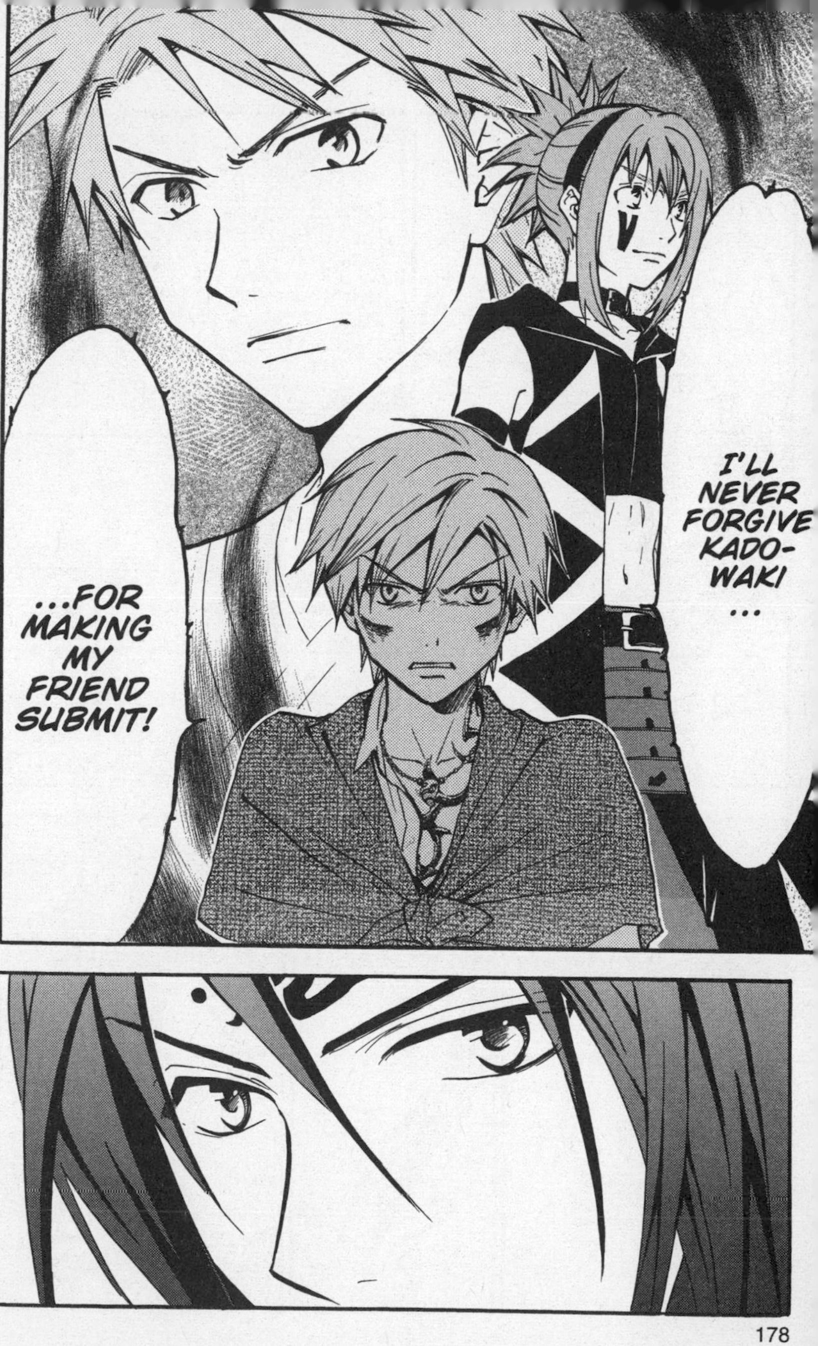
I'LL NEVER FORGIVE KADO-WAKI ...
...FOR MAKING MY FRIEND SUBMIT!

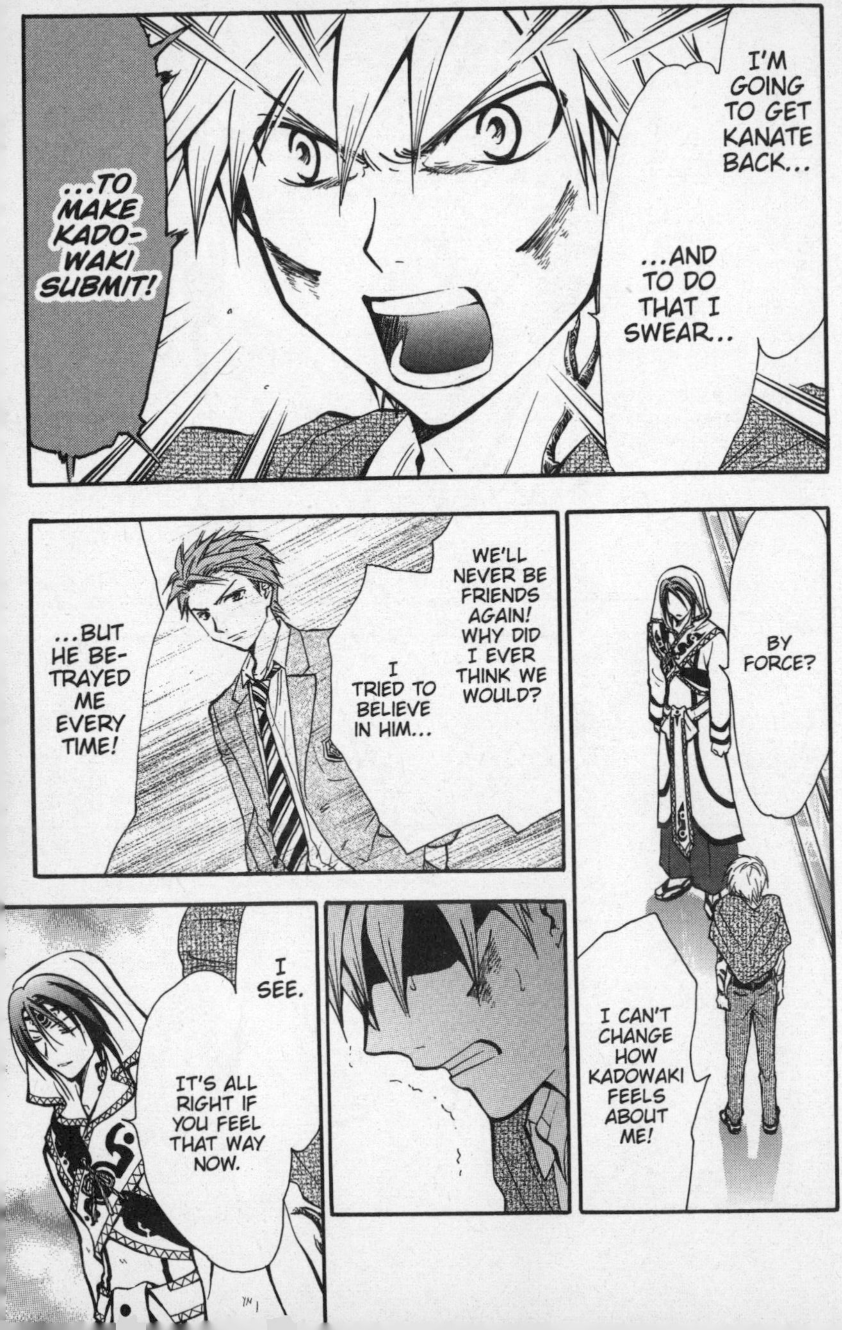
I'M GOING TO GET KANATE BACK...
...AND TO DO THAT I SWEAR...
...TO MAKE KADO-WAKI SUBMIT!
BY FORCE?
I CAN'T CHANGE HOW KADOWAKI FEELS ABOUT ME!
WE'LL NEVER BE FRIENDS AGAIN! WHY DID I EVER THINK WE WOULD?
I TRIED TO BELIEVE IN HIM...
...BUT HE BE-TRAYED ME EVERY TIME!
I SEE.
IT'S ALL RIGHT IF YOU FEEL THAT WAY NOW.

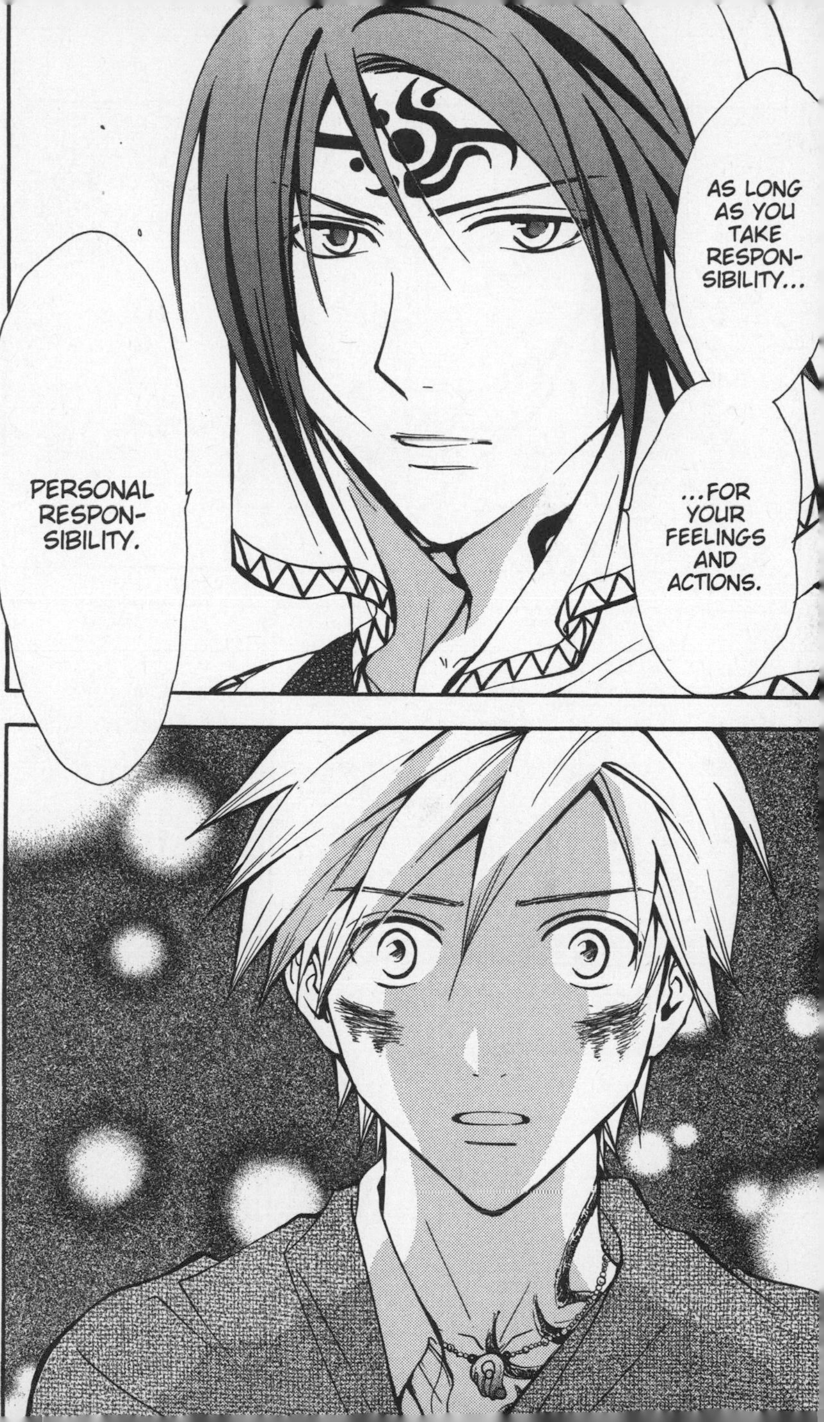
AS LONG AS YOU TAKE RESPON-SIBILITY...
...FOR YOUR FEELINGS AND ACTIONS.
PERSONAL RESPON-SIBILITY.

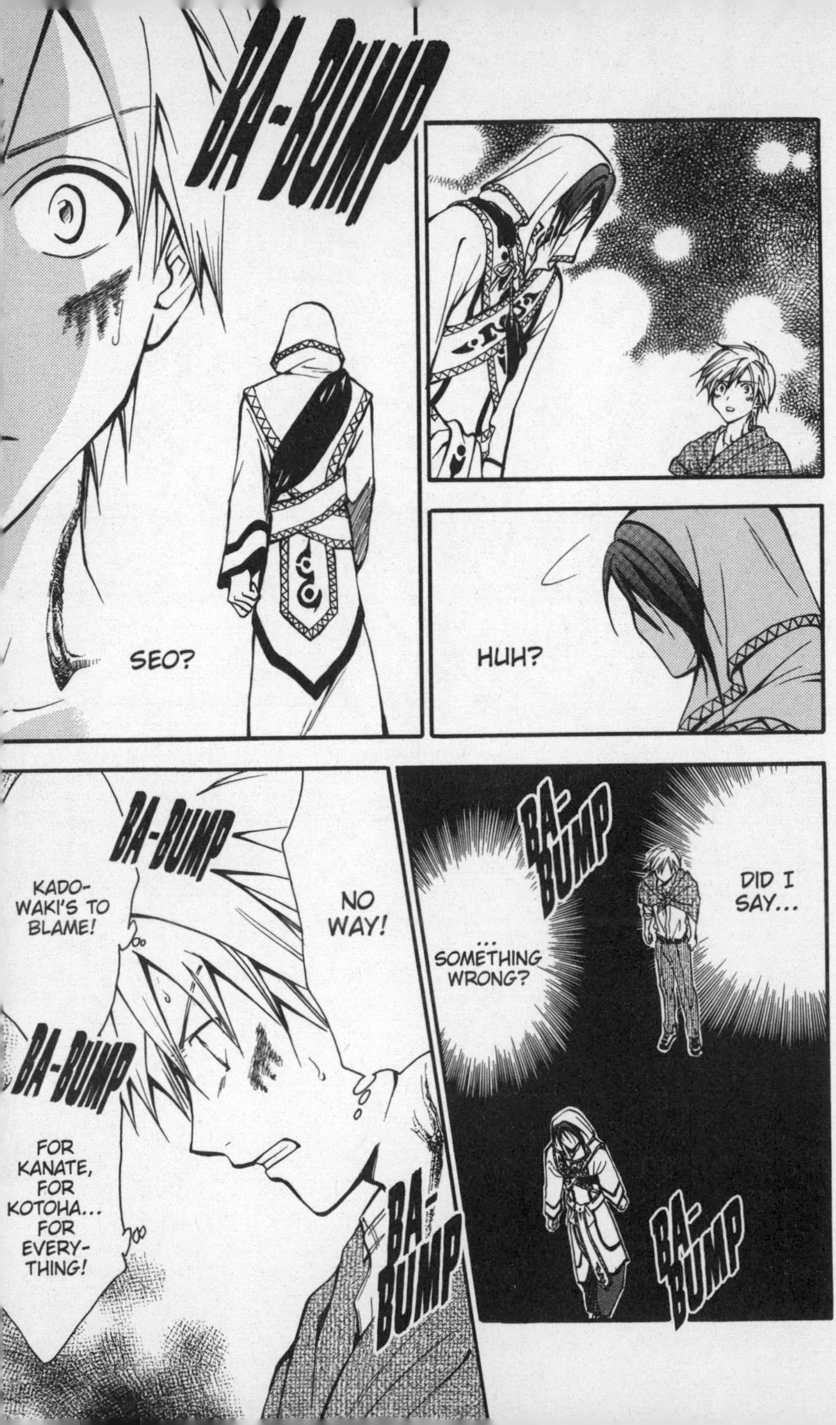
HUH?
BA-BUMP
SEO?
DID I SAY...
BA-BUMP
...SOMETHING WRONG?
BA-BUMP
NO WAY!
BA-BUMP
KADO-WAKI'S TO BLAME!
BA-BUMP
FOR KANATE, FOR KOTOHA... FOR EVERY-THING!
BA-BUMP

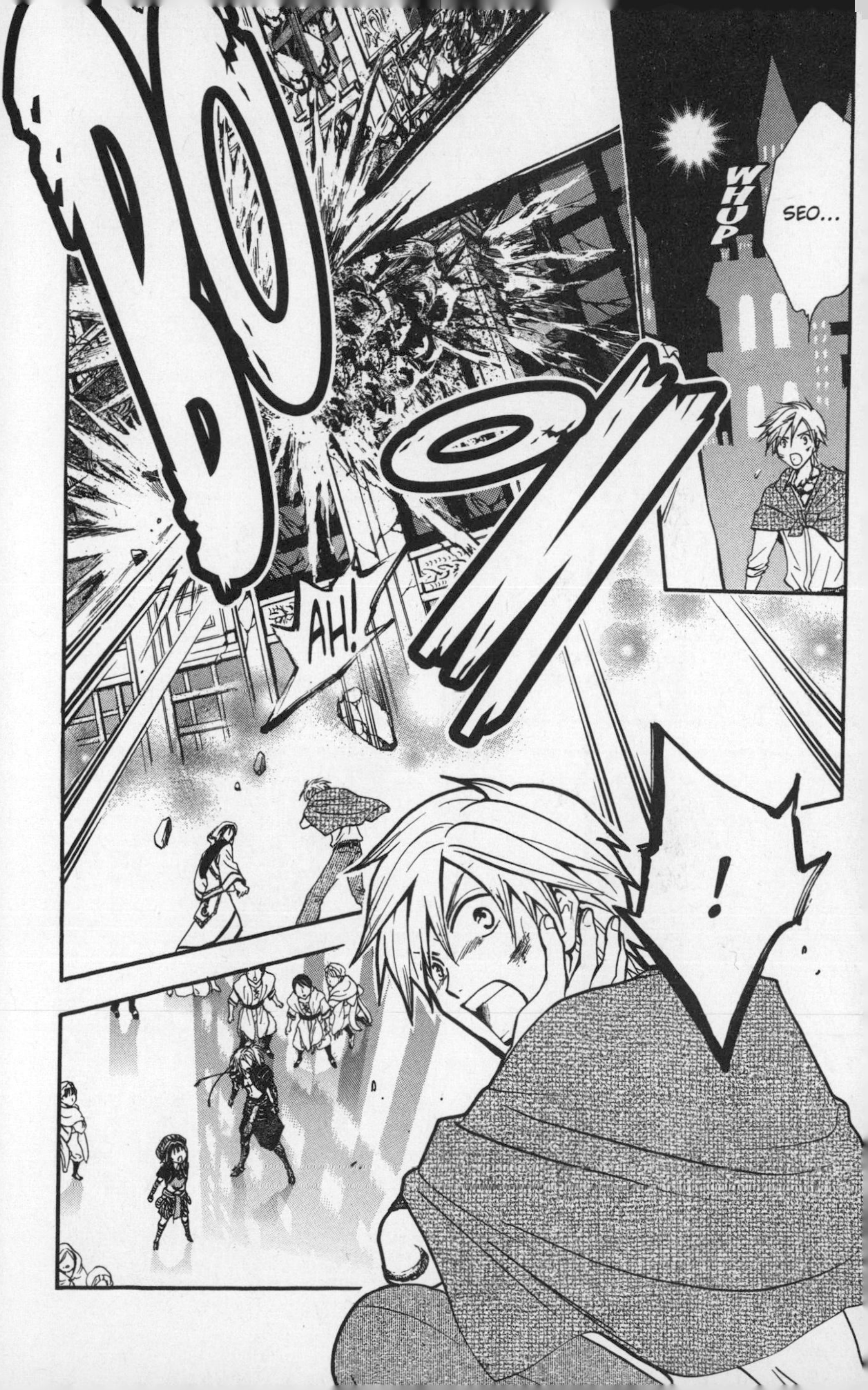
WHUP
SEO...
AH!
!

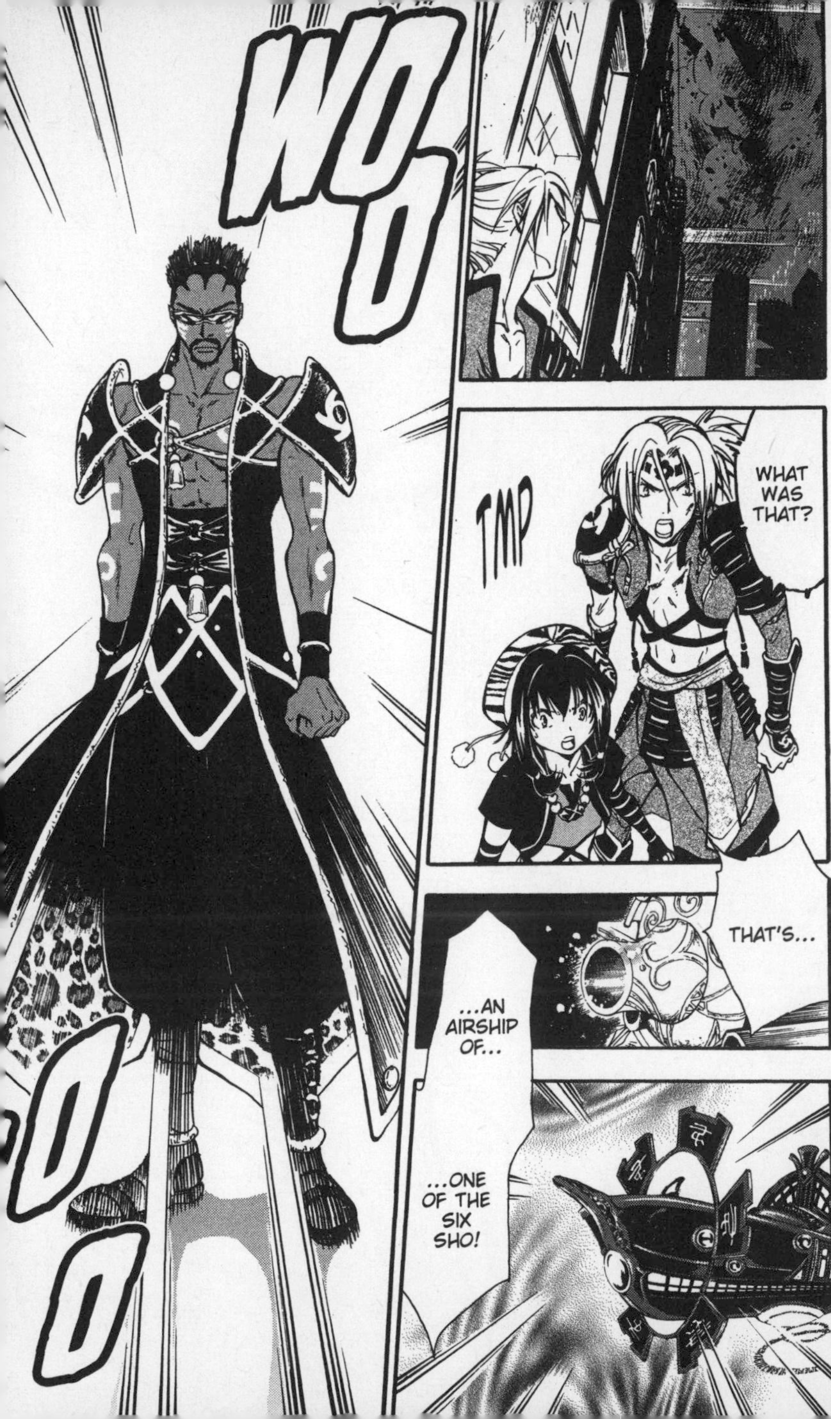
WHAT WAS THAT?
TMP
THAT'S...
...AN AIRSHIP OF...
...ONE OF THE SIX SHO!
WOO
OO

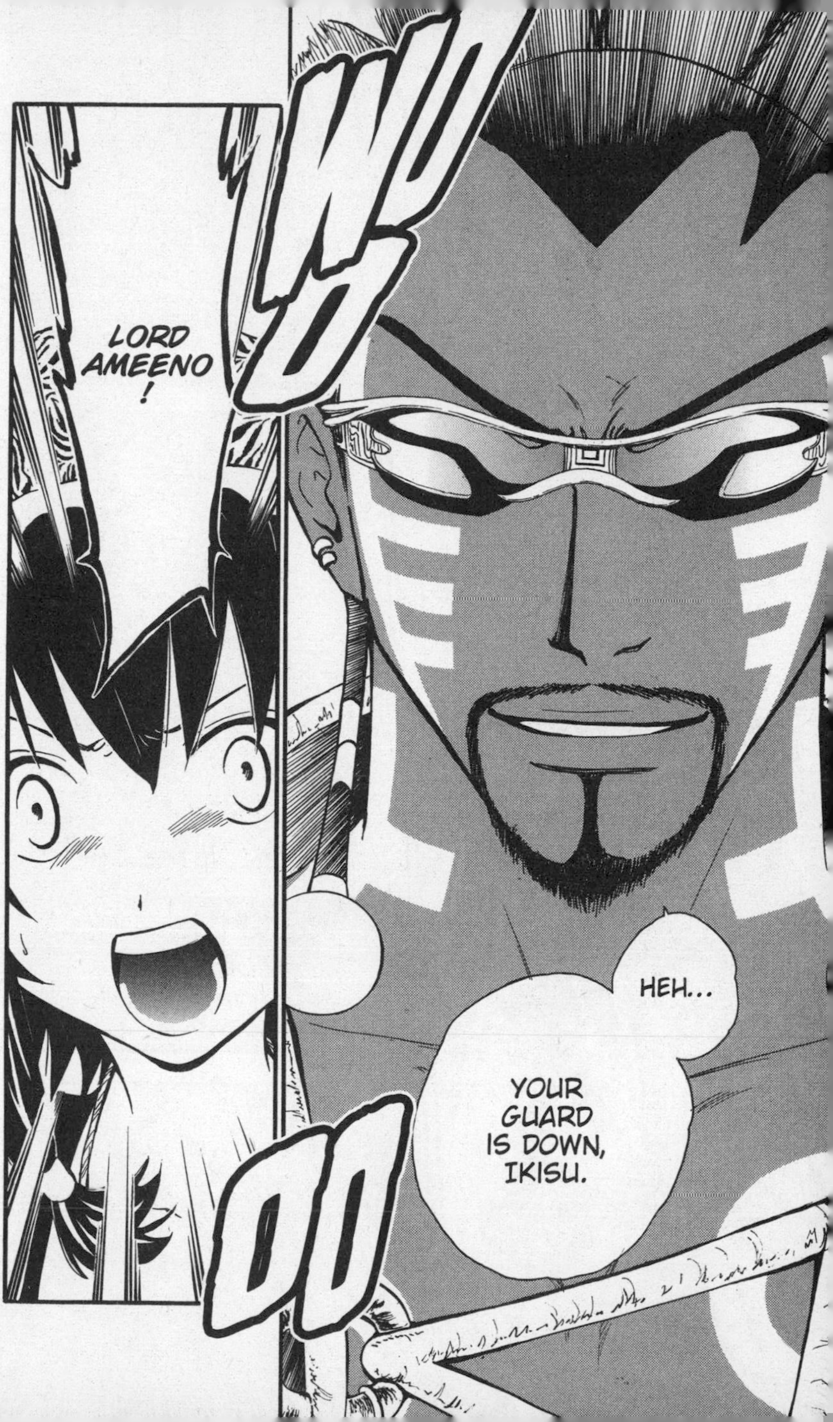
HEH...
YOUR GUARD IS DOWN, IKISU.
LORD AMEENO!

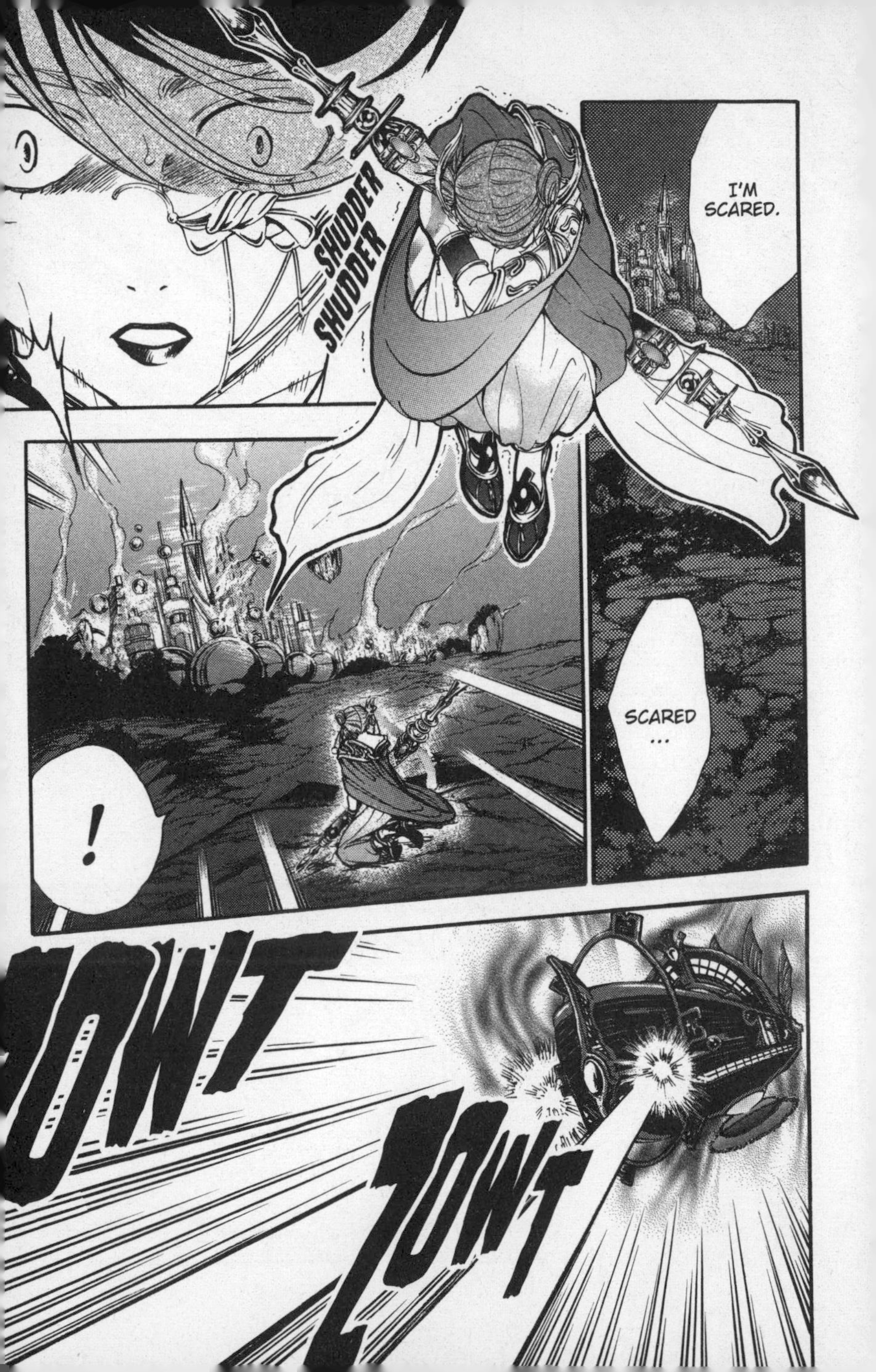
I'M SCARED.
SHUDDER SHUDDER
SCARED ...
!

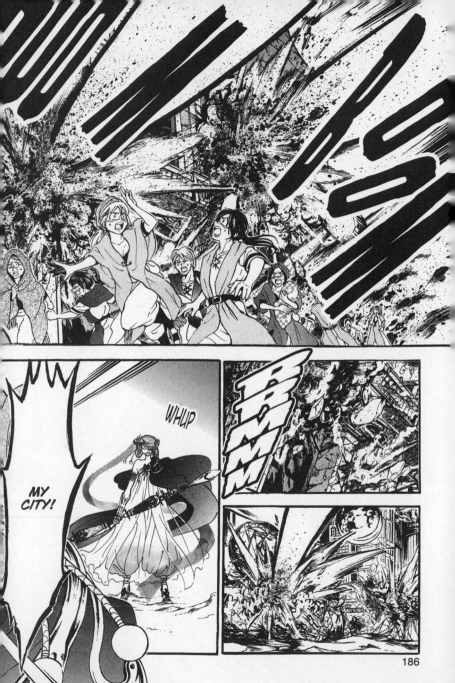

WHUP

MY
CITY!

BRAMM

186

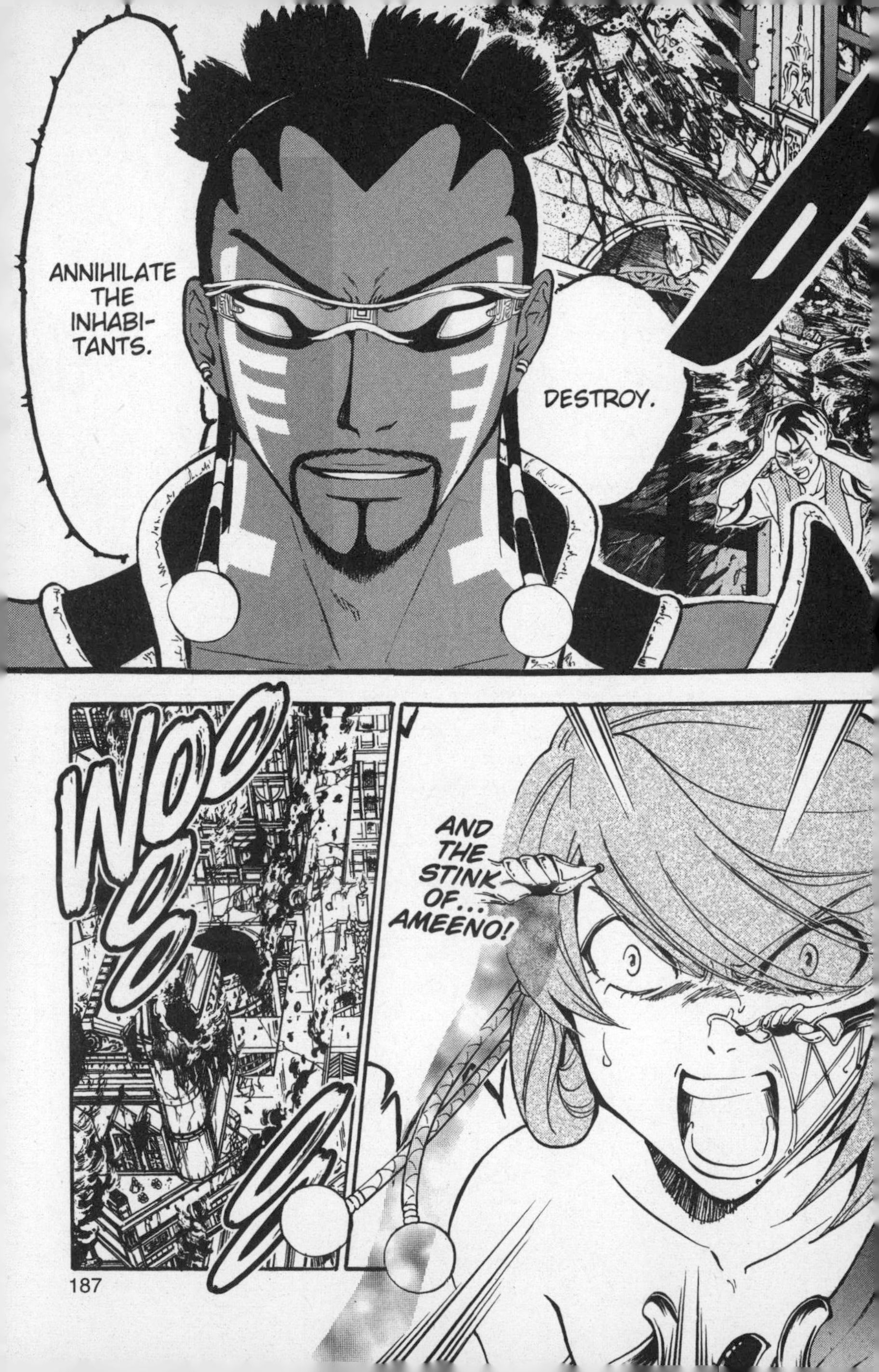
DESTROY.
ANNIHILATE THE INHABITANTS.
AND THE STINK OF... AMEENO!
WOOOO

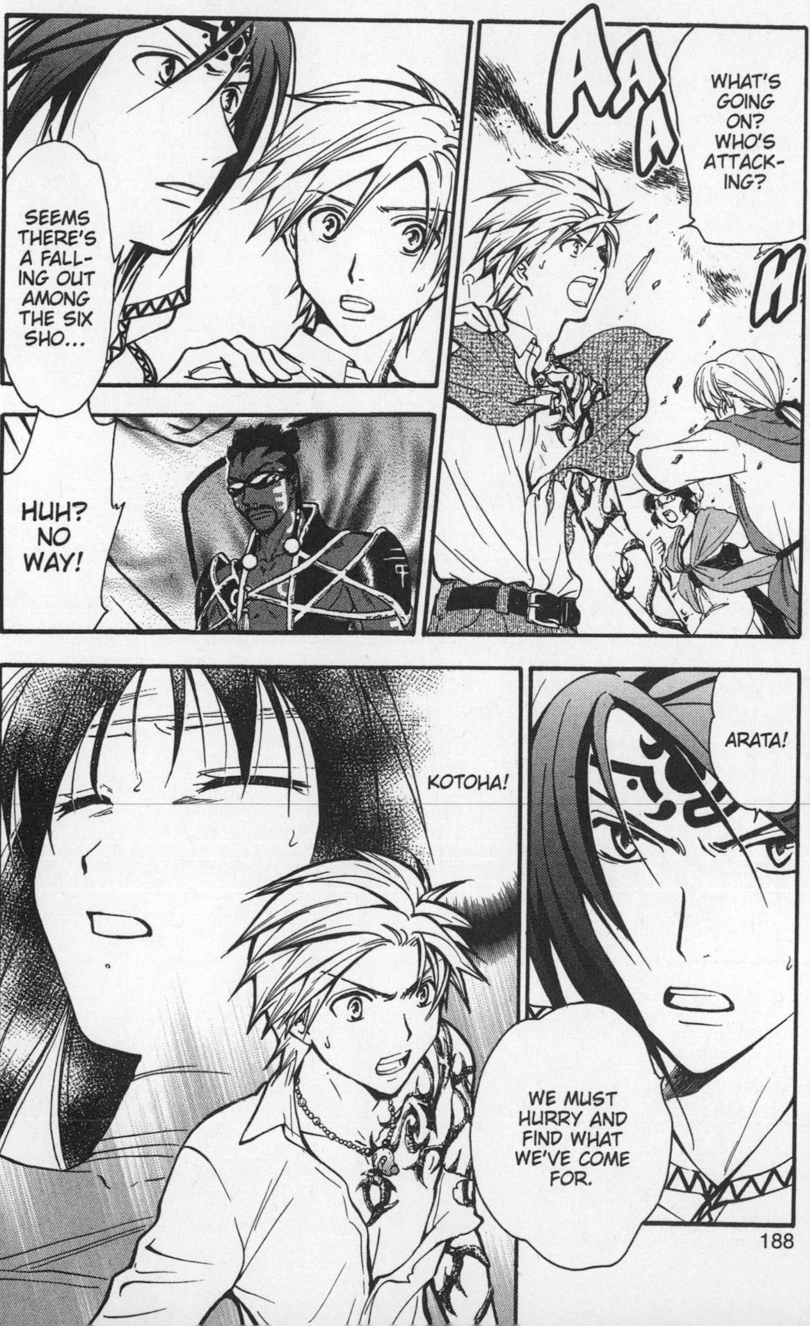
AAAH
WHAT'S GOING ON? WHO'S ATTACK-ING?
SEEMS THERE'S A FALL-ING OUT AMONG THE SIX SHO...
HUH? NO WAY!
ARATA!
WE MUST HURRY AND FIND WHAT WE'VE COME FOR.
KOTOHA!

ARATA: THE LEGEND 21 (THE END)

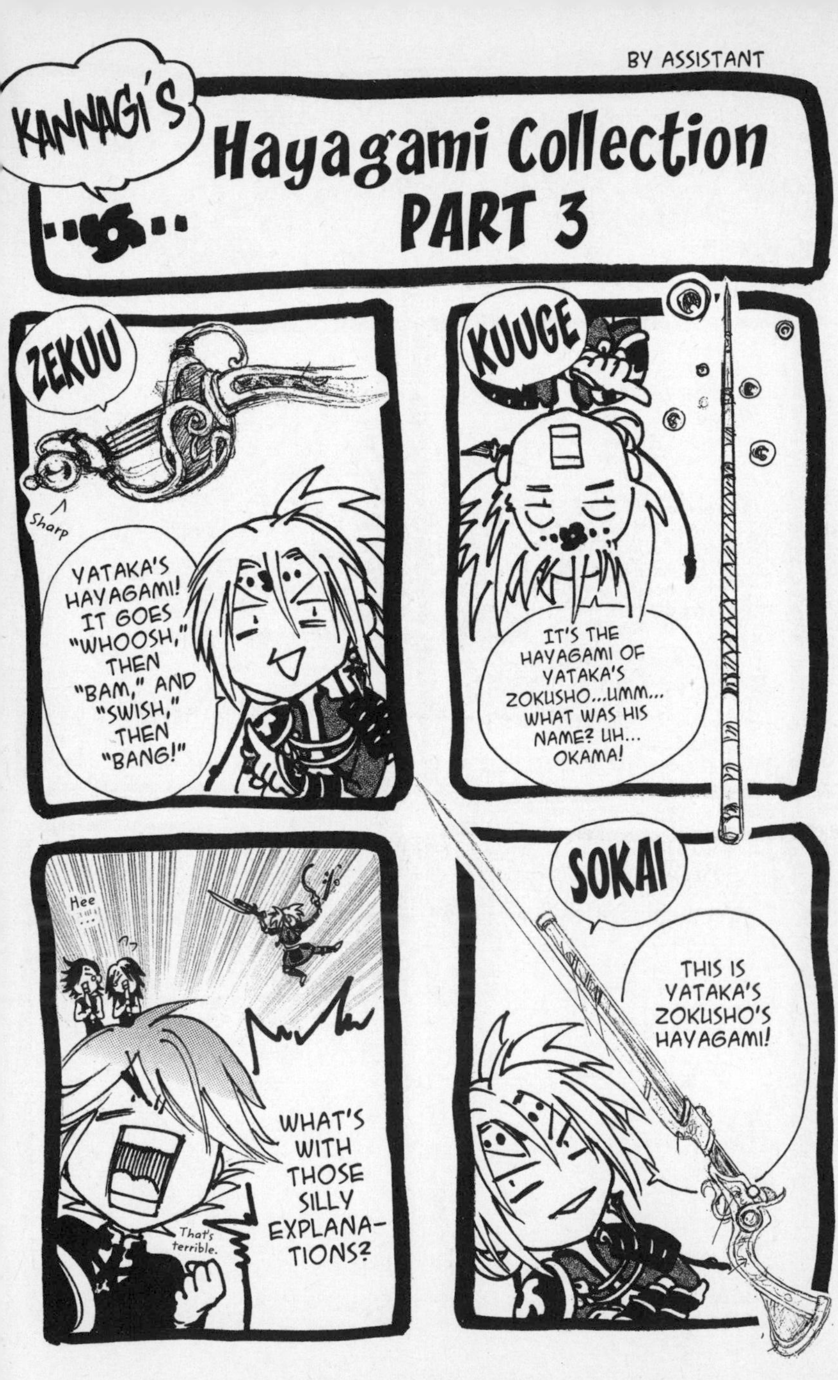
BY ASSISTANT
KANNAGI'S
...!...
Hayagami Collection PART 3
KUUGE
IT'S THE HAYAGAMI OF YATAKA'S ZOKUSHO...UMM... WHAT WAS HIS NAME? UH... OKAMA!
ZEKUU
Sharp
YATAKA'S HAYAGAMI! IT GOES "WHOOSH," THEN "BAM," AND "SWISH," THEN "BANG!"
SOKAI
THIS IS YATAKA'S ZOKUSHO'S HAYAGAMI!
Hee
WHAT'S WITH THOSE SILLY EXPLANATIONS?
That's terrible.

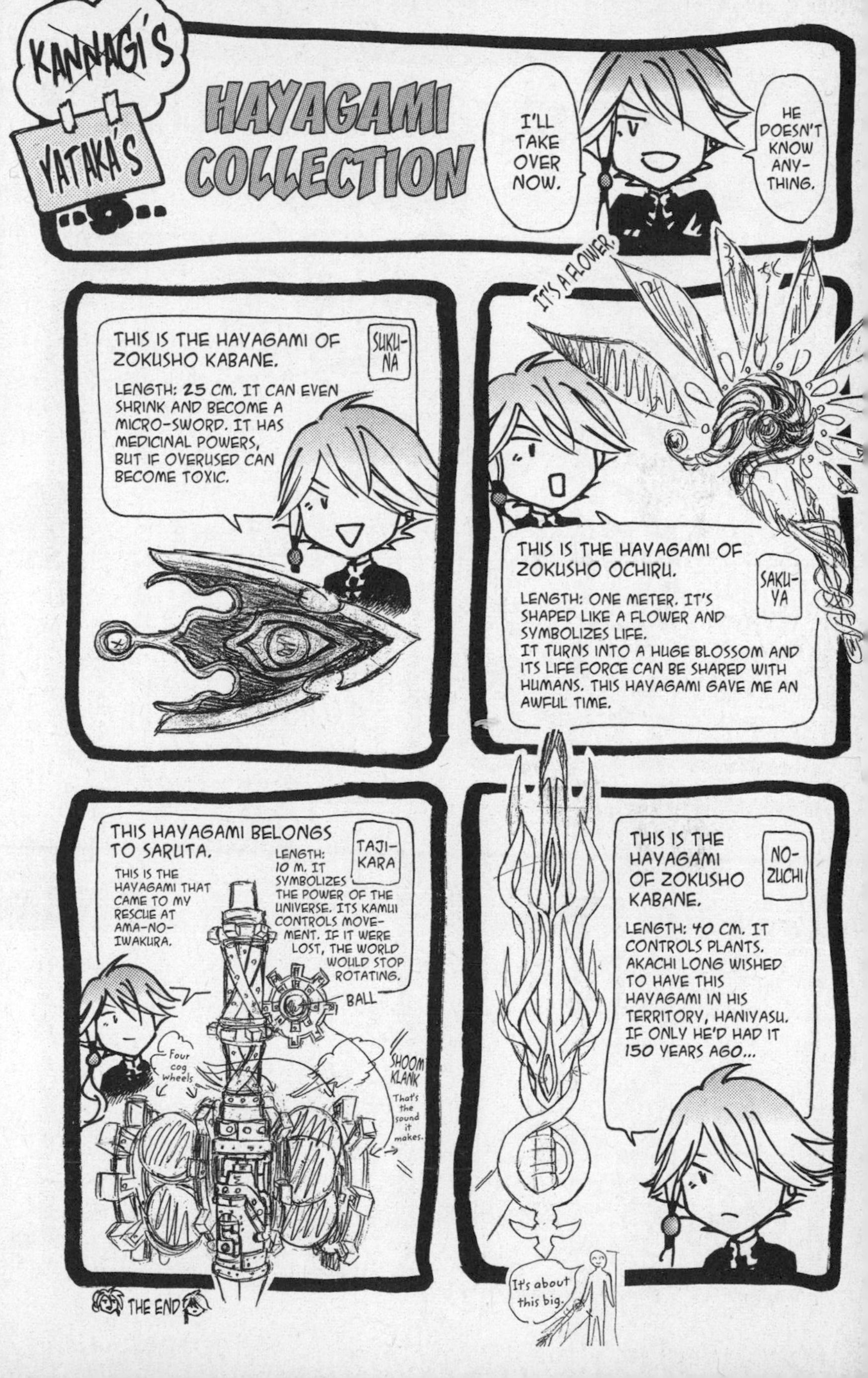
KANNAGI'S
YATAKA'S
HAYAGAMI COLLECTION
5
HE DOESN'T KNOW ANYTHING.
I'LL TAKE OVER NOW.
IT'S A FLOWER.
SAKUYA
THIS IS THE HAYAGAMI OF ZOKUSHO OCHIRU.
LENGTH: ONE METER. IT'S SHAPED LIKE A FLOWER AND SYMBOLIZES LIFE. IT TURNS INTO A HUGE BLOSSOM AND ITS LIFE FORCE CAN BE SHARED WITH HUMANS. THIS HAYAGAMI GAVE ME AN AWFUL TIME.
SUKUNA
THIS IS THE HAYAGAMI OF ZOKUSHO KABANE.
LENGTH: 25 CM. IT CAN EVEN SHRINK AND BECOME A MICRO-SWORD. IT HAS MEDICINAL POWERS, BUT IF OVERUSED CAN BECOME TOXIC.
NOZUCHI
THIS IS THE HAYAGAMI OF ZOKUSHO KABANE.
LENGTH: 40 CM. IT CONTROLS PLANTS. AKACHI LONG WISHED TO HAVE THIS HAYAGAMI IN HIS TERRITORY, HANIYASU. IF ONLY HE'D HAD IT 150 YEARS AGO...
It's about this big.
TAJIKARA
THIS HAYAGAMI BELONGS TO SARUTA.
LENGTH: 10 M. IT SYMBOLIZES THE POWER OF THE UNIVERSE. ITS KAMUI CONTROLS MOVEMENT. IF IT WERE LOST, THE WORLD WOULD STOP ROTATING.
THIS IS THE HAYAGAMI THAT CAME TO MY RESCUE AT AMA-NO-IWAKURA.
BALL
SHOOM KLANK
That's the sound it makes.
Four cog wheels
THE END

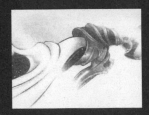

I took my family to an *onsen* hot spring in Shuzenji. We all need a break sometimes! As well as family time!

...I had nothing pending during the week I reserved the rooms for. (Or so I thought.) I worked up until the day we were to leave! Oh no, will I make it?! Uh-oh (°д°;), I nearly panicked! We somehow managed to go on our trip, and it was divine. The hot spring was amazing. The food was delicious. But upon returning home, I was faced with deadlines again! The negatives made the plusses turn to zero. But it became an even bigger – (minus). I just wasn't feeling physically well. Long story short, I collapsed and landed in the hospital. Don't put up with it until it's too late! I've never had so many IVs in my life!

I'm usually quite healthy.

Even my chiropractor says, "You have a sturdy body."

...There's nothing scarier when your stamina goes!

It's a stretch to keep my body in good health!

I'll do something about it before the next volume!

–Yuu Watase

AUTHOR BIO

Born March 5 in Osaka, Yuu Watase debuted in the *Shôjo Comic* manga anthology in 1989. She won the 43rd Shogakukan Manga Award with *Ceres: Celestial Legend*. One of her most famous works is *Fushigi Yûgi*, a series that has inspired the prequel *Fushigi Yûgi: Genbu Kaiden*. In 2008, *Arata: The Legend* started serialization in *Shonen Sunday*.

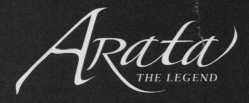

Arata
THE LEGEND

ARATA: THE LEGEND

Volume 21
Shonen Sunday Edition

Story and Art by YUU WATASE

ARATA KANGATARI Vol. 2
by Yuu WATASE

Original Japanese edition
English translation rights i
Kingdom and Ireland arran

English Adaptation: Lance Caselman
Translation: JN Productions
Touch-up Art & Lettering: Rina Mapa
Design: Veronica Casson
Editor: Gary Leach

Printed in the U.S.A.

Published by VIZ Media, LLC
P.O. Box 77010
San Francisco, CA 94107

10 9 8 7 6 5 4 3 2 1
First printing, March 2015

RATED T FOR TEEN

PARENTAL ADVISORY
ARATA: THE LEGEND is rated T for Teen and is recommended for ages 13 and up. This volume contains fantasy violence.

ratings.viz.com

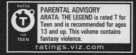

viz media
www.viz.com

MANGA STARTS ON SUNDAY SHONEN SUNDAY
WWW.SHONENSUNDAY.COM